# NUGGETS ON THE DIAMOND

# NUGGETS ON THE DIAMOND

PROFESSIONAL BASEBALL IN THE BAY AREA
FROM THE GOLD RUSH TO THE PRESENT

DICK DOBBINS
JON TWICHELL

**WOODFORD PRESS**

*SAN FRANCISCO*

Published by
**Woodford Press**
A division of Woodford Publishing, Inc.
660 Market Street, Suite 206
San Francisco, California 94104


ISBN: 0-942627-00-8
        0-942627-01-6
Library of Congress Card Catalog Number: 94-60296


First printing April 1994

Book design: Laurence J. Hyman
Editor: Jon Rochmis

Pictured on front cover, top row (l-r): Arky Vaughan, Artie Wilson, Harry Wolverton, Mel Duezabou. Back row: Ernie Lombardi, Rickey Henderson, Joe DiMaggio and Lefty O'Doul, Willie Mays, Casey Stengel.

Pictured on back cover: Billy Martin, Frank Crosetti, Orlando Cepeda, Ray Dandridge, Dario Lodigiani.

Pre-press by ScanArt Graphics, Richmond, California.
Color separations by Riverside Scans, West Sacramento, California.
Printed and bound by Rand McNally Inc., Taunton, Massachusetts.

# CONTENTS

# ACKNOWLEDGMENTS

In writing *Nuggets on the Diamond*, we have attempted to meld the myriad available records with the human, colorful side of the game. Written accounts in the daily newspapers were very helpful to us. City libraries in Oakland, San Francisco and Pleasant Hill, plus the California Historical Society and Bancroft Library at the University of California, Berkeley, allowed us to become intimate with their versions of the past.

For more than three years, these libraries became a haunt for us. We learned the idiosyncrasies of each and every microfilm machine. Our primary sources included the *San Francisco Chronicle*, the *San Francisco Call-Bulletin*, the *Oakland Tribune* and the *San Jose Mercury*. *The Sporting News, Who's Who in Baseball, The Baseball Encyclopedia* and Society for American Baseball Research (SABR) *Minor League Stars, Volumes I-III*, helped to provide the statistical record.

There were human interest stories in almost every edition of these newspapers from the earliest days of recorded Bay Area sports history. Many of the stories found their way into this book. But the greatest sources were people. We interviewed a multitude of former players, staff and just plain fans. Many of them helped establish the statistical record. Others helped establish the atmosphere of Bay Area baseball.

We drank beer with some of our interviewees; we had meals with others. We even completed a scrapbook for one retired player, a real pleasure in itself. We were enthusiastic about our project and we received enthusiasm in return.

One of our most gratifying moments came at the conclusion of a player interview when it was time to leave. The 90-year-old asked, "Do you really have to go so soon?" It's doubtful he realized how long we had already spent with him. It had been an enchanting afternoon and he appreciated someone listening to him.

We were lucky enough to interview five players who played in the Coast League more than 60 years ago. Frankie Crosetti, Bernie DeVivieros, Smead Jolley, Gus Suhr and Charlie Wallgren told of sandlot games in the vacant lot and professional games at "Old Rec"—Recreation Park, home of the San Francisco Seals and the Mission Bells.

John "Dutch" Anderson was a visiting batboy at "Old Rec." He later was the coach at the University of San Francisco and a long-time scout for the New York/San Francisco Giants. Dutch took us on a revealing mental excursion of this early home of the Seals and Missions.

During the Depression years, Leo Kintana, Dominic DiMaggio, Mel Duezabou, George McDermott, Eddie Joost, Lou Chericoni, Bob Jensen, Dario Lodigiani, Billy Raimondi, Nanny Fernandez, Bill Rigney, Bob Cole, Steve Barath, Rugger Ardizoia and Emil Mailho all broke into professional baseball. Some became stars and major leaguers. Many played through the 1940s and a few made it into the 1950s. Others had a short, but challenging career. But they all had wonderful memories they were willing to share.

We were fortunate to interview an assistant trainer and a batboy from this period. Pete Chinn was an assistant to Red Adams of the Oaks and Bobby Arieta was an Oaks batboy for several years before World War II. Their anecdotes and observations provided valuable contributions to this work. Chuck Symonds was an Oaks batboy during the 1940s. The insights of these three helped to give us a perspective of baseball in the clubhouse.

Lou Dials, a Cal graduate in engineering, offered a perspective held by few others. Because he was unable to get a job in his chosen field, he was forced to play baseball in the Negro Leagues. This courageous man came within one door slam of being the first black player of the modern era to play in the Pacific Coast League.

Tony Gomez was also gracious in relating his tale of heartache at being denied, because of race, his chance to play for his hometown Seals. His youthful exploits at shortstop were legendary in the city, but that wasn't enough to get him a contract.

Larry Jansen, Gene Woodling, Damon Hayes, Bobby Bragan, Russ Rose, Don Ferrarese, Artie Wilson, Bud Watkins, Roger Bowman, Jack Brewer, Walt Pocekay, Jose Perez, George Vico, Con Dempsey, Tom and Will Hafey, Eddie Lake, Bud Beasley, Frank Seward, Tom Munoz and Ed Cereghino offered rich stories about the prosperous days after World War II.

On several occasions, we had the pleasure of having the player's wife join us. Their perspective and/or memory often was very helpful in filling some of the gaps created by time or selective memory. They remembered the three strikeouts to go with the winning hit. Grace Wallgren, Fran Raimondi, Jackie Duezabou, Connie Perez, Lola Mailho and Dorothy Brewer all echoed the enthusiasm their husbands showed for the game.

A distinct pleasure was the interview with Helen Kelly, Mrs. George L. "Highpockets" Kelly, and their son, Walter. Helen Kelly and her husband were born in the Bay Area and retained permanent residence on the Peninsula. Kelly played less than one full season in the Pacific Coast League, but his heart and his legacy belonged to the Bay Area.

To provide different perspectives of the game, interviews were held with Leo "Doc" Hughes, former trainer for both the Seals and the Giants; Cecil Carlucci, veteran Coast League umpire; Bob Stevens, baseball writer for the *San Francisco Chronicle*; and Don Klein, veteran sports announcer and "Voice of the Seals" in the late 1940s and early 1950s.

Another special afternoon was held at the home of Kay Miller. Her husband, Damon Miller, was the savior of the Seals when he and seven other employees acquired the franchise after Paul Fagan turned it back to the league in 1953. Mrs. Miller was helpful in providing research material and insights to this critical period.

And bless the fans! Several folks gave us a different slant on the game, including Walter Wells, Clarence Amaral, Bob Levin, Bob Schroth and Carl Haas, who passed up an opportunity to sign with the Seals in the late 1930s. In his retirement, Schroth reconstructed a four-foot-square model of Recreation Park from memory and research. Seeing the park in three dimensions was very helpful in drawing new perspectives.

Of invaluable help was Bill Weiss, long-time statistician for the Pacific Coast League who probably has the most extensive "fingertip" knowledge of the league. We needed to know the most finite details surrounding the PCL and its players, and it became a challenge to see if Bill knew it all. He didn't, but he came close. And he always knew where to look it up. We cannot thank Bill Weiss enough for his contributions.

Doug McWilliams grew up in the Bay Area and used to sneak into Oaks and Seals games with Dick Dobbins. Doug later became a photographer for Topps Baseball cards and he developed an outstanding photographic library on the Oakland Oaks. Thanks to Doug for his great friendship and for his assistance in selecting photos for this project.

Also providing excellent photographs were Mark Rucker of Transcendental Graphics, Lew Lipset, Vern Sappers, Dennis King and Lloyd Feinberg.

The State Archives of Hawaii and the Bishop Museum Archives in Honolulu were very helpful in locating photographs of Alexander Cartwright. The California State Library promptly located an 1870s photograph for us as well.

John Spalding, author of *ALWAYS ON SUNDAY, The California Baseball League, 1886 to 1915,* helped provide inspiration for our project. John's scholarly work set high standards for us. He was also helpful correcting those mistakes authors miss when they read their own manuscripts. Thanks as well to Lefty O'Doul biographer Richard Leutzinger for his insights on "The Man in the Green Suit."

Thanks also go to Robert Whiting, author of *You Gotta Have Wa* and other books on Japanese baseball, for his comments and encouragement. If it weren't for Rosser and Yin-Wah Brockman—our Tokyo/San Francisco connection—we would not have had the privilege of meeting Mr. Whiting.

The Fisher family told us what they remembered of "Uncle Mike" Fisher, player, team owner and organizer of the Reach All-Americans, first American baseball team to barnstorm the Far East. No wonder they felt moved to participate in the effort to keep the Giants in San Francisco.

Thanks also to Tony Khing and to Dick Beverage. Tony, a native San Franciscan, played ball at San Francisco State and was affiliated with the Giants' media office for several years. Beverage has been a guiding light of the PCL Historical Society. Both were enthusiastic in their support of the project and helped hone the work with their sharpened pencils.

A special acknowledgment goes to Pat Gallagher and Maria Jacinto of the San Francisco Giants and Andy Dolich and Jay Alves of the Oakland A's for their encouragement of our project. Their participation was our connection to the present.

The final form and shape of this book was created by the San Francisco publishing house, Woodford Press. We placed our labor of love in the expert hands of Publisher and Art Director Laurence J. Hyman and Editor Jon Rochmis, who understood our passion and took great care in making us feel at ease as they took our materials and created this book. We also appreciate the dedicated help of Woodford's Jim Santore, David Lilienstein and Kate Hanley.

And we must thank the Dobbins family: Judy and the kids, Pete, Anne and Annette; and the Twichell family: Linda Evans Twichell, son Olu Evans —the Oakland A's loyalist—and Baseball Ben, who took in his first game when he was three months old. You gave your time, your patience and your inspiration. We appreciate you for it, and we love you for it.

Dick Dobbins
Jon Twichell

# INTRODUCTION

Frankie Crosetti, Eddie Joost, Lou Chericoni and I all had at least one thing in common when we were young: We all went searching for diamonds in the San Francisco Bay Area. This was long before Little League and years before television. Yet we were never bored. We always found our diamonds, we always had baseball. Baseball has tugged at the hearts, souls and minds of a large percentage of children, as it did for Crosetti, Joost, Chericoni and me. It was, and is, a special game for us and became the centerpieces of our lives. Little did we know then, or realize just how lucky we were, that we were growing up in the richest baseball center in the world. The game may have been "invented" in upstate New York and played professionally for the first time in Ohio, but the true heart of American baseball is right here in the Bay Area.

Care to argue? Let's start at the beginning. Alexander Cartwright himself stopped in the Bay Area to help introduce the game well before the Civil War. Teams first organized here in the 1860s. And Bill Lange, who the experts say was greater than Ty Cobb, got his start here in the 1890s.

Some of the greatest players of all time either grew up in the Bay Area or got their professional starts here, and the list extends far beyond Joe DiMaggio, the most famous of all San Franciscans. How about Billy Martin, Frankie Crosetti, Harry Heilman, Tony Lazzeri, Paul Waner, Lefty O'Doul? Or Frank Robinson, Willie Stargell, Jackie Jensen, Curt Flood, Joe Morgan? And don't forget that Willie Mays, Willie McCovey, Juan Marichal, Catfish Hunter, Rickey Henderson, Rollie Fingers and Reggie Jackson all played most of their careers in the Bay Area. Casey Stengel managed the Oakland Oaks to the Pacific Coast League championship in 1948, one year before he began his long, storied, title-filled tenure with the New York Yankees. The list can fill a book. In fact, that's what we've done.

There was tremendous elation when the New York Giants announced their intention to move to San Francisco for the 1958 season. But many local fans remained unimpressed. The 1957 San Francisco Seals, playing in one of the finest stadiums in the United States, had just won the PCL championship and some oldtimers—remembering the great Seals championship teams three decades earlier—sneered, "Shucks, we've had major league baseball here for years!"

Because there were three local Pacific Coast League teams and thousands of youngsters hoping someday to play for one of them, a dedicated cadre of baseball scouts scoured our diamonds, looking for the gems who could play professionally. The early phenomenon of sandlot baseball—a term that originated in San Francisco—became an institution here.

Damon Runyon, writing in a Los Angeles paper in 1927, marveled at the sandlot activity taking place in the Bay Area during the late 1920s. A friend of Runyon's by the name of Hap O'Connor talked of a trip to the Bay Area where he "saw diamonds laid out on every sandlot in the bay district, but while there is plenty of vacant pasturage in Los Angeles, the lads there do not take advantage of it.

"It seems to me," O'Connor continued, "that the kids here in Los Angeles and Hollywood are much softer than those of San Francisco and Oakland."

Growing up in Oakland in the 1930s, Lou Chericoni's life revolved around the search for diamonds. The vacant lots were good enough when he was younger, but Lou eventually graduated to local fields where he played his pick-up games.

As a teenager, Chericoni and a dozen or so of his friends decided it was time to form a team and play in an Oakland recreation league. The most important step in this venture was finding a sponsor. The kids approached the owner of a local mortuary who agreed to help, and he sent them to Maxwell's Hardware to order uniforms from a man named Abe Rose, who became an Oakland youth league legend. The team representatives were so excited, they forgot to take uniform measurements for their teammates before running all the way to Maxwell's. Still, that wasn't enough to prevent the Oakland Casket Company baseball team of the Tribune Newspaper League from being born.

Getting settled into an appropriate league and establishing a schedule and field assignment brought the boys into contact with the legendary Al Erle. Erle worked at Hirsch & Price Jewelers in central Oakland, and he was also the secretary for amateur baseball in the East Bay. Erle had played ball at St. Mary's College and later played with Tacoma of the Pacific Coast League in 1904. For many years he served as secretary for the Northern California Scouting Association where he was famous for his annual crab feed for local scouts.

Each team was responsible for reporting their game results to Erle every Sunday. Erle would provide game assignments for the following weekend, and naturally, the higher classes and more successful teams received the better fields and times. Teams played in Alameda, Pinole, Walnut Creek and points more central. These leagues continued around the calendar; only rain could cancel a game.

Players would have to dress at home because there were no locker facilities at the parks. It was routine to see players in full uniform traveling on the trolleys, equipment bags slung over their shoulders.

The kids learned by emulating the older and more experienced players in the league or by going to PCL games at Oaks Ball Park in Emeryville. There were few coaches in these leagues, so the players had to learn through their own trials and errors.

Young Vernon "Lefty" Gomez would travel by trolley from Pinole to pitch for the H&F Grocers of Oakland, the trip being quite an ordeal in itself. There he faced the likes of Harry Lavagetto or Ernie Lombardi or one of the Hafey brothers on the East Bay diamonds. After the Coast League season ended, local Coast League players would enter the more advanced winter leagues, thus providing stiff competition and positive examples for the younger players to follow.

The local bush league games gained their share of publicity. The *Oakland Tribune*, along with San Francisco's many newspapers, reported the box scores and standings of the various leagues. After Sunday's games, somebody from the winning teams would take the highlights down to the KRE radio offices on San Pablo Avenue, and at 6 p.m., broadcaster Charlie Tye would provide his listeners with the results.

The broadcast would include a short segment offering baseball tips. Frequently, Tye would bring in a guest celebrity, such as Bernie DeVivieros or Jimmie Reese. Tye would also urge the best prospects to show their civic pride by signing with local baseball clubs rather than with "those carpetbaggers" back east. Joe Devine, the New York Yankees' scout for the Bay Area, complained that these public editorials made it more difficult to convince local prospects to sign with a major league team over the Seals, Oaks or Missions. But Devine always came away with more than his share of local prospects.

Lou Chericoni took this route in an attempt to achieve his dream of playing major league baseball. Like hundreds of Bay Area baseball players, Chericoni was good enough to sign with a local team—in his case, the Seals. But when the Seals optioned him to some far-off corner of the country for added seasoning, Chericoni decided to stay home and give up his chase.

Frankie Crosetti's search for diamonds initially found only corn fields. Crosetti was born in San Francisco but moved to Los Gatos, near San Jose, when he was 2. The family became farmers, and Frank's and his older brother's duty was to irrigate the fields. By turning the water on slowly, they could escape to a neighboring field to play "one-o-cat" while their field was being irrigated.

They crafted their bat from spare wood. The ball was the stub end of a corn cob. Thus, the boys had an endless supply of pseudo-baseballs to use. By seventh grade, Frankie was pitching and playing shortstop with older kids. In his early teens, the Crosettis moved back to San Francisco and Frankie enrolled at Lowell High School, where he played on the varsity baseball team.

Crosetti quit school at 16 and went to Montana to play semi-pro ball for the Montana Power team. In between playing three games a week, he cut pipe for the local electric power company. He told his employer that he was 19 in order to hold the job.

After the summer he returned to San Francisco and played ball for the Young Mens Institute. YMI games were played at Recreation Park, where the Seals spotted him and signed him to a contract.

Like many other youngsters, Crosetti had little coaching. He had to learn the game by watching others play. Also like many others, he played hundreds of games on makeshift diamonds before he was discovered by a scout. But his years of experience allowed him to jump right into the starting lineup as a Seals rookie in 1928, playing four excellent years before going on to the Yankees and a distinguished major league career.

Eddie Joost, who would play for 17 years in the major leagues, searched for his diamonds south of Market Street. Young Eddie grew up in a blue-collar area where men were proud of their heritage, their family and their ability to drink and fight. Joost could play with the best of them even though he was small and he wasn't much of a hitter.

Joe Baerwald of the Missions had followed Joost's exploits and wanted to sign him. At 16 Joost dropped out of Mission High School to play for the Missions, but was discovered by a truant officer who forced him to return. A compromise was then worked out between the school district and the Joost family, with Eddie being able to finish his education at continuation school.

Joost earned $150 a month playing for the Missions. With the Depression in high gear, this was a lifesaver for the whole family.

Joost and hundreds of youngsters like him were helped by men like Rose and Erle in Oakland. In San Francisco, the patron saint of young amateurs was Edward "Spike" Hennessy. Hennessy frequented the local playgrounds in the city where he coached, offered advice and provided moral support. He also tipped off Seals officials and interested scouts about prospects. Hennessy is said to have helped 135 San Francisco youngsters into professional or semi-pro baseball.

Hennessy frequented the playgrounds throughout San Francisco, but on Sunday his interest turned to "Big Rec," the sunken diamond in Golden Gate Park. Here the most promising youngsters would join seasoned professionals for an intense game of baseball. Even in the dead of winter, the game would draw large crowds.

Hennessy helped orchestrate the choosing of teams. Each player would ante up a small fee to be put into a winners' pot. Pitchers and catchers would get a "cut-and-a-half" while field players would get a "cut." The winners' pot wouldn't match that of a World Series, but the intensity of the game might. This Hennessy-developed institution helped generate the continued flow of future stars out of the sandlots of San Francisco.

It also created or reinforced the Bay Area's passion for baseball.

Bay Area citizens often knew more about major league teams than did their Eastern city counterparts. After all, local boys were featured on almost every Eastern team. Local newspapers kept us well-informed of their exploits.

"First class." This was the quick answer given by Artie Wilson, Oakland's first black player, to the question, "What was so special about the Pacific Coast League?" Similar comments were heard from almost every other contributor to this book. It may have been stated differently, but the thrust was the same: baseball here was special. The PCL certainly was not a typical minor league.

Former *San Francisco Chronicle* baseball writer Bob Stevens called the Coast League "comfortable." Whether it was better pay, nicer hotels, the most modern transportation available or concern about accommodations for a player's family, Pacific Coast League teams seemed to do it better than their so-called major league counterparts.

Veterans on the way down preferred to play in the Pacific Coast League even though there were as many as 50 more games per season than in the majors. Players knew they could get as much as $500 more a month than they would receive from teams in the American Association or International League. Gene Woodling, the great hitter of the 1948 Seals, was given a raise when he was "demoted" by the Pittsburgh Pirates to San Francisco. Seals first baseman Ferris Fain had to fight for a raise when he was drafted by the Philadelphia Athletics after the 1946 season.

Major league veterans also knew the West Coast climate would not drain them of their waning energies the way the East Coast and Midwest would. The travel schedule was also kinder. It was a "comfortable" way to age.

Coast League teams became a blend of crafty veterans and youngsters yearning for a chance to play. For the fan, the mix was just right. The veteran provided the home team with name association and some degree of star quality, while the home-grown rookies engendered home-town pride. Whenever one of the locals was sold to a major league team, fans were both saddened by the loss of a local boy but heartened because another of "our own" made it to the bigs.

The Coast League also had comfortable stadiums. True, Lane Field in San Diego and Vaughn Street Park in Portland were worthy of condemnation, but the parks in Los Angeles and Seattle, and Seals Stadium in San Francisco, were up to major league standards. Oaks Ball Park in Emeryville was cozy and a wonderful place to watch a baseball game.

We all have special memories of our days on the sandlots. Mine center in and around the Berkeley foothills, where I grew up. The only "real" diamonds there were on the school playgrounds, but most of us learned to play the game on the many vacant lots. I will never forget chiseling a diamond out of a rough lot. Unfortunately, it was a rectangular lot. From home plate, it was probably 200 feet down the left field line. A grove of eucalyptus trees served as a porous wall at the end of the field. The trees created a unique barrier that caused balls to bounce in any direction. The field did not work to my advantage at all, since I was a left-handed batter. Ten feet behind first base the ground took an abrupt upward pitch. Any fly ball I hit would strike ground approximately 100 feet from home plate. The rightfielder could play in closer than the second baseman.

We manicured the lot fairly well, but each ground ball still was an adventure; the fielder had to keep low and be ready to react to the inevitable bad hop. We made our bases out of burlap sacks filled with grass trimmed from the infield. Home plate was made out of a piece of plywood. The game ended when the boy who owned the ball had to go home.

A singular event brings a chuckle whenever I think back on those times. I'm not even sure of the boy's name; I think it was Teddy. He was a short, chunky kid. On this particular day we had a large group of about 20 playing the game. With two outs, runners on base and a full count on him, Teddy turned to bunt! The ball hit him squarely in the stomach, and Teddy went down like an over-the-hill fighter.

We rushed to home plate, not to see how Teddy was but to argue whether the inning was over or not. As Teddy writhed in pain on the ground, we hovered above in heated argument over the outcome of the play. The argument went unresolved and the game abruptly ended. Somebody must have helped Teddy to his feet, but I don't remember it.

I thought Teddy was out. Of course, I was on the other team.

Searching for diamonds in the Bay Area may not always have been profitable, but it was enriching and fulfilling. And passionate. Extremely passionate.

It wasn't always easy to root for the Oaks or Seals. Through the years there were always threats of one or the other team leaving . . . another dubious Bay Area tradition. Several years before the Seals finally left, the threat was very real. In a last-ditch, grassroots campaign to save the team—joined by politicians and the media—the Seals offered their stock to the public at $10 per share.

As a 17-year-old high school student, I purchased 10 shares in San Francisco Seals, Inc. That $100 was a lot of money, but there was no question I had to do it. I could not let my beloved Seals cease to exist without a fight.

The effort ultimately failed, but we did save the team for a brief period. After they were gone, I received a check for $20 from San Francisco Seals, Inc.—the return on my investment—along with a letter of apology that it couldn't have been more.

It was still the best investment in the stock market I ever made.

Dick Dobbins
Alamo, California
1994

# NUGGETS ON THE DIAMOND

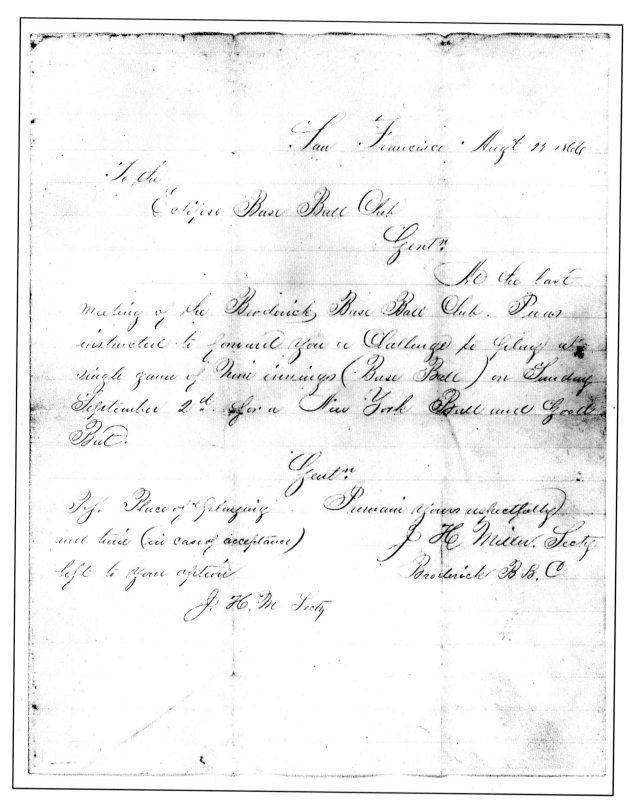

A letter, dated August 22, 1866, from the Broderick Base Ball Club of San Francisco, challenging the Eclipse Base Ball Club of Oakland to a 'single game of nine innings (Base Ball) on Sunday, September 2 for a New York Ball and good bat.' Both teams were 'crack nines' and members of the first Pacific Convention of Base Ball Clubs. Unfortunately, there is no indication the game was ever played.

CHAPTER **1**

# GOLD RUSH SANDLOTTERS

In true California pioneer fashion, the first baseball club organized in San Francisco—and in all of California, for that matter—was formed in a bar.

Dan Driscoll and a group of his buddies got together in early 1858 at Dan's Oyster Saloon, on Montgomery Street between Clay and Commercial, to create the San Francisco Base Ball Club. They elected officers, met every other Tuesday, bellied up to the bar for libations . . . but never did get around to playing a game.

Base Ball, as Dan and his cronies knew it, was essentially the same as we know it, play it and love it today (the single word "baseball" would come later). The game was organized in 1845 in New York City by Alexander Cartwright of the Knickerbockers, the very first baseball team. Bitten by the gold bug, Cartwright carefully carried west with him his original rules, ball and diary as he trekked from Newark, New Jersey, to Sacramento, California.

Cartwright organized a few games in San Francisco, it is said, as he had all across the prairies with settlers and mountain men alike. But he didn't stay long in Gold Rush country or in San Francisco, because he soon sailed to Hawaii where he made a long and fruitful life for himself.

San Francisco was chartered as a city in 1850 and by 1853 already had 50,000 residents. Although baseball was not popular at first among the rough-and-ready 49ers, the sport came west with the second wave of pioneers as

tradesmen, artisans and mechanics—many of them baseball fans—emigrated to service this booming area.

A great number of baseball clubs had been organized in the first decade of the sport's formal existence, which in turn led to the formation of the National Association of Base Ball Clubs in May 1857. The National Association also began annual conventions in 1857 to formally codify baseball, resolve disputes and recognize clubs. The organization was the unifying force in the sport until the rise of professional players in the later 1860s.

The original envelope sent to the Eclipse Base Ball Club.

Alexander Cartwright (center, back row) and some of his teammates from the 1845 New York Knickerbockers. Cartwright stopped through the Bay Area to help introduce the game before sailing on to settle in the Hawaiian Islands.

Meanwhile, back in California, the first truly active baseball club was organized November 11, 1859, as the Sacramento Base Ball Club. This immediately got San Francisco's competitive juices flowing, and the November 19 edition of the *Spirit of the Times* newspaper exhorted the locals to generate their own baseball clubs as the manly and clean-living thing to do.

**THE GAMES BEGIN**

It took just nine days for another version of the San Francisco Base Ball Club to be formed—primarily from a group of cricket players—and on January 28, 1860, they challenged "any nine base ball players to a match game" scheduled for February 22 at Centre's Bridge. The Red Rovers, a second San Francisco team, responded first. The Sacramentos, who had gotten everyone excited in the first place, also scheduled a game for February 22, 1860, against the Union, another club from the state capital.

The February date was chosen since it was Washington's Birthday; Lincoln had not even been inau-gurated as President yet. The San Francisco match was in the morning, laying claim to the title of California's first official baseball game. The Sacramento teams played in the afternoon.

Sacramento beat the Union club in gentlemanly fashion, 20-14. The umpiring was pronounced "satisfactory and impartial." The Union club hosted a banquet and presented a game ball to the winners. All very polite.

Given San Francisco's reputation as the last refuge of eccentrics, the first game played in the city had no such genteel theme. One apocryphal tale had the ballplayers fashioning a ball from a rubber overshoe. The game started late, ran long, reached the end of nine innings a 33-33 tie, and was finally forfeited by the Red Rovers when they refused to continue unless the San Franciscos changed their pitcher. Finally, the Red Rovers refused to pay for the post-game dinner, which the loser was supposed to do according to a pre-game agreement. The San Franciscos had to split the $75 dinner cost at Peter Job's Ice Cream Saloon.

The site of "Centre's Bridge" is uncertain. The most geographically sensible explanation relates the spot to the

Mission Dolores Plank Road Company, whose president in the late 1850s was John Center.

Most of San Francisco at that time was sand dunes and creeks draining the hills. Mission Dolores, center of the farming area (and at the corner of Centre Street and Dolores Street), was at the end of a plank road. Centre Street was later 16th Street, which would become the home of the San Francisco Seals in 1931.

In the late 1850s a new plank road was constructed along what became Folsom Street, including a good half-mile across swamps from Third to Eighth streets. Since the footing under these plank roads was precarious in more than one spot, the locals would facetiously call them "bridges." So, a spot of hard ground somewhere along the plank roads south of Market probably is the spot of California's first formal baseball game.

## THE EAGLES—FIRST CALIFORNIA CHAMPIONS

The next month, the San Franciscos changed their name to the Eagles in deference to member Marvin Gelston, formerly of the New York Eagles, the third baseball club formed in New York. More teams bloomed that spring, particularly the Stockton Base Ball Club and the Live Oaks, also of Stockton.

On August 29, 1860, the San Joaquin District Agricultural Fair was held, which included a one-day baseball tournament. The Sacramentos showed up and won their two games, trouncing Stockton 49-11 and the Live Oaks 73-7.

Full of themselves now, the Sacramentos proposed a tournament as part of the State Agricultural Fair, with substantial cash prizes. On September 24-25 the Sacramentos and the San Francisco Eagles played for the state crown. In front of 2,000 spectators, the Eagles won two games, 36-32 and 31-17. Both games were interrupted by darkness. After some grumbling, the Sacramentos paid up and faded from the baseball scene.

The State Agricultural Society awarded the Eagles a silver game ball, an artifact that disappeared following the 1906 earthquake and fire.

Over the next few years, the Eagles became California's dominant baseball club, but by 1863 a group of their players broke away to form the Pacifics. The Eagles and Pacifics first played each other on February 23, 1863 behind Mission Dolores—perhaps at Centre's Bridge—where the Eagles prevailed 27-18.

## THE PACIFIC BASE BALL CONVENTION

Despite a decrease in baseball popularity in California during the Civil War—largely because of the absence of able-bodied men—the Eagles and the Pacifics maintained their rivalry. By the summer of 1866, there were so many new clubs that rules and regulations became necessary.

BANCROFT LIBRARY

Rare photograph of silver ball awarded by the State Agricultural Society to the San Francisco Eagles, first California State Champions, 1860. This photograph is from an equally rare book, *Base Ball, 1845-1871*, written and published in 1902 by Seymour H. Church of San Francisco.

THE " PACIFICS," 1866

| J. SHEPARD | S. H. WADE | W. SHEPARD | W. F. HALE, JR. | J. H. WETMORE |
| FIRST BASE | SECOND BASE | THIRD BASE | PITCHER | RIGHT FIELD |

| H. T. WHITBECK | J. KERRIGAN | J. W. HARRISON | T. CAMPBELL, JR. |
| CENTER FIELD | SHORT STOP | CATCHER | LEFT FIELD |

The San Francisco Pacifics were the state's championship team of 1866 and first holders of the Championship Bat.

The National Association, created in 1857 when the first 20-odd teams to be formed were primarily from greater New York City, had helped to standardize and popularize baseball. The championship teams through the early 1860s had hailed from Brooklyn, but in 1866 the Philadelphia Athletics, great-grandfather to the present Oakland A's, became the first non-New York team to win a championship.

The Eagles called for a convention of California baseball clubs—similar to those being held by the National Association—and the first meeting was held in August 1866. By the next year there were 25 member clubs at the convention, primarily from San Francisco and Oakland, and an estimated 100 baseball teams statewide.

Despite this burst of activity, the Eagles and Pacifics maintained their superiority over other teams. Their matches were bold and exciting. Gold Rush cavorting had not died off; between the drinkers and the gamblers, baseball still had a rough, bawdy, brawling quality.

One of the gamblers' favored ploys was to empty their six-shooters into the air just as a fielder was settling under a fly ball. Between no gloves, a very lively ball and gunsmoke in the background, errors—and scores— remained high. On April 18, 1867, for instance, the Eagles defeated the Pacifics 65-42.

Their games were usually close and bitterly contested. An extended set of 15 games between the Eagles and Pacifics from early 1866 into 1869 showed the Eagles winners eight times and the Pacifics seven times. Other rivalries arose, among them City College of San Francisco and the Live Oaks of Oakland. In a three-game set played in April 1866, the Live Oaks scored 131 runs yet lost two of the three games—the last one 84-39.

By the time of the second Pacific Convention in February 1867, there were 16 baseball club members from San Francisco, a half-dozen from Oakland and others from Santa Clara and San Jose. The Pacifics, led by the Shepard Brothers, were declared champions for 1866, and the

Championship Bat, crafted of Spanish cedar, was created. The bat was capped top and bottom with silver—this was the era of Nevada's silver Comstock Lode—and contained a silver plaque at the center of the bat. As with the silver game ball awarded to the Eagles for winning the State Agricultural title, this trophy did not survive 1906.

## RECREATION GROUNDS

Although the Pacific Convention was not held again until 1870 and the Sunday laws continued to interfere with practice and games, there were two significant developments that occurred towards the end of the 1860s. First, a pair of Australian immigrants, the Hatton brothers, bought a plot of land in what was then a remote section of the city—between Folsom, Harrison, 25th and 26th Streets—and built the West's first enclosed ballpark, Recreation Grounds.

The present-day site belies its pedigree. Half of the area is a green but slightly tattered park attached to nearby public housing, while the half closer to the former main entrance at 25th and Folsom contains worn-down, century-old Victorians.

In 1868, though, the Recreation Grounds were just what latter-day San Franciscans would love: a new ballpark. Although it was frequently windy, sandy and cold, the Outer Mission location also provided warm, sunny days. The playing surface consisted of a rolled dirt infield and a good grass outfield. There were also stands and concessions. Along with baseball and cricket, footraces, circus shows and other events paid the rent.

Opening Day on Thanksgiving, November 26, 1868, drew 4,000 spectators and featured a game between the Eagles and the Wide Awakes of Oakland. Box scores of the time showed outs made and runs scored, rather than at-bats and hits.

May 1869 saw the completion of the Transcontinental Railroad, which forever transformed baseball, among many other things. Now a trip that formerly took months could be completed in relative comfort and safety within days, with no Indian attacks and no suffering on the open plains or through the Western mountains.

As early as 1864 the Philadelphia Athletics had hired Al Reach at the then-amazing salary of $1,000 a season. The gentlemanly and amateur nature of the game of baseball in the 1840s and 1850s was rapidly being supplanted in the late 1860s by rough and aggressive semi-pro and finally professional teams as the post-Civil War man sought to earn or supplement his living through sport.

The final step occurred in 1869, when the first fully professional team, the Cincinnati Red Stockings, was formed. It took only a few months for the Hattons to arrange for the Red Stockings to visit. The Red Stockings

---

## SANDLOTS, KRANKS AND MUFFINS

One of the great charms of baseball is that it has changed so little in the past 150 years. Of course, there have been subtle changes, particularly in the terminology.

"Sandlot" baseball is a term that originated in San Francisco. In 1850, when San Francisco was chartered as a city, what is now the greater Civic Center area was then a large sand hill designated as Yerba Buena Cemetery. By 1860 the Board of Supervisors authorized the removal of the graves and the leveling of the hill, making the area a somewhat bare park. By 1869 the city was ready to move City Hall from Portsmouth Square to the Civic Center, but in the intervening 10 years the "Sand-Lot" had become a training ground for young ballplayers. San Francisco sportswriters coined the term "sandlotters" for young ballplayers, and by the beginning of the 1900s the term had spread everywhere.

Other baseball terms didn't make it. The term "muffin" once was used to describe a mediocre or error-prone player; today it survives in a different form, as in, "he muffed an easy catch."

Another unique 19th century term is "kranks" for fans. Its usage developed as a word out of the installation of turnstiles in eastern ballparks in the 1870s: One "crank" of the turnstile let in one customer. Kranks then were much like devoted fans now, not only attending games but keeping score, tracking statistics and players and reading newspaper accounts of the game.

"Hippodroming" meant play-acting and throwing the game, usually for gamblers. Hippodroming and drunkenness were factors—along with the lure of money—that led to repeated efforts to properly regulate the game in the latter part of the 19th century.

The ultimate humiliation in early baseball was to be "Chicagoed," or shut out. On July 23, 1870, the New York Mutuals defeated the Chicago Club by the then-remarkable score of 9-0. In all of 1870 there were only three "Chicagos," while in 1871, the National Association's first year, there were all of six shutouts.

The reasons for the high scores seen in early games are logical. Fielders did not wear gloves, playing surfaces were primitive, balls were sheepskin-covered rubber and yarn; pitchers still tossed underhand and the batter could request the placement of pitches.

spent the year barnstorming the entire country playing any and all teams, and generated a record of 65 wins, one tie and no losses. In 1870 they went 68-6. Finally, 1871 saw the formation of the first major league—the National Association of Professional Baseball Players—which lasted five seasons. In 1876 the National League was born.

The Red Stockings arrived in San Francisco on September 23, 1869 for a six-game series against local teams and all-stars. There were also cricket and baseball exhibition games. A final seventh formal game was played in Sacramento on October 5.

Thousands of spectators, braving the sand-ladened winds and traffic jams created by carriages and omnibuses, crowded Recreation Grounds for every game. The pavilion seats cost $2 in gold and the package tour of omnibus transportation and bullpen standing room went for $1 in gold.

Unfortunately, the play wasn't even sterling. After the first inning of the first of two games against the Eagles—by now a decade-old club—the Red Stockings held a 12-0 lead. They went on to post victories by scores of 35-4 and 58-4, then defeated the Pacifics 66-4 and 54-5,

the Atlantics 76-5, and the California All-Stars 46-14 and 50-6. It wasn't at all difficult to determine that the Eastern professionals were far advanced over their counterparts on the West Coast.

## THE 1870s—TRANSITION TO PROFESSIONALISM

The real agent of baseball progress turned out to be urbanization. The East and Midwest now had real cities with urban populations which could generate enough sustained baseball fans—then called "kranks"—and enough gate receipts to support professional teams.

Only the San Francisco Bay Area, in all of the west, had the urban population to keep up with Eastern cities. Los Angeles was still a mission and farm town; rail connections between the two cities were not even completed until 1887. So it fell upon the Bay Area to support the continued growth of baseball in the west.

One immediate result of the Red Stockings' visit was a resurgence of interest in organizing the game of baseball. Despite the shifting mobility of the general Bay Area pop-

The Oakland Grand Centrals (formerly the Wide Awakes) were recognized as one of the state's best teams in the early 1870s.

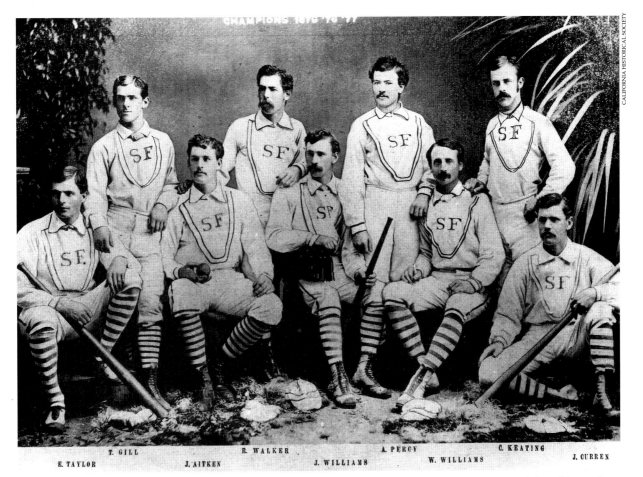

T. GILL     R. WALKER     A. PERCY     C. KEATING

E. TAYLOR     J. AITKEN     J. WILLIAMS     W. WILLIAMS     J. CURREN

The San Francisco Base Ball Club in an 1875 photograph taken by Thomas Houseworth. The San Franciscos and the Athletics of San Francisco vied for championship honors in 1875, 1876 and 1877.

ulation, there was enough stability in San Francisco and Oakland to hold the Convention of Base Ball Players for the Pacific Coast on June 14, 1870.

The Championship Bat moved to Oakland in 1871 when the Wide Awakes took the title. By 1874 they were called the Grand Centrals and were considered the best team in California. "Bay Ball" continued to be played with enthusiasm, if in a somewhat haphazard manner. The Athletics of San Francisco and the San Franciscos vied for local honors from 1875-77. A Pacific Slope championship tournament was organized at the Recreation Grounds in 1877, with the San Franciscos triumphant.

Professionalism had crept into the Bay Area game. For an August 12, 1877 match, the Athletics and San Franciscos bet $100 on the outcome, with the players sharing two-thirds of the gate receipts. The San Franciscos possessed the first real home-grown star, Ed "Live Oak" Taylor, who regularly turned in brilliant defensive plays in the outfield. Taylor, who played into the late 1880s with local teams and even got into a couple of major league games during his long career, was credited with introducing gloves to the outfield.

The Bay Area was lurching forward into a new era of professional baseball. ❖

CHAPTER **2**

# MIGHTY CASEY AT THE BAT

The best-known baseball star of all time began his career in the San Francisco Bay Area in 1888, with notices of his prowess first appearing in the *San Francisco Examiner* on June 3.

He is, of course, Mighty Casey of "Casey at the Bat."

"Casey" started his career inconspicuously tucked into page 4 of that Sunday's edition of the *Examiner*, lodged between editorials on the left and Ambrose Bierce's column on the right.

A minor blip of interest caused several newspapers in the East to reprint the poem. The *New York Sporting Times* reprinted it on July 29, 1888, changing the locale from Mudville to Boston, and Casey to Mike "King" Kelly, the most flamboyant ballplayer of the day. But as one of literally thousands of pieces of doggerel which were published in the many newspapers and magazines of the time, "Casey" seemed headed for quick oblivion.

### "CASEY" HITS THE NEW YORK STAGE

An improbable sequence of events then headed the ballad on its path to lasting fame. A New York novelist, Archibald Gunter, had visited San Francisco during the summer of 1888. Liking "Casey," he tucked a clipping of it in his wallet. Two months after returning to New York City, he was chatting with his friend, comic opera star De Wolf Hopper.

Hopper was appearing in "Prince Methusalem," a comic opera at Wallack's Theater at Broadway and 30th Street. Hopper was also a krank—a serious baseball fan—who had developed a close friendship with members of the New York Giants. At his instigation, James Mutrie's Giants and Cap Anson's Chicago White Stockings were invited to the show as guests of the management.

Hopper wanted to perform something special in honor of the two baseball teams but wasn't sure what would be appropriate. Gunter quickly pulled the ragged newspaper clipping from his pocket.

So on the evening of August 14, 1888 in the midst of the second act—with the Giants in box seats on one side of the theater and the White Stockings in boxes on the other—De Wolf Hopper recited "Casey at the Bat" for the first of an estimated 10,000 times during his career. Hopper wrote in his memoirs, "When I dropped my voice to B flat, below low C, at 'the multitude was awed,' I remember seeing Buck Ewing's gallant mustachios give a single nervous twitch. And as the house, after a moment of startled silence, grasped the anticlimactic denouement, it shouted its glee."

The next day's review in the *New York Times* noted that the poem was "uproariously received" by the audience. Six weeks later, Hopper delivered a second recital at a dinner honoring the Giants for winning the 1888 National League pennant.

There was such a strong bond of friendship between the team and Hopper that the actor was given a gold-tipped cane by the Giants as a memento of the occasion. That cane appeared in San Francisco in a 100th anniversary exhibition honoring "Casey" in 1988. In addition, Hopper got his photograph taken with Giants players, appearing in a set of cabinet cards. It was a forerunner of modern-day baseball cards.

Wherever Hopper went, whatever show he was appearing in, the crowds called for "Casey" as an encore. With a four-octave range and a stage actor's grand gestures, Hopper became the undisputed champion, as well as introducer, of "Casey" recitation.

Hopper constantly experimented with slight variations in emphasis and gesture during his readings. He had it down to exactly five minutes and 40 seconds of delivery. A recording of Hopper reciting "Casey" may strike today's listeners as somewhat excessive, but to the stage and vaudeville patron of the late 1800s, it was a stirring and gripping tale of our National Pastime.

Well aware that the ballad was his claim to lasting fame, Hopper had impressive things to say about "Casey." He asserted the poem was the only truly great comic poem written by an American.

"It is as perfect an epitome of our national game today as it was when every player drank his coffee from a moustache cup," he wrote. "There are one or more Caseys in every league, bush or big, and there is no day in the playing season that this same supreme tragedy, as stark as Aristophanes for the moment, does not befall on some field. It is unique in all verse in that it is not only funny and ironic, but excitingly dramatic, with the suspense built up to a perfect climax. There is no lame line among the fifty-two."

## AUTHOR! AUTHOR!

The author of "Casey at the Bat" was Ernest Lawrence Thayer, although that was not clear for a number of years. Thayer was reluctant to claim parentage or to think much of his child.

Thayer was born the son of well-to-do parents in 1863; his father owned and ran the American Woolen Mills. After a privileged early life in Worcester, Massachusetts, young Thayer went off to study philosophy under William James at Harvard, where he demonstrated an exceptional mind. He wrote the annual Hasty Pudding play, was editor of the *Harvard Lampoon* and avidly followed the Harvard baseball team.

While Thayer was graduating magna cum laude and Phi Beta Kappa in 1885, his friend, William Randolph Hearst—the *Lampoon's* business manager—was thrown out of the college. Hearst's father, who had recently purchased the *San Francisco Examiner* as a vehicle to promote his candidacy for the U.S. Senate, then appointed William Randolph as its publisher.

Meanwhile, Thayer went to Paris. Hearst tracked him down and offered him a job in San Francisco writing a humor column for the Sunday supplement. Thayer's work, mostly unsigned, began appearing in 1886. From October through December 1887, he wrote a series of ballads which ran in the Sunday edition about every other week. He signed these "Phin," a derivative of his Harvard nickname "Phinny."

Thayer took ill and returned to his family back east but continued to send in material to the *Examiner* for several months. The very last piece, "Casey at the Bat," signed by "Phin," was written and submitted in May 1888. Thayer, 25 at the time, was paid $5 for "Casey."

Back home, Thayer ran one of his father's mills for many years. "Casey" was far from his mind as he kept a decidedly modest attitude towards claiming his great work. Even Hopper didn't know who the author was for five years after he began reading the poem. Finally, one night after having performed in a Worcester theater, Hopper was invited to a local men's club to meet Thayer. There he heard the author's somewhat uninspired reading of his own poem.

Thayer attended his 10th class reunion at Harvard in 1895, where he read "Casey" and delivered what was called an eloquent speech. In the meantime, copies of the poem were constantly being printed, revised and misprinted. Many different "authors" stepped forward and every second-rate player nicknamed Casey claimed the ballad was written about him. The "Casey at the Bat" phenomenon was only beginning.

By the turn of the century practically everyone in America had read or heard "Casey," but hardly anyone knew its author. Thayer continued to have a low opinion of his own work. "During my brief connection with the *Examiner* I put out large quantites of nonsense, both prose and verse, sounding the whole newspaper gamut from advertisements to editorials," he wrote. "In general quality 'Casey' (at least in my judgment) is neither better nor worse than much of the other stuff."

Between his own modesty and lack of need for money, Thayer did not go out of his way to claim authorship or royalties. Correct attribution was finally worked out in January 1909—21½ years after it was written—when Thayer authorized printing of a slightly revised version of the poem in *The Bookman* magazine.

Over the years "Casey" has been endlessly copied, parodied and corrupted. Grantland Rice, *Mad* magazine and science fiction author Ray Bradbury have done

## CASEY AT THE BAT
### (Original version)

A Ballad of the Republic, Sung in the year 1888

The outlook wasn't brilliant for the Mudville nine that day;
The score stood four to two with but one inning to play.
And then when Cooney died at first, and Barrows did the same,
A sickly silence fell upon the patrons of the game.

A straggling few got up to go in deep despair. The rest
Clung to that hope which springs eternal in the human breast;
They thought if only Casey could but get a whack at that—
We'd put up even money now with Casey at the bat.

But Flynn preceeded Casey, as did also Jimmy Blake,
And the former was a lulu, and the latter was a cake;
So upon the stricken multitude grim melancholy sat,
For there seemed but little chance of Casey's getting to the bat.

But Flynn let drive a single, to the wonderment of all,
And Blake, the much despis-ed, tore the cover off the ball;
And when the dust had lifted, and the men saw what had occurred,
There was Johnnie safe at second and Flynn a-hugging third.

Then from 5,000 throats and more there rose a lusty yell;
It rumbled through the valley, it rattled in the dell;
It knocked upon the mountain and recoiled upon the flat,
For Casey, mighty Casey, was advancing to the bat.

There was ease in Casey's manner as he stepped into his place;
There was pride in Casey's bearing and a smile on Casey's face.
And when, responding to the cheers, he lightly doffed his hat,
No stranger in the crowd could doubt 'twas Casey at the Bat.

Ten thousand eyes were on him as he rubbed his hands with dirt;
Five thousand tongues applauded when he wiped them on his shirt.
Then while the writhing pitcher ground the ball into his hip,
Defiance gleamed in Casey's eye, a sneer curled Casey's lip.

And now the leather-covered sphere came hurtling through the air,
And Casey stood a-watching it in haughty grandeur there.
Close by the sturdy batsman the ball unheeded sped—
"That ain't my style," said Casey. "Strike one," the umpire said.

From the benches, black with people, there went up a muffled roar,
Like the beating of the storm-waves on a stern and distant shore.
"Kill him! Kill the umpire!" shouted someone in the stand;
And it's likely they'd have killed him had not Casey raised his hand.

With a smile of Christian charity great Casey's visage shone;
He stilled the rising tumult; he bade the game go on;
He signaled to the pitcher, and once more the spheroid flew;
But Casey still ignored it, and the umpire said "Strike two."

"Fraud!" cried the maddened thousands, and echo answered fraud;
But one scornful look from Casey and the audience was awed.
They saw his face grow stern and cold, they saw his muscles strain,
And they knew that Casey wouldn't let that ball go by again.

The sneer is gone from Casey's lip, his teeth are clenched in hate;
He pounds with cruel violence his bat upon the plate.
And now the pitcher holds the ball, and now he lets it go,
And now the air is shattered by the force of Casey's blow.

Oh, somewhere in this favored land the sun is shining bright;
The band is playing somewhere, and somewhere hearts are light,
And somewhere men are laughing, and somewhere children shout;
But there is no joy in Mudville—mighty Casey has struck out.

"Casey" spoofs. Movies have been made and records of dramatic readings have been released. Even an opera, *The Mighty Casey*, was written in the 1950s.

### SO WHERE'S MUDVILLE?

Mudville and its baseball nine were largely a product of Thayer's imagination. Although Thayer insisted the town and players were all invented, this does not seem to be totally true. During the period of Thayer's stay in San Francisco, the four-team California League included an entry from Stockton, about 90 miles away. The quickest way to reach Stockton from the Bay Area was by Delta steamboat, and because the trip included scraping over muddy shallows along the way, the locals derisively called Stockton "Mudville." Furthermore, many Stockton players bore names suspiciously similar to those in the poem, often with only a letter or two changed.

As for the great Casey, he was nowhere to be seen in Stockton. Thayer claimed in a letter to the editor of the *Syracuse Post-Standard* that Casey was actually a big Irish lad who had threatened Thayer in high school. A decade later, Thayer got his revenge in the poem. ❖

# CHAPTER 3

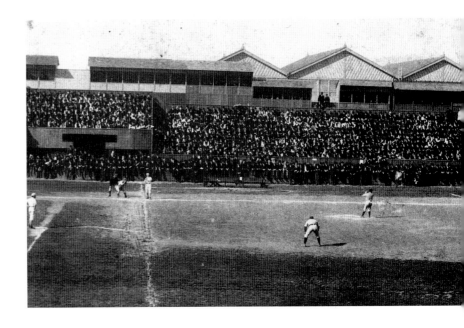

# DISORGANIZED BASEBALL

The first two decades of baseball in California could be called an "Age of Innocence." Games were played as social get-togethers as well as to soothe men's competitive urges. Although the local version of the National Pastime lacked refinement, it nonetheless attracted society's upper crust as well as its roughnecks. Bay Area kranks loved their baseball. Even women were enthusiasts and were normally allowed free admission.

Fans all along the West Coast had gained an appetite for more and better play. Major league junkets to California helped educate and excite both players and fans, and the outcome of the most recent local games became the subject of conversation in saloons and salons throughout San Francisco.

**PLAY FOR PAY BEGINS**

The region was ready for advancement to the next level of sophistication—playing the game for pay. A group of prosperous and interested San Franciscans inaugurated the Pacific Baseball League in 1878. The league's unique feature was its manner of hiring players to fill its rosters; the PBL was strictly semi-professional. Four teams—the Athletics, Californians, Eagles and Renos—

played weekend games at Recreation Grounds. After expenses, the gate receipts were split among the players. During the remainder of the week, the players had to work at regular jobs.

The Pacific League proved so popular with the citizens of San Francisco that there appeared room for expansion. For the following season, 1879, entrepreneurs formed a rival circuit which they named the California League, thus providing competition to the Pacific League and offering kranks a choice of games.

The Californians and the Athletics both jumped to the new California League, giving it instant credibility. They were joined by the Mutuals of San Francisco and the Oaklands from across the bay. The Californians and Athletics were replaced by the Stars and the Knickerbockers, keeping the Pacific League an all-San Francisco entity.

The California League played its games at the Center Street Park in downtown Oakland while the Pacific League continued at San Francisco's Recreation Grounds. Both leagues were relatively successful, occasionally playing before crowds of 5,000 spectators. At season's end, the champions of the two leagues met at the Recreation Grounds for an exhibition playoff. The Knickerbockers of the Pacific League defeated the Californians 6-5.

## THE BAY CITIES NINE SHOCKS CHICAGO

The Cincinnati Red Stockings returned to California in the winter of 1879 after a 10-year absence. They were joined by the Rochester Hop Bitters and the Chicago White Stockings. Although the visitors won on the field, the junket was a financial disappointment because of poor attendance; many games were played mid-week and local fans couldn't attend because they were at work.

But there was one significant development to arise from that tour: Cal McVey, a talented player for Cincinnati who had participated as a 19-year-old during the 1869 tour, remained in San Francisco after the exhibitions ended. McVey became active in baseball circles and organized the Bay Cities Nine, a group that quickly became the powerhouse of Bay Area baseball.

During the winter of 1880, future Hall of Famer Cap Anson brought his Chicago team, the National League champions, to San Francisco for an exhibition series. The Bay Cities Nine trounced the mighty champs by winning four of six games but folded shortly thereafter. McVey continued to organize various teams before eventually retiring from the game.

While the game continued to grow in popularity through the early 1880s, it still lacked a strong foundation. Teams in both the Pacific and California leagues often formed and disbanded within the same season.

In 1882 John J. Mone, a San Francisco attorney, became president of the California League and provided some desired stability. A four-team league with strict rules was re-established. The league played a limited schedule over the next four years. Outside the league, other teams organized and played pick-up type schedules.

## THE HAVERLYS AND THE G&Ms ARE FORMED

The Haverlys team dominated the California League from 1883 to 1886. Many of Northern California's best players joined the Haverlys, with several later going east to play in the major leagues. Catcher Lou "Pop" Hardie, pitcher-outfielder Jim Fogarty, infielder Pete Sweeney and pitcher Pete Meegan—all local residents—were members of the 1883 Haverlys and ultimately went on to play in the major leagues.

In mid-season 1885, a group of local players formed the Pioneers. This new San Francisco-based team was to become the arch-rival of the Haverlys. The Pioneers sported several exciting players on their roster, including the Smith brothers—Hugh and "Big John." The Smiths anchored the corners of the infield and were fearsome hitters. Mike Finn was the team's star pitcher and manager.

In 1886, the California League aligned itself with the National League of Professional Baseball Clubs, an organization formed by team owners a decade earlier. The "National Agreement," as it was called, prevented players from jumping contracts and established a major/minor league structure. Affiliating with organized baseball gave owners some feeling of security; still, various outlaw teams were ready to pirate away a team's best player.

For the 1886 season, league organizers determined to invite the popular Altas team of Sacramento to join the California League. The Altas were an exciting nine, and the owners of the three San Francisco based teams—the Stars, Haverlys and Pioneers—saw the presence of the Altas as a means to stimulate gate receipts.

In a pre-season conflict over rental fees for the use of Central Park, Mone pulled his league out of the facility, negotiating the use of a park yet to be built on Alameda island. To fill the void at Central Park, D.R. McNeill, the commissioner of the Central Park Association, leased the diamond to yet another fledgling league, the California State League. The four-team league was composed of three San Francisco teams—the Californians, Damianas and Knickerbockers—with an Oakland entry, the Greenhood & Morans, rounding out the new circuit.

As the 1886 season began, two leagues once again were competing for the allegiance of the fans, with the California League acknowledged to have had better players than its rival. But in early May several events changed the course of the season as well as the future of baseball in San Francisco.

One of the most significant involved the well-known Stars pitcher, Jimmy Mullee, who became a martyr for the team and the league by trying to foil a plan by two men to take over the team. Mullee learned of the plan and proceeded to make such a mockery of a game against the Haverlys that most observers were convinced he was trying to throw the game. Mullee was blacklisted and the Stars were expelled from the league as a result of this incident. Mullee later tried to defend his actions through public apologies and eventually signed with the Californias in the California State League. A week later, the Greenhood & Morans jumped leagues, replacing the Stars in the California League.

The Greenhood & Morans were sponsored by owners of an Oakland clothing store, Jacob Greenhood and James T. Moran. Hired to manage the team was Colonel Tom Robinson, a shrewd promoter who seemed to flit from one controversy to another. While the sponsorship of the G&Ms continued only three more years, Robinson remained as team manager and later its owner for several additional seasons.

The G&Ms were a popular draw around the league and boasted a lineup including several future major league players. The most popular was lefty George Van Haltren, the team's pitcher and top hitter. Van Haltren was the first great baseball star to come out of the Bay Area. He would play in the major leagues for 17 seasons, primarily with the New York Giants, compiling 2,536 hits

Right, four surviving members of the 1887 Greenhood & Morans of Oakland, taken 50 years later on Old Timers Day, September 12, 1937. Van Haltren and Knell were solid major leaguers before the turn of the century, and Lange gained fame by writing *A History of Baseball in California and the Pacific Coast Leagues* in 1938. Top, an 1888 publicity photograph of the G&Ms.

OLD TIMERS DAY ∽ SEALS STADIUM ∽ SEPT. 12, 1937.
Members of the Greenhood & Moran team of 1887
PHIL KNELL, P    TOM McCORD, SS    GEO. VAN HALTREN, CF    FRED LANGE, C

and a .316 lifetime batting average. Although mainly an outfielder in the big leagues, Van Haltren also managed to win 40 games.

Van Haltren played the 1904 season at Seattle and came to bat 941 times, creating a PCL record that will stand forever. In 1905 at age 39, Van Haltren returned to Oakland for a five-year stint as player-manager of the Pacific Coast League's Oakland Commuters before turning to umpiring, again in the Coast League.

Van Haltren's teammates included outfielder Danny Long, who enjoyed a distinguished career with Oakland teams. He later managed the San Francisco Seals and then became the West Coast scout for the Chicago White Sox. Willard "California" Brown was the team's catcher. After the 1886 season, Brown, a San Franciscan, graduated from the G&Ms to the New York Giants for a seven-year major league stint.

Brown had replaced catcher "Dolan" early in 1886. "Dolan" in reality was Fred W. Lange, a teenager playing under an assumed name so his parents wouldn't find out he was playing such an uncivilized game. His parents nevertheless learned of the ruse but allowed him to continue playing ball under his true name. Lange had a well-

traveled career, but his legacy to Bay Area baseball came from the writing of a book, *History of Baseball in California and the Pacific Coast Leagues, 1847-1938*.

When the G&Ms jumped to the California League, it became a more regional operation as Sacramento and Oakland teams guaranteed broader appeal for the league and gave it more credibility.

## BIGGER CROWDS, LARGER PARKS, SAME OLD CHAOS

Baseball was so popular in 1886 that no field was large enough to accommodate the throngs. During the subsequent winter league, officials negotiated a lease of property at the eastern end of Golden Gate Park to build a larger stadium. The result was the construction of the Haight Street Grounds. For the next seven years Haight Street Grounds was home to San Francisco teams, drawing crowds approaching 20,000 for crucial games.

Between 1887 and 1893, the California League was plagued by yearly team shifts. The Altas left the league after the 1888 season to become a part of a local circuit

A California League game played at the Haight Street Grounds, near Golden Gate Park, between the Pioneers and the Haverlys on October 9, 1887. Crowds of 15,000 to 20,000 were common at the games between the crosstown rivals. The Pioneers edged the Haverlys for the championship by one game that year.

A publicity photograph of the 1889 Oakland Base Ball Club.

The 1891 Oaklands, managed by Colonel Tom Robinson, in his suit in the middle row. Robinson was an excellent promoter of his teams and of himself. He was highly controversial due to his hiring and arbitrary firing of his players.

where they could play a more dominant role. They were replaced by Stockton. Teams were placed in San Jose, returned to Sacramento, and even located in Los Angeles. Concurrently, the league was challenged by competing leagues that usually were established in the spring but gone by the fall.

As California moved into the last decade of the 19th century, it was obvious that the league hadn't yet established itself as a permanent fixture on the sporting scene. Owners refused to treat their players fairly, often reneging on financial promises. Players therefore felt little loyalty to their teams. To compound the problem, a period of nationwide economic stagnation plagued the early 1890s. People didn't have money to spend on baseball.

In preparation for the 1892 season, league owners had to deal with a major problem: The Sacramento franchise had been on the verge of collapse for more than a year and had suffered through a series of owners. The league decided to drop Sacramento in favor of Los Angeles.

Los Angeles at that time was a small but rapidly growing community in Southern California. Even with

the distance, its potential for success was greater than any other applicant requesting admission to the league. But it would also cost more to travel there and back.

These additional costs made the 1892 season a losing one for the league. But there were interesting developments on the field. A split-season schedule created two winners and the opportunity for a playoff series. San Jose won the first half and Los Angeles fended off a surge by Oakland to win the second half. Los Angeles concluded the season with games in San Jose and Colonel Robinson loaned San Jose his top lefty pitchers, Van Haltren and Charles DeWald, in an effort to drop the Looloos into second place behind Oakland.

Yes, they were called the Looloos.

Robinson's ploy didn't work; the prospect of a playoff series loomed. League directors gathered to formulate the playoff only to be thwarted when San Jose Owner Mike Finn refused to pay to send his team to Los Angeles. Finn wouldn't relent even when Los Angeles Owner G.A. Vanderbeck offered to pay San Jose's travel costs.

The San Jose players, seeing a big payoff by playing

# THE GREAT BILL LANGE—STAR OF THE 1890s

Many local baseball historians and fans feel Lefty O'Doul deserves to be in Baseball's Hall of Fame. O'Doul was a great hitter, exceptional nurturer of talent and a fine international ambassador of the game.

The other San Franciscan recognized as one of the truly great players of the game who will never get to Cooperstown is Bill Lange. A robust 6-foot-2 and 200 pounds of muscle, Lange—nicknamed both Big Bill and Little Eva—played a stellar seven years for the Chicago White Stockings during the 1890s.

Brought up in the Presidio District of the city, Big Bill learned his baseball on Golden Gate Park

Bill Lange was a San Franciscan who many observers felt was the best baseball player in the game at the turn of the century. He was big, fast and powerful. In seven seasons with the Chicago Nationals from 1893-99, Lange hit .330 and stole 399 bases.

diamonds. He dropped out of high school in 1889 to sign a contract with Port Townsend, Washington. Two years later he moved to Seattle of the Pacific Northwest League. When that team folded in late 1892, Lange returned to the Bay Area and played for Oakland of the California League. By 1893 he was a starter for the Chicago team of the National League.

Lange became a truly sensational player on a mediocre team. He batted .389 in 1895 and constructed a .330 lifetime average in his seven years in the majors. Not only was he big and strong, he was fast: He stole 84 bases during the 1896 season, and averaged almost 60 steals a year—399 steals in seven seasons.

His defensive skills were at the same superlative level. His size and speed, as well as his cannon of an arm, drew praise from his contemporaries who put his overall abilities on the same plane as Ty Cobb's. Lange has been variously described by baseball authorities as "the fastest player of the 1890s," "the greatest defensive outfielder of the decade" and the "greatest player of the era." Wrote one: "Bill Lange stands as the finest everyday, all-around player to retire from baseball at the peak of his career."

The immortal Albert Spalding named Lange to his all-time All-Star team over Tris Speaker, saying, "Both men could go back or to either side equally well. Both were lightning fast in handling ground balls. But no man I ever saw could go forward and get a low line drive like Lange."

Old-time star Tim Murnane's all-time All-Star outfield consisted of Ty Cobb, Joe Jackson and Lange. Al Spink, founder of *The Sporting News*, considered Lange the equal of Ty Cobb.

Lange was handsome, warm and outgoing, with a wit that would get him into and then out of trouble. He became Chicago's captain after just his first season. His most celebrated exploit came in a game against Baltimore in 1897. Chicago led the Orioles 6-5 in the eighth inning as twilight descended. The White Stockings wanted to call the game, but the umpires ignored their pleas. When Lange came up to bat that inning, he struck a match to see where the plate was, a jest that cost him a $10 fine.

He got his revenge in the last of the ninth, with a man on second and two out. The Orioles' Joe Kelly hit a fly ball that cleared the left field fence, but it was so dark that neither the umpires nor the spectators could see it. Lange shouted to left fielder Jimmy Ryan, "Put her here, Jim." Ryan threw an imaginary ball to Lange, who made believe he stuffed it in his back pocket as he ran off the field.

At the height of his game, Lange tired of playing for a second-division team. The White Stockings finished no better than fourth during his tenure there and twice finished ninth in a 12-team league. Although he was making a phenomenal salary for the period—$3,300 per year—Lange quit after the 1899 season.

Chicago offered to double his salary, but Lange returned to San Francisco, married well and became wealthy in Peninsula real estate. He still loved baseball, though, and frequently attended Seals Stadium until his death in 1950.

## THE FISHERS—FIRST FAMILY OF BAY AREA BASEBALL

When Gap Inc. Owner Donald Fisher and his son, John Fisher, bought into the San Francisco Giants in 1993, many people wondered where their interest in baseball had come from. "Uncle Mike" is the answer.

A native San Franciscan, Mike Fisher moved to Sacramento in 1884 to play for the Altas. That team, along with the Haverlys and the Pioneers of San Francisco, as well as the Greenhood & Morans of Oakland, would play each other on a regular basis.

The California League was their home. As Mike recounted in a newspaper article in the 1920s, one of the rules of the league at the time

To play for the Sacramento Altas, Mike Fisher, a native San Franciscan, was required by league rules to live in California's capital.

was that a player had to live in the town where he played. Mike was given a job in the Southern Pacific machine shops in Sacramento.

"It was a great place to work—when we won," said Mike. "The master mechanic would say, 'Now take it easy, Mike. Don't work up a sweat. You've got a hard game coming up Sunday.' But when we lost, not a man in the shop would speak to me, and I'd get the toughest, meanest job the master mechanic could dig up for me."

Mike survived the shops and enjoyed Sacramento baseball so much he stuck around for many years. When the Pacific Coast League was formed in 1903, Mike was the manager of Sacramento's entry, the Sacts, which included catcher Charlie Graham, later to own the San Francisco Seals.

In 1904, the franchise was shifted to Tacoma, replacing a team which had performed in the recently defunct Pacific Northwest League. The 1904 Tacoma Tigers were the league power-house, winning the first half of a split season and defeating Los Angeles for the pennant in a post-season playoff.

Pacific Coast League turmoil caught up with the Tigers despite their first-half title in the 1905 split season. The team tailed off in the second half and was forced to relocate back to Sacramento to stay afloat financially. After losing the 1905 play-offs, the team once again moved—to Fresno—and Mike found himself running the Fresno Raisin Pickers. After a last-place finish in 1906, compli-cated by the earthquake's effect on the league, Fresno folded.

Mike's greatest success was in 1908, when he organized the Reach All-Americans, the first base-ball team to barnstorm through Japan, China, Hawaii and the Philippines.

in Los Angeles, arranged a playoff themselves. But sever-al key San Jose players decided at the last minute not to travel. Without them, the team dropped the eight-game series five games to two with one tie. The league directors refused to recognize the playoff results and dropped the Looloos from the league.

### DISORGANIZATION AND DISASTER

Keeping with the disorganized tradition of the California League, a new season found a new mixture of franchises. San Jose had been a financial dud in 1892 and Finn moved his team to Stockton. Al Lindley of Los Angeles convinced the directors of the importance of his

city in the league and the Looloos were readmitted. It had been Los Angeles' attendance in 1892 that had saved the California League from financial disaster. Oakland and San Francisco rounded out the four-team circuit.

The 1893 season started out poorly as early atten-dance was down in both Oakland and Stockton. In Oakland Colonel Robinson was threatened by a player boycott after missing two payrolls and finally sold his interest to a pair of more well-heeled Oakland business-men. Stockton was also troubled. A potential player boy-cott over a roster change and poor attendance caused Finn to give up and sell out.

With three new owners taking seats at the league directors' meeting, Lindley initiated a revolt against Mone and his presidency. Lindley contended the public had lost

HAIWAII. JAPAN. CHINA. MANILA.

1908.
1909.

The Reach All-Americans were the first baseball team to tour throughout the Pacific and Asia. The ballclub, organized by Mike Fisher, barnstormed through Japan, China, Hawaii and the Philippines. The team's mascot was Mike's nephew, Sydney (foreground).

Mike's nephew, Sydney, grew up to become a San Francisco home-builder and lifelong Seals and Giants fan, as well as father to Don, Bob and Jim Fisher. Don's son John, a fourth-generation San Franciscan, is involved with the partnership owning the Giants. Mike moved back to San Francisco in the 1920s and became a resident authority on old-time baseball in the Bay Area.

One great Fisher mystery remains: the identity of Mike's father. A John M. Fisher was one of the charter members of the San Francisco Eagles in 1859. John M. was their regular shortstop for the next decade at least, playing in the first California baseball game of substance, against the Sacramentos in 1860. He also played in the inaugural game at the original Recreation Grounds in 1868, represented the Eagles at the Pacific Base Ball Convention in 1866 and was the Eagles' shortstop against the Cincinnati Red Stockings in 1869.

Fisher owned the silver ball that had been awarded the Eagles for their victory in 1860, and at the turn of the century was being touted as "The father of base ball in California" in S. R. Church's history of early baseball. Was he the great-great grandfather of the present-day John Fisher?

confidence in the traditional leadership, convincing his first-year colleagues to oust Mone. Mone's 11-year tenure ended in mid-season with Bob Weiland, a local businessman and fan, replacing him.

Also at mid-season 1893 the Stockton franchise collapsed and was replaced by Sacramento, which itself lasted just five weeks. Its owners wanted a financial guarantee from Los Angeles before traveling south for a series. The guarantee was not offered, Sacramento refused to travel and both teams disbanded.

Not all was without promise. Oakland produced a young 23-year-old pitcher named Clark Griffith who won 30 games, pitching 425 innings. He would go on to notch 240 wins in the majors and ultimately own the Washington Senators of the American League.

On July 2 in Los Angeles, the Looloos and Stocktons attempted to play a night exhibition game at Athletic Park. The teams had played a regular-season game in the afternoon and came back later for the night-time experiment. Before a packed house, the teams played a frivolous contest; the field was illuminated by a multitude of kerosene lamps and a theatre arc lamp was focused on the ball as it moved around the field of play.

The game's most entertaining event came when a dog ran away with the game ball. The conclusion from this experiment was that Thomas Edison's technology wasn't quite ready yet.

While it was presumed the California League would organize again for 1894, this didn't happen. Mismanagement of the league by its director-owners and a soft economy were the main culprits. Local fans had so often been turned off by the antics of greedy owners and the turmoil created by disenchanted ballplayers that they began seeking their entertainment elsewhere.

## A VAST WASTELAND

During the next four years, organized baseball did not exist in the Bay Area. All the good players went elsewhere to ply their trade. Summer and winter leagues were organized, but they were much less formal and were generally manned by younger players.

During the winter of 1895, a four-team professional league was organized by Charles Comiskey of the Cincinnati Red Stockings. When it became obvious the league was not going to be a financial success, Comiskey pulled up stakes and headed east.

To fill the void, the *San Francisco Examiner* sponsored a tournament during the winter of 1896 to determine the state's top amateur youth team. The tournament was highly successful and its concept was expanded for 1897 to include players of all ages.

The 1897 tournament drew several excellent amateur teams from around the state, becoming very competitive and the center of controversy. Two of its finest teams, Gilt

Doc Moskiman pitched for both Oakland and San Francisco.

Edge of Sacramento and Reliance of Oakland, were disqualified because they had played an exhibition game before the tournament opened. Rather than getting angry, the two clubs invited teams from San Francisco and Stockton to join them in the California Winter League, a weekend semi-professional circuit. This league was a big step towards the return of professional baseball to Northern California.

## LEAGUE PLAY RETURNS

After four years without quality baseball in the Bay Area, fans were ready for the return of an organized league. And there were businessmen prepared to take the risks necessary to bring it about. Two leagues formed simultaneously for the 1898 season, each sporting six teams. Often there were competing teams in the same community attempting to attract the same fans.

Both leagues played weekend schedules but they also had teams filled with young and inexperienced players. The quality of the baseball was much lower than in the pre-1893 era.

It became rapidly apparent that competition between the two leagues, the Pacific States League and the new California League, would cause the demise of both. They quickly united to form one eight-team league, named the Pacific Coast League, with Eugene F. Bert serving as its president. Its season was abbreviated to approximately 40 games per team.

Some of the stronger teams from the previous leagues entered the new league virtually intact, while others merged with each other, taking the best players from several teams. The contracts signed by many players led to questions of eligibility if National Agreement guidelines were strictly followed.

About the same time as the league was consolidating, the Spanish-American War broke out. Newspapers designated their prime space to the war, and readers' attention was focused on the events in Havana Bay, not those in San Francisco Bay. Without the help of newspaper publicity, it was difficult to fill the grandstands.

Although the 1898 version of the PCL attempted to play by the National Agreement, a multitude of illegal players filled the rosters, play was shoddy and umpiring was inconsistent and sometimes suspicious. The fact the league survived was a compliment to the tenacity of its owners' determination to resurrect organized baseball and the desire of kranks to watch it.

Sacramento's Gilt Edge was one of the teams that came into the PCL from the PSL with its original lineup intact. In fact, Gilt Edge won the championship. Gilt Edge teammates Charles "Demon" Doyle, at 10-5, and Erwin "Silent" Harvey, 14-8, were the league's top pitchers, alternating between the mound and the outfield.

Baseball games have been written about in the daily newspapers for more than a century. The style of writing used for reporting the results of a ballgame underwent several major changes throughout the 20th century.

Today's style of investigative reporting is relatively new, having replaced a more simplistic reporting by observation.

A report on a game at the turn of the century would be brief, but effusive, and devoid of detail. A box score was seldom seen. This made compiling statistics more difficult.

For pitchers, winning percentage was a key statistic. The earned run average was not calculated until 1914. Runs batted in was not a statistic until 1922.

It was common for editorial opinion to be injected, sometimes to extremes, to provide the reader with a flavor of the game.

The following was the complete report of a game played on July 8, 1888, as reported in the *San Jose Mercury*.

"A SNIDE GAME: San Francisco, July 8— The game at the Haight Street Grounds this afternoon between the Greenhood & Morans and the Pioneers was a veritable farce, the men in both clubs playing very poorly. The majority of those present left the grounds in disgust before the game was half over. It was probably the poorest exhibition of professional ball-playing ever given in San Francisco."

---

The presence of so many illegal players led to a multitude of protests over their eligibility, but the outcome of many of these protests was never announced, making an official finish unclear. Artistically—and in many cases financially—the league was a failure, but it still ushered in a successful return from four years without professional baseball in California. Bert, the league president, announced the circuit would be reorganized for 1899. The league title reverted to "California Baseball League," and the six-team league applied for membership in the National Association. However, San Jose disbanded at mid-season and Watsonville was dropped, making it a four-team league once again.

It was apparent the only way the league could be a financial success was to go with the four largest cities in the area: San Francisco, Oakland, Sacramento and Stockton. This was the makeup of the league as the California League moved into the 20th century.

## NEW CENTURY, OLD PROBLEMS

The league in 1900 entangled itself in a contractural mess when Jay Hughes jumped from the Brooklyn Superbas to become Gilt Edge's stellar gate attraction. This illegal player move forced the California League to abrogate its National Association agreement.

Hughes had led Brooklyn of the National League in 1899 with a 28-6 record. But Hughes' wife was not happy in New York and did not want to return to Brooklyn for the 1900 season. When Hughes was rebuffed in his effort to get a pay raise after his fine season, he decided to stay home in Sacramento.

Local businessmen convinced Hughes to play for Sacramento by chipping in the equivalent of his previous season's salary. They were not disappointed when Hughes went 23-9 to lead Gilt Edge to its third consecutive championship.

The problem was that as a member of the National Association of Professional Baseball Leagues, the California League should have returned Hughes to Brooklyn. Instead, the league dropped its membership, thus protecting Hughes and keeping his gate appeal at home. It was no surprise, then, that the National Association gave the California League no support when an outlaw league in Montana started luring players away from the West Coast during the season.

Still, 1900 had been a marvelous success. The quality of baseball had improved and money was made around the league with the exception of Stockton. Stockton's team wasn't very good and few owners had confidence the small community could support a team, good or bad.

The Stockton problem was solved when Jim Morley of Los Angeles applied to join the league for the 1901 season. Much had changed in Los Angeles since the city last played in the California League. Los Angeles now was second only to San Francisco in population and it offered an untapped market much as Sacramento had in 1886. The directors accepted Morley's application and dropped Stockton from the league.

Entering the 1901 season, the California cities that would inaugurate Pacific Coast League play in 1903 were now in place. Likewise, many of the future PCL leaders were in positions of control. Cal Ewing was at Oakland, Morley owned Los Angeles, and Henry Harris controlled San Francisco. Moran and Bert, the first two presidents of the league, were also in positions of influence.

The inclusion of Los Angeles meant extended road trips up and down the coast for every team. To cut down on the wear and tear, league directors expanded all series in Los Angeles to include games on Thursday, making it a long four-game weekend.

Herman 'Ham' Iburg was one of the most effective pitchers in the California League. He also pitched for the San Francisco Wasps in 1903, their first year in the Coast League. The San Franciscan pitched in the National League in 1902 but preferred to stay on the West Coast.

The Looloos were accepted enthusiastically by the fans around the league. Their roster was made up of California League veterans, but the pitching staff was recruited from the east. The team finished second with an 81-67 record, 13 games behind San Francisco's Wasps, who were led by Ham Iburg's 37 wins and Jimmy Whalen's 36.

Flush from the successes of the 1901 season, the California League moved to improve its product. The schedule was expanded and each park was improved to increase seating space and provide more amenities for the fans. Umpires were paid more to ensure higher quality.

For once, the 1902 California League opened with the same alignment of teams as in the previous season.

Oakland, the cellar-dweller in 1901, made some key acquisitions that vaulted it into first place in 1902. There was no weakness in any facet of the Oakland roster and it consistently pulled away from the second-place Looloos. With a 108-74 record, Oakland won the flag by 13 games over Los Angeles.

When the pennant was presented to the Oakland team, it was inscribed to read, "Oakland Baseball Club—1903 Champions—Pacific Coast League." This was not a misprint. Oakland served as the defending champions until a new champion was crowned at the end of the 1903 season. But in 1903, Oakland would be a member of the new Pacific Coast League. ❖

# CHAPTER 4

# TUMULTUOUS BEGINNINGS

Although separated by only a few miles of water, San Francisco has always been vastly different from Oakland. This was especially so around the turn of the century. San Francisco, the Hub of the West, was the largest city west of the Mississippi in 1900. Oakland was a sleepy village with a small population of farmers and merchants. San Francisco was privileged class, Oakland was working class. Oakland marked the end of the line for the Transcontinental Railroad, but few people stayed there. Usually, newcomers immediately hopped on a ferry to get to San Francisco.

San Franciscans did travel to Oakland, however. Many of the city's elite had summer homes in the foothills of Oakland in order to escape the summer fog for the warmer climate of the East Bay.

As different as they were and still are, both cities liked their baseball. The rivalry between them began as soon as baseball took hold in California. Fans attended weekend games in droves, with crowds of several thousand patrons becoming the norm for Sunday contests. Club teams played each other regularly, and games pitting one community against another were guaranteed to swell audiences. Not only was some trophy, like a silver bat, ball or cup at stake, but so was community pride.

The seamy side of baseball was always present. In many ways, the game emulated the downside of life in the Bay Area. The ballplayers played, drank and lived hard. Gamblers were constantly present, always looking for an angle to secure their wagers. Players signed contracts to play, then jumped clubs to accept better offers elsewhere.

Owners often reneged on promised compensation and released players at their whim.

The situation certainly did not encourage the loyalties of baseball fans.

## NATIONAL ORGANIZATION VERSUS LOCAL LEAGUES

The formation of the American League in 1901 had caused the National League to abrogate its agreements with all minor leagues. This act removed any protections the minor leagues had received from the one previously existing major league. Now, two leagues threatened to raid the minors of their stars.

To fill the vacuum, Tom Hickey of the Western League hastily called minor league presidents to Chicago for a meeting on September 5. From this meeting came the formation of a brand-new National Association of Professional Baseball Leagues, more commonly called the "National Association." The Association classified leagues along lines of population, established rules to secure the services of players under contract and set penalties for players and teams who broke those rules. Players who jumped their contractual obligations would be banned from participation with other member teams or leagues and heavy fines would be imposed as penalties before they would be reinstated.

The California League and the Pacific Northwest League quickly became members of the National

Freeman's Park, located at 55th and San Pablo in Oakland, served as home for the California League at the turn of the century. It was also frequently the home of the Oakland Commuters of the Coast League before the park in Emeryville was constructed for the 1913 season.

Association. Membership in the association provided needed structure and order for its members but it was helpless to deal with teams and leagues that remained outside its jurisdiction. These were "outlaw leagues," a status retained by the California State League.

In 1902, the California League consisted of teams from San Francisco, Oakland, Sacramento and Los Angeles. To distinguish it from the rival California State League, the California League was often referred to as the Pacific Coast League. For the 1903 season, the fledgling league's owners took the ambitious step of structuring a circuit that would act as the dominant baseball organization on the West Coast. They formed a true Pacific Coast League—the four California cities were the nucleus, joined by Portland and Seattle.

Portland and Seattle already had entries in the Pacific Northwest League, and National Association bylaws dictated territorial rights to the PNL for these cities. This meant the Pacific Coast League planned to go head-to-head with the PNL for control. The PCL directors dropped their membership in the National Association—which they had just joined a year earlier—immediately becoming an "outlaw" league.

The PNL countered the attack on their territory by placing teams in San Francisco and Los Angeles. In the battle for fan allegiance, the Coast League prevailed and the PNL teams in San Francisco and Los Angeles folded before season's end. With their territory firmly established, the Pacific Coast League rejoined the National Association in 1904.

San Francisco's inaugural PCL game was played on Thursday, March 26, 1903, on the Recreation Grounds at 8th and Harrison streets. The local newspapers had promoted the new league and the opening game. The locals even sported a new name. Gone were the Wasps, replaced by the Stars.

The Stars' opponent for the 1903 opener was called the Portlands. The afternoon game was preceded by the normal pageantry, with league President James T. Moran delivering the ceremonial first pitch. A paid crowd of 5,235 swelled to more than 5,500 by women who were admitted free. They saw the Stars defeat the Portlands 7-3 behind the pitching of George Hodson.

Rosters for the inaugural season were set at 12 players. The Stars were managed by Charlie Irwin, their third baseman. Ham Iburg, Jimmie Whalen and Ira Lindsay joined Hodson in the pitching duties. Iburg and Whalen had previously pitched for San Francisco, among other teams, in the California League.

Iburg was a San Franciscan who, like many other fledgling players, had been discovered playing in the *Examiner* Newspaper Tournament. He broke into professional baseball in the California League in 1898, winning 15 games. From 1899 through 1901, he continued to pitch well for the hometown nine.

After the 1901 season, Iburg traveled east where he joined the Philadelphia club of the National League. He had a strong first season in 1902 and returned to San Francisco for the winter. When his contract was sent to him for the 1903 season, Iburg declined to sign it, prefering to remain in San Francisco. He was 27-23 in 1903, second to Whalen's 28-21 record. Lindsay was 20-21.

The Stars' leading batter in 1903 was right fielder Patty Meaney at .309. Center fielder Henry Lynch was the home run leader with four. Double digits in homers weren't reached by a San Francisco player until Ping Bodie accomplished the feat for the 1909 league champions. Danny Shay, the shortstop, stole a remarkable 83 bases.

Oakland opened its season at Sacramento. Many local businesses closed their doors at 2 o'clock, which allowed workers to attend. Governor George Pardee was the guest dignitary and 3,000 fans watched Sacramento defeat Oakland 7-3.

Below, the Oakland team rides through Sacramento to help commemorate Opening Day 1903. The players are right outside the State House Hotel at K and 10th Streets, billed as 'The Best Family Hotel in the City.' Parades such as these were common around the turn of the century.

The following are excerpts from the *San Francisco Call* during the first week of play in the Pacific Coast League.

April 2, 1903: "There have been good ball games and bad ball games of almost every kind and variety decided in this city, but the one at Recreation Park yesterday afternoon established a record that will probably never be broken and, let us hope, never be equaled. After almost two hours and one half of good, valuable time had been wasted, the awful farce finally showed signs of diminishing, and then it could easily be seen that Seattle was a winner 11 to 3 (over Oakland at San Francisco)."

April 8, 1903: "Across the water on the uncivilized Oakland Baseball diamond, the San Francisco and Seattle players met for the first time in their lives. Long before the finishing period was at hand the ordinary fan could easily see that Seattle was not going to get in the running.

"Score 5 to 0.

"The weather came pretty near being sublime and a large crowd turned out to view the struggle. The weather was superior to the game.

"It was surprising that more errors were not committed, for large holes and ruts decorated the fields and made the lives of the players a burden while the contest was in progress.

"Nothing worth mentioning happened (save it be the twirling of Ham Iburg)."

For Oakland, Pete Lohman was the manager and catcher. Oakland's record in 1903 was 89-126, 46 games behind Los Angeles, in last place.

The bulk of Oakland's pitching was done by Jack Lee (17-17), Oscar Graham (27-26), Curley Cooper (18-30) and Doc Moskiman (12-25).

Moskiman, who doubled as an outfielder when not on the mound, was the team's leading hitter at .313 and home run slugger with four. Outfielders Billy Murdock and Brick Devereaux provided the bulk of the offense for Oakland.

A major problem the league faced was an imbalance of teams. Los Angeles ended up as league champion and was the only team with a winning record. The Angels were 133-78, 27½ games ahead of Sacramento at 105-105. San Francisco was fourth with a record of 107-110.

The new league had survived its first year, but it was far from being easy. Some cities didn't support their teams, and numerous franchise shifts took place over the next 20 years.

After the 1903 season, Mike Fisher, owner of the Sacramento team, moved his franchise to Tacoma, Washington. The team was highly successful but the city didn't support it. Two years later, Fisher moved the team again to Fresno for the 1906 season. The move didn't help and the franchise collapsed.

In those early years, each season seemed to have its own set of adventures. In 1903, it was the league's outlaw

Sepia postcard of Recreation Park, sent in 1911 by Seals pitcher Harry Sutor to his mother.

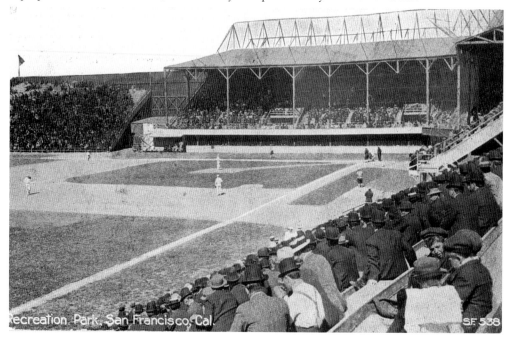

status and the battles for survival with its two neighboring leagues. In 1904, it was continued fighting with the California State League and the financial instability of the Sacramento/Tacoma franchise.

Coast League rosters fluctuated greatly from year to year. It was not unusual for more than 50 percent of the players to be gone after one year or less. Only the local players remained.

The 1905 season offered several problems. Each year the league schedule had expanded. By 1905 it was a full eight months, ending in early December. There was simply too much baseball and fans quickly reached the saturation point.

The nadir of attendance records was set on November 8, 1905, when one patron paid to watch Portland beat Oakland 3-2. Oakland's weather was bad, San Francisco was playing at home and both teams were out of contention. Legend says the umpire who would customarily announce the lineups to the crowd greeted the lone man, "Dear Sir."

This game had some ironic significance to it. At the previous day's game, Oakland had scored a run on an overthrow into the stands. The ground rule stipulated the ball was in play and the Oakland batter scored before the ball could be retrieved. Portland Manager Sammy Vigneaux requested a change in the ground rules to allow the advance of only one base on an overthrow into the stands, but Brick Devereaux, Oakland's captain, would have none of it.

Devereaux, stationed at third base the following day, threw a batted ball past Richards at first base into the stands. While the ball was rolling along the empty grandstand, the Portland batter rounded the bases with the winning run.

The paucity of fans forced the Oakland team to go on the road throughout the Central Valley. This created situations where Oakland would play Seattle in Sacramento or host Portland in Bakersfield. Such were the economics of baseball at the time.

Bill Lauterborn, Seattle's third baseman by way of New York, commented to a writer in Seattle about the poor attendance he found in Oakland: "Well, there were just nine men and boys in the grounds one day we played there. Some of them got in for nothing, and a few did not stay for the finish. I can't see where the California towns have anything to howl about the lack of attendance in Tacoma when a town like Oakland, claiming 80,000 inhabitants, turns out a magnificent crowd of nine persons to see two teams play ball. Oakland ought to be in a trolley league . . ."

The difference was Oakland had financial backing to survive the lean years. Tacoma didn't.

The league had stabilized itself at six teams going into the 1906 season. On April 7, the season opened at Recreation Park with San Francisco winning the opener 4-0

over Seattle—its first of six consecutive season-opening wins.

Team nicknames changed frequently in the early years. Early that season, the fans and newspapers started calling the team the "Young Americans." The team persisted in wearing "Fourth of July" caps—white caps with red and blue stripes. After the games of Tuesday, April 17, the "Young Americans" had a 9-2 record, a full game ahead of Los Angeles.

But at 5:15 the next morning, a massive earthquake rocked San Francisco, immediately turning large sections of the city into rubble. The water system was disrupted, major thoroughfares were impassable and fire broke out and raged uncontested through large portions of the city.

Recreation Park at 8th and Harrison, Central Park at 8th and Market and the Haight Street Grounds next to

A tongue-in-cheek subpoena issued by the Alameda County Board of Directors exhorting fans to attend the April 24, 1906 baseball game between Oakland and San Francisco at Idora Park. Because of the earthquake one week earlier, the game was not played.

Golden Gate Park all were destroyed. Across the bay in Oakland, the earthquake had been felt but the city was largely undamaged.

The quake also rocked local baseball, because even though only one team had been directly affected, it was in the league's most important city. The league offices, after all, were located in San Francisco. Play was suspended for two weeks as league officials decided what to do. The league offices were moved to Oakland and teams were cajoled into sticking together.

But players were uncertain about the league's future and many of them jumped to other leagues.

## CAL EWING RESCUES THE PCL

The San Francisco earthquake could have been the final blow to a struggling Pacific Coast League. Without Cal Ewing's efforts, the league would not have survived.

James Carroll "Cal" Ewing was born in Solano County in 1866, but his family moved to Oakland when Cal was six. Even as a boy, Ewing was organizing the kids on the block into local teams. At age 10, he was a player on the "Merry Macks," named after Mack Street in Oakland. The youngsters even had uniforms made by their mothers. Whether it was the uniforms or natural disagreement engendered by baseball, the games always seemed to end with a fight. For Cal this was fine. He loved a good scrap.

Cal continued as an amateur baseballer and around 1888 he became athletic director of the Reliance Club, one of the best known of the local baseball nines. Cal was captain and manager of the team, playing right field or first base. In 1890, Ewing joined the Reliance team in the California State League, a loose-knit circuit at the time. In 1893, the Reliance team became the Oakland entry in the semi-pro league.

The league would flourish, fail and be re-established. In 1898, Cal took his first fling at team ownership, financing and managing the Oakland club. His 1902 Oakland team was a good one. Pete Lohman was the team's manager, and Walter McCredie, Brick Devereaux, Heinie Schmidt and Kid Mohler, the left-handed second baseman, were some of its stars.

Before the 1903 season opened, McCredie, Schmidt and Mohler all jumped the team to play elsewhere. This incident convinced Ewing of the necessity for a structured league within the guidelines and protections of the National Association of Professional Baseball Leagues.

Ewing was instrumental in the negotiations to establish the Pacific Coast League in 1903, although he turned down its presidency. By 1904, it had become a member of the National Association.

Eight days before the 1906 earthquake struck, Ewing and his uncle, Frank Ish, finalized negotiations to buy the San Francisco Young Americans. Ewing turned his ownership in the Oakland club over to a trustee, Ed Walter.

When the quake hit, Ewing guaranteed the financial stability of both Oakland and San Francisco, sent a check for $750 to Mike Fisher in Fresno to fund his payroll and found investors Henry and Clarence Berry to resurrect the Los Angeles club.

Ewing evidently also helped Seattle, but it is not clear how much. The only team not receiving assistance from Ewing was Portland . . . and it was Portland that won the league pennant.

While it would have been reasonable to cancel the remainder of the 1906 season after the quake, PCL officials realized the importance of holding the league together. Additionally, fans were in need of a diversion from their misery. Within a month's time, the league had stabilized to the point where play could be resumed.

Games began again on Wednesday, May 23, as San Francisco—playing for the rest of the season in Oakland and bedecked in new gray uniforms with more traditional caps—defeated Mike Fisher's Fresno Raisin Pickers 4-3. For the most part, the post-quake lineups were similar to those before the quake.

Portland, the team least affected by turmoil, won the pennant by 19½ games over Seattle. San Francisco finished with a winning season, 91-84, in fourth place. Oakland was fifth, 77-110, 10 games ahead of cellar-dwelling Fresno.

This would be the end for Fresno and Seattle. Their seasons had been financial disasters and both teams turned their franchises over to the league when the season concluded. Rights to their players were distributed throughout the PCL for 1907.

With the destruction of the league office, many records from earlier Coast League seasons were lost or destroyed and some remain incomplete. While many records from the 1906 season have been painstakingly reconstructed, there are still serious gaps, especially in fielding and pitching statistics.

In 1907, Ewing assumed the league presidency and San Francisco Manager Danny Long was named secretary (the team was now known as the Seals). For the three years of Ewing's tenure and the first of Judge Thomas F. Graham, team statistics and many individual statistics were not kept. Starting with 1911, statistics were religiously kept, and while many errors undoubtedly exist, records of the Pacific Coast League are the most thorough of any minor league.

## "OLD REC"

In order to return the team to San Francisco in 1907, construction quickly started on another Recreation Park, located in the Mission District between 14th and 15th

The 1907 Oakland Oaks. George Van Haltren's team, which took third place in the league, had several stars. Van Haltren is in the middle of the picture with Brick Devereaux at far left and Truck Eagan to the right. Heine Heitmuller is the tall player in the back row. Willie Hogan is in the front row, far right.

Streets on Valencia. Recreation Park, later affectionately called "Old Rec," was a cozy park. A wooden grandstand was elevated to allow for several rows of bleachers placed at ground level behind chicken-wire fencing. This area became known as "the booze cage." Here, only males dared tread. The price of admission included the choice of a sandwich or a shot of whiskey.

The spectators who frequented the booze cage were knowledgeable, loud and often abusive. Home plate was close to the grandstands, so umpires, visiting players and a few home players were unable to find refuge from the boorish spectators in the "cage."

Behind the home plate area and out to the dugouts, the upper grandstand was covered. Grandstand seats had planks for backrests. Along the foul lines in the bleachers, spectators had to be content with open boards over a wooden framework. Bleachers were added to the left field area after the 1910 season.

The dimensions of the field were 345 feet down the left field line, 385 feet to center field and only 235 feet down the right field line. But the chicken-wire fence in right was 50-feet high, requiring high fly balls to clear it.

Outside the bleachers were the dugouts consisting only of a bench with a plyboard cover to prevent the players from receiving regular showers of beer, soft drinks or food items. Players would select their bat from a group neatly lined up on the ground adjacent to the dugout. The batter was then faced with having to walk close by the fans congregated in the booze cage.

The clubhouse was located in deep center field at the corner of the lot. It was a two-story building and its very presence served as an obstacle course for any center fielder chasing a ball hit over his head.

Ewing invested $90,000 to construct Recreation Park. The grand opening of the park was to feature a weekend series with John McGraw's New York Giants two weeks before the league opener. Then the rains came.

March 1907 was unseasonably wet, curtailing Spring Training activities throughout the state. The Giants were greeted in San Francisco with a heavy rain. The players got off the train and went directly to the racetrack. They explored the city the next day and then boarded the train for an exhibition series in Los Angeles. It had been too wet even to work out.

The steady rain prompted league directors to postpone the opening of the season by one week. Rain

George Hildebrand played in the outfield for the Seals from 1904-08 after a career in the California League. Hildebrand later became a distinguished major league umpire.

Orval Overall formed the Seals' 'reverse battery' with Nick Williams. One would pitch and the other catch in the first game of a doubleheader, and then switch for the nightcap.

Oakland right-hander Jimmy Wiggs (left) was the losing pitcher in the 1909, 24-inning game to the Seals. San Francisco won the marathon 1-0. Willie Hogan (right) could play anywhere. In 1907 he won 20 games; in 1909 he hit 50 doubles and 11 home runs.

George Van Haltren was one of the earliest superstars to play baseball in Oakland. He also enjoyed a marvelous 17-year major league career during which he collected more than 2,500 hits.

Kid Mohler was a left-handed second baseman and also captain of the 1909 champion Seals.

delayed the finishing touches on Recreation Park as well. Four days before the 1907 season began, workers were still completing the final touches: painting the grandstands and left field bleachers, and mixing a final batch of loam into the infield.

The park opened on Saturday morning, April 6, 1907, to a standing-room crowd of 10,000, and Seals pitcher John Hickey hurled a complete-game victory over Portland.

After all the problems in 1906, only four teams remained in the league for 1907 and 1908: Los Angeles, Portland, Oakland and San Francisco. Los Angeles won the pennant both years.

## THE SEALS BUILD FOR THE FUTURE

The Danny Long years began for San Francisco in 1907. Long was a long-time resident of Oakland and an outfielder on the Oakland G&Ms during the 1890s. His tenure with the Seals lasted through 1913, including San Francisco's first PCL pennant in 1909.

In 1907, the Seals finished in second place, 18 games behind Los Angeles with a 104-99 record. The Seals again finished 18 games back in 1908, this time in third place with a 100-104 mark.

Some very talented players performed for the Seals in 1907 and 1908. Charles "Gabby" Street developed into an excellent catcher and was traded to Washington for the 1908 season. Bill Killefer came to San Francisco during 1908 on his way to a 13-year major league career. Two other future major leaguers joined the Seals in these years—Rollie Zeider in 1907 and Frank "Ping" Bodie in 1908—after jumping from the California League.

George Hildebrand, Seals outfielder from 1904-1908, is the same person who umpired in the American League for 23 years starting in 1912. With the Seals, Hildebrand was a fearsome base stealer and a strong left fielder.

Versatile Richard "Nick" Williams was one of the Seals' most valuable players from 1906-1910. Williams' nickname, one with certain racial connotations, was coined due to his curly, dark hair. Williams had played baseball at the turn of the century for Cal where he formed a unique battery with Orval Overall. While one pitched, the other caught. In the second game of a doubleheader they would reverse their playing positions.

Overall pitched seven years in the National League, twice a 20-game winner, before returning to the Seals in 1913. Williams never played in the major leagues but had a long, distinguished career with the Seals as player, scout, assistant manager, farm club manager and finally as manager of the Seals. He was credited with advancing many of the Seals' finest recruits, and his teams won two Coast League championships.

Also teammates on the University of California nine were Jack Bliss and Heine Heitmuller. Bliss was a reserve

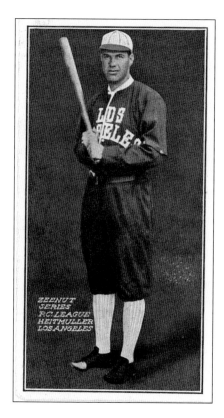

Heine Heitmuller and Truck Eagan were two of Oakland's finest hitters in the 1900s, although both played with other teams as well. Heitmuller's career was cut short when he died of typhoid fever; he won the 1912 batting title posthumously.

catcher for the St. Louis Cardinals from 1908 through 1912 before returning to the coast for brief stints at Sacramento and Vernon. William F. "Heine" Heitmuller was a native San Franciscan. He graduated from Lick-Wilmerding High School, where he played both baseball and football. At Cal he again played both. In baseball he was a pitcher and outfielder.

Heitmuller signed out of college with Seattle in 1906, but was sold to Oakland. He stayed with the Commuters into the 1909 season when he was purchased by Connie Mack of the Philadelphia Athletics. With Oakland, Heitmuller led his teammates in every offensive category at least once. In 1908, he batted .284, leading the league with 791 at-bats, 225 hits, 39 doubles, 12 home runs and 302 total bases. He led his team with 39 stolen bases and 31 sacrifices.

After two years in Philadelphia, he returned to the coast with Los Angeles. In 1912 his roommate, Hughie Smith, contracted typhoid fever. Smith left the team while Heitmuller played on. Heitmuller and his teammate, Pete Daley, were in a tight race for the batting title when Heitmuller was hospitalized with Smith's malady. Within two weeks, Heitmuller was dead.

The trauma affected the Angels as they dropped out of first place and finished third. Daley's production also was affected and his batting average dropped below his dead teammate's. Heitmuller won the league batting crown posthumously at .334, three points ahead of Daley.

At the 1907 winter baseball meetings, the smallness of the Coast League became a point of contention. The Eastern League made a concerted effort to get the National Association to drop the Coast League from Class A to Class B status. Their feeling was that such a small, isolated league was not deserving of the top classification in the minors. Logically, with the state of affairs on the West Coast, the Eastern League had a point. It was only through Ewing's efforts that the Eastern League's proposal was defeated.

During the 1908 season, Walter McCredie of Portland proposed an eight-team league composed of four southern and four northern teams. McCredie felt he held the key to the league's future success. Without Portland, the league would be a local entity without much clout.

The league meetings were held in Portland and McCredie promised Northwest League representation from groups in Seattle, Spokane and Tacoma. But at the end of the meeting, two new California teams, Sacramento and Vernon in Southern California, had been granted franchises for the 1909 season.

Transportation concerns and weak franchises were the drawbacks for the northern teams. It would be 12 years—in 1919—before Seattle would re-enter the Coast League. McCredie's Portland team would remain the only northern team in the league through the first World War.

In the previous six years of the Coast League, neither Bay Area team had made a serious run at the pennant. The league was dominated by Tacoma and Los Angeles. That, however, would change. ❖

# CHAPTER 5

# SUCCESS!
# THE FIRST PENNANTS

Danny Long's San Francisco Seals won the Bay Area's first pennant in 1909. By his third season as manager, Long had put together the nucleus of a solid, competitive unit. Excellent pitching and superb defense compensated for below-average hitting.

On the mound, the Seals had two stellar right-handers. Clarence "Cack" Henley was the ace. The 25-year-old pitcher hailed from Sacramento and originally signed with the Seals in 1905. When the earthquake hit, he jumped the team, finishing with Pueblo in the Western League. Obeying organized baseball's National Commission—an arm of the National Association—he returned to the Seals in 1907.

Frank "Pete" Browning was a diminutive 5-foot-5 southerner who didn't get the same publicity as Henley but was equally effective. It was Browning who ran off 16 straight victories, a string ended when Santa Rosa's Walter Nagle, pitching for the Angels, beat him 2-1 on August 15, 1909. In the middle of his streak, Browning pitched a 3-0 no-hitter against Sacramento. Browning closed at 32-16 for the league high in wins.

On June 8 at Freeman's Park, Henley matched up with Jimmy Wiggs of the Oaks in what has been called the most remarkable game in Pacific Coast League history—a 24-inning shutout that took just three hours, 35 minutes to complete. Henley gave up nine hits, struck out six and allowed only one walk. Wiggs walked six, gave up 11 hits and whiffed 13.

Although the game was in Oakland, the Seals were the home team. They scored the winning run in the bottom of the 24th inning with two out. Rollie Zeider, the Seals' third baseman, lined a double to left center for his third hit in 10 at-bats. He advanced to third on an error but held there when Frank Carroll caught Kid Mohler's fly ball to center field and threw a strike to catcher Carl Lewis. First baseman Tom Tennant laid down a bunt but Zeider was caught in a rundown. Tennant sprinted to third before Zeider was tagged out. Nick Williams, who had replaced Ping Bodie in left field in the 20th inning, then roped a double to end the game.

The *San Francisco Chronicle* reported the following day, "The crowd at the start was not of immense proportions, but increased as the game progressed, and before the end, there was a mob of howling fans who yelled at every play made and went home to cold suppers satisfied that they had had their money's worth."

Coincidentally, on the same day in Portland, Sacramento and the Beavers played to an 18-inning, 1-1 tie. Henley and Wiggs both took their normal turns in a Sunday doubleheader five days after the marathon, but not against each other.

On June 24, two weeks after the 24-inning game,

Browning pitched 19 innings at Old Rec to defeat the Angels 5-4. At that point in the race, the Angels were dogging the Seals, and the contest brought out 13,362, the largest crowd to date at Recreation Park.

Backing up the pitching staff was a superb infield. First baseman Tennant, a talented fielder, was the only new player. A position switch seemed to tighten up the defense on the left side: Harry McArdle, the regular third baseman in 1908, flopped with Rollie Zeider at shortstop.

This simple switch made greater use of McArdle's range, and Zeider's quickness was an asset around the hot corner. Many observers felt McArdle was the greatest shortstop who had been developed in the league to that point and that the infield was the best defensively in the league's short history.

Zeider was also the infield's offensive strength, batting .289, third best in the league. He scored 141 times and stole 93 bases, a league record, and went on to play the next nine seasons in Chicago for the American League,

Federal League and National League clubs beginning in 1910. He returned west for the 1919 and 1920 seasons where he starred for the Vernon Tigers, who won the championship both years.

Seals right fielder Henry Melchior was the league's top batter at .298, the second straight year no regular batted above .300. Melchior and Zeider shared most of the team's offensive burden, although Bodie led the Seals in home runs with 10.

The Seals won 132 games, losing 80, to beat second-place Portland by 13½ games.

## OAKLAND STARTS SLOWLY IN THE PCL

Oakland endured losing seasons under George Van Haltren from 1905 to mid-1909. In May 1909, pitcher Bill Reidy replaced Van Haltren and ultimately moved the team up to fifth place.

The 1909 San Francisco Seals won the Bay Area's first pennant. Managed by Danny Long, they were led by pitchers Cack Henley and Pete Browning and sluggers Ping Bodie and Nick Williams. The Seals went 132-80 and won the championship going away.

Using 'state of the art' graphics in 1909, an artist was able to superimpose members of the championship Seals baseball team onto the bodies of the frolicking animals. This is a photograph of a postcard that was quite popular at the time.

Other than Heitmuller, the only real power on the Oaks was provided by Willie Hogan and Charles "Truck" Eagan. Hogan, nicknamed "Lucky Bill" after he won 11 games in a row for Oakland in 1907, was switched to first base because Van Haltren wanted his bat in the lineup every day. Hogan led his team in at least one offensive category each year but had difficulty finding an adequate defensive position. He later played third base and then moved to center field.

Truck Eagan was another great Oakland player. Eagan, like many others, starred in the *Examiner* Tournament, making his way into the California State League with San Jose before he jumped to the Pacific Coast League.

Eagan played with Sacramento before graduating to the majors. After a rather unsuccessful year divided between Pittsburgh and Cleveland, Eagan returned to Sacramento as he preferred the West Coast climate to the heat and humidity in the east. When the Sacramento franchise was transferred to Tacoma after the 1903 season, Eagan went with them for the 1904 and 1905 seasons. Eagan won the PCL's home run title all three years; his 25 homers in 1904 stood as the Coast League record until Ping Bodie broke it with 30 as a member of the Seals in 1910. When Tacoma/Fresno returned its franchise to the

league in 1906 because of the lack of community support, Eagan's contract was assigned to Oakland.

Truck was only with the Commuters in 1907 and 1908, but in 1907 he led the league in batting at .335 with 237 hits. His 45 doubles and 316 total bases were also league highs. Eagan's aggressive play at shortstop and his prowess with the bat made him a fan favorite.

The Commuters had a young star in their midst when they picked up George E. "Duffy" Lewis from the Alameda team in the outlaw California State League. Lewis had grown up in the East Bay, went to school at St. Mary's College and joined Alameda in 1907. He jumped to Oakland during the 1908 season and was sold to the Red Sox by 1910. In 1909, Lewis batted .279 in 200 games, showing enormous potential for a 21-year-old.

## THE BAY AREA'S FIRST HALL OF FAMER

The Red Sox had also negotiated a deal with Harry Hooper from Charlie Graham's club in Sacramento in the State League one year earlier. Hooper was born in Santa Clara and also played at St. Mary's College before joining the Oakland entry in the California State League in 1907. Graham purchased him from Oakland during the season for $25. In 1908, Hooper hit .344 at a time when pitching thoroughly dominated hitting.

Lewis and Hooper joined Tris Speaker in Boston to form one of the greatest outfields of all time. Hooper and Speaker were elected into Baseball's Hall of Fame and many experts feel Lewis is equally as deserving.

Harry Bartholomew Hooper was the earliest Bay Area player to enter the National Baseball Hall of Fame. A civil engineeering graduate from St. Mary's, Hooper initially thought of himself as an engineer who happened to play baseball. While playing for Charlie Graham's Sacramento team, he also worked for the Western Pacific Railroad as a surveyor. At the end of his stellar 1908 season, Red Sox Owner John I. Taylor negotiated a contract with Harry. Because Graham's club was in the outlaw California State League, he couldn't simply purchase Hooper's contract.

The speedy Hooper quickly became recognized as one of the great outfielders and leadoff hitters in baseball. John McGraw said of him, "For years Harry Hooper has been considered one of the greatest outfielders that ever lived. He is also one of the most dangerous hitters in a pinch that the game has ever known."

Hooper played on one of the all-time great teams. The Red Sox won pennants in 1912, 1915, 1916 and 1918, winning all four World Series against four different National League teams. Tris Speaker and Babe Ruth were in the outfield with him at one time or another on a team that also featured Smokey Joe Wood and Dutch Leonard, but Hooper was the only one to play on all four World Championship teams. He collected 2,466 hits in his 17-year major league career.

## OAKLAND ON THE UPSWING

The 1910 pennant race was the most exciting in the league's brief history. At one time or another five of the six teams held first place, Sacramento being the exception. The race was complicated by the uneven number of games played by different teams. While Portland was a narrow winner, second-place Oakland lost 11 more games than McCredie's Beavers. Portland had played 201 games and Oakland 210, while Los Angeles played the most at 222.

Demonstrating the tumult of the race, on July 1 the Seals held a 4½-game lead over Portland but went into a

### 'MYSTERIOUS' MITCHELL

In the heat of the 1910 pennant race, the Seals signed talented right-handed pitcher Fred Mitchell, a Nebraska alumnus who had pitched in the "Three I" League.

The Seals won the first four games in which he pitched. He was signed August 31, and on September 1 he pitched five innings against Vernon before he left with a 6-2 lead. Using an effective mixture of fastball, curveball and spitter, Mitchell threw a complete-game victory against the Tigers six days later.

On September 10, he won both games of a doubleheader against the Angels. But people were uneasy about Mitchell, and were starting to ask questions about his background: "Why hadn't Mitchell been heard of before? Why is he unwilling to socialize with the other players or talk about his past? Who is he?"

A carnival atmosphere was present for his debut at Old Rec. A large, curious crowd came to watch this new star. The photographers were also waiting but Mitchell refused to leave the clubhouse while any photographers were on the field.

It was no surprise he was quickly referred to as "Mysterious" Mitchell. Writers and fans speculated about his true identity. Some felt he was Bob Mitchell, who was offered a job with the Cubs, but that theory was discarded when it was remembered Bob Mitchell was left-handed. Others felt he

was McQuillen, a pitcher suspended by the Philadelphia Nationals.

A San Francisco Chronicle photographer with a new telescopic device took several photos of Mitchell, and these were compared to the photographs of a University of Chicago player named Fred Walker. The comparison was obvious. The mystery had been solved.

Mitchell-Walker started the season with Cincinnati and had gotten himself in trouble with the law over a woman. He bolted the team, disappeared, and resurfaced in Portland, Oregon, where the Seals discovered him.

With all the intrigue surrounding him, Mitchell became an instant favorite with the fans. The same couldn't be said about his teammates. Mitchell did as he pleased, arrived when he pleased and disdained his teammates as inferior to him intellectually and talent-wise. He created so much dissension on the team that many felt he was directly responsible for the team's drop in the standings.

Finally, on October 11, less than six weeks after he had signed with the Seals, Long released him. The last straw was Mitchell's unwillingness to carry his own bags to the ferry for a game in Oakland. The team was better off without him, but it was too late.

Mitchell-Walker returned to the major leagues, pitching in both the National and Federal Leagues. His nickname went with him. There, he was "Mysterious" Walker.

Team Secretary Herb McFarlin and Oaks Manager
Bud Sharpe at 1912 Spring Training.

skid to fall behind the Beavers. By August 1, the Seals had climbed back into first place. At the end of the month, they were six games out in third place.

On the other hand, Oakland started slowly. As the season continued, the Oaks began to play consistently and sufficiently closed the gap by November 1. At that point, they faced three doubleheaders in a row against the arch-rival Seals, hoping to make two games on the Beavers. However, their championship hopes were dashed when the Seals swept the second doubleheader. But it was great excitement right up until the end.

## SEALS SLOWLY SLIDE DOWNHILL

Danny Long's 1910 Seals were much the same team as his champions from the previous year but the results were different. The Seals slipped to third place at 114-106. There were a few highlights, though. Cack Henley went

---

**REPORTING THE GAME—III**

Into the 20th century, literary style became more descriptive. The style didn't impart more information; it did become more effusive.

From the *San Francisco Chronicle*, July 3, 1910, Seals catcher Claude Berry catches a foul popup:

"Berry kept his peepers on the sphere, which was carried by the wind in his direction, and he shouted to his aids to back away while he ate it up without apparent effort."

---

34-19, his second consecutive 30-win season. Ping Bodie cracked 30 home runs to lead all of baseball and was crowned "World Champion of Home Runs." He also scored 110 runs, statistics which led the Chicago White Sox to draft him for 1911.

The 1911 season was also disappointing for the Seals. Many writers felt they would be the team to beat. Besides boasting a formidable pitching staff, roaming the infield were two future major leaguers: George "Buck" Weaver at second base and Oscar Vitt at third. Weaver had been purchased from the York, Pennsylvania baseball club after the 1910 season. Vitt was a product of the the San Francisco sandlots.

Weaver, who played with great enthusiasm, hit .271, stole 29 bases and led the team in doubles (38) and home runs (nine). Vitt batted .269 with 44 stolen bases.

But most of the other players had only average years and the team finished in fifth place at 95-112.

Both Weaver and Vitt advanced to the major leagues, Weaver as a shortstop with the Chicago White Sox and Vitt as a utility infielder with the Detroit Tigers. Later in their careers both gained an ignominious place in the sport's history books. Weaver had nine productive years in Chicago before he was implicated in the infamous Black Sox scandal of 1919. Weaver was banned from baseball because he had knowledge of the fix.

Vitt played 10 years and later managed in the majors and on the coast. It was Vitt who had to deal with the rebellious 1940 Cleveland Indians, whose constant bickering cost them a pennant.

Long's 1912 Seals got progressively worse, finishing fifth for the second straight year. No starting pitcher had

## BASEBALL MEETS VAUDEVILLE

To encourage fans to watch them play, the Stars hired Joe Copeland, "The Human Megaphone," to ride through the streets on a horse, calling out to people and urging them to come to the ballpark. Copeland had wide experience working in the National, Interstate and Texas leagues, and had recently been employed in the Pacific Northwest.

"Through the medium of his remarkable voice, whose foghorn ability to make itself heard half a mile away," stated the *San Francisco Bulletin*, "has been the cause of much wonderment to those who have come within his range."

Thus, a San Francisco tradition—getting a personality to "hype" the day's game—was established. Other personalities followed. Doc Frost would announce the day's lineups, then during the games retrieve errant balls in flamboyant, acrobatic fashion. In one of his many colorful uniforms, Frost became an integral part of the day's entertainment package.

Around 1911, Foghorn Murphy started promoting Seals games. Like Copeland before him, Murphy would ride the streets of the city, but unlike Copeland, Murphy used a megaphone.

While Copeland disappeared from the scene rather quickly, Doc Frost and Foghorn Murphy practiced their trade long enough to gain legendary status in this city of legends. In the 1920s and for three more decades, Walter "The Great" Mails carried on their tradition.

---

a winning record and offensive production was off as well. Much of the team had been new to San Francisco in 1912, and most of them would not return in 1913.

## 1912: OAKLAND'S FIRST PENNANT

Harry Wolverton was hired to manage the Oaks in 1910 and immediately elevated the team into second place with a 122-98 record. But the Oaks were anemic at the plate, batting a collective .224. Center fielder Willie Hogan was the top batter at .261 on 193 hits.

Pitching was the Oaks' strength. Jack Lively was the league's top pitcher at 32-13, Walt Moser was 28-19, Tyler Christian 20-16 and Slim Nelson 19-14.

Wolverton brought added excitement into the season over a running battle with umpire Eugene McGreevy. The conflict blew out of control in mid-September when McGreevy awarded a forfeit victory to Los Angeles against the Oaks. After a controversial call by McGreevy at first base, Oaks first baseman Don Cameron erupted in anger at the umpire, Wolverton egging him on. Both were thrown out of the game and fined $25.

Wolverton was ordered to return his team to the field but refused, compelling McGreevy to order the game forfeited. At this point fans poured onto the field and police had to come to the rescue of the embattled umpire. Wolverton and Cameron were suspended and McGreevy received a rebuke from Judge Graham for his handling of the incident. From that point on, Graham attempted to assign McGreevy to games not involving Oakland. This incident helped bring the institution of the two-umpire system to the Coast League.

Wolverton returned to the helm in 1911 and had to rebuild his Oaks pitching staff after losing Lively and Moser to the American League. Slim Nelson had to retire because of rheumatism and several others were released. Tyler Christian was the only pitcher to return from the previous year.

As the season started, the pitching staff was still unsettled. Jimmie Wiggs rejoined the team but was not effective. The Oaks picked up Oregonian "Hub" Pernoll. The young lefty developed as the season progressed, fin-

Harry 'Rube' Sutor was one of the best pitchers for the Seals. This posed shot was taken in 1911, not a particularly successful year for San Francisco baseball.

The 1911 Oakland Oaks and their families picnic on Angel Island.

ishing at 23-16 with 340 innings pitched. This earned Pernoll a Spring Training tryout with the Detroit Tigers in 1912 but he was returned to Oakland.

Lefty Harry Ables was acquired from the Yankees early into the 1911 season. He had been an accomplished Texas League pitcher but failed in his trial in New York. Ables led the staff at 22-11 with 324 innings pitched, 218 strikeouts and only 88 walks, also a team high from a stingy pitching staff. Ables pitched a no-hitter for the Oaks, and Pernoll was the victim of a 1-0 no-hitter by the Seals' Rube Sutor .

Howard "Pop" Gregory was picked up from the St. Louis Browns after he failed a tryout as well. Gregory chipped in with 16 wins and the veteran Christian compiled his second 20-win season, 20-12.

The Philadelphia Athletics acquired Willie Hogan from Oakland, creating a void at first base. The position remained a problem for Oakland and was filled by the committee of Elmer Zacher, John Tiedemann, Monte Pfyle and anybody else willing to give it a try. The rest of the infield was ably manned by George Cutshaw at second, Clyde "Buzzy" Wares at shortstop and Wolverton at third, backed up by Gus Hetling.

Cutshaw led the league in stolen bases with 90 and

was sold to Brooklyn after the season. Wares was acquired by the St. Louis Browns.

Wolverton's 111-99 record earned Oakland a third-place finish in 1911 and earned him a promotion to manage the New York Yankees for 1912. But he left a nucleus of talented players for his successor, Bayard "Bud" Sharpe.

Sharpe, a veteran minor leaguer with a couple of years of major league experience, was known as a smart baseball man and an effective leader. Sharpe was also a talented first baseman, so he could also take over the 1911 Oaks' weakest position.

The 1912 race was an extremely exciting one until the death of the Los Angeles Angels' Heine Heitmuller cast a pall over its conclusion. The typhoid fever outbreak struck in September, whereupon the Angels plummeted out of contention.

As the Oaks came out of Spring Training, the team was balanced and talented at all positions. The pitching staff returned Ables, Christian, Gregory, Pernoll and Bill Malarkey from the 1911 team. This list included three 20-game winners.

The pitching staff was bolstered by the acquisition of Cy Parkin from Newark and Jack Killilay, at mid-season,

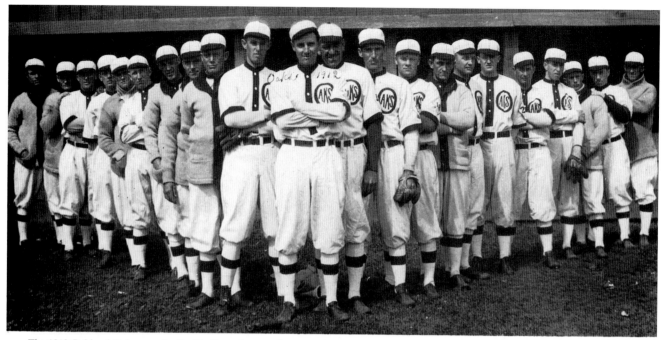

The 1912 Oakland Oaks won the Pacific Coast League championship in an exciting race with the Los Angeles Angels. Manager Bud Sharpe, who missed part of the season because of illness, is situated front and center.

The 1912 Seals were a conglomeration of new players who did not mesh well together and the team placed fifth in the league for the second season in a row.

Oaks first baseman Gus Hetling receives a 1912 Chalmers automobile at Freeman's Park for being selected the league's MVP.

from the Boston Red Sox. Ables went 25-18, Malarkey was 20-11, and the remainder of the staff was remarkably consistent. Killilay was 15-4 for the last five months of the season, Parkin was 13-8, and Christian finished 16-10. Gregory was 18-14.

Honus Mitze, a tough veteran, and John Tiedemann shared the catching load. Mitze batted only .228, but his strength was in handling the pitchers. The Oaks had to fill the shoes of Cutshaw and Wares, which was accomplished by the acquisitions of Bill Leard from Seattle of the Northwest League and Al Cook from Austin in the Texas League.

Sharpe was expected to play regularly at first base and he did bat .300 in 101 games, but he contracted a virus early in the season, limiting his play. Tiedemann filled in effectively for Sharpe, batting .288 with 10 home runs. Mitze served as acting manager during Sharpe's illness, giving him experience for his eventual appointment as Oaks manager in 1913.

Leard and Cook were an effective combination in the middle of the infield. Leard stole a league-high 80 bases and scored 122 runs.

The real surprise was at third base, where Hetling was a seldom-used reserve in 1911. Sharpe had tried to sell him during Spring Training, but with the loss of Wolverton, Hetling got a chance to play. As a regular, he fielded exceptionally well, batted .297 in the clutch, played in 202 of the team's 203 games, and was selected the league's Most Valuable Player, for which he received a new Chalmers convertible automobile.

In the outfield, Bert Coy had a career year with a league-high 19 home runs. He also scored 110 times while batting .297. Zacher played center field, hitting .277 with 11 home runs, and right fielder Claire Patterson led the team at .305 with 30 stolen bases.

As the season progressed, the Oaks and Angels took turns holding the league lead. Vernon was within attacking distance in third. The Seals started slowly and never challenged, finishing a dismal fifth.

On October 1, the Oaks held a four-game lead over Los Angeles and seven games over Vernon. With the typhoid epidemic in full swing, the Angels lost 14 of their next 22 games to fall out of contention. Meanwhile, the Tigers closed the gap on the Oaks. On October 21, with the Oaks starting a critical series at San Francisco, the Tigers were four games behind.

The Seals won four of seven from the Oaks while Vernon took five of seven from Sacramento, closing to two games back with one week to play.

Seals right fielder Rabbit Mundorff had a spectacular series against the Oaks, throwing out four runners at first base and costing Oakland two victories.

The end of the race came down to the last day of the season. In the final week Oakland played host to Los Angeles while the Tigers greeted Portland. By Friday, the Oaks' lead had slipped to a half game.

Friday's results found the Angels beating Oakland 4-3 while the Tigers played to a 9-9 tie in a game halted by darkness. At the end of the day's activities, Vernon had vaulted into first place by percentage points, .58376 to .58291. With four games to play, Vernon's Happy Hogan, never one to be modest, told the world, "The Tigers have it in the bag."

On Saturday, the Oaks blanked the Angels twice while the Tigers split with Portland. Oakland had a one-game lead with a doubleheader to go.

More than 11,000 fans jammed Sunday morning's game at Freeman's Park. The scene was repeated in the afternoon, as more than 18,000 filled Old Rec. Anxious eyes watched the scoreboard to see the scores from Southern California. The Oaks won their morning game and trekked to the ferry for the trip to San Francisco. On the way, someone perpetrated a cruel hoax, telling the team the Tigers had lost their first game. The Oaks and their fans celebrated their championship, only to find when they arrived in San Francisco that the Tigers had won the first game.

The Tigers won the second game too, but so did Oakland. Now the celebration began in earnest. Each player was presented with a solid gold ring with the Oaks emblem on top and the players presented Sharpe with a diamond pin. Shortly thereafter, Sharpe turned in his resignation; doctors had advised him to sit out at least a year to recover from his illness.

Despite winning the 1912 pennant, the Oaks suffered greatly. Patterson was drafted by the St. Louis Browns at season's end but died of tuberculosis in March 1913, his death creating a ghoulish dispute over whether the Oaks were required to return the draft price. Jimmy Frick, the reserve infielder, died in November 1912, presumably from an accident. Sharpe never returned to baseball and died in 1916.

As was the tradition, the league directors allocated money for the making of a pennant. This pennant, more of a silken plaque, hung in the Oakland offices for the rest of the franchise's lifetime. For the fans of Oakland, it served as a banner of pride. San Francisco's little brother could also win big. ❖

CHAPTER **6**

# BALL PARK BUILDING

With the success of the 1912 Oaks and the continued popularity of the Seals at the gate, the adequacy of the local ballparks came into question. Both Freeman's Park and Old Rec were too small.

The pennant-winning season of 1912 convinced Oaks management to construct new facilities for the team. Al Walters decided on a plot of land about a half-mile from the bay in Emeryville, a tiny, industrial community squeezed between Oakland and Berkeley. Oaks Ball Park was constructed on the west side of San Pablo Avenue at Park Street. Included as part of the grounds was land from the original Emery family homestead.

In 1912, construction of a ballpark was not a complicated matter. Ground was broken on December 15, 1912, actual construction of the buildings, bleachers, grandstands and fences started on February 1, 1913, and the park was completed by March 15.

The slowest part of the process was the growth of the turf on the field. An automatic sprinkler system was installed, but the grass couldn't be rushed. Still, the field was ready by Opening Day.

The ballpark was attractive but simple. The main grandstands had 19 sections of seats, all stadium chairs. The nine sections behind home plate were covered. Past the dugouts down both foul lines, bleachers were nothing more than planks on a wooden framework extended out to the fences. Seating capacity approximated 10,000.

The playing field was symmetrical except for a rectangular building in center field which served as the clubhouse. The business and ticket offices were enclosed in a brick structure behind the left field bleachers. This area also served as the entrance area to the park.

The Oaks Ball Park normally had excellent weather conditions. A light breeze would sometimes blow off the bay, discouraging left-handed hitters from powering the ball out of the park. But the flatlands location guaranteed that winds would never be overbearing. The park was conducive to watching baseball and it would serve the franchise for more than 40 years.

## PRECURSOR TO CANDLESTICK

One year later, the Seals ownership felt the need to move from Recreation Park. Old Rec had served as home of the Seals for only seven seasons before Ewing and Ish, after a dispute with the park's owners, decided to bolt the scene and take their ballgames elsewhere. Ewing and Ish signed a 20-year lease on a plot of land near the foot of Lone Mountain, one block south of Geary Boulevard where it intersected with Masonic Avenue.

The March 22, 1914 *San Francisco Chronicle* said of the site, "The only possible drawback to the new location is the possibility of meeting with bad weather conditions. In

Ewing Field. This ballpark was built in a foggy, windswept section of the city, near the current campus of the University of San Francisco, and lasted as the Seals' home for just one season.

the Mission, the diamond play was in the warm belt, but out by Lone Mountain, wind and fog may be experienced in the afternoon." Nothing could have been more true.

Unlike Oaks Ball Park, construction on Ewing Field would not be as simple. Major excavation and grading had to be performed before foundations could be laid. Construction started on November 20, 4½ months before Opening Day. However, construction took six months, and the Seals were forced to open the season against Happy Hogan's Vernon Tigers at Old Rec, where they played their first few homestands of the season.

Ewing Field, a monument to the savior of the Coast League and the owner of the Seals, was intended to be the finest minor league park in the country. Its lines were similar to Oaks Ball Park; entry to the park was located behind the left field bleachers and the grandstand was similar in appearance, also covered. Gone was the "booze

cage" and in its place were field-level box seats, extending down the right field line into the corner. Bleachers extended down the left field line and continued behind left and center fields. The park could seat 18,000 fans— 9,000 in the grandstands and 9,000 in the bleachers.

The park's dimensions were 340 feet to left, 400 feet to center and 336 feet to right field. The park had about five more feet than Oakland to each field. Gone was the short drive to the right field fence found at Old Rec. Left-handed batters found the wind came from behind the right field fence, but at Ewing Field it was more intense than at Oaks Ball Park.

On May 16, six weeks into the season, the Seals opened Ewing Field—which the *Chronicle* called "home of the Seals for the next 20 years"— in front of an overflow crowd for an afternoon game against Oakland. The Oaks ruined the day as Jake Geyer tossed a 3-0 shutout. While

Another view of Ewing Field, taken of the left field stands during a game against Oakland.

the day remained sunny, gusts of wind made fly balls in the outfield an adventure and gave fans a sampling of what they could expect at Ewing Field.

The Seals had a new manager, Del Howard. Howard had been a major league first baseman for five years and had been a fan favorite as the Seals' first baseman during the previous two seasons. But this season, the Seals had a pretty good first baseman in Joe Cartwright and the 36-year-old Howard seldom inserted himself into the lineup.

Over the winter the Seals made a blockbuster trade, at least in 1914 terms. They sent Cack Henley and Roy McArdle to Venice for pitcher Charles "Spider" Baum. Baum, a slender right-hander, was a native San Franciscan and an excellent pitcher. He had gone 23-19 with 361 innings pitched for the Tigers in 1913. He would become San Francisco's ace for the next four years.

Giving up Henley was difficult; he had been a consistent winner since 1905. Trading McArdle wasn't as hard. McArdle was one of the finest fielding shortstops in all of baseball, but his hitting was poor. In 1913, Roy Corhan showed great skills at short, making McArdle expendable.

In fact, the Seals were loaded with middle-infield material, with Jerry Downs at second base and Charlie O'Leary from the Cardinals at third. Young Bobby Jones quickly developed into a major league prospect.

The 1914 season was complicated by the development of a third major league—the Federal League. The new league had no scruples in pirating away star players from any team, major or minor, but the effects in the Coast League were lighter than expected. For example, Corhan rejected a handsome offer from the Federal League—almost twice his Seals contract—because he preferred to stay on the West Coast. Other players were presented with feelers but there was little movement.

## THE OAKS WITHER

The Oaks' fortunes turned quickly after winning the 1912 pennant. Although their roster was almost the same in 1913, the champions plummeted to the basement in 1913 and 1914. Manager Bud Sharpe had resigned and catcher Tiedemann, infielder Jimmie Frick and outfielder Bert Delmas didn't return to the champions. Ables, Christian, Killilay, Malarkey and Pernoll all returned to the pitching staff, but the team's batting dropped from .272 in 1912 to .241 in 1913.

The loss of Sharpe's managerial skills was a hindrance. Honus Mitze took over in 1913 and was very unhappy in the manager's role. He returned to his catch-

Biff Schaller, the Seals' slugging left fielder from 1913-1916.

Seals shortstop Roy Corhan played on two pennant-winners.

ing duties in 1914, spending nine more years in the league, mostly with the Oaks.

The league remained at six teams through 1918, with Oakland's loftiest finish at fifth, in 1915 and 1917. In 1919, the Oaks again finished fifth, but with the re-entry of Portland and Seattle into the league, there were now eight teams in the league.

The highlight of this period for Oakland was first baseman Jack Ness' 49-game hitting streak in 1915. Ness, a slender right-handed hitter, began the streak on May 31 and hit safely in every game before he was finally stopped by Vernon pitcher Art Fromme on July 21.

Ness eclipsed Chester Chadbourne's previous league record of 28 and broke Wee Willie Keeler's "world record" of 44. Ness had 81 hits in 184 at-bats for a stylish .440 average. The Oaks, in a battle for the cellar at the start of the streak, climbed into third place, only to fall back into fifth when Ness cooled off.

He finished the season at .339, second to outfielder Jimmy Johnston's team-leading .348. Ness' contract was picked up by the White Sox for 1916 and Johnston went to Brooklyn. Johnston compiled a lifetime .294 batting average in 13 major league seasons, but Ness lasted only one year with Chicago. His Coast League hitting mark lasted until it was broken by a teenaged Joe DiMaggio in 1933.

## A SECOND PENNANT FOR THE SEALS

The 1914 season was a costly one for the Seals ownership. Moving from Old Rec to Ewing Field proved to be a mistake as fans chose to stay away from the windy site. The Seals' box office woes forced Ewing and Ish to sell their interest in the club. Henry Berry from Los Angeles purchased control and he immediately returned the club to Old Rec for the 1915 season.

Berry also needed a manager to replace Del Howard. He chose Harry Wolverton, the former successful Oaks manager and capable third baseman who had managed the Sacramento Wolves in 1913 and 1914. He was available because the Sacramento franchise had gone into receivership and was returned to the league.

The 1914 Seals had won 115 games with the nucleus of the team returning for 1915. Many experts predicted a championship for the 1915 Seals especially after the franchise made some strategic acquisitions. Wolverton's major worry was pitching. Although he had two of the league's best in Spider Baum, 21-12 in 1914, and Charlie Fanning, 28-15 in 1913, every other pitcher on the staff was new to the Seals. Curly Brown, Johnny Couch and Luther "Chief" Smith made the club out of Spring Training.

Smith became a big winner, 17-9, while Brown, 11-8, and Couch, 6-5, were used in spots. Couch would be a future star. Baum was a magnificent 30-15 and Fanning went 25-15 in 1915.

Two mid-season pitching acquisitions from Detroit were instrumental in the Seals' 1915 pennant drive. The two franchises had an informal working agreement in which the Tigers would get the first choice of players off the Seals' roster for the following year, and the Seals had first crack at purchasing or trading for Detroit players. The Seals took advantage at mid-season, purchasing veteran right-hander Bill Steen. He went 10-5. The Seals also acquired tall lefty Tiller "Pug" Cavet in a trade for rookie infielder Bobby Jones, who was allowed to remain with the Seals through the end of the season. As the regular third baseman, he hit .282. The Tigers optioned him back to San Francisco in 1916 as well. After that, he played the next nine years for Detroit.

## THE NEXT HALL OF FAMER

Detroit's biggest contribution to the Seals was in optioning young Harry Heilmann to San Francisco. In 1913, a teenaged Heilmann was working in San Francisco as a bookkeeper when a friend asked him to fill in at third base in an industrial league game. A scout for Portland in the Northwest League saw Heilmann play, he was signed to a contract and Portland sold him to the Tigers in early 1914. Heilmann made the major league squad but played only sporadically. Team management decided he needed

Harry Heilmann is in the Hall of Fame.

more seasoning and optioned him to San Francisco for the 1915 season.

Heilmann got off to a marvelous start for the Seals, batting .364 in 98 games before falling ill with a mysterious malady. He collapsed while riding in a parade honoring the Seals at the Pan Pacific Exposition and missed the rest of the year.

Heilmann recovered sufficiently to return to the Tigers in 1916. After five years of unexceptional numbers, the lefty-hitting Heilmann won the 1921 American League batting championship with a .394 average and 237 base hits. He won three other batting titles, hitting .403 in 1923, .393 in 1925 and .398 in 1927. He played 15 years in the majors, batting .342 lifetime. He was elected to the Hall of Fame in 1952.

Harry Heilmann is the answer to a Bay Area baseball trivia question, in that he was the only local player ever to hit above .400 in the major leagues. Although they came close, neither Joe DiMaggio nor Lefty O'Doul accomplished that feat.

Heilmann had ample batting help from the 1915 Seals lineup. As a team, the Seals powered 99 home runs, more than double their previous high of 42. Outfielder Biff Schaller hit 20, Ping Bodie 19, Heilmann 13, Molly Meloan 11, Justin Fitzgerald 10 and Jones 9.

Meanwhile, the Oaks were a disappointing fifth in 1915 at 93-113, and they finished in the cellar in 1916. Oakland was not a rich franchise and improvement without money was extremely difficult.

In 1916, the Seals' Ping Bodie enjoyed a year that led to his promotion to the majors. Bodie played in all 206 games, batting .303 with 20 home runs, and was sold to the Philadelphia Athletics for $5,000 and players.

## ANOTHER PENNANT FOR THE SEALS IN 1917

Wolverton's third season as manager, 1917, came to an early and abrupt end, the result of philosophical differences with the owner, Henry Berry. Berry selected Jerry Downs as his new manager and Downs, a popular choice with the players, led the team to another championship by going 119-93 to finish two games ahead of the Angels.

Red Erickson was the big winner, 31-15, with Baum at 24-17. George "Chief" Johnson, a workhorse pitcher with experience in the National and Federal Leagues, added 24 wins while losing 23. The second "Chief," Luther Smith, was 17-15.

The hallmark of this team was speed. As a team, the Seals hit only 20 home runs, but they stole 385 bases. Third baseman Charlie Pick, with 66 thefts, was high on the team.

As a footnote to the 1917 season, the Seals signed a young left-handed pitcher named Francis Joseph O'Doul who was tearing up the Sunday sandlot leagues. The club optioned him to Des Moines in the Western League where he put together an 8-6 season.

After the Seals' championship season, both local clubs experienced downslides for the remainder of the decade. The impact of The Great War had a detrimental effect on the whole league. The attention of fans was on the war effort and the fate of loved ones, not on the pitching and hitting of baseballs. Attendance up and down the coast tailed off significantly.

With players being called into the service and owners taking an increased financial beating, it was little surprise the league directors called a halt to league play after the games of Sunday, July 14, 1917. The league had played only slightly more than half its schedule, but nobody seemed to care.

## CHARLIE AND LEFTY COME TO THE SEALS

The Charlie Graham years in San Francisco began in 1918. Berry had incurred substantial debts during his three years as owner and he was delighted to sell to Graham, Dr. Charles Strub, a local dentist, and George Alfred Putnam, a local sportsman.

Graham was born and raised in Santa Clara and played baseball on several West Coast teams. In 1901 Graham joined the San Francisco Wasps and went to Sacramento a year later. In the middle of that season, Sacramento Owner Mike Fisher fired his manager and appointed Graham, just 24, manager for the rest of the season. The Sacramento franchise was transferred to Tacoma in 1904, with Fisher taking over as manager. After the franchise folded, Graham fielded a team in Sacramento as part of the outlaw California League. When Sacramento returned to the Coast League in 1909, Graham, along with Bill Curtis, were part owners. Graham was also the manager and the catcher. He managed again in 1910, then sold his interest in the ballclub in 1912.

In 1918, Putnam convinced Graham to become a partner in the purchase of the Seals. The new owners quickly reversed the financial downslide. Graham took over the daily business operations while Jerry Downs continued as field manager, captain and second baseman. But it became quite evident that Graham wanted an active role on the field. Downs found his influence eroding as the season progressed. Finally, on July 1, Downs resigned and retired from baseball. Graham took over as field manager and third baseman Charlie Pick became team captain.

Unfortunately the season ended two weeks later, again because of the war. Major league teams were losing players to the war effort and looked to the Pacific Coast League to bolster their depleted rosters. The National Commission assured all minor league owners that they would continue to own, at season's end, the rights to any player who advanced to a major league team.

Seals second baseman Charlie Pick and Manager Harry Wolverton, 1917. Wolverton quit at mid-season and was replaced by Jerry Downs. The Seals won the pennant.

Pick, the Seals' leading batter, was sold unconditionally to the Cubs, so he didn't return in 1919. Francis "Lefty" O'Doul, in his first full season with the Seals, was 13-9 as a pitcher and was immediately drafted by the Yankees. Hack Miller of Oakland signed with Boston for the remainder of the 1918 season, returning to play for Oakland in 1919.

But most players wondered how they could receive a military deferment and continue to play ball. "Shipyard leagues" quickly formed. Local shipyards signed up players to work a shift and play for their team. Moore and Hanlon's shipyards joined with other Alameda and San Francisco shipyards to form a four-team league. But 3½ months later, worldwide hostilities ceased and the shipyard leagues gave way to winter industrial leagues.

## THE DECADE COMES TO A CLOSE

Out of the ashes of war came a revitalized Pacific Coast League, larger and stronger than ever before. The 1919 season saw the return of two Pacific Northwest teams to the league, Portland and Seattle. Portland had been dropped in 1918 because of wartime restrictions on travel, with Sacramento taking its place.

Seattle got a late start and went with younger players plus over-the-hill veterans. It didn't work and the team finished a distant last. As a footnote, the Seattle team's official nickname was the Purple Giants, but newspapers and fans alike continued to call them the Siwashes, their earlier name.

Portland finished seventh, with the Seals taking sixth and Oaks in fifth. Vernon took its second of three consecutive pennants.

Other than the return of baseball, it was a generally dismal season for local fans. For the Seals, Graham introduced a rookie third baseman, William Kamm. Kamm was a San Francisco boy, another of Spike Hennessy's Golden Gate Park projects. Hennessy, as he had done for so many other San Francisco youngsters, served as an unofficial adviser to Kamm and ultimately recommended him to the Sacramento Solons.

The Solons signed Kamm for the 1918 season but he was released when the season was cut short. He returned to San Francisco and played industrial league ball at Recreation Park. There, Graham spotted him and signed him to a contract for 1919.

Graham installed Kamm as the team's regular third baseman. Nobody questioned his glove, but there was speculation he would not hit well enough. In 1919, he batted only .235, and in 1920, .237. But Kamm started filling out, and his batting average fattened up as well: .288 in 1921 and .342 in 1922. Kamm was eventually sold to the Chicago White Sox for $100,000 plus players, one of the first of Charlie Graham's blockbuster sales.

The 1919 team was a transitional one for the San Francisco and Oakland clubs. Several older Seals were ending their careers and Graham had acquired younger players Jimmy Caveney and pitchers Jim "Death Valley" Scott and Johnny Couch, who would bring the team great successes in the 1920s.

For Del Howard's Oaks, the fifth-place finish in 1919 was viewed as an improvement because there were now eight teams in the league instead of six. Plus, there were several solid players forming the nucleus of the club. Carl Mitze and Rowdy Elliott anchored the catching staff, Harry Krause and Ray Kremer were excellent pitchers, and a young Buzz Arlett became a workhorse on the mound. Sammy Bohne, Louie Guisto, Rube Gardner, Roxie Middleton and Rod Murphy were all fine players. The 1920s would treat the Oaks a little better. ❖

# CHAPTER 7

# FRONT OFFICE TRIALS

If there were any period of time when West Coast baseball qualified to be considered as competitive with major league baseball, it was the 1920s. Some of the greatest players and teams were located in the Bay Area during this decade.

Front-office activities moved to the forefront of baseball news during that same decade. Seemingly endless bickering took place among the league directors, the team presidents and other officials. William H. "Bill" McCarthy of San Francisco was stationed at the center of many of these controversies.

McCarthy served four tumultuous years as Coast League president in the early part of the decade. Like the owners of the eight teams in the league, he had a strong will and a large ego. His major failing was that his approach was not as diplomatic as it needed to be.

## GAMBLING TAINTS BASEBALL

The huge cloud of the Black Sox scandal descended upon baseball as the 1920s began. In the Coast League, several critical problems demanded courageous action by the president—not the least of which was the credibility of the game. In the majors, Judge Kenesaw Mountain Landis

was hired as baseball commissioner to return confidence in the game to the fans of America.

The scandal was revealed in 1920 and players were prosecuted in 1921. Landis dealt firmly—but apparently unevenly—with players in meting out justice. While the participants in the Black Sox scandal were summarily banished from baseball, star players suspected of other gambling activity were ignored.

Long-time Sacramento Solons shortstop Ray French revealed in the early 1970s how Landis practically pleaded with "Shoeless Joe" Jackson of the White Sox to deny knowledge of the World Series scandal. When Jackson declined, Landis had no other choice but to include him in the banishment.

On the Pacific Coast, rumors of scandal shrouded the end of the 1919 pennant race. Many players were alleged to have been bribed by members of the Vernon club, guaranteeing the Tigers the pennant. McCarthy completed an arduous investigation and pressed charges in civil court against a half-dozen players including Casey Smith of the Seals. However, evidence was inconclusive and the charges were dropped. McCarthy still banned all six players from the Pacific Coast League.

Salt Lake's Bill Rumler, the 1919 league batting champion, was one of the banned players. Bees President Bill

Recreation Park in San Francisco, circa 1920, had a 'booze cage' like the earlier field. This ballpark was not as enclosed and had a larger seating capacity.

Lane and his secretary, Jack Cook, strongly opposed McCarthy and his presidency as a result of the scandal. Both became leaders of a conspiracy to oust McCarthy.

The 1920 winter meetings, held in Sacramento, offered McCarthy's opponents an issue upon which they could push for his removal. McCarthy had taken the job on the assumption he would be able to continue his law practice. But with all the problems in the league, the presidency had developed into a full-time job. McCarthy was earning half-time pay—$5,000 a year—which he felt was insufficient.

When the meeting was called to order, McCarthy startled his detractors by issuing a prepared statement announcing his resignation. The thrust of McCarthy's remarks were twofold: The owners had to end their divisive bickering, and the president's position commanded a larger salary. Upon delivery of his statement, McCarthy left the meeting.

The owners were so shocked by McCarthy's move that they offered him a three-year contract at $10,000 a year and pleaded for him to return. After a week of refus-ing, McCarthy accepted the offer and returned with a much stronger hand. His detractors were silenced, at least temporarily.

McCarthy's action against players alleged to be on the take preceded Judge Landis' Black Sox rulings by two years. McCarthy was able to declare his league clean and he assured the public it could have complete confidence in the integrity of the game. He also led occasional sweeps of Coast League ballparks to arrest the gamblers who fre-quented them.

McCarthy's heavy-handedness had alienated him from a number of owners, and by 1923 they were working to replace him with Harry Williams, sportswriter and columnist for the *Los Angeles Times*. For some owners, the issue was simply one of north vs. south. Underlying this division was a deep hatred that had developed between Oakland's Cal Ewing and the Seals' Doc Strub. Ewing favored McCarthy's ouster.

When the ultimate vote was taken at the 1923 winter meeting, Williams had four votes to McCarthy's three. The eighth vote belonged to Seattle, whose representative favored McCarthy's ouster. But before nominations were taken, McCarthy had declared the Seattle representative ineligible because, in a clear violation of league by-laws, the Chicago Cubs' William Wrigley had secretly invested in the Seattle franchise. McCarthy, in his capacity as president, voted the proxy—for himself.

Lane then stated, "Mr. President, we recognize that Seattle has a right to vote here, and we recognize Mr. Williams as president of this league from now on. Mr. Williams, take the chair."

At this point, McCarthy left the meeting, followed by the directors from Sacramento, San Francisco and Vernon.

The election was referred to the National Board of Arbitration, the judicial branch of minor league baseball. They decided in Williams' favor, thus ending one of the more dynamic and divisive periods in Pacific Coast League history.

McCarthy became president of the Mission Bells in

Bill McCarthy and Wade 'Red' Killefer of the Missions talk at Old Rec. McCarthy was a former league president and Killefer led the Reds to their only first-place finish in 1929.

1926 and was again nominated for the league presidency in 1928, but ultimately lost in a long, drawn-out and spiteful vote.

## LOCAL BOY MAKES BAD

Although major league baseball had attempted to clean up its image by hiring Judge Landis, rumors of gambling still periodically surfaced. In 1924, just as the baseball world was focusing on the upcoming World Series, scandal returned. An attempted fix centered around a local boy, Jimmy O'Connell.

O'Connell was going to college at Santa Clara. When he decided not to return to school in the fall of 1919, Alfie Putnam, co-owner of the Seals, quickly signed him to a contract. After three years with the Seals, Charlie Graham sold O'Connell, who had excellent speed and was a solid hitter, to the New York Giants for $75,000—a record for a minor league player.

O'Connell was only 22 when he reported to the Giants for Spring Training in 1923. As a naive country kid wanting to be accepted by his teammates, he was a perfect foil for clubhouse pranks.

Near the end of the 1924 season, several Giants players were joking around in the clubhouse before a game with the Phillies. The team needed just one game to clinch the pennant. Somebody suggested, most likely as a practical joke, the possibility of fixing the game to guarantee a Giants' victory. Giants coach Cozy Dolan told O'Connell to talk to Heine Sand, the Phillies' shortstop, and offer him $500 to guarantee a Giants victory that day. Sand was from San Francisco and O'Connell knew him from their PCL days.

O'Connell took the comment seriously and approached Sand on the matter. Sand immediately told his manager, Art Fletcher, who informed Commissioner Landis of the incident.

An immediate investigation was held and O'Connell told the commissioner the full story. Dolan's answers, however, were evasive. Implicated in the scandal, but later exonerated, were Frankie Frisch, Ross Youngs and George Kelly. Landis expelled O'Connell and Dolan from baseball for life, and a bewildered O'Connell returned to San Francisco.

American League President Ban Johnson reacted to the scandal by publicly claiming that graft was rampant among western players, implying gamblers regularly affected the outcome of PCL games.

An angry Williams, the new Coast League president, challenged Johnson to back up his statement with facts. "His charge is an insult to every man who wears a uniform in this circuit, and his assertions are unbelievable. No man, especially one in a prominent position in the game, should make such blanket statements. He should

Jimmy O'Connell, once a promising hitter for the Seals, was banned from baseball for allegedly plotting a fixed game.

The top minor leagues and the major leagues continued to squabble over the draft. In an unusual show of strength in 1919, the minor leagues demanded and got some relief from the major leagues on that subject. As part of the new National Agreement, minor leagues would be allowed to exempt themselves from the draft. None of their players could be drafted, but neither could they draft from minor leagues inferior to them.

Minor league clubs could now wait to sell their players on the open market, thus allowing the owners to receive premiums for star players. There was a negative side to this, however; players could be held back from advancement simply because an acceptable price could not be agreed upon. The draft exemption lasted about three years before the major league owners reinstated the major league draft.

## THE MISSIONS COME TO TOWN

Two Pacific Coast League franchises were shifted between the 1925 and 1926 seasons. Bill Lane had grown tired of substandard attendance and expensive trips. He yearned to move the Salt Lake franchise to somewhere in Southern California.

In addition, Eddie Maier of Vernon had seen his club suffer from a second-class image in Southern California, and hoped to sell. A triumvirate of Herbert Fleishhacker, a wealthy San Francisco banker; Stanley Dollar of shipping fame; and ex-PCL President McCarthy negotiated a complicated deal that would bring the Vernon franchise to San Francisco. But Salt Lake City, Los Angeles, Vernon, San Francisco and Oakland had to be satisfied with the arrangement. The partnership paid Maier $300,000 and moved it to San Francisco.

The idea of transferring the Vernon team to San Francisco had been floated for the first time after the 1924 season. It was presumed Ewing's opposition would be enough to defeat such a transfer, but Ewing was swayed by monetary concessions from fighting the shift. The Oaks received immediate cash payments of $25,000 from both the Angels and the Seals. The Oaks were also to receive $10,000 a year for the next six years. The total package to Oakland was $110,000.

The transfers were ratified on January 13, 1926, less than three months before Opening Day. As soon as the Vernon franchise was transferred to San Francisco, they adopted the team name of Mission Bears, intending to adorn themselves in blue and gold. The University of California at Berkeley, with a distinguished tradition behind their school colors and mascot, filed suit against the baseball club. It was then the Mission club accepted "Bells" as its team name.

But the new Mission Bells would continue their struggle for an identity. The team remained in San Francisco

name the guilty, if there are such, and not cast suspicion on the game generally."

Ironically, the betting line on that day's World Series game was but two columns over from Williams' statement in the *San Francisco Bulletin*.

At Emeryville and at Recreation Park, greater efforts were made to prevent the gamblers from passing money for their bets. But in time the furor subsided, and it was back to business as usual in the gambling sections at the two ballparks.

## MINORS VERSUS MAJORS

The PCL moguls' most serious concerns about their business revolved around the continued ability of major league owners to draft talented, exciting young stars from their league's rosters at a mere fraction of their potential market value.

As long as a draft was imposed on the minor leagues, there would be no chance for the Pacific Coast League to become truly competitive with the major leagues.

Pacific Coast League President Harry Williams.

through 1937 and was consistently outdrawn at the gate by the Seals, in some cases by close to 100,000 fans a season. The identity crisis continued in other ways as well. The team was alternately called the Bells, Reds and Monks, but mostly the Missions.

Bill McCarthy became president and spokesman for the Mission franchise and was welcomed back as a director of the league in an ironic twist. McCarthy's reputation and esteem were excellent in San Francisco so he was the logical person to promote and lead the new Mission Bells. Owner Fleishhacker opened his wallet to acquire a competitive team, and the fans of San Francisco—although not easily swayed from their partisanship to the Seals—seemed willing to give the new team a chance.

Finding a manager was another matter. The Missions went through five in their first two seasons alone.

Walter McCredie, "The Tall Scot," had previously signed to manage the Vernon Tigers for 1926, and McCarthy honored his contract in San Francisco. But McCredie had to resign in ill health after just one month and was replaced by veteran catcher Walter Schmidt.

Schmidt had caught five years for the Seals from 1911 to 1915 before going to the major leagues. He was an excellent handler of pitchers and had been acquired from the St. Louis Cardinals to bolster the Bells' catching. As a

manager, however, his management of pitchers was widely criticized. On August 13, three months after his appointment, he was replaced by "Wild Bill" Leard, a former infielder for the Oaks and the Seals during the 1910s.

The *San Francisco Call and Post's* wrote, "Bill Leard is a fire-eating, scrapping pilot of the old school."

More appropriately, he was an Irishman who could not hold his temper or his drink. Leard provided added excitement around the ballpark but was unable to improve the Bells' standing.

Leard managed into 1927, but the first game of the season proved to be a harbinger of the chaos to follow. Leard was thrown out of the game by umpire Carl Westervelt for arguing a called third strike. His ranting was soon eclipsed by his refusal to leave the home plate area. It was only when Westervelt took out his watch, threatening the Bells with forfeiture of the game, that Leard withdrew to the clubhouse.

Eighteen days into the season, Leard was fired in one of the most bizarre removals in baseball history. The team was in Seattle when McCarthy started getting reports that all was not well. At mid-week, he rushed north to find that Leard had been on a drunken binge and absent from the previous day's game. The team was on the verge of rebellion. McCarthy fired Leard on the spot and issued a release stating Leard had been responsible for "conduct unbecoming a manager, and failure to live up to the training rules demanded of the players themselves."

McCarthy appointed catcher Al Walters as interim manager and embarked on a thorough search for a permanent one. Three weeks later Harry Hooper was appointed player-manager. Hooper, the future Hall of Famer, came out of retirement to take the job. He had been living in Capitola selling insurance.

Hooper's career spanned 17 years with the Red Sox and the White Sox and he played in four World Series. His activity with the Bells as a player was limited to 79 games, many as a pinch-hitter. He concluded the season with a .288 average and then decided he preferred selling insurance to managing.

Stability in the dugout arrived in 1928 when Wade "Red" Killefer bought into the Mission club and became its manager. He served three years, including the 1929 season when the Missions had the best record in the league. However, they lost the pennant to Hollywood through a playoff series of the split-season winners. Before the 1931 season started, Killefer became ill and had to resign his positions as league director and manager.

## McCARTHY'S COMEBACK FAILS

When Killefer was voted in as president of the Missions at the conclusion of the 1928 season, McCarthy's resignation from the board of directors was accepted.

McCarthy had tendered his resignation earlier when Killefer had purchased into the ownership, but at that time his letter of resignation was not accepted. Now there was no place for him.

Immediately, several owners started campaigning for McCarthy's return as league president. Harry Williams' term of office was up after the 1928 season, so the timing was right.

McCarthy's adversaries were still members of the league board, and the prospect of his return to leadership was unacceptable to them. They had not forgotten his previous tenure of office.

The election of a president was on the agenda at the next board meeting, held in November 1928 in Portland. San Francisco, Los Angeles, Sacramento and the Missions were firmly committed to McCarthy's return, and the other four were equally opposed.

It was not that Williams had done a poor job, but many viewed him as a caretaker, nothing more. With McCarthy there certainly would be dynamic—albeit controversial—leadership.

Five names were put into nomination: McCredie of Portland, McCarthy, former President A.T. Baum, John J. Sullivan of Seattle and Williams. The first ballot showed four votes for McCarthy and one each for McCredie, Baum, Sullivan and Williams.

Eight more ballots were held in the morning with McCarthy gaining four votes on each, but not a fifth. Seeing the futility of the process, Williams was called back into the room to conduct other business.

In the afternoon session, four more ballots were taken. McCarthy's supporters remained at four. On one ballot, Baum had four votes. On two other ballots, McCredie had four. Again, the directors went on to other business, postponing the vote until the next morning.

When the morning session convened, the directors agreed to limit themselves to 10 ballots. If no selection was made within this limit, the issue would be postponed until January's meeting. The 10 ballots were taken, and the two favorites, McCarthy and Williams, ended in a deadlock. So, after 23 ballots, there was no resolution and the issue was dropped.

This election effectively ended McCarthy's baseball career. He had resigned as director of the Missions and he had been rejected by the PCL directors. At the January directors meeting, Williams' name was put into nomination and he was unanimously confirmed for an additional two years.

As a sidelight to the November 1928 meeting, the directors were asked to approve a recommendation of the Major-Minor League Advisory Council. The council had recommended an increase in compensation to $7,500 for any player taken in the draft by a major league club from a Double-A league. In their general opposition to the draft as an institution, the league unanimously turned down the recommendation.

## MORE BALLOT BICKERING

At the end of 1929, Cal Ewing took his first step towards retirement from baseball. He sold his interests in the Oaks to Victor Devincenzi and A. Robert Miller. Also taken in as a minor partner was Carl Zamloch, coach of the University of California baseball team and a former Coast League and major league player and manager. Because Ewing had purchased the Oaks Ball Park property from the Key System Transit Lines two years earlier, he no longer owned the team but did own the ballpark.

As a result of selling the team, Ewing had to resign from the PCL Board of Directors. Ewing had been the league's primary contact with major league owners. This was a loss, because his motives were always in the best interests of baseball and he was respected because of it.

With Harry Williams' term of office ending in a year, several owners approached Ewing about seeking the league presidency. He was receptive, and when the directors met in November 1930, Ewing, Williams and John Sullivan were nominated.

The first ballot found Williams earning the votes of San Francisco, Portland, Los Angeles and Sacramento. Ewing received three votes, and Sullivan received one, from Seattle. Three additional ballots in the morning and one in the afternoon brought similar results, so the directors, remembering 1928, moved on to other business.

A December directors meeting found a similar stalemate. Finally, in January 1931, the directors voted to extend Williams' presidency for an additional year, effectively removing Ewing from the inner workings of the Pacific Coast League.

For the next few years he served as a consultant to the league in their dealings at the winter meetings. Ewing's wife was killed in 1935 when a gas stove exploded. Cal never seemed to recover from the shock of her death, and he died within two years. ❖

CHAPTER **8**

# FOUR FLAGS FOR FRISCO

The 1920s provided quality baseball and tight pennant races and proved to be an unusual time as five championship pennants flew over local ballparks. The Seals were winners in 1922, 1923, 1925 and 1928. The Oaks put together a marvelous squad that challenged in 1926 and won in 1927. Even the Mission Bells finished at the top in 1929 before losing a seven-game championship series to the Hollywood Sheiks.

The Seals were one of the top franchises in all of baseball during this decade; there were many who believed the San Francisco team would have been competitive in either major league. At the turnstiles, Seals fans supported their team as fervently as in any major league city. Attendance surpassed 446,000 in 1922—a minor league record until after the second World War.

The Seals graduated four players from the decade who became Hall of Famers. Two other Hall of Famers, Joe Cronin and Tony Lazzeri, grew up in San Francisco but played elsewhere.

In Oakland, Ernest Lombardi was knocking balls lopsided, and bespectacled Charles "Chick" Hafey spent the off-season in Berkeley, his birthplace.

The PCL was primarily an independent league in which each team owned its players outright. The teams aggressively scouted players in their own backyards and occasionally sent scouts into untapped areas such as the southwest or the Pacific Northwest.

The major league draft, to which the Pacific Coast League directors strongly objected, limited the league's ability to build strong teams. At the end of each season, major league teams could draft as many players as it wanted from the minor leagues. However, each minor league team could lose only one player in the draft, for whom it would receive a mere $5,000. The low price tag greatly bothered minor league owners because the system dictated the pre-draft selling of star players for a higher premium. It was not unusual to find a minor league team selling a player or two to the major leagues and then lose another player in the draft.

This concept helped minor league franchises balance their budgets but also guaranteed they would remain subservient to the major leagues.

When selling players to the majors, minor league teams usually insisted on receiving players along with a reduced amount of cash. Minor league owners wanted major league veterans because they were gate attractions. These veterans also served as instructors or role models for the younger players on the team, as teams seldom had coaches at this time.

In the Bay Area, baseball was still the only game in town. Seals and Oaks games were headline material in the local newspaper even when Cal, St. Mary's and the other colleges played football in September and October. The World Series would come and go and fans would still flock to see the Seals and Oaks play the last few games on their schedule.

## THE GRAHAM YEARS

Charles H. Graham, along with Charles Strub and George "Alf" Putnam, had purchased the San Francisco Seals from W.H. "Hen" Berry of Los Angeles in 1918. Graham was the baseball man, and he would run the team until his death during the 1948 season. Graham was tight-fisted at contract time, but he was respected and admired by the players because of his ability to judge talent and his compassion towards the players' needs.

Graham was manager that first year and led the club to moderate success through the next four seasons. But 1921 was particularly devastating to Graham when the Seals plunged to third late in the season after leading the league. At that point, Graham decided to run the club from the front office, not the field.

The Seals opened the 1921 season by winning their first 10 games. As the season progressed, the Seals continued to play solid ball and kept a comfortable lead over the field. Jimmy O'Connell, Ike Caveney, Justin Fitzgerald and Bert Ellison were all batting over .300 for a team that would ultimately have a cumulative team batting average of .293. O'Doul, who had come over in a trade from Vernon after the Tigers acquired him from the New York Yankees, was pitching admirably after getting off to a slow start. But the rest of the pitching was inconsistent.

The Seals held a 6½-game lead over Sacramento on September 1, but they went 12-20 during the last month and watched the Angels and the Senators pass them at the finish. Graham retired as field manager after the season, vowing to rebuild the team for 1922. As the first step, he hired John B. "Dots" Miller as his manager. Miller had a distinguished major league career concluding with the Phillies in 1921.

Miller was a quiet man who apparently lacked the desire to play up to reporters or influential personalities. Still, the players swore by him. He motivated them and used them effectively in the situations where they could display their strengths. If results were the major criteria, Miller was wildly successful. His 1922 team won the pennant, and his more talented 1923 squad made a shambles

Charlie Graham, long-time owner of the San Francisco Seals, was one of the most respected men in the history of the PCL.

of the pennant race when Miller was forced to leave the team in August.

Miller started the 1923 season in good spirits and apparently good health. By June, he didn't seem to be his normal self. He wasn't sleeping well at nights and his eating habits deteriorated. A medical diagnosis determined Miller was suffering from tuberculosis. He left the team in mid-August, returning to his home at Saranac Lake in

Golf proved to be a valuable training tool for the 1922 Seals. Trainer Denny Carroll would give players a club and a ball, then have them run the full 18 holes during the game. Manager Dots Miller is in the center of the picture.

New York to recuperate. In late August he contacted the Seals front office to say that he was feeling better, but just weeks later, on September 5, he died.

Bert Ellison, Miller's first baseman, was appointed interim manager for the last two months of the 1923 season, and was named full-time manager during the winter for the 1924 season.

In rebuilding for 1922, Graham knew he had to focus on his pitching staff, which had blown more than a few leads in 1921. Only Jim "Death Valley" Scott and Herb McQuaid survived the winter, and they had accounted for only 24 victories between them. Lefty O'Doul, who was 25-9 with a 2.39 ERA in 1921 despite a chronically sore elbow, was drafted by the Yankees for $5,000, and Johnny Couch, who worked 345 innings and was 25-15, was sold in a package with Caveney to the Cincinnati Reds.

Graham acquired workhorse Ernie Alten from Oakland, Harry Courtney from Washington, and Doug McWeeney and Clarence "Shovel" Hodge from the White Sox. Rookie Oliver Mitchell was 24-7 in 1921, Scott 25-9, Bob Geary 20-9, and McWeeney 15-7. Alten won 13 and

Fritz Coumbe 10. These six pitchers accounted for all but 20 of the team's 127 victories, the strongest front line in the league. This staff dominated the league through 1923.

The 1922 Seals were solid. The infield of O'Connell at first, Pete Kilduff or Dee Walsh at second, rookie Hal Rhyne at shortstop and Willie Kamm at third was better than most major league infields.

Outfielders Joe Kelly and Justin Fitzgerald were joined by veterans Charlie See, Pete Compton and rookie Gene Valla. Ellison could play almost any position with great skill, and Dots Miller still had a few games in him as a utility infielder. The catching was solid with Sam Agnew and Archie Yelle, both able handlers of pitchers and both experienced hitters.

The Seals won the 1922 pennant by four games over Vernon in an exciting race. The Tigers actually won 18 of the 28 games against the Seals, but San Francisco's hitting was too strong to overcome over the course of a season. The Seals' team batting average was .298. Kamm batted .344 with 21 homers. O'Connell was at .338 with 13 homers. Kelly hit .332 with a league-leading 141 RBIs.

## THE KING OF TRAINERS

If there ever were to be a Hall of Fame for athletic trainers, Denny Carroll would be its Babe Ruth.

Carroll was not out of the traditional mold of athletic trainers of the day. He was highly educated and made a detailed analysis of each pitcher's mechanics and the potential for arm ailments. It is said that "Doc" Carroll could spot potential ailments before they presented themselves by noticing slight changes in a player's mechanics. During the winter, major league players would come to San Francisco to have Carroll work with them.

Carroll joined the Seals in 1909 and for five years he served as trainer for both the Seals and the Oaks. He continued with the Seals until the end of the 1931 season when he and Manager Nick Williams got into a violent, drunken argument on the train bringing them back to San Francisco. Charlie Graham didn't tolerate such action and immediately fired both men. Carroll went on to a distinguished career as trainer for the Detroit Tigers.

In 1921, the Seals trained at Byron Hot Springs, outside of Monterey. This was to be Graham's last year managing the Seals. Conditioning in the early weeks was turned over to Carroll.

Carroll was given responsibility for setting up the Spring Training regimen. Each player had to be up by 7:30 every morning and was to drink two to four glasses of the water from the sulphur springs. Breakfast was served at 8:30, and the players were to be on the diamond at 10:30 for the first of two workouts. The second workout began at 2:30 p.m., and was followed immediately by a hot sulphur bath at 4 p.m. Dinner was served at 6:30, everyone properly dressed, and all players were to be in bed by 10.

The terrain at Byron Hot Springs was hilly, with two golf courses nearby. It was not unusual to see the full Seals team jogging over the fairways as an early morning conditioner. Carroll occasionally added a wrinkle to the routine, one the players particularly enjoyed. Each player received one golf club and two golf balls. Twosomes would tee off and run to the location of the ball, hit it again and repeat the process. Several players previously not golfers became smitten by the game through this exercise.

---

Five others hit higher than .300, contributing to the Seals' 1,085 runs—slightly better than five runs per game. The Seals also had speed on the bases. O'Connell stole 39, Kamm 32, Kelly 31.

The development of Hal Rhyne into a superior shortstop and the discovery of Gene Valla gave the Seals four of the finest young players in America. Kamm and O'Connell were sold to the majors at the end of the season.

### A REPEAT IN 1923

The 1923 Seals won the pennant by 11 games. Eddie Mulligan moved in to third base for the departed Kamm and Bert Ellison returned to first base for O'Connell, who had been sold to the Giants.

The only major addition to the club was a rookie outfielder from Oklahoma named Paul Waner. Graham had sent his talent scout, Nick Williams, to the Southwestern states in search of young pitchers. After several weeks of frustration, Williams was, by chance, turned on to a prospect by a fellow train traveler. The pitcher turned out to be Paul Waner, whose record with the Ada team was 24-3 with 278 strikeouts and only 29 walks and a 1.70 ERA. Williams wasted no time in signing Waner to a Seals contract.

But when Waner reported to the Seals' 1923 Spring Training, it became obvious that he was too much of a hitting prospect, so he was converted into an outfielder. In 112 games in his rookie campaign with the Seals, Waner hit .369—second in the league—and showed total command of the strike zone.

## HOW PAUL WANER CAME TO SAN FRANCISCO

Paul Waner explained the unlikely circumstances of his sojourn to the San Francisco Seals in an interview for Lawrence S. Ritter's classic, *The Glory of Their Times*:

"How did they find me? Well, they found me because a scout went on a drunk. Yes, that's right, because a scout went on a bender. He was a scout for the San Francisco Seals of the Pacific Coast League, and he was in Muskogee looking over a player by the name of Flashcamper that Frisco wanted to buy. He looked him over, and sent in a recommendation—that was late in the summer of 1922—and then went out on a drunk for about 10 days. They never heard a thing from him all this while, didn't know anything about him or where the heck he was.

"He finally got in shape to go back to the Coast, but on the way back a train conductor by the name of Burns—you know how they used to stop and talk with you and pass the time of day—found out that this fellow was a baseball scout. Well, it so happened that I went with this conductor's daughter—Lady Burns—at school. So naturally—me going with his daughter and all—what the heck—he couldn't wait to tell this scout how great I was. How I could pitch and hit and run and do just about everything. He was such a convincing talker, and this scout needed an excuse so bad for where he'd been those 10 days, that the scout—Nick Williams was his name—decided, 'Doggone it, I've got something here.'

"When he got back to San Francisco, of course they wanted to know where the heck he'd been and what had happened. 'Well,' he said, 'I've been looking over a ballplayer in Ada, Oklahoma. His name is Paul Waner and he's only 19 years old, and I think he's really going to make it big. I've watched him for 10 days and I don't see how he can miss.'

"Then Nick quickly wrote me a letter. He said, 'I've just talked to the Frisco ball club about you. I heard about you through this conductor, Burns. I told them I saw you and all that, and I want you to write me a letter and send it to my home. Don't send it to the ballclub, send it to my home. Tell me all about yourself: your height, your weight, whether you're left-handed or right-handed, how fast you can run the 100, and all that. So I'll know, see, really know.'

"So I wrote him the letter he wanted, and sent it to his home, not really thinking too much about it at the time. But the next spring, darned if they didn't send me a contract. However, I sent it right back, 'cause my Dad always wanted me to go to school. He didn't want me to quit college. My father was a farmer and he wanted his sons to get a good education.

"But they sent the contract right back to me, and even upped the ante some. So I said, 'Dad, I'll ask them for $500 a month, and if they give it to me will you let me go?'

"He thought about it awhile, and finally said, 'Well, if they'll give you $500 a month starting off, and if you'll promise me that if you don't make it good you'll come right back and finish college, then it's OK with me.'

"'Why surely, I'll do that,' I said.

"So I told the Frisco club about those conditions. But it didn't make any difference to them. Because they could offer you any salary at all and look you over, and if you weren't really good they could just let you go and they'd only be out expenses. They had nothing to lose.

"So I went out to San Francisco for Spring Training. That was 1923. I was only 19 years old, almost 20, just an ol' country boy. I didn't even know, when I got there, that they had a boat going across to San Francisco. My ticket didn't call for any boat trip. But after the train got into Oakland you got on a ferry and went across San Francisco Bay. Boy, as far as I was concerned that was a huge ocean liner!

"I had hardly arrived out there before I met Willie Kamm, Lew Fonseca and Jimmy O'Connell. Those three used to pal around together a lot, because they all came from the Bay Area. I was anxious to be friendly and all, so I said to them, real solicitous-like, 'Well, do you fellows think you'll make good up here?' (All the while thinking to myself, you know, 'Gee, you sure don't look like it to me.')

"How was I to know that all three of them were *already* established big leaguers? It turned out they were just working out with the Frisco club until their own training camps opened. But I didn't know that. That was a big joke they never let me forget—a kid like me asking them did they think they'd make good!

"Anyway, there I was, a rookie who'd never played a game in organized ball, at Spring Training with the San Francisco club in the Coast League, which was the highest minor league classification there was. I was a pitcher then, a left-handed pitcher. At Ada I'd played first base and the outfield when I wasn't pitching, but the Frisco club signed me as a pitcher.

"The first or second day of Spring Training we had a little game, the Regulars against the Yannigans—that's what they called the rookies— and I was pitching for the Yannigans. The umpire was a coach by the name of Spider Baum. Along about the sixth inning my arm started to tighten up, so I shouted in, 'Spider, my arm is tying up and getting sore on me.'

"'Make it or break it!' he says.

"They don't say those things to youngsters nowadays. No, sir! And maybe it's just as well they don't, because what happened was that, sure enough, I *broke* it! And the next day, gee, I could hardly lift it.

"I figured that was the end of my career, and in a few weeks I'd be back in Ada. I was supposed to be a pitcher, and I couldn't throw the ball 10 feet. But just to keep busy, and look like I was doing something, I fooled around in the outfield and shagged balls for the rest of them. I'd toss the ball back underhanded, because I couldn't throw any other way. I did that day after day, but my arm didn't get any better.

"After the regular day's practice was over, the three big leaguers—Willie Kamm, Lew Fonseca, and Jimmy O'Connell—would stay out an extra hour or so and practice hitting, and I shagged balls for them, too. I figured I'd better make myself useful in any way I could, or I'd be on my way back to Oklahoma.

"I don't know which one of them mentioned it to the others, but after about a week or so of this they decided that maybe I'd like a turn at hitting. Especially since if I quit shagging for them, they'd have to go chase all those balls themselves. And they didn't relish the idea of doing that.

"So they yelled, 'Hey kid! You want to hit some?'

"'Sure I do,' I said.

"So they threw, and I hit. They just let me hit and hit and hit, and I really belted that ball. There was a carpenter building a house just beyond the right field fence, about 360 or 370 feet from home plate. He was pounding shingles, and he had his back to us. Well, I hit one, and it landed on the roof, pretty close to him. He looked around, wondering what the devil was going on. The first thing you know, I slammed another one out there and it darned near hit him. So he just put his hammer down and sat there and watched. And I kept on crashing line drives out there all around where he was sitting. Of course, they were lobbing the ball in just right, and heck—I just swished and away it went.

"When we were finished, we went into the clubhouse and nobody said a word to me. Not a word. And there was only dead silence all the while we showered and got dressed and walked back to the hotel. We sat down to dinner, and still not a single one of them had said 'You looked good' or 'You did well' or anything like that.

"But when we were almost through eating dinner the manager, Dots Miller, came over to my table. He said, 'Okie, tomorrow you fool around in the outfield. Don't throw hard, just toss 'em in underhand. And you *hit* with the regulars.'

"Well, boy, that was something! I gulped, and felt like the cat that just ate the canary. And from then on I was with the regulars, and I started playing.

"Luckily my arm came back a month or two later, a few weeks after the season started. We went into Salt Lake City, and was it ever hot.

"Suddenly, during fielding practice, my arm felt like it stretched out at least a foot longer, and it felt really supple and good. It caught me by surprise and I was afraid to really throw hard. But I did a little more each time, and it felt fine!

"Duffy Lewis was managing Salt Lake City and he knew about my bad arm, so he'd told his players, 'Run on Waner. Anytime the ball goes to him, just duck your head and start running, because he can't throw.'

"There was a pretty short right-field wall at Salt Lake City, and in the first or second inning one of their players hit one off the wall. I took it on the rebound and threw him out at second by 15 feet. Someone tried to score from second on a single to right, and I threw him out at home plate! I threw about four men out in nothing flat, and after that they stopped running on me. I never had any trouble with my arm after that. It never bothered me again.

"I had a good year in the Coast League that first season; hit about .370. Then the next season I did the same thing, got over 200 hits and batted in about 100 runs. I was figuring by then that maybe I should be moving up to the big leagues. Joe Devine, a Pittsburgh scout, was trying to get the Pirates to buy me, but the San Francisco club wanted $100,000 for me, and the Pittsburgh higher-ups thought that was a little too much for a small fellow like me. I only weighed 135 pounds then. I never weighed over 148 pounds, even, in all the years I played.

"So Joe said to me, 'Paul, it looks like you'll have to hit .400 to get up to the majors.'

"'Well then,' I said, 'that's just exactly what I'll do.'

"I was kidding, you know. But darned if I didn't hit .401 in 1925. I got 280 hits that season, and at the end of the year the Pirates paid the $100,000 for me. San Francisco sold Willie Kamm to the big leagues for $100,000 in 1922, and then did the same thing with me three years later."

"So that's the way it was. Those 24 years that I played baseball—from 1923 to 1946—somehow, it doesn't seem like I played even a month. It went *so fast*. The first four or five years, I felt like I'd been in baseball a long time. Then, suddenly, I'd been in the big leagues for 10 years. And then, all at once, it was 20.

"You know—sitting here like this—it's hard to believe it's more than a quarter of a century since Lloyd and I played together. Somehow—I don't know—it seems like it all happened only yesterday."

Nick Williams returned to Ada the next winter to sign lefty Guy Williams to a Seals contract. The following winter, it was Lloyd Waner, Paul's younger brother.

The 1923 San Francisco Seals boasted a .319 team batting average. It was not a team of sluggers, but one that could move runners along and score them. Ellison led the team with 65 doubles, 23 home runs, 139 runs batted in and 427 total bases.

But Ellison enjoyed tremendous support. Nine players who played in 100 or more games batted above .300 for the Seals. Paul Waner's .369 was tops, followed by Ellison's .358, Kelly's .348, Tim Hendryx's .339, Valla's .336 in 194 games, Mulligan's .329, Kilduff's .328, Compton's .324 and Agnew's .312. Dee Walsh batted .343 in 78 games, and young Pete Ritchie (later Ricci) batted .322 in

57 games. It was the pitching staff and shortstop Rhyne at .296 who brought the team average down.

The starting pitching had great balance with Courtney (19-6, 2.80 ERA), Hodge (18-15, 3.48), Shea (21-10, 3.62), Geary (21-11, 3.64) and McWeeney (20-9, 3.91). The five regular starters won 99 games, and with the exception of Pat Shea's 291 innings, pitched between 251 and 262 innings each.

Oliver Mitchell and "Death Valley" Scott didn't receive the pitching opportunities they were used to in previous years and tailed off to 10-9 and 11-9, respectively. Scott did pitch a 5-0 no-hitter at Oakland, however. There was no place on the staff for Ernie Alten, winner of 33 games over the past two seasons, so he was shipped to Vernon. The Seals' pitching staff turned in 112 complete games during the 201-game season.

Below, members of the 1923 Seals infield relax before a game (l-r): Second baseman Pete Kilduff, third baseman Eddie Mulligan, shortstop Hal Rhyne, utility man Dee Walsh and first baseman Bert Ellison. Bottom, the 1923 Seals.

## NO CIGAR IN 1924

The 1924 season concluded with one of the most exciting finishes in PCL history. The Seals, fielding practically the same team as in 1923 except for the pitching staff, were prohibitive favorites to repeat, and indeed, they led the race most of the way.

Throughout the season, four teams remained in the fight: San Francisco, Oakland, Seattle and Los Angeles. On October 7, the Seals took a 4½-game lead over Seattle into the Pacific Northwest, where they opened a critical series against the Indians.

The Indians took six out of seven from the Seals in a series filled with come-from-behind performances and extra-inning games. At the end of the week, the Indians had taken a half-game lead over the Seals and Angels.

## 1924's FUTURE STARS

Three youngsters who went to Spring Training with the Seals in 1924 would each become distinguished in his own particular way. Jimmie Reese, a former Angels bat boy, was brought north as a Seals "recruit." A skinny 19-year-old, Reese came to camp with a reputation for being able to field almost any ball batted between second and third base. He also was known as a light hitter.

When the Seals broke camp, Jimmie was gone, but by the end of the 1924 season, he had caught on with Oakland. Reese would later be moved to second base where he combined with Lyn Lary to form one of the most highly publicized double-play combinations in Coast League history.

Another rookie was 18-year-old San Franciscan Gus Suhr, who was sent north with Nick Williams to play with Eureka in the Humboldt League, an industrial league. When Suhr finally broke in with the Seals in 1926, he started out as a shortstop, played some at third base, but found the most playing time at second base. Even through the 1928 season, Suhr was the regular second baseman, playing infrequently at first. In 1929, Suhr was moved to his more natural position at first base, the position he played for 10 years with the Pirates.

Suhr played a solid four years with the Seals before being sold to the Pittsburgh Pirates. He later came out of retirement during World War II to fill in for Ferris Fain during Fain's three-year stint in the service.

Another recruit on the 1924 spring roster was Eddie Montague, a graduate from San Francisco's Polytechnic High School. Although highly touted as a rookie prospect, Montague was released before Spring Training ended. Montague is the same man who later signed Willie Mays to a contract with the New York Giants.

Then in the last week of the season, the Indians defeated the hapless Portland Beavers six times in a seven-game series while the Seals took five of seven from the Oaks, giving the pennant to Seattle by 1½ games. The Angels, meanwhile, took five of seven from Vernon and finished in second place, ahead of San Francisco by .001. The Oaks dropped seven games off the pace to fourth place.

## ONE OF THE GREATEST TEAMS EVER

The 1925 Seals won their third championship in four years. With Ellison managing and playing first base, the Seals took the pennant by 12½ games over a powerful Salt Lake team that featured two San Franciscans: Lefty O'Doul and Tony Lazzeri.

The 1925 Seals were one of the greatest PCL clubs of all time. They won the pennant in a rout over Salt Lake City and had four 20-game winners on the pitching staff.

Lazzeri took advantage of Salt Lake City's rarified climate to hit 60 home runs, which remains a Coast League record. Practically every player in the league was pulling for Lazzeri to reach the magical goal of 60 in order to break Babe Ruth's 1921 record of 59 home runs. Veteran PCL outfielder Ray Rohwer told how the Solons were slow to react to a long hit by Lazzeri at Moreing Field during the last week of the season, allowing Lazzeri to round the bases before the ball was relayed to home plate.

The Bees led the league in batting at .321 led by O'Doul's .375, but San Francisco's Paul Waner won the PCL batting championship at .401. "Turkey" Brower provided 36 home runs and a .361 average, batting cleanup behind Waner.

The Seals had four 20-game winners. McWeeney was 20-5 and led the league with a 2.70 ERA. Mitchell had a 20-8 record, Williams 21-10 and Geary 20-12. Marty Griffin was 16-4, and veteran Jeff Pfeffer, back in the Pacific Coast League after 13 solid years in the major leagues, was a sturdy 15-15.

The Seals faced a dilemma of wealth in their outfield, a picture that became more complicated when they acquired young Smead Jolley from the Texas bush leagues. Jolley only got into 38 games, but he hit 12 home runs and batted in 43 while hitting .447 in his abbreviated stay. Lost in the multitude was 19-year-old Lloyd Waner, whose rookie season found him batting only 45 times, hitting a puny .244.

Inevitably, this team was broken up at the end of the season. Paul Waner and Rhyne were sold to the Pirates for $95,000 and players, while McWeeney was drafted by Brooklyn. Over the winter Ellison became ill with tuberculosis and resigned as manager.

## FROM FIRST TO WORST

The 1926 season proved how quickly things could turn around in professional sports when the Seals finished last. The pitching went sour and the infield was initially

Gus Suhr (left) and Vernon 'Lefty' Gomez were two local products who played for the Seals and then went on to have successful major league careers. Gomez is a member of the Hall of Fame.

weak. Still, the Seals, under the leadership of former superscout Nick Williams, put together a team that captured the imagination of San Francisco's dedicated fans. Attendance at Recreation Park was tops in the league.

By July, three rookies had filled in admirably. Twenty-year-old Gus Suhr got his first break at shortstop, but Williams quickly moved him to second where he became a fixture. Lori Baker would only hit .258 as the regular shortstop, but he was agile and had a strong arm. Nineteen-year-old Adolph Camilli, out of Sacred Heart High School, was smooth around first base. With Ellison still ill, he could play every day. When Ellison returned in mid-August, it was Ellison who got the greater share of playing time. Both finished over .300; Camilli at .311 and Ellison at .303.

## THE ALL-TIME OUTFIELD

Towards the latter stages of the 1926 season and during 1927 and 1928, the San Francisco Seals assembled the finest minor league outfield ever: Smead Jolley, Earl Averill and Roy Johnson.

Jolley was the first player acquired for this super outfield, purchased from Corsicana of the Texas Association in 1925. In 1926, he was the regular right fielder, batting .346 with 25 home runs and 132 RBIs in 174 games. Jolley would remain with the Seals through 1929 before being sold to the White Sox. In 1925, Ellison had started Jolley on the mound at Salt Lake. When Jolley won his own game with a home run in extra innings, Ellison knew he was too valuable to be wasted as a pitcher.

In his four full seasons with the Seals, Jolley had 1,070 hits and 642 RBIs in 733 games. He collected 309 hits and 188 RBIs in 1928 and had 314 hits the following season. He hit .346 in 1926, .397 in 1927, .404 in 1928 and .387 in 1929. He led the league in hitting in 1927 and 1928.

Jolley and Suhr took the brunt of much razzing from the spectators in the booze cage at Old Rec. Whether it was due to their size and rather awkward appearance or their apparent defensive limitations, they took an unmerciful hounding from the hometown fans.

Stories of Jolley's defensive inadequacies have become legendary and most of them are true. Just before he died in 1991, he admitted he wasn't the best fielder, but he also said his reputation was largely exaggerated. He was quite proud of his rifle arm and his high number of assists from the short right field at Old Rec. He was doubly proud of having regularly thrown runners out at first base on hard ground balls to right field—but he failed to mention that he was an occasional victim of the same play.

In his five years with the Seals, Jolley stole 22 bases. In his first year with the Seals, after a failed steal attempt, a fan commented, "Surely Jolley will be the most honest man in San Francisco."

Smead Jolley was one of the greatest hitters in all of baseball, but his defensive liabilities kept him from playing for long in the major leagues. This picture was taken around 1929.

Earl Averill was found playing industrial league baseball in Snohomish, Washington and came to Spring Training with the Seals in 1926. Averill became a replacement for the overmatched Lloyd Waner after the first six games of the season. For three years, Averill was a fixture in the Seals' outfield before being sold to Cleveland in 1929. A rather intense and competitive player, Averill was also a fluid athlete, making everything look routine.

Young Lloyd Waner wasn't able to crack the Seals' outfield of 1925 or 1926. He came to the Seals in 1925, and brother Paul insisting on a "no-option" clause in his contract. At the time Lloyd was small, possibly weighing 130 pounds, and he got into just 31 games while his brother was hitting .401 in 1925. But with Paul playing for the Pittsburgh Pirates in 1926, Lloyd was on his own. It quickly became evident that Lloyd would not start, so Graham and Lloyd wired Paul for his advice. Paul wired back, "Ask for your release." Reluctantly, Graham gave Lloyd the release, and Lloyd was picked up by Colombia of the South Atlantic League. He had a solid season there and went on to play in the same outfield with his brother at Pittsburgh for the next 14 years.

Roy Johnson joined Averill and Jolley in the Seals' outfield near the end of the 1926 season. Johnson was another of the Seals' Oklahoma finds. His presence made Frank Brower, who hit .361 in 1925 and .328 in 1926, expendable in 1927. Brower brought $7,500 when he was sold to Baltimore of the International League.

The 1927 Seals, with practically an entirely new infield, rebounded nicely to win 22 more games than in 1926, but they still finished 14½ games behind the runaway Oaks.

Dolph Camilli, heir-apparent to the first base job, lost his hitting eye and batted only .244. By mid-season he had been optioned to Logan, Utah, and after the season he was cut loose. History showed the Seals erred with Camilli, who went on to have a fine major league career topped by his winning the 1941 National League Most Valuable Player award for the Brooklyn Dodgers.

The biggest story of the 1927 Seals was Lefty O'Doul, whom the Red Sox had sent back to the minors after the 1923 season. At Salt Lake in 1924, O'Doul first made the transition from pitcher to outfielder. His arm, once strong and his finest asset, was nearly shot. As a pitcher for the Bees, he was 7-9. But as an outfielder, he batted .392, good enough to tie for the league batting title with his manager and fellow San Franciscan, Duffy Lewis, who had 100 more at-bats and 40 more hits than O'Doul.

O'Doul had played for Hollywood in 1926 after the Salt Lake franchise transferred there following the 1925 season. He came to San Francisco in 1927 for $7,500 after hitting .338.

Back home, Lefty captured the hearts of fans young and old alike. In the process, he also captured the PCL's Most Valuable Player award despite the fact that his teammate, Jolley, led the league in hitting at .397 and runs batted in with 163. O'Doul, meanwhile, led the league with 164 runs and 279 hits. O'Doul's popularity and better defensive skills were the difference in his winning the award over Jolley.

During the 1927 World Series, O'Doul was drafted back into the majors by the New York Giants. In the next seven years, O'Doul earned himself a reputation as being one of the finest hitters in the game. He twice won the National League batting championship, hitting .398 for the Phillies in 1929 and .368 for the Dodgers in 1932. He had 254 hits in 1929, a National League record tied by the New York Giants' Bill Terry the very next season. The record remains intact.

For Graham, O'Doul's departure was bittersweet—it was the second time O'Doul had been drafted away from him. Graham not only lost his top draw at the gate, but the $5,000 he received for O'Doul's contract was $2,500 less than he had paid for O'Doul's services just one winter earlier. This represented a striking example of the minor league owners' hatred of the major league draft.

## A FOURTH FLAG FOR SAN FRANCISCO

The climax to the 1928 season was extremely unusual. The league decided to experiment with a split-season format, with the first half ending July 1 and the second half ending October 4. The winner of the first half would play the winner of the second half if they were different teams. If the same team won, it was declared the champion.

The Seals won nine of their first 10 games and were never in danger during the first half. They went 58-34, five games ahead of the Hollywood Sheiks. The Missions were 49-43 in fourth place and the Oaks went 40-52 to finish the first half in sixth place.

The second half turned into a dogged race between the Sheiks, the Solons and the Seals. For the three months of the second half, no team was able to take more than a two- or three-game lead.

On September 16, the Solons and Sheiks were tied at 50-30 with the Seals two games behind. By September 22, the Solons had moved to a three-game lead over Hollywood and a four-game lead over San Francisco. The next six days saw the Seals pick up four games to tie the Solons while the Sheiks dropped to third.

As the Sheiks dropped off the pace, the Solons and Seals battled to the finish. Going into the last day of the season, the Solons were up by one game but couldn't hold the lead. The Seals and Solons finished the second half at 62-37, necessitating a three-game playoff.

The Solons won the first game 5-1 at Moreing Field before a record crowd exceeding 11,000. The teams traveled to Recreation Park in San Francisco to conclude the series. Before a record gathering of 17,000, the Seals' pitching deserted them and the Solons swept the pre-play-off 10-7 to win the second half of the regular season.

Now the teams had to play each other in a seven-game series for the league championship. After splitting the first four games before capacity crowds in both cities, the Seals won Game Five at Old Rec and the teams traveled to Sacramento for Game Six. Before another capacity crowd, the Seals won a slugfest 9-5 with Dick Moudy, previously sidelined with strained ribs, turning in a heroic relief performance.

The Seals players divided $9,000 as the winners' share, while the Solons shared a $6,000 runner-up prize.

Ed R. Hughes, beat writer for the *San Francisco Chronicle*, concluded his game report: "The Seals came here fully determined to win this game, for they brought

Top, the 1928 Seals, winners of the PCL title for the fourth time. Left, Bert Ellison, Gene Valla and Paul Waner examine a piece of wood. Above, a 1923 Zeenut card depicting Paul Waner.

Above, Seals infielders Gus Suhr, Babe Pinelli, Ike Caveney and Frankie Crosetti. Below, Manager Bert Ellison accepts a car at Recreation Park in recognition of the Seals' third pennant of the 1920s.

Above, Opening Day at Old Rec. Left to right: Gus Suhr, Pop Penebsky, Gene McIsaac, Babe Pinelli, Manager Nick Williams, Ike Caveney, Jerry Donovan. Left, Earl Averill.

along their shotguns to go duck hunting tomorrow. Had they lost today they would have had to go back to San Francisco to play tomorrow, and that would have spoiled the duck hunt."

Five Seals made the 11-man PCL All-Star team, including the entire outfield. Jolley was an automatic choice after winning the Triple Crown with a .404 average on 309 hits, 45 home runs and 188 runs batted in—arguably the finest season in league history. Johnson, meanwhile, hit .360 and Averill hit .354 with 173 RBIs, 36 homers and scoring a league-leading 178 runs.

Also representing the Seals on the all-league team were Dutch Ruether, the league's top pitcher at 29-7 with 28 complete games, and Hollis "Sloppy" Thurston as the utility player.

Another footnote to the 1928 Seals: Third base was shared between the veteran Ralph "Babe" Pinelli and 17-year-old Frank Crosetti.

With the successes of 1928, it was impossible to expect the nucleus of the team to return in 1929. The Cleveland Indians offered San Francisco $100,000 for their full outfield, a deal Graham turned down. The Indians reportedly offered to trade outfields intact with a few dollars included, but this too was rejected.

## BATBOY AT OLD REC

Dutch Anderson was a local schoolboy who happened to know the home batboy. One day, he was asked if he wanted to help out at Old Rec by tending the bats for the visiting team. Anderson accepted immediately.

Batboys were there to help the players and otherwise remain invisible. That didn't stop an impressionable kid from observing and remembering. Anderson smiled as he recalled the charming old park. "The wind blew in over the left field fence. Sluggers like (Dave) Barbee and (Wes) Schulmerich would come in and hit blue darts over the left field wall. Fuzzy Hufft (the Missions' left fielder) would go back to the wall and wait. Sure enough, here comes the ball back to him.

"Right field was short and there was a tall screen above the wall. Buzz Arlett wasn't doing anything right-handed in a game, so he turned around and hit left-handed. He hit one out of there. That was a poke; it had to be hit real high."

Hitting a foul ball always created a mad scramble among the children outside Recreation Park. "They had a bell up there (on the roof). One bell was for the Valencia side and two was for 15th Street. He could see where the ball was and direct the employee to it. If you got the ball and their guy didn't get it, they'd let you into the game for the ball."

As a batboy, Anderson didn't have a uniform, but he still had a chance to play catch with the players and help out in other ways. In earlier times at Recreation Park bats were laid out next to the dugouts, but by the late 1920s bat racks were in place, down close to home plate.

"Dutch" recalled a day Jack Fenton of the Oaks had a particularly disturbing at-bat. "I had already put the bat back up," Anderson recalled. "Fenton comes back, grabs the bat and he— Bang—tries to break it. So I say, 'Hey Jack, if you don't want that bat, I'll take it.' Then he looked at me and kind of smiled, and put the bat back and went back to the dugout. Those bats were good wood and hard to crack."

Elmer Jacobs pitched for the Seals from 1928-31.

Finally, Graham accepted $50,000 from Detroit for Johnson and $50,000 from Cleveland for Averill. Jolley was sold to the White Sox for $35,000, but actually was returned to San Francisco for the 1929 season before rejoining the Sox in 1930. Averill went on to post Hall of Fame credentials and Johnson became a major league 10-year man with a .296 career average.

Graham later regretted selling Jolley to the White Sox, feeling the expanse of Comiskey Park's right field was not in Jolley's best interests. A more cozy park might have allowed Jolley to become a star. As it was, Jolley accumulated a lifetime .305 major league average, but he stayed in the majors only four years.

Possibly the most distressing loss to the Seals was Hal Rhyne. Rhyne wasn't indispensable because he opened a spot for Crosetti, but the way he was lost was through the draft. The Seals purchased Rhyne's contract from the Pirates after the 1927 season for $7,500. At the end of the season, he was drafted by the Red Sox for $5,000. With the drafting of O'Doul the year before, the Seals were 0-for-2.

Also lost for 1929 was Dutch Ruether. Ruether, the league's top pitcher in 1928, wanted more money than the Seals were willing to pay. The Seals allowed him to shop his services around and the Mission Reds picked him up.

### MORE STARS

The highlight of 1929 was the play of Gus Suhr, now switched to his natural position of first base. Suhr batted .381 with 51 homers and 177 RBIs and scored 196 runs.

Frankie Crosetti, a local product who played shortstop for the Seals and later the New York Yankees.

These numbers catapulted him to the Pittsburgh Pirates, where he played 10 years without substitution, compiling a consecutive game streak of 822 games.

Nineteen-year-old Vernon "Lefty" Gomez, was 18-11. Gomez was so slight of frame and with such large feet that nobody expected him to be able to throw as hard as he did. But by the time each team had played the Seals, Lefty was the talk of the league. At the end of the season, Graham sold Gomez to the Yankees for $65,000.

In the end, the Seals had an excellent year, finishing with a 114-87 record. But in a split-season schedule, this was only good enough for second place in the first half and fifth place in the second. The crosstown-rival Mission Reds were nine games better than the Seals and 10 games better than Hollywood, but lost the championship playoff to the Sheiks, four games to three.

The decade was one of unparalleled success. The 1920s convinced people the Pacific Coast League was something special. ❖

# CHAPTER 9

# IT WAS A DIFFERENT GAME

The true beauty in baseball is that it tantalizes the imagination, creating questions that can never be answered, arguments that can never be resolved. Who was better, DiMaggio or Williams? Hubbell or Marichal? The 1927 Yankees or the 1973 Oakland A's?

Here's another question: What was a baseball game like back when there was no television, primitive radio and long-winded yet uninquisitive sportswriters? When salaries necessitated the players' obtaining winter jobs? When there was not yet a Bay Bridge or a Golden Gate Bridge? When every man in the crowd wore a white shirt, a tie and a hat?

Through the first half of the 20th century, Bay Area fans learned and experienced their baseball by following the Pacific Coast League, a cozy, comfortable circuit for players and spectators. That era ended in 1957 when the Seals fell victim to major league expansion into San Francisco. Since then, baseball has experienced tremendous changes in the places it is played, the money it costs to watch it and the media that report and transmit it. Baseball, like everything else, became "state of the art."

Baseball in the 1920s is a fuzzy, worn-out photograph that freezes undiscernable, faraway action, begging for details long since forgotten. Just what was it like to go to a game in the Bay Area in the 1920s? What is the story inside that vintage photograph?

All it takes to answer is a little imagination.

It's a sunny, electric spring afternoon at Old Rec or Oaks Ball Park. Hundreds of people arrive early for the 3 p.m. game, some having opted to leave work early or to shorten their lunch so they could get to the game on time. Public transportation is efficient and cheap, so many fans come on the local streetcar. Others walk. The game will be played in under two hours, so everybody will be home in time for dinner.

Schoolchildren scurry up the streets after successfully badgering their teachers to let them out early so they won't miss the first pitch.

Box seats cost $1, but it's better to save 15 cents by buying chair seats or grandstand seats, located immediately behind the box seats. The backless bleacher seats, down the right and left field lines, cost 30 cents.

Kids buy a 10-cent bleacher ticket unless it's "Kids Day," when they'll get in free. Some will try to sneak into the grandstand when the guard isn't watching.

Ladies are admitted for free on weekdays but must sit at least four rows deep in the grandstands unless they are accompanied by a gentleman. The male spectators wear coats and ties, and almost everybody wears a hat.

Rent a seat cushion and buy a scorecard for a nickel apiece. The cushion is practically a necessity in the bleachers, where splinters from the bench can easily damage a new pair of pants. And leave the cushion at the end of the game; kids will collect them and be paid off with a ticket to a future game. But occasionally an umpire's call will anger the crowd so much that they can't restrain themselves and the air will be filled with sailing cushions, causing the game to be delayed while the field is cleared.

The players arrive at the ballpark the same way as the fans. Because most of the players are locals, they are easily recognizable. Fans have their favorites and can recite their playing records and recount memorable plays.

The ballplayers are friendly, talking and joking with fans, signing autographs, searching out the attractive young women in the crowd. Very few of the players are college graduates; in fact, quite a few have dropped out of high school, usually at the age of 16, so they can play ball. And although their salaries are generally higher than the fans', they still must supplement their earnings with winter employment.

Their uniforms are heavy wool with sleeves extending below the elbow, although the players have cut the sleeves to facilitate the act of throwing and catching. The home uniforms are white, sometimes with blue pinstripes; the road uniforms are gray, sometimes with the same pinstripes. The under-sleeves are navy blue as are the socks, although some teams will have the bottom third of their socks in white. The caps are navy blue, usually without any logo or symbol. The pants are "knicker" style, falling just below the knee. Often, the players leave them untied at the knee for greater comfort.

There are no numbers on their backs, and there won't be until the early 1930s. Nevertheless, each player is designated by a number in the program and on the scoreboard above the outfield fence. This number indicates his position in the batting order.

Each player is issued one home and one road uniform for the season. If he is traded or released, his replacement gets that same uniform. In the early season the uniforms are fresh and clean, but by season's end, the home uniforms look nearly as gray and dingy as the road uniforms. The pants of active baserunners have undoubtedly been repaired several times; luckily, most of the players are wearing quilted sliding pads.

The player's glove is his pride and joy. There is not much to it: two pieces of leather with some padding around the thumb, little finger and palm. Some players feel the glove is already too restrictive, so they cut a hole through the pocket to feel the ball better when it is caught. Other players are so superstitious they use the same glove throughout their careers. When the padding wears out it will be re-padded, and when the leather wears out it will be replaced.

After each inning, the players in the field drop their gloves on the outfield grass when it is their team's turn to bat, although the pitcher places his glove and the catcher puts his mitt off to the side of the diamond. Yes, strange bounces do occur when batted balls hit gloves temporarily abandoned by their owners.

Sometimes a player leaves a little "present"—usually in the form of used chewing tobacco—in the finger holes of his counterpart's glove. Occasionally abandoned gloves have ended up in the stands, the result of a frustrated player taking out his revenge for a spectacular defensive play or an umpire's undeserved call.

Each player takes great care of his bat. It has been lathed out of aged hardwood, and he has bone-rubbed it to depress the soft spots in the wood. Its thick handle has undoubtedly been roughed up or taped to allow the player's calloused hands to get a better grip. Some players soak the bat in water or a mineral substance to make it heavier. The player plans to use the same bat all season and won't let anyone use it. After all, there are only so many hits in each bat. Before the game, the batboy will line up the bats on the dirt outside the dugout so each batter can easily find his own piece of wood.

At the plate, the batter probably spreads his hands an inch or two apart on the bat handle for better bat control.

## FUNDAMENTALS: ESSENTIAL ELEMENTS

If the count goes to two balls and one strike, or two balls and no strikes, the batter will probably take the next pitch. If the count is three balls and no strikes, he must take the next pitch, no exceptions. If he swings, his teammates will treat him with disdain and the opposing pitcher will likely give him a pitch in the ribs on his next at-bat.

If there's a runner on, he'll probably sacrifice, and there is no doubt as to his intentions: He faces the pitcher with both feet planted, the bat hanging menacingly over the plate as he waits for the pitch. His only concern is to avoid a high, hard pitch on the inside of the plate.

With a runner on third and less than two outs, the third baseman expects the bunt to come his way. The runner takes a lead off of third base and he can score easily if the third baseman throws the ball to first base.

The pitcher works quickly. His job is to deliver pitches that the batter can hit and let the fielders do their job. He knows he is expected to pitch a complete game, so wasting pitches is not something he wants to do. With this attitude in mind, there will be few walks and few strikeouts. He is very protective about "his" plate. He had better not see an opposing batter dig his cleats into the dirt to get better footing, or else he'll place his next pitch under the batter's chin.

Some pitchers are still allowed to throw a spitball. This pitch was declared illegal in 1920 because many felt it was too hard to control and thus dangerous to the batters. Players new to the league are not allowed to throw it, but if the pitcher had used the pitch as a major weapon before that time, he is allowed to continue.

The fact that the spitball is illegal to most pitchers doesn't mean they don't throw it. Concealing a foreign substance or having a teammate rough up the ball for him has become an art. Because only two or three balls will be used during a game, a crafty pitcher might gain a certain advantage with a doctored ball.

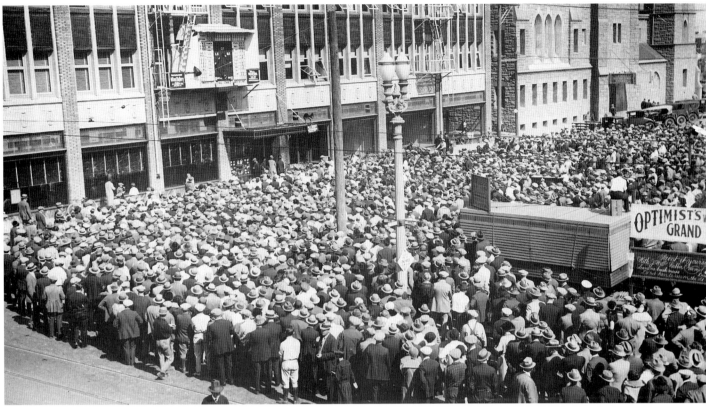

San Francisco baseball fans congregate on Market Street to keep up with the progress of the 1921 World Series. Wire reports would reach an operator, who then would move players on a diamond-shaped board.

Most players use chewing tobacco, an appropriate expectorant for the spitball pitcher. For other players, it serves as a lubricant for their gloves, all the while leaving stain marks on their uniforms. It is not unusual to see batters with stains on their shoes, socks or pant legs, the target of a squatting catcher or a first baseman holding the runner close to the bag.

The manager stands at the corner of the dugout. He doesn't expect the friendship of his players, just their respect. He is a good teacher and has seen every trick in the game, sometimes deploying them himself. He is a good motivator and tactician, and his players play well for him. Because he has no coach, he must handle all the pregame chores himself.

The team is fundamentally sound. The players have been schooled by experience to hit the cutoff man, throw to the right base, back up the proper base for the overthrow and carry out the defensive nuances flawlessly. They have been instructed to think ahead so their action will be quick and without hesitation. Their years of experience have ingrained most of these plays in their minds, but the presence of an angry manager when they come off the field will serve as a reinforcement.

The manager has low tolerance for a player who joins his team and has to learn the many fine points. The player was supposed to have learned them in the lower leagues.

When a rookie first joins the team, it will be a lonely time for him. Most veterans on the team aren't about to make him feel welcome or help him to become a better player because he is there to take away their job.

The veteran, shipped down from the major leagues, has experience and know-how. He has an automatic advantage over any rookie coming to Spring Training. The rookie's best hope is to have an impressive spring and make the club at the start of the season. If he can prove himself then, he will be accepted by the veterans.

In the stands, there is quite a bit of drinking going on even though Prohibition is in effect in the United States. And although baseball is still recovering from the cloud created by the 1919 Black Sox scandal and gambling is publicly forbidden, a large group of fans sits in the same area every game to bet. They will bet on the outcome of the game, the exploits of a certain batter, or whether the next pitch will be a strike or a ball. They make no effort to hide what they are doing, and likewise, no effort is made to stop them.

Plenty of refreshments are hawked at the park. A bag of peanuts costs a dime. So does a soft drink. Most candies are a nickel. The Rainier Company, formerly a popular brewery, sells ginger ale and a refreshing drink called Blue Moon. Also available are Hires Root Beer and Sun Crush Orange.

"Ric Rac Twins," candies that come in "the Ball Park size," cost a dime, but most other candies will be a nickel. Three kinds are most popular with the kids: "Zeenuts," a Cracker Jacks-like product; "Ruf Neks," chocolate marsh-mallow bars; and "Home Run Kisses," salt-water taffies. The real attraction is the Zeenut baseball card of a local hero inside. Each card has a coupon attached to the bottom of the photograph that can be collected and redeemed for prizes. A baseball, a whistle, a cap gun, knife, billfold, bat or glove are among the prizes available.

The kids gamble too, but usually after they go home. Each player tosses a Zeenut card, one at a time, against the closest wall, hoping it will land by touching the vertical plane of the wall, but not leaning on it. It is similar to penny-pitching, complete with shouting and arguing.

"Sharpies" try to get an edge by waxing a "shooter" card so it will carry more weight. Others roll their card into a cylinder so it can roll closer to the wall. World Championships are proclaimed each day by kids, who win large quanties of Zeenuts from the other kids.

The players have Monday off after the homestand concludes with Sunday's doubleheader. But they have to be at the railroad station by 8 p.m., to start the next road trip. Train life helps the players become a more cohesive group. Poker and bridge games start even before the train pulls out of the station. The Pullman car provides sleeping quarters for the team. Veterans get the lower berths.

Not all players accompany the team on the road trips. By the end of the first month, rosters have been trimmed to league specifications, which vary from 18-25 depending upon the season. It will not be a surprise if the last player or two on the roster does not make the trip. This is an economy measure.

The team arrives at the host city early in the morning. Players will either stop off at the hotel or go directly to the ballpark, depending on the time. They can unpack their suitcase and hang up their suits, for they will be in town for the full week.

Boredom often becomes a factor. There are only so many vaudeville shows or movies. The card games start up again, often extending late into the evening past the team curfew. Rainouts occur frequently during early or late-season games in the north. This means more leisure time around the hotel, more boredom.

It is not surprising, then, that drinking becomes a problem for some players. Although the consumption of alcoholic beverages is against national law, this doesn't seem to stop any group, let alone ballplayers. It will not be too surprising to find a selected player or players arriving at the ballpark the next day with a hangover. The manager may overlook the situation, but he always expects the player to perform to a high standard. The fact the manager might have been out drinking as well could help explain his rather passive attitude towards the drinkers. And in many cases, the manager is also active as

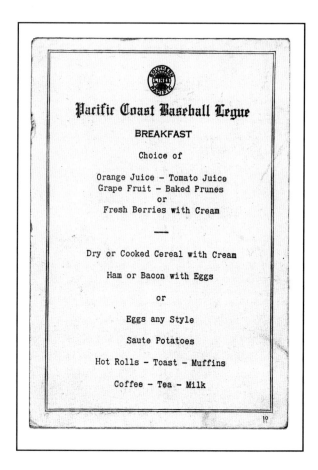

a player, an economy device owners use particularly during the Depression.

The season is long, and often more than 200 games are played. An early April start stretches to a conclusion in late October, a few weeks after the World Series has been decided. Players, particularly veterans, play hard and always play when they're hurt, because there is always a youngster right behind him ready to take his job. The career of an older player may be over if he has lost his starting job because of an injury.

The team breaks up for the winter as soon as the season ends. Many players live in the Bay Area or Northern California. Most will take a few days off, then go right to work. Winter leagues are already in progress, but the team sponsor has held a position on the roster for the returning professional. His presence will make the team more competitive and draw more attention.

Winter league play allows the player to pick up a few bucks and keep his batting eye sharp. His heart isn't necessarily in the game, but his employer sponsors the team and expects a solid effort on the field. Fortunately, it will rain during some weekends, allowing time for fishing on the bay or duck hunting in the delta.

As spring approaches, fans and players start getting itchy. It's been a long winter. Players sign contracts and the first day of Spring Training finally arrives.

Some things don't change after all. ❖

CHAPTER **10**

# MORE EXCITEMENT IN THE '20s

Whille the Seals were wildly successful in the 1920s, the Oakland Oaks and the new Mission Bells also played entertaining baseball. The Oaks had a more restricting budget, but that didn't keep them from being aggressive in signing players off the East Bay playgrounds. Management was also willing to search outside of the immediate area to acquire players.

However, the Oaks languished in the second division for much of the decade. It wasn't that the Oaks weren't competitive. They were. It wasn't that the Oaks didn't have excellent players. They did. Their lack of successes was simply a classic case of not putting everything together at once. Excellent pitching would be wasted by poor hitting or average fielding. Players would have a great season followed by a sub-par year.

The Oaks had two winning seasons between 1920-1925. In 1921 under co-owner Del Howard, the Oaks were 101-85 for a fifth-place finish. After the 1922 season, Howard handed the managerial reins to his brother, Ivan, who in 1924 led the Oaks to a fourth-place finish at 103-99.

The Oaks finally became a home team in 1922. For the previous two decades, they played most of their "home" games in San Francisco. Generally, they played only two games each week at the Emeryville park, on Thursday and the morning game of the Sunday double-header. The other five games were played at Old Rec.

Cal Ewing and Del Howard had previously felt the Oakland community wouldn't provide consistent support for seven games a week. Only in 1922 did the Oaks feel they could equal their attendance in San Francisco.

Ewing proceeded to put money into cleaning up the Oaks park and constructing additional box seats between the dugouts. A concerted effort was made to gain support from the Oakland business community, resulting in a strong fan base. Attendance figures didn't exactly equal attendance in San Francisco, but it was strong enough to support the team.

### BUZZ ARLETT—OAKLAND'S FINEST

A small nucleus of players spent many years with the Oaks and were immensely popular with the fans. The most popular was Buzz Arlett, who joined the Oaks in 1918 and played with the team for 13 seasons.

Russell Lewis Arlett, born in 1899, learned the game

Four members of the 1921 Oaks ham it up during Spring Training. Left to right: Harry Krause, George Boehler, Buzz Arlett and Hack Miller. Arlett, one of the most prolific hitters in baseball history, and Miller were power hitters for the Oaks.

on the playgrounds of Oakland and signed his first contract with the Oaks. He could pitch, and at the plate he was a switch-hitter.

From 1919 through 1922, Arlett was a mainstay of the Oaks' pitching staff, pitching more than 300 innings each year. In 1920, he pitched 427 innings, winning 29 and losing 17. As a pitcher, Buzz batted in the mid-.200s. But when he wasn't pitching, he played the outfield and put on tremendous displays of hitting.

Even though Arlett won 96 games for the Oaks during those four years, he was shifted to right field when Ivan Howard became manager. He pitched sparingly over the next six years and accumulated a 9-13 record. But during the next eight years, he was a terror at the plate; Arlett's poorest average was a .328 in 1924. He still drove in 145 runs and scored 122 that year.

Arlett's most productive year was 1929 when he played in all but two of the Oaks' 202 games. He batted .374 with 189 RBIs, 70 doubles and 39 home runs. He also scored 146 runs and pitched in 17 games that year.

But Arlett was a defensive liability as an outfielder, which helped keep him out of the major leagues for all but the 1931 season. That year, with the Philadelphia Phillies, he batted .313. Also in that year, Phillies pitcher "Jumbo" Jim Elliott purportedly asked Manager Burt Shotton to deliver a rocking chair to Arlett in right field, reasoning that the chair wouldn't affect Arlett's range, so he might as well be comfortable.

Another immensely popular Oaks player was graceful first baseman Louie Guisto. Guisto, a graduate of St. Mary's College, was formerly property of the Cleveland Indians, for whom he played in 1917 and 1918 before

being sent to Oakland for the 1919 season. He stayed three seasons with the Oaks before the Indians recalled him for 1922. Guisto remained in Cleveland 1½ more years before the Indians gave up.

Guisto wanted to play only in Cleveland, informing his owners he wouldn't report if he were to be traded or waived and picked up by another organization. He preferred to return to Oakland. Finally in 1923, the Indians obtained permission from the commissioner's office, allowing Guisto to avoid waivers and return to Oakland.

Guisto hit more for average than for power, but with a batting order including Arlett, Hack Miller and Ted Cather, Oakland had no problem scoring runs.

Left, Buzz Arlett strikes a handsome pose. Bottom left, Oaks first baseman Louie Guisto, who preferred playing PCL ball on the West Coast to the major leagues. The St. Mary's College baseball field in Moraga is named after him. Below, Hack Miller takes a swing.

Harry Krause was a left-handed pitcher for the Oakland Oaks who helped stabilize the team's pitching staff for about 10 years. Armed with a legal spitball, he was a workhorse who usually pitched more than 300 innings a year. He was traded across the bay to the Missions in 1928.

Harry Krause, a San Franciscan with a wicked spitball, was the anchor of the Oaks' pitching staff for more than a decade. He broke into professional baseball in 1907 with San Jose of the California State League, played five years in the American League—mostly with Philadelphia—and arrived in Oakland at age 30 in 1917. Krause could always be counted on to pitch at least 300 innings with 30 or more decisions every year before the Oaks traded him to the Missions in 1928.

Oakland-born Ray Kremer pitched for the Oaks from 1919 through 1923 before going to the Pittsburgh Pirates. He was a starting pitcher with the Bucs for nine years before returning to Oakland for the 1933 and 1934 seasons. Kremer's best season for the Oaks was 1923 when he was 25-16 in 357 innings.

Lawrence "Hack" Miller was the Oaks' left fielder from the late 1910s into the early 1920s. After a four-season stay with the Cubs, Miller returned to Oakland and was the Oaks' power hitter before Arlett was switched to the outfield. In 1925 and 1926, the two were in the same outfield, providing the lineup with a solid one-two punch.

When the Coast League season was cut short in 1918 by World War I, Miller jumped to the Boston Red Sox for the remainder of the year. He returned to Oakland in 1919 as part of the National Commission's contract stipulations. Miller played in just 12 games for the Red Sox in 1918, but managed to get into one World Series game that year.

Ray Brubaker was another popular Acorn. He joined the Oaks in 1920 and continued to be an active player through the 1934 season. Brubaker's strength was his versatility. He could play any infield position well and he often filled in as an outfielder. He was a natural No. 2 hitter, a good bunter who usually made contact. Brubaker was the regular shortstop during the first half of the 1920s and later shifted to second base. But the fine double-play combination of Reese and Lary relegated Brubaker to the role of utility player by the middle of his career.

Brubaker was a smart player who regularly batted between .270 and .280. His intelligence and versatility allowed him to stay around for 15 years, which earned him a shot at managing the team toward the end of his playing career.

Jimmie Reese and Lyn Lary formed one of the most effective double-play combinations in the PCL during the 1920s. They were sold as a package to the New York Yankees in 1928.

## THE MISSIONS COME TO TOWN

The transfer of the Vernon franchise to San Francisco after the 1925 season meant there was always one team playing in the city, making the rivalry for fan attention intense. The Missions associated themselves with the citizens of the Mission District, generally acknowledged as being of lesser economic means and social graces.

The Missions were never fully accepted by the people of San Francisco, who generally looked down on the Missions and their fans. This was regularly demonstrated in attendance figures. Throughout their 12-year stay in San Francisco, the Missions were generally outdrawn by the Seals by more than 100,000 patrons per season. Both called Recreation Park and later Seals Stadium their home, and crowds were always large when the two teams met during the regular season.

All three Bay Area teams were hit hard at the turnstiles during the early years of the Depression. Missions attendance fell below 100,000 four consecutive years (1932-1935). The Seals, meanwhile, dropped below 100,000 in attendance just once, in 1934 when they drew 99,493. This was still 11,000 better than the Missions.

Oakland attendance was directly proportional to its successes on the field. And it was the Oaks who drew the poorest during the Depression. In 1934, a particularly bad year for the league, the Oaks drew slightly less than 56,000. Attendance problems helped explain Oakland's lack of competitiveness on the field. The money simply wasn't there to acquire and pay the better players.

In their inaugural season in San Francisco, 1926, the Missions climbed into third place while the Seals crashed into the cellar. The Seals had won the championship in 1925 while the Vernon team occupied the cellar. Still, the Seals won the war of the turnstiles.

Many regulars came north with the Vernon franchise, but several new players made spectacular contributions to the new Missions.

## IKE BOONE CRASHES THE FENCES

Foremost among the new stars was Isaac M. "Ike" Boone, a husky left-handed outfielder. Recreation Park, with its short right field fence, was aptly suited to Boone's power. In 1926, he clubbed 32 home runs and hit a crisp .380. Boone had been acquired from the Boston Red Sox, and his successes at Recreation Park earned him another trial in the majors via the draft, this time with the Chicago White Sox.

After one year in Chicago he was returned to the West Coast and ended up with the Missions. Boone put together one of the most spectacular seasons in minor league history in 1929, winning the Triple Crown and leading the league in most offensive categories. He batted .407 with 55 home runs, knocked in 218 runs and scored 195. His 323 hits was another league high, and 553 total bases a record for all of organized baseball. All of this was accomplished in 198 of the Missions' 201 games.

However, like Buzz Arlett in Oakland, Boone lacked defensive skills. Center fielder Evar Swanson was forced to shade slightly towards right field for all batters, taking anything within his reach.

Boone hit .448 in the Missions' first 83 games of the 1930 season, compelling Brooklyn to give him another try. He spent parts of the next three years in Brooklyn and several more in the International League, but his brief stay in the Coast League earned him legendary status.

Swanson also had star qualities. He came north with the reputation of being the fastest man in the league, having led Vernon in stolen bases. In San Francisco, he led the Coast League in thefts with 43 in 1926 and 49 in 1928. During the Missions' inaugural season, Swanson batted .320 as the leadoff batter and scored a league-leading 156 runs. Two years later, Red Killefer sold him to Cincinnati in a deal that brought Walter "Seacap" Christensen to the Missions to play center field.

Evar Swanson was a speed-demon for the Mission Reds.

(continued on page 105)

Above, assorted premium baseball cards from Creole Cigarettes. Right, an 1890s souvenir badge for fans of the San Francisco Base Ball Club.

The 1902 Oakland Oaks, champions of the California League.

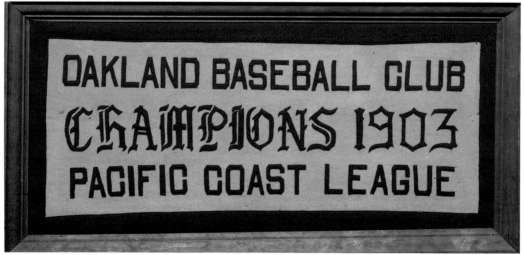

Although the 1902 Oaks won the pennant in another league, they played the 1903 season as the champions of the new Pacific Coast League.

Three cigarette premium baseball cards, redeemable through the mail. Top left, the San Francisco Seals' Buck Weaver, who would later be banished from baseball in the Black Sox Scandal. Top right, Cack Henley, who pitched a 24-inning shutout against the Oaks. Bottom, Harry Wolverton, player-manager of the Oaks and later manager of the Seals.

This collection of cigarette baseball cards features Oaks and Seals players.

A pennant commemorating Seals Opening Day in 1915.

Ewing Field Opening Day pennant, 1914.

A 1912 advertisement for I.W. Harper whiskey. On the back is a PCL game schedule.

Several companies, primarily cigarette manufacturers, attempted to increase sales by including cards featuring images of local baseball players.

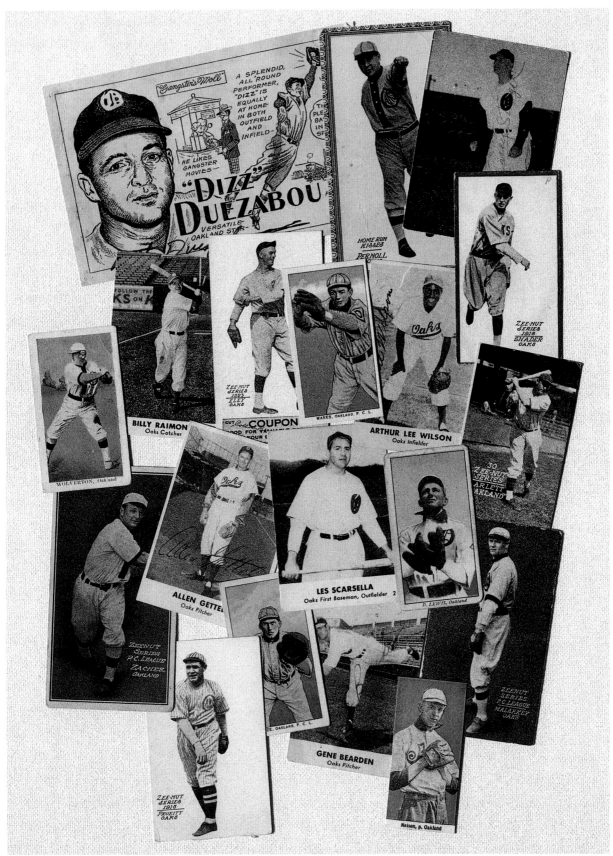

Children would gamble with their baseball cards, playing games similar to penny-pitching in an effort to win their friends' collections.

Below, a Mission Reds uniform, circa 1930. Right, bats used by three of the finest hitters in PCL history (l-r): Smead Jolley, Lefty O'Doul and Buzz Arlett.

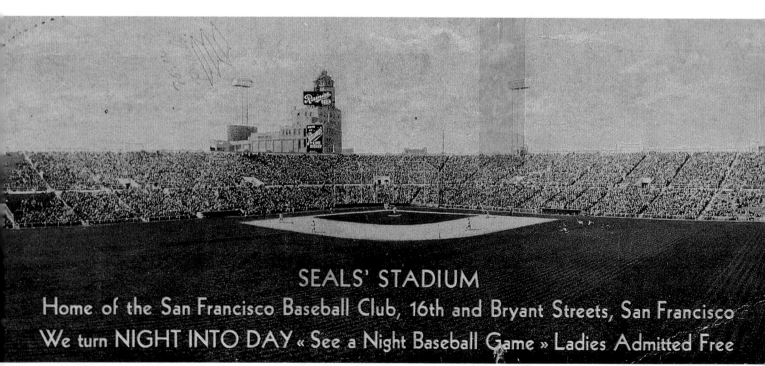

SEALS' STADIUM
Home of the San Francisco Baseball Club, 16th and Bryant Streets, San Francisco
We turn NIGHT INTO DAY « See a Night Baseball Game » Ladies Admitted Free

Before the advent of ball-point pens, blotters such as this 1930s version were used to absorb excess ink.

## Uniform Agreement for the Assignment of a Player's Contract to or by a Major League Club

### IMPORTANT NOTICE

Six (6) counterpart originals of this Agreement to be executed. One copy is to be retained by the Minor League Club, and five copies are to be mailed to the Secretary-Treasurer, Office of the Baseball Commissioner, 122 S. Michigan Avenue, Chicago, Ill. He will send a copy to the President of the American League, Fisher Building, Chicago, Ill.; the President of the National League, 8 West 40th Street, New York, N. Y.; and the Secretary of the National Association, Auburn, N. Y. The copies sent to the Secretary-Treasurer must be accompanied by a check for the consideration, which check, in the case of a payment due a Minor League Club, shall be to the order of the "Secretary of the National Association." If the payment is due a Major League Club, the check sent the Secretary-Treasurer shall be to the order of the Major League Club. If agreements are not filed with the Secretary-Treasurer within 30 days after the transfer is effected, he shall collect a penalty of $25 from the club responsible, or from each of the parties, if both Clubs are responsible for such non-filing.

**This Agreement**, made and entered into this **3rd** day of ... **August** .... 192**5**.

by and between ... **SALT LAKE BASEBALL CLUB** ..................................
(Party of the First Part)

and ............ **AMERICAN LEAGUE BASE BALL CLUB OF NEW YORK** .............
(Party of the Second Part)

**Witnesseth:** The party of the first part hereby assigns to the party of the second part the contract of Player ... **ANTONE LAZZERI** ..........................
according to the Rules adopted under the Major League Agreement and the Major-Minor League Agreement and upon the following conditions (including any provisions set forth upon the back of this agreement):

1. That said New York Club shall pay said Salt Lake Club the sum of Fifty Thousand ($50,000.) Dollars, payment of said sum to be made as follows:

   $10,000. on execution and delivery of this agreement.
   10,000. November 1st, 1925.
   10,000. February 1st, 1926.
   10,000. May 1st, 1926.
   10,000. August 1st, 1926.

2. That said New York Club shall transfer, outright, to said Salt Lake Club, players Alex Ferguson, Mack D. Hillis and Martin Autry, on or before April 1st, 1926; provided, however, that if any of the five players cannot be delivered on or before the dates specified, said New York Club shall then pay said Salt Lake Club the sum of Five Thousand ($5,000.) for each player not delivered.

3. That all players transferred as provided in Clause No.2 hereof, shall be subject to selection in all respects as provided in the Major-Minor League Agreement and Rules, notwithstanding any club that may acquire title to their services shall otherwise be exempt from selection.

*5 PLAYERS ACCEPTABLE TO SAID SALT LAKE CLUB.*

BASEBALL COMMISSIONER — AUG 21 1925

BASEBALL COMMISSIONER — AUG 10 1925

**In Testimony Whereof**, we have subscribed hereto, through our respective Presidents or authorized agents, on the date above written:

Witness: *Cal Baum*

**SALT LAKE BASEBALL CLUB**
Club
By _____ President
(Party of the First Part)

**AMERICAN LEAGUE BASE BALL CLUB OF NEW YORK**
Club
By *Jacob Ruppert* President
(Party of the Second Part)

Corporate name of Company, Club, or Association of each party should be written in first paragraph and subscribed herein.

Tony Lazzeri, who hit 60 home runs for Salt Lake City, was sold to the New York Yankees in 1925 for $50,000, payable in five installments.

(continued from page 96)

The pitching star of 1926 was Bert Cole. As a youngster with the Seals in 1920, Cole impressed Ty Cobb, who encouraged the Tigers to purchase his contract. Cole pitched five unspectacular seasons in the American League before he was acquired by the Missions, for whom he was extremely successful.

Cole acknowledged that he was not ready for the major leagues in 1921. With the Missions, he was 29-12 with a 2.63 ERA in 325 innings. He was back in the major leagues in 1927.

Another pitcher who gave stability to the Missions was Herman "Old Folks" Pillette. Pillette pitched in the Pacific Coast League for six teams over 23 years and won 226 games.

## OAKLAND'S TIME

Fifteen years had passed since the last pennant flew over Oaks Ball Park. The Oaks finished strong in 1926, taking second place. The nucleus of that team was back and several newcomers strengthened the team. Pitchers Bob Hasty, George Boehler and Wilbur Cooper were key acquisitions. Boehler and Cooper, both 35, had extensive major league experience, as did Hasty, 31. Boehler, known throughout his career as a workhorse, led the league with 22 wins, losing 12 and striking out a league-leading 160 batters in 296 innings.

Meanwhile, lefty Harry Krause was in his 21st season of professional ball, and although he needed more rest

Four Oaks in 1927: Catcher Al Bool, first baseman Louie Guisto, outfielder Ralph Shinners and outfielder Buzz Arlett.

between starts, he went 15-6 on the season. Krause also set a positive example for the younger players by working hard to stay in top condition.

The Oaks used only 10 pitchers throughout the season, but they accounted for 120 victories. Everyone contributed to the effort.

The Oaks were also blessed with a suffocating defense, especially up the middle with second baseman Jimmie Reese and shortstop Lyn Lary. Reese hooked on with the Oaks in the later stages of the 1924 season. Lary joined the Oaks in 1925. He was scheduled to enroll at Cal but changed his mind and signed with the Oaks. It was a smart choice because midway through the season, Lary emerged as the regular shortstop.

Reese and Lary worked together in 1925 and 1926 and became known as the top second base-shortstop combination in 1927 in a league blessed with excellent middle infielders. They led the league in fielding percentage, as did first baseman Jack Fenton.

Pete Read caught 110 games and led the league in putouts. Al Bool and Del Baker were the backup catchers. All three were veterans of previous Coast League seasons and knew the enemy batters well. The Oaks were so deep in catchers that Ernie Lombardi, a 19-year-old Oakland boy, couldn't make the team and was sent to Ogden in the Utah-Idaho Class C League.

While Ike Caveney was not a statistical leader at third base, his many years of experience helped stabilize the three youngsters who manned the rest of the infield. Lary and Reese each played in 191 of their team's 195 games.

The outfield was comprised of center fielders Ralph Shinners and Tony Governor, Buzz Arlett in right and Joe Bratcher in left.

The Oaks did not overpower their opponents, although a collective .291 team batting average was much more than adequate. Howard's main concern as manager was protecting his only legitimate power source, Arlett, from being walked intentionally all season. His batting order usually consisted of Governor or Shinners leading off, followed by Reese, Lary and Arlett. Fenton and Caveney batted fifth and sixth, which gave opposing pitchers little choice but to pitch to Arlett. With this batting order, Arlett batted in 123 runs and Fenton 110. Lary scored 124 times, Reese 112.

Offensively, the year was Arlett's. Even though he endured a bout of pleurisy at mid-season, Arlett led the Oaks in batting (.351), hits (231), doubles (a league-leading 54), home runs (30), RBIs (123) and even stolen bases (20).

The Oaks broke open a tight race in August when they won a franchise-record 14 straight games and took a 7½-game lead over the field. During an 18-game period, Howard got 17 complete games from his staff. The win-

Ernie Lombardi, later a member of Casey Stengel's 1948 'Nine Old Men,' played briefly for the 1927 Oaks.

ning streak effectively removed all challengers and the Oaks coasted to the pennant by 14½ games.

The pennant returned to San Francisco in 1928 as the Oaks dropped to fifth place with a 91-100 record. The stars were Arlett, who hit .365 with 113 RBIs while scoring 111 runs, and Lombardi, who hit .377 in 120 games.

Reese and Lary continued to play well in the field amid rumors of pending sales to the Pirates or the White Sox. Instead, the Howards sold their "Gold Dust Twins" to the Yankees for a reported $125,000. Lary, 23, hit .309 in 80 games in 1929 but Reese returned to Oakland for another year of seasoning.

Top, the 1927 Oakland Oaks await the start of the annual parade that signaled Opening Day. During that season, the Oaks enjoyed a franchise-record 14-game winning streak and went on to win their first PCL pennant in 15 years, which they celebrated the next season (below).

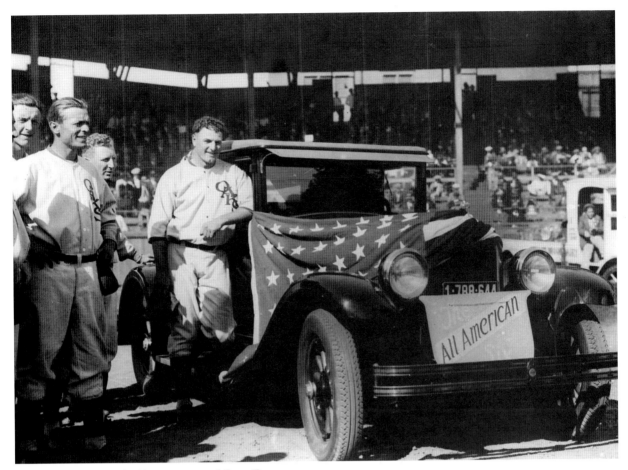

Buzz Arlett is presented with a new automobile on 'Buzz Arlett Day' in 1927. Although he had given up pitching, Arlett went to the mound that day and treated his fans to a complete-game victory, the only game he pitched all season.

In 1930, Reese and Lary were reunited with the Yankees. Lary was the regular shortstop and Reese was a utility infielder. Both players returned to the Yankees in 1931 but Reese only saw limited playing time. He was waived and picked up by the St. Louis Cardinals for 1932, his last season in the major leagues. With the acquisition of Frankie Crosetti from the San Francisco Seals after the 1931 season, Lary's value to the Yankees diminished. Early in the 1934 season, Lary was traded to the Red Sox for Freddie Muller, who had grown up in the East Bay community of Newark.

In later years, the Yankees regarded their acquisition of Lary and Reese as one of the worst in the history of their franchise. It forced the Yankees to re-evaluate the manner used to acquire new players.

Colonel Ruppert hired George Weiss to emulate the lead of Branch Rickey of the St. Louis Cardinals by building a farm system for the Yankees. In this fashion, the Yankees would not have to depend on the acquisition of players from the independent minor leagues. The Bay

### RUSSELL LOUIS "BUZZ" ARLETT AS AN OAK

| YEAR | POSITION | G | AB | R | H | 2B | 3B | HR | RBI | PCT. |
|---|---|---|---|---|---|---|---|---|---|---|
| 1918 | 1B, P | 26 | 71 | 9 | 15 | 4 | 0 | 1 | 8 | .111 |
| 1919 | P | 58 | 144 | 15 | 42 | 8 | 2 | 1 | 19 | .292 |
| 1920 | 1B, P | 64 | 178 | 26 | 45 | 5 | 4 | 5 | 26 | .253 |
| 1921 | P | 64 | 128 | 12 | 28 | 5 | 1 | 3 | 14 | .219 |
| 1922 | OF, P | 74 | 174 | 23 | 42 | 9 | 4 | 4 | 21 | .241 |
| 1923 | OF, P | 149 | 445 | 76 | 147 | 31 | 5 | 19 | 101 | .330 |
| 1924 | OF, P | 193 | 698 | 122 | 229 | 57 | 19* | 33 | 145 | .328 |
| 1925 | OF | 190 | 710 | 121 | 244 | 49 | 13 | 25 | 46 | .344 |
| 1926 | OF,1B,P | 194 | 667 | 140 | 255 | 52 | 16 | 35 | 140* | .382 |
| 1927 | OF, P | 187 | 658 | 122 | 231 | 54* | 7 | 30 | 123 | .351 |
| 1928 | OF, P | 160 | 561 | 111 | 205 | 47 | 3 | 25 | 113 | .365 |
| 1929 | OF,1B,P | 200 | 722 | 146 | 270 | 70* | 8 | 39 | 189 | .374 |
| 1930 | OF, P | 1176 | 618 | 132 | 223 | 57 | 7 | 31 | 143 | .361 |
| OAKS TOTALS | | 1735 | 5774 | 1055 | 1976 | 446 | 89 | 251 | 1188 | .342 |
| MINOR TOTALS | | 2390 | 8001 | 1610 | 2726 | 598 | 107 | 432 | 1786 | .341 |
| MAJOR TOTALS | | 121 | 418 | 65 | 131 | 26 | 7 | 18 | 72 | .313 |

### PITCHING RECORD

| YEAR | GAMES | IP | W | L | H | R | ER | BB | SO | ERA |
|---|---|---|---|---|---|---|---|---|---|---|
| 1918 | 21 | 153 | 4 | 9 | 150 | 60 | 46 | 43 | 34 | 2.70 |
| 1919 | 57* | 348 | 22 | 17 | 315 | 172* | 116 | 112 | 79 | 3.00 |
| 1920 | 53 | 427* | 29* | 17 | 430 | 162 | 137 | 134 | 105 | 2.89 |
| 1921 | 55 | 319 | 19 | 18 | 371 | 180 | 155 | 115 | 101 | 4.37 |
| 1922 | 47 | 374* | 25 | 19 | 396 | 171 | 115 | 112 | 128 | 2.77 |
| 1923 | 28 | 149 | 4 | 9 | 182 | 106 | 84 | 47 | 34 | 5.76 |
| 1924 | 2 | 4 | 0 | 0 | | | | | | — |
| 1926 | 5 | 14 | 2 | 0 | | | | | | — |
| 1927 | 1 | 9 | 1 | 0 | | (Pitched on Buzz Arlett Day) | | | | — |
| 1928 | 7 | 27 | 1 | 0 | | | | | | — |
| 1929 | 17 | 61 | 1 | 4 | 83 | 46 | 40 | 17 | 17 | 5.76 |
| 1930 | 3 | 3 | 0 | 0 | | | | | | — |
| OAKLAND | 296 | 1864 | 108 | 93 | 1927 | 897 | 693 | 580 | 498 | 3.45 |

Below, 'Wild Bill' Leard, manager of the 1926-27 Mission Reds.
Right, Ping Bodie. Bottom, Mission pitchers Jack Knott,
Wilbur Hubbell, Clyde Nance and Ernie Nevers.

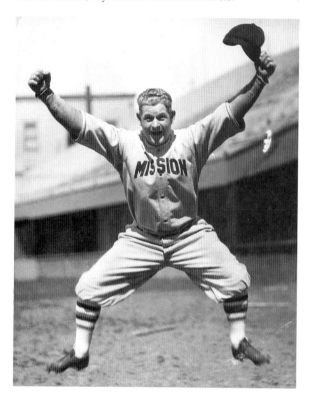

Area would continue to be one of the Yankees' richest gold mines in the years to follow, but only under their direct control.

## THE MISSION REDS GAIN RESPECTABILITY

The 1928 season marked some excitement for the Missions. Ernie Nevers, All-American football hero from Stanford University, joined the team early in the season. He had experienced minimal success during the previous two seasons with the St. Louis Browns and his acquisition by the Missions was looked upon as a box-office coup.

The season also brought stability to the Missions. Wade "Red" Killefer, popular manager of the Seattle Indians the previous five seasons, bought into the Missions and became their manager. In his first season, he directed the club to a 99-92 record. After the 1928 season,

Top left, Johnny Vergez broke in with the Oaks in 1928 and returned to manage the team in 1939. Below, the 1929 Oaks. Note a young Ernie Lombardi on the far left of the top row.

Left, Missions outfielder Fuzzy Hufft was one of the league's most feared sluggers. Above, the 1929 Missions took first place in the Pacific Coast League but lost a playoff series against Hollywood. This picture was taken in front of the Recreation Park clubhouse.

Killefer was elected president of the club by the other owners. This dual role placed him in the enviable position of both acquiring and managing the players on the team.

Killefer's presence was also responsible for the team's new nickname, "Reds." The "Bells" had never really caught on. Still, most fans were happy to know the team as the "Missions."

Nevers was the top pitcher in 1928 with a 14-11 record. Swanson had a fine year, leading the Reds with a .346 batting average, 256 hits, 53 doubles, 151 runs scored and a league-leading 51 stolen bases.

The Reds were heavily favored to win the 1929 pennant after Killefer made several big off-season moves. In March, Killefer sold his fine center fielder, Swanson, to the Cincinnati Reds for $15,000 and outfielder "Seacap" Christensen. Swanson had just completed a career year but Killefer felt Christensen was a superior outfielder. Plus, he gained an extra $15,000 out of the deal. Killefer then purchased pitcher Bert Cole from Portland for $10,000 and used the other $5,000 to acquire outfielder Pete Scott from Pittsburgh. He later purchased crafty third baseman Eddie Mulligan from the Pirates.

Killefer also pulled a coup by getting from the Seals Dutch Ruether, the PCL's Most Valuable Pitcher in 1928. Ruether went 29-7 to price himself out of the Seals market. Charlie Graham allowed Ruether to shop himself around with the caveat that the Seals were to receive $7,500 before releasing him. Killefer jumped at the opportunity, which angered the Seals tremendously because they had an agreement with the Reds not to tamper with their players.

Why did the Seals let Ruether go? For one thing, the Seals didn't want to pay a large contract, especially to a 36-year-old pitcher whom Manager Nick Williams felt was losing his touch. Besides, the Seals had five promising young pitchers: Curtis Davis, Val Glynn, Elmer Knight, Hal Turpin and Lefty Gomez.

Williams went so far as to predict that his ace, Elmer Jacobs, would win more games during the season than Ruether. His prediction was correct: Jacobs won 21 and Ruether won 14. Still, Ruether was a significant addition to the Reds' pitching staff, which also featured crafty veterans such as former major leaguer Wilbur Hubbell and ex-Seals pitcher Herb McQuaid plus youngsters Clyde Nance and Mert Nelson.

Tragedy interfered early with an otherwise successful season when Nance was killed in an automobile accident outside of Merced after a Sunday game.

Offensively, the Reds boasted a powerful lineup. Batting in the heart of the order, Ike Boone (.407), Fuzzy Hufft (.379) and first baseman Jack Sherlock (.336) combined to knock in 541 runs.

Around the infield the team of Sherlock, Finn, Slade and Mulligan were all iron men. Slade and Finn developed into a double-play combination as good as the Oaks'

Reese and Lary. In fact, like Reese and Lary, the two Mission Reds stars were sold as a package to Brooklyn after their marvelous 1929 season. Sherlock was drafted by the Phillies, so three of the four infield regulars were promoted to the majors for 1930.

The 1929 season was played with the split-season format. The Reds won the first half easily but fell into a dogged battle with Hollywood for the second-half championship. On October 1, with only one week remaining in the season, the Sheiks held a two-game lead over the Reds.

The Sheiks hosted a difficult Portland team while the Reds entertained Seattle. Seattle was the doormat of the league at 25-71, and it was conceivable the Reds could pick up two games in the standings.

On Saturday and Sunday, the Reds and Indians played doubleheaders. In Saturday's first game, Pillette pitched a no-hitter. The Reds took the second game as well, pulling to within one game of the Sheiks.

On Sunday, the Sheiks did their part by blowing a doubleheader. Junk Walters, the former Seals pitcher who was released because he was too heavy, pitched both ends of the doubleheader for Portland, batted sixth in the line-up, and got three hits on the day.

But the Reds also lost two, ultimately winning four games in the seven-game series. But against such a lowly team, winning five or six games was a must.

The end result was a seven-game playoff between the Reds and the Sheiks. In a series highlighting the pitching and batting prowess of Hollywood's Frank Shellenback, the Sheiks won, four games to three. This was as close as the Reds ever got to winning it all. ❖

# CHAPTER 11

# THE DEPRESSION
# HITS SEALS STADIUM

For years, it had been evident that Recreation Park had outlived its usefulness as San Francisco's baseball stadium. The overflow crowds who witnessed the excellent Seals teams of the 1920s deserved better. Strub, Putnam and Graham knew this and contracted for the purchase of land in the Mission District to construct a modern ballpark. Since plans were formulated before the Depression reached its zenith, the owners decided to go ahead with the project.

The choice was a sloped plot located between 15th and 16th streets, with Bryant Street on the west and Hampshire Street on the east, primarily because it was located in one of the warm belts of San Francisco and free of fog during the playing season. There would be no repetition of the Ewing Field fiasco of 1914. In addition, Potrero Street, a major thoroughfare from downtown, was just one block east of Hampshire.

Coincidentally, in pioneering days three-quarters of a century earlier, a land claim had been filed on this plot in the name of the "Home Plate Mine."

The owners committed more than $300,000 to purchase the land and they secured further bank loans to construct the stadium. The total project—land and structure—would end up costing slightly more than $1 million, further complicated by the fact that the owners were still

obligated to five years on a contract for the use of Recreation Park.

The stadium project was initiated in the spring of 1930 and took less than one year to complete. Before construction could be started, 84,000 yards of rock had to be excavated and removed. The rocky base necessitated the use of tile drain which was then covered by sand and the proper top soil to guarantee hearty grass growth for the playing surface.

Seals Stadium, a cement structure, was constructed with the era's finest technology. It had an official capacity of 25,000, but 21,000 was probably more accurate. The stadium consisted of 16 rows of lower box seats and 26 rows of grandstand seats, divided by a wide aisle parallel to the field. The last row of seats was elevated 46 feet above the playing surface and 130 feet away from it. The most modern seats available were individually bolted to the risers.

It offered excellent visibility and proximity to the field, and was a convenient park to move around in and exit from. Home plate was 56 feet from the curved backstop, and the grandstand angled closer to the foul lines as it moved into the outfield. The foul line and the grandstand met in right field at the wall, 385 feet away from home plate. In left field the fence was 365 feet from home plate. The left center field corner was 404 feet away, and right center field was a prodigious 424 feet from home plate. To make things more challenging, the outfield wall was a uniform 20 feet high.

Another popular innovation was the public address system, located in center field. No longer did the umpire have to use a megaphone to announce the lineups.

When construction was finished, Seals Stadium was unquestionably the finest baseball park in America. Now the task was to attract fans to it. Its owners had obligated themselves to a hefty mortgage at a time when baseball fans were finding it difficult to put food on the table.

The first game at Seals Stadium was played on Friday, March 13, 1931 against the Detroit Tigers and future Hall of Famer Waite Hoyt. Sam Gibson, recently acquired by the Seals in the Frankie Crosetti deal, worked the first five innings for the win. The league opener on April 7 against Portland brought the stadium's first packed house. The fans left happy after Gibson blanked the Beavers 8-0.

But the Depression was coming on strong. Every area of American life was being hit. Baseball's position was unique; owners were feeling the pinch like everyone else, but baseball offered relief from the miseries for the American people.

Seals Stadium glistened its first few years. But the Depression necessitated a cutback on maintenance and little upkeep could be accomplished during World War II. The clean white cement turned to a shabby gray.

## THE COAST LEAGUE SURVIVES

One miracle out of the Depression was that, while many minor leagues collapsed, the Pacific Coast League was able to continue operations despite enduring at least one crisis a year that threatened one or more franchises, and thus the league.

There were serious concerns during the winter of 1930 regarding the potential loss of one of the Pacific Northwest teams. If one team suspended operations, it would not be feasible to make a road trip north to play just the other; the other team would be forced to cease operations as well.

Contingency plans were adopted to add franchises in California cities, probably Fresno or San Diego. But Portland and Seattle were able to stay afloat to guarantee the continuation of a normal playing schedule for at least another year.

Back in the Bay Area, Seals Owner Charlie Graham, Oaks Owner Cookie Devincenzi and Missions Owner Joe Baerwold dug in for the long haul. The price of admission was halved and the number of Kids Days, where youngsters were admitted free, was increased.

Seals Stadium featured six light towers 125 feet above the playing field (the PCL had inaugurated night baseball

to instant success one year earlier). Four were located behind the grandstand and two were behind the outfield. Westinghouse had developed a new high intensity lamp featuring glass reflectors made especially for Seals Stadium. The contractors boasted Seals Stadium was the best lighted park in the world, although many who played there were less complimentary. While the lights were better than other stadiums, it was still easy to lose fly balls in the night sky.

Night baseball was encouraged as a way of increasing attendance. Seals Stadium's new lighting system would be used often in 1931. The first night game at Seals Stadium took place on April 23 when Gibson defeated Sacramento 5-1.

## ONE STEP AHEAD OF THE BANK

The Missions were sinking deeper into the red each season. With a stadium mortgage to consider, the Seals were near the brink each year as well. The only way the Seals could survive was by selling off their young players.

For Graham, the bank's attitude toward the mortgage on the stadium complicated his effectiveness as an owner. The sale of at least one player a year to a major league club was necessary to meet his expanded obligations. If the Seals got too much cash in the deal, however, the bank would insist on the greater part of it. Then Graham wouldn't have enough cash to acquire an able replacement. To compensate, Graham had to insist on a substantial percentage of the sale price being delivered in players.

The Seals moved 13 players into the major leagues in the 1930s either by player transaction or through the major league draft. After the 1930 season, Frankie Crosetti was sold to the Yankees for delivery in 1932. He brought $75,000 and the contracts of pitchers Gibson and Bill Henderson. Gibson won 28 games for the Seals in 1931, promptly earning himself a return trip to New York—this time to pitch for the Giants.

At the end of the 1933 season, the Seals sold pitcher Lee Stine to the White Sox, Augie Galan to the Cubs and Prince Henry Oana to the Phillies.

Also, right-hander Curtis Davis was lost in the major league draft. Davis had joined the Seals in 1929 and won 90 games over the next five years. In 1932 Davis was 22-16 and in 1933 he went 20-16. Major league scouts wouldn't recommend him for purchase because of his age, but the Phillies took a chance and drafted him for $7,500. As a 30-year-old rookie in 1934, Davis won 19 games for the Phillies. He spent a total of 13 years in the National League and won 158 games.

Of the four transactions, the Galan deal was the blockbuster. The Seals received $25,000 plus the contracts of seven players: pitchers Leroy Herrmann, Gibson again, Win Ballou and Walter Mails, catchers Larry Woodall and

Hugh McMullen and infielder Lenny Backer. All were veterans, well past their prime playing years, but several would form the nucleus of the Seals for years. Herrmann returned to the major leagues after one successful year. Woodall served as assistant manager for several years, and Gibson and Ballou would be mainstays of the Seals pitching staff for another 10 years.

Herrmann went 27-13 in 1934 and was taken by the Reds in the major league draft. His stay in Cincinnati lasted only one year, after which he returned to the West Coast. Before the decade was concluded, Herrmann would wear the uniforms of all three Bay Area teams.

The sale of Joe DiMaggio after the 1934 season, for delivery in 1936, turned out to be one of the Yankees' greatest heists. In June 1934, DiMaggio injured his leg in a freak, non-baseball incident, so most scouts shied away from him as a viable prospect after that.

But Joe Devine of the Yankees watched DiMaggio's progress closely, and after arranging a secret visit with a doctor for a progress report, recommended DiMaggio's purchase to George Weiss and Ed Barrow of the Yankees.

Charlie Graham's hopes of a $100,000 sale were dashed by the injury and he settled for $25,000 and five players. But of the players received for DiMaggio, only Ted Norbert played a major role for the Seals.

The sale of outfielder Joe Marty during the 1936 winter meetings in Montreal was undoubtedly Graham's most critical deal. Graham knew the franchise would be insolvent if he couldn't generate some capital. Marty, a Sacramento native, was his best hope because the remainder of the Seals roster was composed of tired veterans and untried rookies.

While Graham was in Montreal, his bank in San Francisco cut off his credit and ordered him home. But then the Cubs purchased Marty for $35,000, saving the Seals franchise. Other players sold to the majors were catcher Joe Becker to Cleveland in 1935, infielder Bill Lillard to the Athletics in 1938 and outfielder Dominic DiMaggio and pitcher Larry Powell to the Red Sox after the 1939 season.

Becker batted .372 in 1935 while sharing the catching duties with Larry Woodall and Vince Monzo. Lillard, who divided time at shortstop with Ted Jennings, batted .335, second in the league, but played in only 81 games. Neither player left a big impression as a major leaguer.

Dom DiMaggio was sold for $75,000—three times what his brother Joe brought. Powell's sale added another $20,000 to the treasury.

On the field, league domination shifted out of the Bay Area during the 1930s. The Seals won pennants in 1931 and 1935, but the Los Angeles franchise won back-to-back pennants in 1933 and 1934 and the Seattle Rainiers were league champions in 1939 through 1941. The Oaks and the Missions spent much of the decade looking up from the second division.

## ANOTHER TRIUMPH FOR THE SEALS

The 1931 season was split into halves. Sam Gibson was 28-12 and led the pitching staff in virtually every category. As a team, the Seals batted .314. Hollywood won the first half in a tight race against the Seals. The Seals ran away with the second half, and then swept the four-game series from the Stars. Nick Williams managed the team to the championship only to be fired two days after the conclusion of the playoffs for "unsatisfactory personal habits." That was the team's euphemism for drinking too much. Also fired at the same time was trainer Denny Carroll, widely known at the time as the best in the business. Williams and Carroll had engaged in a wild, drunken brawl, conduct which Graham found intolerable.

In 1932, the popular veteran, Jimmy "Ike" Caveney was promoted to manager. His selection was somewhat of a surprise as the owners were supposed to be looking for a high-profile man to take over. Caveney remained manager for the next three years.

His teams finished in the middle of the pack, but several excellent players emerged to make San Francisco an attractive draw around the league. Most notable was Joe DiMaggio, who played the last three games of the 1932 season as Galan's replacement at shortstop.

Jimmy 'Ike' Caveney played shortstop for the Seals and Oaks before becoming Seals manager in the 1930s.

Walter Mails, left, delivers a Spring Training 1933 message to Leroy Hermann, Larry Woodall, Joe DiMaggio, Ike Caveney and Roy Frazier while Owner Charlie Graham listens in.

This was Galan's first season in baseball and he was only a couple of years older than the 17-year-old DiMaggio. The Berkeley-born Galan was slender and quick. He possessed good speed and had smart instincts. In 1933, Galan batted third in the lineup, hitting .356. DiMaggio hit fourth, batting .340, but he drove in 169 runs. Of the two, it was Galan who was chosen the team's most valuable player. This earned him a promotion to the Chicago Cubs for 1934.

The Seals lacked the youth that carried them to great success in the 1920s. There were good, young players—outfielders Jerry Donovan, Mike Hunt and Ernie Sulik and catcher Bill Brenzel among them—but there were too many players winding down their careers.

Two veteran pitchers established long second careers with the Seals after being acquired by the Cubs: Win "Pard" Ballou and Sam Gibson. Ballou grew old pitching in relief for the Seals, finally retiring at the conclusion of the 1944 season just a few weeks before his 47th birthday. Ballou, whose best pitch was the spitter, found his career extended because of the manpower shortage created by the second World War.

"Sad Sam" Gibson matched Ballou season for season. He retired, along with Ballou, after the 1944 season, then came out of retirement to pitch for Oakland. After an unsuccessful comeback, Gibson retired again.

As a starter, Gibson won more than 20 games five times for the Seals. A right-handed pitcher, he had an unorthodox motion leading to a sidearm pitch. When he pitched, Gibson was one of the most intense and intolerant craftsmen in the game. He was never satisfied with a

large lead, constantly extolling his teammates to "More tallies, more tallies." If a player made an error behind him, Sam would get very angry, extending his wrath to the offender for all to see. On the field, Gibson trained as hard as any player; off the field he drank as much as most.

### YET ANOTHER PENNANT WINNER IN 1935

In 1935, Graham brought Francis "Lefty" O'Doul back home to manage. While Caveney hadn't produced any winners, he had still done an adequate job. O'Doul's selection initially had as much to do with box-office appeal as it did with managerial skill.

O'Doul hit .316 for the Giants in 1934 at age 37, but he was through. His arm was gone and he was a defensive

| | SAMUEL BRAXTON "SAD SAM" GIBSON | | | | | | | | | | |
|---|---|---|---|---|---|---|---|---|---|---|---|
| YEAR | TEAM | G | IP | W | L | H | R | ER | BB | SO | ERA |
| 1931 | S.F. | 41 | 337* | 28* | 12 | 338 | 108 | 93 | 59 | 204* | 2.48* |
| 1933 | Port. | 33 | 234 | 15 | 14 | 248 | 118 | 104 | 60 | 132 | 4.00 |
| 1934 | S.F. | 47 | 313 | 21 | 17 | 297 | 116 | 103 | 74 | 171 | 2.96 |
| 1935 | S.F. | 38 | 252 | 22 | 4 | 269 | 122 | 97 | 48 | 121 | 3.45 |
| 1936 | S.F. | 39 | 298 | 18 | 15 | 297 | 115 | 93 | 70 | 172 | 2.81 |
| 1937 | S.F. | 35 | 260 | 19 | 8 | 263 | 102 | 82 | 55 | 146 | 2.83 |
| 1938 | S.F. | 38 | 284 | 23 | 12 | 243 | 96 | 84 | 59 | 151 | 2.66 |
| 1939 | S.F. | 34 | 265 | 22 | 9 | 242 | 96 | 66 | 51 | 136 | 2.24* |
| 1940 | S.F. | 35 | 263 | 14 | 14 | 245 | 106 | 83 | 57 | 126 | 2.83 |
| 1941 | S.F. | 22 | 163 | 13 | 7 | 150 | 73 | 60 | 41 | 72 | 3.31 |
| 1942 | S.F. | 34 | 259 | 22 | 12 | 277 | 84 | 77 | 41 | 87 | 2.78 |
| 1943 | S.F. | 20 | 125 | 6 | 5 | 122 | 41 | 34 | 27 | 34 | 2.45 |
| 1944 | S.F. | 18 | 114 | 4 | 8 | 124 | 51 | 50 | 26 | 27 | 3.95 |
| 1945 | Oak. | 18 | 65 | 2 | 3 | 76 | 37 | 23 | 14 | 17 | 3.14 |
| PCL TOTALS | | 452 | 3221 | 229 | 140 | 3191 | 1265 | 1049 | 682 | 1596 | 2.93 |
| MINOR TOTALS | | 661 | 4469 | 307 | 200 | 4460 | 1860 | 1413 | 1073 | 2195 | 3.08 |
| MAJOR TOTALS | | 131 | 594 | 32 | 38 | 676 | 351 | 280 | 249 | 208 | 4.24 |
| * Led League | | | | | | | | | | | |

## OX ECKHARDT—MINOR LEAGUE LEGEND

Texas farm boy Oscar Eckhardt was one of the finest hitters in PCL history. He was a 6-foot-1, 185-pounder with a legendary following in Texas for his football exploits. His brute strength, gained from punching cattle, gave him the nickname of "Ox."

Eckhardt was a left-handed batter with a stance that seemed to put him 10 feet down the first base line before he hit the ball. His slap-style hitting found the defensive holes even though the defenders regularly shifted to the left to reduce his odds of hitting safely. But Ox had speed and he beat out many of those hits.

Eckhardt won four PCL batting titles, including a .414 average for the Missions in 1933. This came after a .371 average in 1930 and .369 in 1931. Still, he could not find a permanent home with a major league team. In a scouting report to his boss, the Yankees' Ed Barrow, in 1935, ex-Missions Manager Devine wrote:

"ECKHARDT: left-handed hitter, right-handed thrower. Eckhardt leads every league he has ever played in in hitting. Eckhardt cannot throw, is not smart, and not a good outfielder. Eckhardt cannot hit a ball to right field, strictly a left field hitter. Eckhardt is fast going to first base. Over one-third of Eckhardt's hits are high hoppers that he beats out. When he gets an extra base hit, he usually runs until he is out. Eckhardt cannot play as a regular on a major league ball club. Eckhardt is not any too good a hitter against good, smart pitching, as a change of pace bothers Eckhardt considerably. The only way Eckhardt may be of some value to a major league club is as a pinch-hitter, and no more."

After Eckhardt's .414 season—an all-time league high—there were still no takers. A discon-solate Eckhardt told a reporter, "They say I'm too awkward to make good. I honestly believe I could go up there if given a decent chance. I've had two trips to the majors, but never played a full game of ball all the time I was in the big show. If something doesn't happen soon, I'm going to throw my bat away and go to coaching football."

Eckhardt batted .378 in 1934, a down year for him, but bounced back to bat .399 in 1935 to win the batting title. Brooklyn gave him a shot in 1936, purchasing both him and pitcher Wayne Osborne from the Reds.

At Brooklyn, Eckhardt played in 16 games, batting .182, before he was sent to Indianapolis in the American Association. He was out of the Pacific Coast League and his major league trials were over.

Eckhardt compiled amazing statistics in his five years in San Francisco with the Missions. In 864 games he had 1,340 hits in 3,461 at bats. His average of 268 hits per season equated to a five-year batting average of .387. Thirty-two of those hits were home runs. He stole 54 bases and scored 629 runs.

Eckhardt played five more years before retiring to Texas and his cattle ranch, joining the ranks of other great PCL sluggers, most notably Buzz Arlett and Smead Jolley, who were Coast League legends and major league flops.

### OSCAR GEORGE "OX" ECKHARDT

| YEAR | TEAM | GAMES | AB | R | H | 2B | 3B | HR | RBI | PCT. |
|------|------|-------|-----|-----|------|-----|-----|-----|------|-------|
| 1929 | Seattle | 161 | 571 | 84 | 202 | 35 | 17* | 7 | 70 | .354 |
| 1931 | Mission | 185 | 745 | 129 | 275* | 52 | 10 | 7 | 117 | .369* |
| 1932 | Mission | 134 | 539 | 80 | 200 | 33 | 13 | 5 | 82 | .371* |
| 1933 | Mission | 189* | 760 | 145 | 315* | 56 | 16 | 12 | 143 | .414* |
| 1934 | Mission | 184 | 707 | 126 | 267 | 36 | 11 | 6 | 106 | .378 |
| 1935 | Mission | 172 | 710 | 149 | 283* | 40 | 11 | 2 | 114 | .399* |
| PCL TOTALS | | 1025 | 4032 | 713 | 1542 | 252 | 78 | 39 | 632 | .382 |
| MINOR TOTALS | | 1926 | 7563 | 1275 | 2773 | 455 | 146 | 66 | 1037 | .367 |
| MAJOR TOTALS | | 24 | 52 | 6 | 10 | 1 | 0 | 1 | 7 | .192 |

* Led League

---

liability. Hiring him to manage was a perfect choice. O'Doul loved the city and was immensely popular in the Bay Area and around the league.

O'Doul ultimately became known as one of the finest teachers in the game, and his gambling style of play succeeded more often than it backfired.

### A GREAT PAIRING

In his first year O'Doul had the privilege and good fortune to work with Joe DiMaggio. Joe was entering his third full season with the Seals and had already been sold to the Yankees. O'Doul was wise enough not to try to change perfection, but his advice and nurturing would not be forgotten by the young player.

Because the Seals received five players from the Yankees in the DiMaggio sale, the 1935 team was reinforced by having both ends of the trade still on the roster. Although the defending-champion Angels overcame a torrid 24-4 start by the Oaks—they won the first half of the split-season schedule—the Seals began playing well for O'Doul in May. At the end of the first half, the Seals and Oaks were tied for second place, five games back.

Los Angeles slumped in the second half, finishing fourth. In a three-team race, Gabby Street's Mission Reds joined the Portland Ducks and the Seals, each trying to hold off the other. On August 15, Mission was in first place by two games, but the lead slipped away. In the final month, the Seals eased past the Reds, ultimately winning by three games. The Oaks faded to sixth.

The Seals won the overall crown in O'Doul's first year as manager, beating the Angels four games to two.

DiMaggio hit .398 but didn't win the batting crown.

That honor went for the fourth time in five years to Oscar Eckhardt, who went 4-for-5 in the first game of a season-ending doubleheader before sitting out the nightcap, finishing at .399.

The Seals led the league in stolen bases with 178. On the mound, Gibson had another brilliant year at 22-4.

## ENTERTAINING, BUT NOT A WINNER

During the remainder of the decade, the Seals were entertaining and generally competitive, finishing second in 1937 and 1939.

The veterans provided stability and the dwindling yet continuous stream of rookies provided the enthusiasm. Among the more prominent youngsters was Brooks

Right, Walter Mails admires Lefty O'Doul's 1936 uniform. Below, Missions Manager Willie Kamm and Seals Manager Lefty O'Doul greet each other at the start of the 1936 season.

Walter Mails, in tails and doffing his top hat, greets the fans at Opening Day ceremonies in 1936. The other dignitaries are (l-r): Mayor Angelo Rossi, Bailey Hipkins, Ty Cobb, Charlie Graham and Police Chief William J. Quinn.

Holder. Holder broke in as an infielder in 1935, was later shifted to the outfield, then was traded to Hollywood for Bernie Uhalt. Holder's popularity in the league was unchallenged for more than a decade.

Frankie Hawkins, Ted Jennings and Dom DiMaggio broke into the lineup in 1937. All three could hit but they had different personalities and styles. Hawkins was volatile, sometimes unpredictable, and hurt himself with a drinking problem. Jennings was sometimes awkward in fielding the left side of the infield and he was slow, but he was an effective batter. Young DiMaggio was quiet, studious and had some necessary physical growth ahead of him. All were very popular with the fans.

**THE 1938 SEALS MAKE THE PLAYOFFS**

The 1938 Seals had few significant changes from the 1937 model. Gene Lillard, a 14-game winner in 1937, had to be offered back to the Cubs, who reacquired his contract for $7,500. Ernie Raimondi was an excellent prospect, but he was young and needed more experience. The Seals had a wealth of young infielders on the left side, so injuries prompted them to let Raimondi go.

Holder led the team in batting with .330 in 1938 while Hawkins hit .309. Harley Boss at first base hit .308 and Dominic DiMaggio batted .307. With the exception of Boss at 28, the team's top hitters were young players.

Among the veterans, Joe Sprinz, who had been purchased from the Missions in the winter, hit .295 while catching the majority of the games. As a team the Seals batted .292.

The Seals finished the season at 93-85 in fourth place, qualifying them for the President's Cup playoff series. Pennant-winning Los Angeles lost to the third-place Sacramento Solons in five games while the Seals took on second-place Seattle in the first round.

The Seals gained entry to the playoffs with a strong, late-season finish, taking five of seven from Sacramento. In the playoffs, they twice faced and beat the league's top hurler, Fred Hutchinson. Only one year out of high school, Hutchinston went 25-7. The Seals proceeded to take four out of five to earn a spot in the championship round against Sacramento.

The Solons defeated the Seals in five games behind the pitching of Tony Freitas, who had gone 6-0 against the Seals in regular-season play. Only Eddie Stutz's 9-4 victory in the second game prevented a sweep.

## MISSION REDS SUFFER

The Mission Reds had few advantages playing in San Francisco during the 1930s and the Depression certainly didn't help. Neither did the new park, called Seals Stadium, to which the Mission owners had to pay rent.

In an attempt to be competitive, President Joe Baerwald decided to take on the Seals at their own game—scouting. Early in 1931, Baerwald brought in scout Joe Devine as an assistant to Manager George H. Burns. The team had invested heavily to acquire top veterans, and the Reds were only playing .500 ball. Before the first half ended, Burns was fired and Devine was elevated to manager. The change made little difference as the Missions finished last during the second half.

Baerwald ordered Devine and assistant Bobby Coltrin to compete with the Seals and Oaks in signing the best players in the Bay Area. When the team went to Spring Training in 1932, its roster boasted 17 players from San Francisco and nine more from East Bay cities.

While some of the locals were veterans—the Pillette brothers, Eddie Mulligan, Pete Ricci, Bert Cole and Jimmy Welsh—most were rookies. Among them were Italo Chelini, a slender left-handed pitcher; Ellsworth "Babe" Dahlgren, a first baseman out of Mission High; second baseman Al Wright from Lowell High and infielder Dick

Herman 'Old Folks' Pillette was a Coast League pitcher for 23 years, starting in 1920. He retired in 1946 at the age of 49.

Gyselman from Polytechnic High. All were legal minors when the season began, and all would eventually play in the major leagues.

Shortly into the season, infielder Mark Koenig, a San Franciscan, was assigned to the Reds by Detroit, and Oscar Eckhardt was returned by the Boston Bees.

Koenig's tenure with the Reds was short. After little more than three months on the coast, his contract was purchased by the Chicago Cubs for their successful drive to the National League pennant. Koenig, the shortstop on the great Yankees teams in the late 1920s, had bolstered the left side of the infield and was hitting .335 when he was sold. His treatment by the Cubs regarding a World Series share was the focus of bitterness expressed by the Yankees after the 1932 Series.

The Reds floundered in 1932 and 1933, finishing eighth and then seventh. Baerwold replaced Devine with popular Freddie Hofmann and a year later replaced Hofmann with Charles "Gabby" Street. Street had experience as a major league catcher after playing for San Francisco in 1906-07 and had been a crafty manager for the 1930 National League champion and 1931 World Champion St. Louis Cardinals.

Street picked up a few veteran pitchers and instilled confidence in the field players, mostly returnees from 1933, that they could win in this league. They did. The Reds won 101 and lost 85, a gain of 22 games over 1933. Still, the Angels won the pennant.

Street's pitching staff featured 18-year major league veteran Clarence Mitchell, the last lefty in the Coast League allowed to throw the spitter. Mitchell went 19-12.

The youngsters carried the load for Street. Dutch Lieber was 19-13 with a league-leading 2.50 ERA. Johnny Babich went 10-3 with a 2.03 ERA but not enough innings to qualify for the league title.

Offensively, despite Eckhardt's "off" season at .378, his fellow outfielders, Louie Almada and Bud Hafey, batted .334 and .322, respectively. First baseman Babe Dahlgren hit .302 with a club-leading 20 homers.

Street resigned after the 1935 season to take a major league coaching position and was replaced by Willie Kamm. The soft-spoken Kamm managed the Reds through their final two seasons in San Francisco and therefore was forced to watch the demise of the franchise. Eckhardt, the only true box-office attraction, was gone. For the most part, the team consisted of over-the-hill veterans with a few untried youngsters.

Attendance remained poor, so there was little cash to acquire proven players. The franchise was losing money and was in deep trouble. The Reds finished at .500 in 1936 but dropped into last place at 73-105 in 1937.

Playing in Seals Stadium made the Reds tailor their hitting style to fit the characteristics of the ballpark. Both Street and Kamm emphasized an offense set up to generate runs one at a time.

Top, the 1937 Seals. Dominic DiMaggio is second from the left in the front row. Right, 'Sad Sam' Gibson was a perennial 20-game winner for the Seals during the Depression years.

## JOE SPRINZ'S BROKEN FACE

The 1939 season was baseball's centennial and Charlie Graham's 50th year in the game. It also marked one of the most infamous publicity stunts in PCL history.

With the Seals in the thick of the pennant chase and the World's Fair being held on Treasure Island in the middle of San Francisco Bay, the great hustler, Walter Mails, negotiated a stunt in which Seals catchers would catch baseballs thrown by Lefty O'Doul from the 450-foot-high Tower of the Sun.

Mails convinced Larry Woodall, Joe Sprinz and Wil Leonard to participate. Leonard dropped out after missing his first chance, watching the ball bounce 20 feet upward off the pavement. Sprinz caught five balls, Woodall three.

The event was a success but Mails, not satisfied at this point, negotiated "The Great Balloon Drop," in which the catchers would attempt to catch balls thrown from a blimp circling 1,000 feet above the baseball diamond on Treasure Island.

A large crowd was on hand to witness the spectacle on a hot August day. Neither Woodall nor Sprinz were enthused about the stunt. When the signal came to start the drop everybody backed away, leaving Sprinz standing alone at the target area.

The first ball landed off target in empty bleachers. The second ball tailed away from Sprinz, embedding itself in the field. That should have been a clue for Sprinz, but he went on. Sprinz went for the third ball, but the wind kept pushing it away from him. With glove held above his head, he tried to keep up with the ball but misjudged it.

The ball glanced off his mitt, crashing into the side of his face. Sprinz awoke in a hospital with 12 broken bones, a badly lacerated face and five teeth knocked out. It was later estimated the ball

was traveling 150 miles per hour, and many observers were amazed Sprinz even got close to it. He spent the remainder of the season in the hospital on a diet of liquids and aspirin.

The accident probably cost the Seals the pennant, as Sprinz was doing most of the team's catching while batting above .300 at the time of the accident.

Sprinz was back in camp the following spring, taking extra hours catching foul pops.

---

The Missions displayed little power and in 1936 hit a grand total of 24 home runs—most of them hit away from Seals Stadium. Their run production established a franchise low of 810, only to be lowered to 770 by the dismal 1937 team.

Fans lost interest that year, and with the ownership on the verge of bankruptcy, there was no hope. The Reds' attendance was 124,052, an astonishing 93,000 behind the Seals' league-leading attendance.

## THE MISSION REDS GIVE UP

The Mission Reds couldn't survive the Depression. Herbert Fleishhacker, the team's principal owner, had taken severe business losses. When Bill Lane transferred

his Hollywood franchise to San Diego after the 1935 season, the Los Angeles area was left with only one team. A clamor arose out of L.A. to acquire the Reds and move them there. At the conclusion of the 1937 season, Baerwald and Fleishhacker negotiated the sale of the team to a group of Southern California businessmen headed by Don Francisco and Harry Young.

A serious hurdle arose over where the new Hollywood franchise would play its games. The Angels were not pleased to welcome the new Stars at Wrigley Field but made the concession on a one-year term.

The transfer of the Mission club to Hollywood relieved pressure faced by the Oakland and San Francisco clubs. It also provided a more balanced league. While San Francisco was a hotbed of baseball interest, it was presumptuous to think the city could support two teams in

Lefty O'Doul was known for many things, among them his ability to teach baseball skills. Above, he demonstrates for Dominic DiMaggio, Charlie Graham and Brooks Holder. Below, he gives fielding tips to infielder Harvey Storey in 1939.

the midst of the Depression. Even in times of prosperity, only so many entertainment dollars were available. With their long tradition, the Seals had those dollars locked up. Economically, the Mission Reds were a bad idea. But with players such as Eckhardt, Fuzzy Hufft, Ike Boone, Boom-Boom Beck, Eddie Joost, the Pillettes and many others, the fans of San Francisco were fortunate. ❖

## CHAPTER 12

# THE OAKS TAKE A DIFFERENT APPROACH

Cookie Devincenzi, Bob Miller and Carl Zamloch purchased the Oaks from Cal Ewing and Frank Ish at the end of the 1929 season. The completion of the sale coincided with the stock market crash and Devincenzi, as managing partner, faced hard times. Prospects for the independently owned franchise in a secondary market at the start of a serious economic downturn were not good. It would take a magician to make a success of this situation.

Carl Zamloch was such a man. Zamloch was serving as coach of Cal's baseball and soccer teams when he was invited to be part of the Oaks' new partnership. He felt confident because the nucleus of the Oakland ballclub looked promising.

Ernie Lombardi and Pete Read returned behind the plate, and infielders Jack Fenton, Monroe Dean, Ray Brubaker and Johnny Vergez were veterans. Buzz Arlett, Tony Governor and Bernie Uhalt were all back to patrol the outfield.

In light of such a strong nucleus, the 1930 season had to be a disappointment for the new management. In a split season the Oaks finished fourth, then sixth, with an overall 97-103 record.

The team incurred several injuries but acquired players to fill the holes. Second base seemed to be especially injury-prone. The team acquired local products Joe Mellana and Bernie DeVivieros to shore up the infield.

Mellana earned the second base role only to break a finger, so the veteran Ray Brubaker filled in.

The big stars quickly left. Lombardi hit .370 and was sold to Brooklyn. Arlett hit .361 and was sold to the Philadelphia Phillies. After hitting .307, Vergez was sold to the New York Giants.

Although the Seals finished ahead of Oakland, the Oaks were the winners at the turnstiles. Oakland's attendance picked up more than 18,000 to exceed 250,000, while San Francisco's dropped to 220,495, a loss of more than 165,000 from 1929, a second-place year. With the increased attendance and the sale of their three stars, Oakland turned a profit even as the Depression kicked into high gear.

To make baseball even more attractive in 1931, the Oaks added lights to the Emeryville park. The Oaks had helped Sacramento and the PCL inaugurate night baseball at Moreing Field in 1930 and were excited about its potential at the gate. Indeed, night baseball helped stimulate attendance in Oakland.

The Oaks made slight profits in 1930, 1931 and 1936 but took losses during the other seasons. Players felt the pinch as well. When contracts were sent out early into the new year, players were often asked to take a cut. Few players held out for more pay, realizing the futility of such a protest. In 1931, Oaks first baseman Jack Fenton held out for a slight increase. Just before Opening Day he met small it was felt a Friday doubleheader would attract more fans than single games on Tuesday and Friday. In the end, the directors voted to keep the traditional format: single games Tuesday through Saturday with a doubleheader on Sunday. When baseball and football overlapped, owners often canceled Saturday dates, playing a doubleheader on Friday to avoid competition with a local college game.

## THE OAKS STRUGGLE TO STAY SOLVENT

Even with night baseball in Oakland, attendance slumped. Maintenance on the park was deferred and equipment orders were cancelled. Cost-cutting moves created a unique situation for Zamloch in 1932. At a directors meeting of the Oakland Association in May, a resolution was adopted that abolished salaries of all officers. Zamloch was an officer of the association as well as manager of the team, but he presumed his manager's salary would still be paid.

However, the club stopped further payments on his $10,000 salary. At the end of the season, Zamloch filed a claim with Judge William B. Bramham, chairman of the National Association, for $7,095 in back wages. To complicate matters, Zamloch and the Oakland Association had neglected to file a copy of the contract with the National Association, which was a fairly common practice between ballclubs and their managers.

Judge Bramham ruled in favor of Zamloch and the Oakland Association had to pay the balance on Zamloch's salary. Whether it was a result of Oakland's seventh-place finish or the increased level of animosity between the parties, Zamloch did not return in 1933.

The 1933 season was an unexpected surprise. Most observers expected the Oaks to occupy the cellar, but the development of four players made it an exciting season. Although the team finished in fifth place under first-year Manager Ray Brubaker, it was a winning year at 93-92.

The Oaks had signed a local youngster off the sandlots, placing him on second base. This was Harry Lavagetto, "Cookie's boy," who batted .312 and earned a promotion to the Pittsburgh Pirates after one season. Lavagetto joined the Pirates shortly after his 19th birthday.

Art Veltman was sent to the Oaks from the New York Giants and became a workhorse behind the plate, batting .322. At the end of the season, the Pirates drafted him back into the National League. Veltman's backup was young Billy Raimondi, a star at Oakland's McClymonds High. Veltman and Raimondi gave the Oaks the best catching combination in the league.

The fourth star was outfielder Bernie Uhalt. Uhalt batted .350, stole 62 bases of the team's 227 league-leading steals and solidified the defense from center field. The Chicago White Sox purchased Uhalt's contract after the

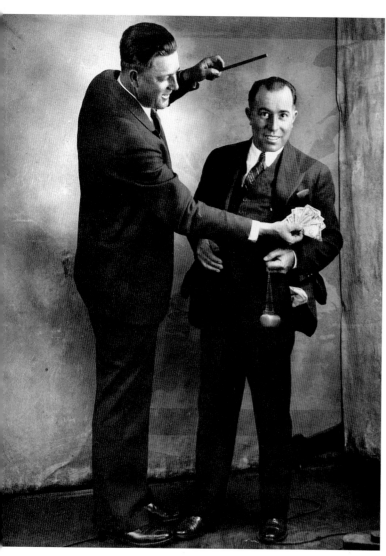

Oaks Manager Carl Zamloch practices some magic tricks on Owner Cookie Devincenzi. It took more than magic for Zamloch or Devincenzi to succeed during the Depression.

with Devincenzi, but Fenton refused to budge on his demands. Jack was immediately suspended until he capitulated to the original offer.

In other economy moves, the league directors voted to reduce roster size early in the Depression from 25 to 21. For long road trips, it became customary for teams to leave two or three fringe players at home to save transportation and lodging costs. Good-hitting pitchers often found themselves in the outfield on their off days.

Curiously, the Pacific Coast League's rosters had been expanded to 25 by 1935, the middle of the Depression. That was two more than were carried in the major leagues and more than any other league in organized baseball. At least five players on the roster had to be classified as rookies.

For the 1935 season, the league directors proposed abandoning Tuesday games. Tuesday attendance was so season, but "Frenchy" would return to the Oaks after Spring Training.

As a side benefit of the Uhalt deal, the Oaks received pitcher Hal Haid from the Sox for 1934. Haid was a veteran screwballer who became a superior relief pitcher for the Oaks. His record was never impressive, but his value as a closer was known to his managers and teammates.

## THE OAKS TURN TO THE YANKEES FOR HELP

While the San Francisco Seals supplemented their income by regularly selling players to the major league clubs, Oakland was always cash poor. At this time of crisis, Devincenzi asked the New York Yankees for their financial assistance.

The Yankees and the Oaks had previously negotiated a working agreement which provided players to Oakland. In return, the Yankees received priority for any young Oaks prospects. In 1934, Devincenzi asked the Yankees' Ed Barrow for a $6,000 loan, to be paid back in three installments over the next few years. The Oaks put up 6,300 shares of their stock as collateral.

Attendance didn't improve, so Devincenzi was unable to meet his first deadline. Rather than acquiring control of the franchise—about which abundant rumors circulated—the Yankees took the contracts of Oakland's finest prospects, Raimondi and Uhalt, as payment.

The financial difficulties incurred by the Oakland franchise guaranteed a decade of second-division teams. The only exceptions were in the 1935 and 1936 seasons. Even with a competitive team, Devincenzi could not count

The 1936 Oakland Oaks. Manager Bill Meyer is in the front row, second from the left. Joe Gordon is in the front row, far right.

Above, Oaks infielders Bernie DeVivieros, Jimmie Hitchcock, Joe Gordon, Roy Anton and Dario Lodigiani. Left, Willie Ludolph, who went 21-6 in 1936, receives a trophy for being the season's best pitcher.

on adequate attendance, which was about 100,000 less per season than in the 1920s.

From 1934 through 1937, the Oaks depended heavily upon the Yankees for players. The agreement was necessary for the Oaks' survival, but it was also responsible for their mediocrity. The Yankees sent their top prospects to Newark and Kansas City, both top franchises, so the Oaks were seldom offered players with experience and good skills. The Oaks continued to own roughly half of their roster while the remainder was supplied by the Yankees.

## THE WORKING AGREEMENT FALLS APART

Neither side felt the other was living up to the spirit of their agreement. On February 10, 1937, Devine wrote a letter to Weiss expressing concern about Devincenzi's handling of the Oaks. The letter said, in part, "Devincenzi will not try to sign any players to build his club up—he proved that in turning down [Harlin] Pool. Pool was well-liked in Oakland and would have made him an ideal

Harlin Pool, who played parts of two seasons in the majors, takes a swing.

Oaks infielder Eddie Mulligan, who also played for the Seals and the Reds during his PCL career.

man at Oakland for $3,000, but he does not intend to put out a dime for signing any players where a little money is involved. He is depending strictly on you to furnish him a club, so George, my advice is make him develop some players for us." Pool, then Yankees property, had been returned on option to Oakland in 1936, but was picked up by Seattle for 1937 after the Oaks declined the chance to purchase his contract.

Devincenzi decided to terminate the Oaks' agreement with the Yankees after the 1937 season. In 1936 and early 1937, Devincenzi felt the Yankees used the working agreement to hurt Oakland. Young, successful Oakland prospects were often recalled and placed at Newark or Kansas City.

Rather than receiving a player from these clubs, or from New York, the replacement invariably came from Class A Binghamton. In essence, Oakland served as No. 3 in the Yankees' Double-A farm system.

The 1938 Oaks, put together after the working agreement ended, was the worst Oakland team of the decade. It finished at 65-113, 40 games behind the pennant-winning Angels.

## THE GOOD YEARS

Oscar Vitt was recommended to Devincenzi by the Yankees to manage the Oaks in 1935, and his upbeat style was both abrasive and motivational. The Yankees provided several players who helped the Oaks drive to a third-place finish under Vitt.

Catchers Chris Hartje and Norman Kies, pitchers Spud Chandler, Hank McDonald, Jim Tobin, Tom Conlon and Jimmy Rego, and infielders Freddie Muller and Frankie Hawkins were all Yankee property. After the season, Raimondi and Uhalt, the Oaks' top prospects, also became Yankee property in lieu of repaying the loan. Raimondi again carried the catching load, receiving credit from the pitchers for his leadership and imaginative pitch selection. At the plate, Raimondi hit .256.

The seeds of 1936 successes were planted one year earlier. Vitt moved on in the Yankees chain and was replaced by Bill Meyer. Meyer had been recommended by the Yankees as a fine teacher and a compassionate man. He was both; his soft-spoken approach to teaching earned him the respect of his players. Meyer stayed through the 1936 and 1937 seasons before the Yankees promoted him to manage their Newark club.

Tobin, an Oakland native, was again loaned to the Oaks by the Yankees. He followed his 11 wins in 1935 with 16 in 1936, earning himself a shot at the major leagues. While the Yankees ultimately gave up on Tobin, who was somewhat of a troublemaker, the Pirates took a chance on him and were rewarded with three years and a cumulative 29-24 record. The Pirates then traded him to

Second baseman Dario Lodigiani was a popular player with the Oaks during the Depression years.

Oaks right-hander Jack Salveson was known for his control. He had several stints in the majors.

First baseman Leroy Anton was a smooth-fielding defensive specialist and a solid hitter for Oakland.

the Boston Bees where he pitched an additional six years. Tobin returned to help the Oaks win the pennant in 1948.

Ludolph won 20 in 1935 and came back with a 21-6 record, tops in the league, in 1936. Douglas won 16 in 1935 and 15 in 1936. And with Haid in the bullpen, the Oaks had the nucleus of a solid pitching staff.

Meyer had several young players to work with, most of them Yankee farmhands.

In putting his team together, the most intriguing area was the infield. Anton was back at first base. At second base was San Franciscan Dario Lodigiani. "Lodi" had been scouted by Vitt when he managed Hollywood in 1934. When Vitt came to Oakland in 1935, he encouraged Devincenzi to sign Lodigiani. Shortstop was manned by the veteran DeVivieros. Nearing the end of his career as a player, DeVivieros was pleased to have a chance to instruct his young teammates on the nuances of infield play and base-running. His season came to an abrupt halt when he broke his finger.

This opened the door for Joe Gordon, a young collegian from Oregon, to step in at shortstop. Meyer had intended to bring Gordon along slowly, but now Gordon had to learn on the job. He played well in the field and hit. 300, then in 1937 was moved to Newark. One year later, he became the Yankees' regular second baseman and

Hugh Luby

Hugh Luby continued the Oaks' tradition of superior infielders at second base in the latter 1930s.

Bill Rigney was another local boy who made good with the Oaks before going on to a long major league career.

capped his career by being named American League Most Valuable Player in 1942. He later returned to the Coast League as player-manager of the Solons and manager of the league-champion Seals in 1957.

The burden of catching fell upon the shoulders of Hartje and Hershberger, both of whom were Yankees property, and both of whom would die by unfortunate circumstances.

Hartje had been one of the Yankees' top prospects. He was blessed with tremendous talent but his desire and heart were lacking. He was a reserve catcher in 1935, then caught the bulk of games in 1936, batting a healthy .322. He was later returned outright to the Oaks, who continued to option him to lower classification teams. He was a victim in a 1946 bus crash that killed several members of the Spokane baseball team.

Hershberger was Hartje's backup. With the Oaks, he batted .263 in 89 games. At the end of the season the Yankees recalled him, later selling him to Cincinnati where he was backup to Ernie Lombardi. After 2½ seasons, a despondent Hershberger committed suicide.

The Oaks finished 1½ games behind the Portland Beavers but lost four out of five in the newly inaugurated championship playoff series. But in 1936 at least, the Oaks were the best of the bay.

For the remainder of the decade, the Oaks were near or at the bottom of the league. Only a miserable Missions team kept the Oaks out of the cellar in 1937, a feat they accomplished in 1938. In 1939, the Oaks finished seventh.

Why were the Oaks so bad? Good players came to the Oaks, but they wouldn't stay long. And the Oaks were only able to afford older players past their prime, retreads like Smead Jolley, Marvin Gudat, Johnny Vergez—back as player-manager in 1939—Jackie Warner and Jerry Donovan.

Devincenzi also signed a multitude of younger players to their first contracts and brought young players like Frank Kelleher, Johnny Lindell, Ernie Bonham and Walter Judnich to Oakland on option.

But Gordon, Jack Glynn, Tobin, Hershberger, Hartje and other optionees were recalled. Anton, Pool, Uhalt and others were moved. Lodigiani was sold to the Philadelphia Athletics. Ludolph went into semi-retirement, pitching only on weekends.

Other than Hugh Luby, Lodigiani and a youngster from Oakland High named Bill Rigney—all of whom would play in the majors—the Oaks signed few youngsters able to compete at the Double-A level. But these few potential stars served as sufficient reason for Devincenzi to keep running the ballclub. ❖

CHAPTER **13**

# BIRD-DOGGING FOR DIAMONDS

For an independent minor league to survive, it was necessary for it to acquire and nurture its own players. The major leagues had not yet developed the concept of farm systems, being more willing to scout the minors and purchase the contracts of their stars.

The San Francisco Seals were always more persistent and certainly luckier than the Bay Area's two other PCL teams in signing local prospects. They had also developed a better reputation for nurturing players and sending them on to the major leagues.

The Oaks and the Mission Reds had scouts working the Bay Area, but the Seals signed the majority of the talent usually by promising the prospect a percentage of any money received if he were sold to the major leagues.

Before 1930 there was little competition from major league teams to sign local talent. There were few major league scouts in the area, and when scouts did come out their primary function was recommending players to be drafted or bought from the teams holding their contracts.

The post-season draft guaranteed local subservience to the major leagues. It also encouraged local owners to try to peddle their young stars. An owner could hope to create a bidding war to drive the sale price upward. Such a sale could bring substantial cash and possibly two or three veteran players to bolster next year's team.

The owner would undoubtedly fail if he tried to conceal a budding young star from the major league scouts because it would take only one scout's recommendation to steal the player away for as little as $5,000. Each team could have a maximum of one player drafted off its roster each year.

When a youngster passed by the locals and signed with a major league organization, the probability existed that the major league club received some tip from a "bird dog," or a friend of the organization. For example, Danny Long recommended a young farm boy from Fresno—Frank Chance—to the Cubs in the late 1890s. San Franciscans Joe Cronin, Lew Fonseca, Harry Heilmann, George Kelly and Tony Lazzeri also started their careers away from the Bay Area.

There was one major exception to the dearth of major league scouts roaming the west—Joe Devine. He lived in San Francisco and scouted for the Pittsburgh Pirates, and it was no accident the Pirates reaped a wealth of Bay Area talent during the 1920s. The Waner brothers, Gus Suhr and Hal Rhyne of the Seals, Ray Kremer of the Oaks, Dick Bartell of Alameda High School and Joe Cronin from the Mission District in San Francisco were all recommended or signed by Devine. In 1929, Devine went to work for the Yankees and the Bay Area became the Yankees' territory.

Joe Devine, left, shakes hands with Joe Cronin after signing him to a contract with Pittsburgh.

## FROM PLAYGROUND TO PCL

The three local teams had an efficient network for scouting local talent. A prospect would be recommended by a coach or friend, or he would be spotted by somebody from the local team. An invitation would then be offered to the player to work out at the ball park before a game.

The field manager was then given a chance to evaluate the player in person. If the prospect impressed the right people, he would be offered a contract on the spot. In all probability, the player was a minor, in which case a parent's signature was required on the contract.

Because the competition was so intense for spots on the local rosters, most youngsters would jump at the chance to sign a contract. It was common for players—Gus Suhr and Frank Crosetti were examples—to drop out of high school to play ball. Billy and Ernie Raimondi both signed before graduation.

The Raimondi family's story was typical. Billy had to work to help support a large family when the Depression hit. As a result, he signed with the Oaks before he had graduated from high school. In 1935, when Billy hurt his arm and could not play, Ernie was forced to skip his senior year of eligibility at McClymonds High School. Ernie's signing with the Seals brought an enormous cry of tampering from the Oakland school district, but there were no other options open to the Raimondi family.

Because young players were thrilled just to be offered a contract, granting bonuses for signing was not necessary along the West Coast. Players also realized the benefits of signing locally. By signing with an independent Pacific Coast League team, that player's chances of being sold to a major league team were greater. If a player signed with a particular major league team, he could get stuck behind an established star and not be advanced for years. This was an effective trump card held by local owners.

Players even frequently played in league games without a contract. At the beginning or the end of a season, a young player would be allowed to play to see if he were worthy of being signed to a contract. Joe DiMaggio is the most dramatic example of this phenomenon. He played the last three games of the 1932 season with San Francisco without a contract, then signed a regular contract for the 1933 season.

## THE FARM SYSTEM

The scouting game changed dramatically during the 1930s when Branch Rickey developed the concept of a massive farm club network. His plan was to stockpile prospects of varying degrees of skill at each level of the minor league structure. If the Cardinals didn't own the farm club outright, they would negotiate a working system with it.

His network consisted of teams at every level of organized baseball, and it was not unusual to find several teams in the same league that had working agreements with the Cardinals. While conditions at some of the Cardinal parks were sub-standard, each park had first-rate lighting because Rickey insisted upon it.

His only invasion into the Coast League was to develop a working agreement with Sacramento in the late 1930s. The Cardinals' administration of the club came close to driving the franchise into receivership.

The other major league teams soon found it necessary to copy Rickey's grand plan. Major league scouts were hired to find prospects and sign them. This was a departure from the previous philosophy of purchasing star players out of the minor leagues. This new approach put enormous pressure on minor league teams to cooperate with the majors, lest they wither and die.

The Yankees hired George Weiss to build their farm system and Joe Devine was given broad responsibilities over most of the western states. Former Vernon Manager Bill Essick was the Yankees' scout in Southern California.

A bevy of bird dogs unearthed prospects and provided leads for Devine and Essick. Bird dogs normally worked on a small retainer, then received commissions only for successful signings.

The Cincinnati Reds had a distinguished scout in Charles Chapman, a professor of history at the University of California. Chapman was not the only collegian of influence. The Boston Red Sox seemed to have a sphere of influence at St. Mary's College, where most of the college's better players were coaxed to sign with the Red Sox.

The Brooklyn Dodgers were a later entry into the scouting derby, but they participated aggressively in the late 1930s. Charlie Wallgren and Justin Fitzgerald, two former Coast League players from the Bay Area, made the Dodgers competitive bidders for local talent.

Devine, in a 1932 letter to Yankees boss Ed Barrow, outlined the scouting network in the western states. He stated there were 28 major league scouts covering the entire area, four of them representing the Yankees. In 1938, in another letter to Barrow, Devine wrote how scouting had become more competitive. "Boston Americans now have three scouts working for them on the Pacific Coast. Detroit Americans also have three scouts. Cincinnati has about four, two of them being regular scouts and two understudies. St. Louis Cardinals have at least six. All the Coast League clubs have representatives also. In fact, there are more scouts than prospects."

Still, Devine managed to sign an abundance of prospects for the Yankees, and their rosters from the 1930s through the 1950s showed a predominance of Bay Area players on them.

But it had become more difficult for Devine and for the Coast League clubs to sign the top players.

For any scout to succeed, he had to develop a trusting relationship with his prospect. It was important for the scout to show an interest in the player, always to be there

giving him suggestions. Dr. Chapman of the Reds had his winter league team, the Orinda Reds. Fitzgerald of the Dodgers had the San Mateo Blues. Every other scout had some semi-pro team available to work out prospects.

## CUTTHROAT SCOUTING

The Yankees' working agreement with the Oaks in the 1930s allowed them to stage tryouts at Oaks Ball Park. This special arrangement was done discreetly because it was controversial and created animosity among other scouts. This wasn't unusual; friction among scouts was routine. In 1937, Chapman wrote to Devine in an effort to redefine some ground rules:

"Do you think it is ethical to attempt to sign a player under any of the following cases:
1. Where the player has already been signed by another scout, but with the contract as yet not filed.
2. Where the player has signed a written agreement with another scout, but not a contract.
3. Where a player is trying out in a camp conducted by scouts or another organization.
4. Where a player is a member of a team sponsored (of course, at some expense) by a scout of another organization."

Chapman found these practices immoral. He hoped the two competing organizations could agree to observe the spheres of influence of others. But it would not be that

Exhibition games featuring local heroes who had gone on to star in the major leagues became popular during the Depression. The games, against local teams, were benefits for service groups and boys clubs. This team, assembled in 1933, was managed by Ty Cobb.

A winter exhibition game in the early 1930s featured a team of local major league All-Stars (l-r): Tony Lazzeri, Ernie Bonham, Gus Suhr, Frank Crosetti and Lefty O'Doul. Note the 'All-Americans' logo on O'Doul's chest. This is the uniform worn on a barnstorming tour of Japan.

easy. In 1940, when the Dodgers held a series of tryout camps along the West Coast, the local teams and other major league organizations cried foul. Was this any worse than the Yankees-Oakland agreement to use the Oaks Ball Park for Yankee workouts and tryouts?

Possibly the most insidious aspect of scouting arose when a prospect and his parents would sign an agreement to sign with a team at a later date. A scout would negotiate a secret agreement with the youngster and his parents, committing themselves to the future signing. In these cases, a prospect with high school eligibility remaining would commit to the team, then sign when his eligibility was concluded. The family would receive cash for its commitment and everybody vowed to keep quiet about the agreement.

The secret agreement was nothing more than a ruse to lock up a player for future delivery. It was commonly used and, if discovered, would have threatened the player's high school and amateur eligibility.

In 1938, the commissioner's office issued a memorandum stating that any team found to sign a player to an undated contract would be fined and the player would be declared a free agent. This simply forced the scouts to be more creative in dealing with prospects because the practice continued.

Late in 1939, Larry Jansen was signed to an undated Red Sox contract by Ernie Johnson, which was promptly lost by the Red Sox front office. When Jansen wondered where he was to report the following spring, he asked a Seals scout what he should do. The commissioner's office was alerted and Jansen was declared a free agent. The Seals promptly signed him.

Jerry Coleman was signed to a secret contract by Devine while still in high school. The contract was not announced until after Coleman had finished his high school baseball career and had graduated. All the time, other scouts were making offers to Coleman and to his parents to get their signatures on a contract.

In early 1937, Devine signed East Bay youngsters Vince DiBiasi and Roy Pitter to secret agreements. DiBiasi still had three more years of school and Pitter had two. The boys received $1,000 immediately and obligated themselves to work under complete charge of Devine and Coltrin. Upon signing an official contract, each boy would receive an additional $1,000. If either went on to college, they would receive the money upon graduation and subsequent signing.

DiBiasi later signed another contract with the Yankees for the summer of 1938 and was optioned to Wenatchee in the Western International League. By 1942, he had worked his way to the Oaks on option before being inducted into the armed services for the remainder of World War II. After the war he had a fine career with the Portland Beavers.

Pitter was the finest pitching prospect Devine had ever seen. Devine's influence with Pitter's parents was a key factor in getting a commitment from Pitter to sign with the Yankees at a later date. While other scouts were hounding Pitter, Devine sat back and smirked. Later, Pitter was a disappointment to the Yankees. He advanced only as far as the Oaks for a few weeks at the start of the 1946 season before being cut.

Helping a prospect with college tuition was another tactic used by scouts to obligate a player for future delivery. Babe Pinelli's son, for example, was helped into Notre Dame by Devine and the Yankees. The colleges closed their eyes to this tactic; after all, it was saving them scholarship money.

Whenever a scout could help a player learn or improve, he had a chance of gaining influence over him. Bernie DeVivieros was one of the more effective scouts in this area. Respected as a teacher and an innovator, he was far ahead of his contemporaries in teaching bunting and base-running skills. Billy Raimondi credited DeVivieros with teaching him all the essential skills of the game.

DeVivieros was an Oaklander who learned the game on the sandlots of Oakland. He played baseball at Oakland Technical High School and was signed to a contract by Joe Devine in 1921. He played briefly with the Detroit Tigers in 1927 but was primarily a journeyman infielder for several PCL clubs, foremost being the Oaks.

Teaching came naturally to DeVivieros. In his tenure with the Oaks, he worked with several rookies who later had distinguished major league careers—Harry "Cookie" Lavagetto, Dario Lodigiani and Joe Gordon.

After a brief attempt at managing, DeVivieros accepted a scouting job with the Detroit Tigers and gained himself some baseball immortality. It was DeVivieros who popularized the bent-knee slide and helped revolutionize the style of chopping-down style of bunting, rather than hitting it squarely. The new style virtually guaranteed that the ball would hit the ground first and not be popped into the air, where it could be caught.

DeVivieros also copied Jimmie Reese's modifications to the popular Bill Doak-style glove. The Bill Doak glove was the one most favored by professional players, but Reese made it more efficient by connecting the fingers together with leather or shoe laces. This helped form a better pocket. DeVivieros copied the idea and induced his young Oaks teammates follow his lead.

While the prestige of being followed by a major league scout carried a certain amount of weight, the local teams had their clout as well. The thrill of playing before family and friends was important, especially when coupled with the possibility of being sold to a major league club. The Seals regularly guaranteed their signees a percentage of any sale to a major league club. The Oaks and the Missions weren't as consistent or as generous.

By the late 1930s, the Seals, Missions and the Oaks were now in direct competition with 16 major league clubs for control over Bay Area prospects. With the expanded use of signing bonuses reaching its zenith in the early 1950s, the death of independently operated minor league baseball teams became a foregone conclusion.

## BIDDING WARS BEGIN

The story of Ed Cereghino of Daly City illustrates the evolution of talent hunting in baseball. Cereghino was the classic example of the high school phenom. A strong right-hander, Cereghino had the physical and mental

Ed Cereghino was signed off a San Francisco sandlot.

attributes to accompany an outstanding fastball. He was on everybody's want list.

Cereghino's indoctrination to baseball was similar to millions of other youths. His father introduced him to the game and encouraged him, but the vacant lot also had its place. As there was no formal program to enter, the youngsters formed their own team, the Daly City Tigers, and searched for teams to play.

As he grew, more of Cereghino's games were played at Big Rec in Golden Gate Park. Here, scouts became aware of his talent.

Baseball protocol of the 1950s allowed scouts to introduce themselves to a prospect, but no overtures could be made until the player had graduated from high school. But one could always find a battery of scouts watching Cereghino's games.

In 1951, Cereghino led his Jefferson High School team to the league championship and he was the star of the annual East-West High School All-Star Game at Seals Stadium. Not only did Cereghino strike out 15 batters in a 5-1 win, but he hit a 380-foot home run. Stakes in the bidding war escalated.

When Cereghino graduated, scouts were now able to make bonus offers for his services. There were a half-dozen serious offers including a four-year scholarship to Stanford offered by the Pirates. The final two bidders were the Pirates, with a cash bid, and the Yankees.

Venerable Joe Devine hadn't lost his touch. He had befriended the family and had kept contacts low-key. When the Pirates had made their final offer, Devine sat down with the family and ultimately offered a $74,000 bonus contract. Ed Cereghino became property of the New York Yankees—but he never pitched for them and in fact never played in the major leagues.

The Seals were in the first year of a working agreement with the Yankees and they negotiated hard and successfully to have the 17-year-old optioned to them. The Seals and the rest of the PCL teams had been forced to sit on the sidelines during the negotiations. They had no other choice; that was how much baseball had changed.

But the Oaks and the Seals didn't give in without a fight. In head-to-head competition, several outstanding prospects signed locally in the late 1940s. The Oaks outbid major league teams to sign Billy Martin from Berkeley High, Ernie Broglio from El Cerrito High and Jackie Jensen from Oakland High and Cal.

The Oaks had also reached tentative agreement with St. Mary's All-American football star Herman Wedemeyer to play for the Oaks in 1948. Wedemeyer was under contract to play football with the Los Angeles Dons of the new All American Football Conference and

Dons G.M. Harry Thayer would not let the Oaks sign him.

The Seals continued to sign local high school players, with Al Fioresi and Joe Sprinz focusing heavily on the San Francisco schools. But the money belts tightened by 1950 and their scouting activities were heavily curtailed.

Jensen's 1949 signing by the Oaks' Brick Laws to a three-year, $75,000 deal was a real coup. It also upset major league general managers. Jensen's salary was to be minimal in 1949, but it had large increases built in for 1950 and 1951. Laws knew he would be able to sell Jensen before the contract was up, so the buyer would be obligated to pay the salary and the Oaks would profit by his sale.

The Yankees purchased the contracts of Jensen and Billy Martin, and Laws' ploy worked. Jensen went on to have an outstanding career, primarily with the Boston Red Sox, and Billy Martin was reunited with Casey Stengel.

But by 1950, searching the diamonds of the Bay Area had produced some serious trends. The Seals and the Oaks lost more products than they could sign. Joe Devine died, but his legacy was apparent on the Yankees' roster. Bay Area products signed or recommended by Devine included Joe DiMaggio, Bobby Brown, Jerry Coleman, Joe Gordon, Duane Pillette, Charlie Silvera, Andy Carey, Art Schallock, Bill Renna and Johnny Lindell.

Add to the list the names of Stengel, Frank Crosetti, Tony Lazzeri, Mark Koenig, Lefty Gomez, Martin, Jensen and Gene Woodling, and it is obvious why the Yankees traditionally had a strong fan base in the Bay Area.

Another trend developed in the 1950s, particularly in the East Bay: The Cincinnati Reds signed the finest black prospects from the area. George Powles, an outstanding teacher and coach at McClymonds High, had gained the confidence of black ballplayers at his school. He coached them, counseled them and opened up his home to them. His influence helped direct them to signing contracts with Bobby Mattick, the Reds' scout in Northern California. Included in this group were Frank Robinson, Curt Flood, Tommy Harper and Vada Pinson.

Bay Area baseball was on the decline. Little League had organized kids, television had diverted them and other sports had gained more of their interest.

In 1965, the Kansas City Athletics drafted the first player in the first free agent draft. His name was Rick Monday, who eventually moved to Oakland when the Kansas City franchise was transferred there. The significance of his selection was that it signaled a permanent change to the role of the baseball scout. His job now became one of a cross-checker of talent. If the Seals and Oaks franchises were still around, the draft would have meant the doors to outstanding prospects would be closed to them. Minor league teams weren't allowed to compete. Their lifeblood had been cut off. ❖

CHAPTER **14**

# THE MAN
# IN THE GREEN SUIT

Lefty O'Doul was simply the greatest hitter, greatest manager and greatest personality and bon vivant in the history of Bay Area baseball. He was also the champion of green clothing.

Ford Frick, who progressed from sportswriter to president of the National League, wrote of O'Doul when he was a star for the New York Giants, "Sing if you will of the glory of Schumacher and Ott, for they deserve it. But for myself, strike up an Irish melody, maestro, and make it lively and quick and twitching, for I would feign lift the lilting lyric to the man in the green suit."

Lefty first became notorious for his Irish green suit in 1929, when he was in the process of winning the National League batting crown for the Philadelphia Phillies with an average of .398. According to an account published in *The Saturday Evening Post* in the late 1940s, he wore the suit one day to Baker Bowl (the Phillies' ballpark) and got three hits, including a home run. The next day he also wore a green shirt and green tie, and proceeded to get four hits, including a triple and a homer. Then he added green socks and green underwear, adding two home runs, a triple and a double to his totals.

Given the superstitious nature of ballplayers every-

where, O'Doul became "The Man in the Green Suit," adding ever more greenery to his closet. Although his attire became more conservative as he matured, Lefty went to his grave known for the green; the inscription on his tombstone reads:

*"The man in the green suit."*
*He was here at a good time*
*and had a good time while he was here.*

### A SAN FRANCISCO HERO

Francis Joseph O'Doul was born in San Francisco on March 4, 1897, in what was then called Butchertown. Now Bayview-Hunters Point—notorious for crime—the neighborhood was just as dangerous before World War II. Because the Italians and the Irish were constantly at odds, Frankie developed a left jab early and could reputedly sling a mean brick before his age reached double digits.

As a seventh-grader in 1912 at Bay View Grammar School, Lefty learned the finer nuances of the manly sport

138

of baseball from his teacher, Miss Rozie Stolz. "It's probably the strangest story in baseball," O'Doul said later in life, "but a woman actually taught me to play the game. Sure, I had always played some ball ever since I learned to walk. But it was Miss Stolz, a teacher and manager of the Bay View ball team, who taught me the essential fundamentals of the game. She taught me to pitch, field and hit."

With a pitching style charitably described as "picturesque," O'Doul pitched the Bay View team to the city championship. Already the subject of the overblown sportswriters' rhetoric of the time, Lefty was pronounced the hero of the game.

At 16 he quit school and trudged off to work for the next three years in the slaughterhouse, just as his father had done. He always spent his days off pitching in the Sunday sandlot leagues. He grew to a strapping 6-foot, 180 pounds, and after a string of 17 straight wins for the Native Sons, was signed by the Seals in 1917.

That year he was farmed out, compiling an 8-6 record for Des Moines of the Western League. After a brief sojourn in the U.S. Navy at the beginning of 1918, he finished the year with a 13-9 mark for the San Francisco Seals. During the off-season he was drafted by the New York Yankees and in 1919 he became the instant Spring Training star. Just like that, Lefty O'Doul, then nicknamed "O'Doodle," was the talk of the Big Apple.


## ATTENTION, BUT NO RESULTS

Lefty's seemingly instant jump to the major leagues amazed many. He became a "Springer"—a Spring Training phenom. In those days a baseball team was covered by a sportswriter from each major newspaper in town, and New York City in the pre-television era had a dozen of them. Fred Lieb observed, "I recall of no recruit kid who ever looked better. He could hit, run and field, and had a great left-handed fastball. He looked like too good an all-around ballplayer to be utilized for pitching." Hy Daab of the *New York Evening Telegram* enthused, "We've got a potential Ty Cobb here . . ."

Some of the writers had a more jaundiced attitude, however. John Kieran said of Lefty's curve, "It fooled every batter—once." The writers actually formed a committee to inform Yankees Manager Miller Huggins that O'Doul should start in the outfield.

Ultimately Lefty threw a few too many curves and ended up with a sore arm. He didn't tell anyone until many years later, however, and made little of his few opportunities to play that year. The arm stayed sore for the rest of his playing career.

Spring Training in 1920 was Babe Ruth's first year with the Yankees. Wrote Lieb: "The Bambino, of course, was the big story, but even Babe had to share some of the spotlight with the personable young rookie from the coast,

Lefty O'Doul. The word 'charisma' wasn't popular at that time, but both Ruth and young O'Doul had gobs of it."

Mister O'Doodle became notorious for joining Ruth's private coterie, slipping peanut shells in Miller Huggins' pockets and developing an affinity for the racetrack.

As in the previous year, the sportswriters insisted O'Doul should be a full-time player and peppered Miller Huggins in print about it. This time Huggins answered

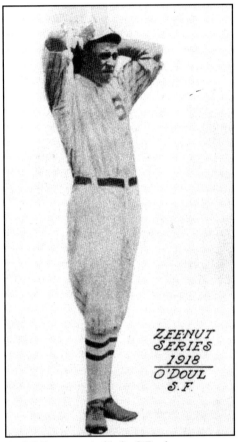

A 1918 Zeenut card of Lefty O'Doul.

back. "I appreciate the fine writers we have on this trip, but I just can't let you pick my lineup," he said. "Furthermore, you fellows have O'Doul confused. I told him regardless of what he reads in the papers, he should consider himself a pitcher, and concentrate on pitching. He once showed me a fastball that was as good as any in the big leagues."

Off the field, Lefty had a great time, but on the field 1920 was another washout. After two full years on the New York Yankees, all he had to show was eight innings pitched, a 0-0 record and a .214 batting average. Finally in 1921, Huggins shipped Lefty back to the San Francisco Seals on option.

Once again, Lefty O'Doul was the local hero. He was sensational in 1921. He compiled a 26-9 record with a 2.39

ERA, pitched more than 300 innings and hit .338 in a total of 74 games. The Seals fell only two games short of winning the Pacific Coast League pennant, and the colorful O'Doodle caught the next train back to the big leagues.

After a sensational third stint as the toast of San Francisco, 1922 was another major disappointment for Lefty. Although his innings pitched increased to 16, his record stayed at 0-0 and his at-bats totaled only nine. The Yankees finally threw in the towel and traded O'Doul as part of one of their annual raids on the Boston Red Sox.

Lefty, despite the support of Boston Manager Frank Chance, endured a fourth year as a mediocre major league pitcher in 1923. By the end of the season he had a 1-1 record with a 5.43 ERA, and his batting average was .143. After seven years in organized baseball and four years in the major leagues, Lefty O'Doul's career was a failure. He was released and ended up playing for the PCL Salt Lake City Bees in 1924.

## IT BEATS THE STOCKYARDS

O'Doul hadn't lost confidence in his athletic gifts. He also had a great desire to continue living the good life of a ballplayer. After all, he was the toast of San Francisco and the Pacific Coast League, and many players had spent a satisfying career playing in the PCL.

The 1924 season was Lefty's last as a pitcher. His arm was so sore he finished 7-9 and never pitched again except in jest. At the plate, he finally became all that people predicted of him, batting .392 in 140 games. In 1925, Lefty played through one of those endless PCL seasons, appearing in 198 games. He compiled league highs of 825 at-bats, 309 hits and 17 triples. He also knocked in 191 runs and had an average of .375. Despite these gaudy statistics, Lefty took a back seat to fellow San Franciscan and teammate Tony Lazzeri, a 21-year-old second baseman from Jackson Playground on Potrero Hill, who became the first professional ballplayer to hit 60 home runs in one— although admittedly long—season. Lazzeri also scored 202 runs, drove in 222 and hit .355. The Yankees bought Lazzeri's contract and added him to their starting lineup in 1926.

Owner William Wrigley of the Chicago Cubs personally acquired O'Doul's contract after the 1925 season for $30,000—half of what the Yankees paid for Lazzeri—and Lefty once again was off to a major league Spring Training. That same year, Joe McCarthy took over as manager, the first of 24 in a career that would lead to the Hall of Fame.

McCarthy, voicing a popular complaint about PCL sluggers, did not feel Lefty's fielding or arm were strong enough to earn him a spot on the team. Lefty was released by the Cubs before Spring Training was over and returned to play yet another season in the PCL.

The Salt Lake City team had moved to Hollywood in the meantime, so Lefty became a Hollywood Sheik in 1926. Even though he hit .338 with 223 hits and 116 RBIs, the season marked the low point in his PCL career. Unclaimed by all major league teams, Lefty, approaching 30, was sold for $7,500 to the San Francisco Seals.

He was home again, and Lefty captured the first PCL Most Valuable Player award and the $1,000 that went with it. He hit .378, led the league in hits with 278 and runs with 164, hit 33 home runs and drove in 158 runs. He even won the stolen base crown with 40.

Hundreds of Butchertown moppets gathered faithfully, game after game, in the left field stands to banter with their hero. In turn, he would stuff his back pockets with baseballs between innings and throw them to the kids as he assumed his defensive position. After several weeks of this, Charlie Graham, torn between the cost of the baseballs and noting how successful this was in cultivating the young fans, worked out a compromise with Lefty. Out of this came the first Lefty O'Doul "Kids Day" in early September, complete with giveaway minature bats and cheap baseballs. At this first event in 1927, 10,000 children were admitted for free and more than 20,000 fans packed the stands, the all-time record for Recreation Park.

As part of the fun Lefty planned to pitch the first two innings. But he wound up throwing a complete-game, two-hit, 3-0 shutout against the Missions. After the game Lefty climbed atop the grandstand roof and threw several dozens of personally autographed balls to the kids below.

## MORE A COMET THAN A STAR

By this point in his career, Lefty O'Doul had become a thoughtful student of the game. There have been better natural hitters than O'Doul, but few ever studied the science of batting so thoroughly. In other facets of his overall game, Lefty had his flaws. He was only an average fielder and his sore arm allowed base runners to take the extra base on him. As a *San Francisco Chronicle* sportswriter once observed, "He could run like a deer. Unfortunately, he threw like one, too."

Lefty always admitted he was never a great defensive player. He liked to tell this story about himself:

"I received a note from the owner of a midtown bar asking when it would be convenient for me to make good on a bouncing $20 check I was supposed to have written. Well, I hadn't written the check, but I decided I had better look into the matter. I pointed out to the owner the signature wasn't mine and he admitted he had never seen me before. I told him to forget it and tossed $20 on the bar. Then I told him the next time someone comes in here and says he's me, take him out back and have somebody hit a few balls to him. If he catches them, you know he's a phony."

The Seals honored Lefty O'Doul with a 'Kids Day' for his great season on September 27, 1927. O'Doul, who started the 'Kids Day' tradition, pitched a two-hit shutout.

## HIS GREATEST SEASON

With Lefty's charming personality and a knack for teaching, Charlie Graham had already decided that he wanted O'Doul to return to the Seals as manager once his playing career was over.

O'Doul's stance was a semi-crouch, with a compact stroke designed to meet the ball cleanly. Like Ted Williams after him, Lefty was blessed with superior eyesight. Sportswriter Red Smith called him "the most dedicated student of hitting in his day." Lefty was more modest: "Hitting was simple . . . I could see the spin of the ball. I'd know when the ball was halfway there whether it was going to be a curve or not."

The New York Giants drafted O'Doul after his MVP season and this time he did not waste his chance. Despite a severe ankle injury in that 1928 season, Lefty hit .319 in 114 games. But because of the ankle injury and Manager John McGraw's conclusion that Lefty couldn't hit left-handed pitching, O'Doul was traded in the off-season to the last-place Philadelphia Phillies for $35,000 and a journeyman outfielder.

By this time every adversity only strengthened Lefty. While the Polo Grounds was a feast for left-handed hitters—its right field foul line was a mere 258 feet away— the Baker Bowl was a veritable banquet. Only 280 feet down the right field line and 315 feet to right center, the Bowl's 40-foot-high right field fence resembled a handball court to O'Doul. "Mel Ott and I would practice nothing but pulling the ball for hour after hour," Lefty said.

In Philadelphia, "Every time I came to bat, I looked at that high fence in right field and felt sure I could hit it. If you take a tennis racquet and a ball and stand about 30 feet from a wall, you just know you can hit it every time. That's exactly the way I felt. I don't guess I hit that fence 20 times all season, but I'd meet the ball and line it out for

Lefty O'Doul receives his MVP trophy from Pacific Coast League President Harry Williams in 1927.

a hit. Maybe I would crack it over the infield, or occasionally over the fence for a homer, but that old fence sure gave me confidence."

Lefty O'Doul's 1929 season was one of those career years that only a Rogers Hornsby, Ted Williams or Babe Ruth would have at their peak. Lefty played the entire 154-game schedule, coming to bat 638 official times and collecting a National League-record 254 hits. The mark, which still stands today, was tied by the Giants' Bill Terry the following season.

O'Doul won the batting title with an average of .398, a mark that has been exceeded only twice in the following 64 years. He scored 152 runs, batted in 122 and hit 32 homers. Most eye-popping of all, he struck out only 19 times. No one else in the history of baseball has hit as many as 32 major league home runs with as few as 19 strikeouts.

His combined total of 330 hits and walks has not been matched in the National League this century; only Ruth and Williams were able to match it with any regularity in

O'Doul banged out a National League record 254 hits and hit a league-leading .398 for the Phillies in 1929.

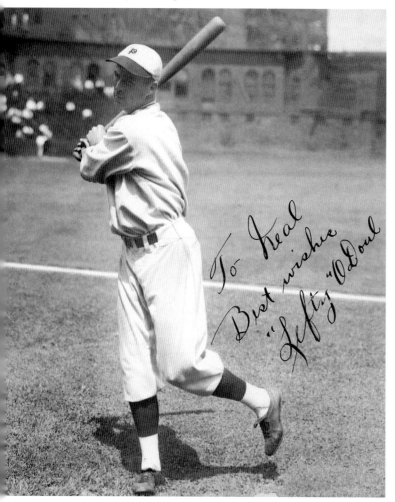

the American League. This meant Lefty was on base an average of 2.14 times every game for the entire season.

Part of what drove Lefty to such heights was his desire to show John McGraw that he could indeed hit left-handed pitching. After battering Giants pitching all year, O'Doul arrived at the last day of the season with 248 hits—two less than Hornsby's National League record set in 1922.

That last day was a doubleheader against McGraw's Giants, who started left-handed Hall of Fame pitcher Carl Hubbell in the first game and left-handed 14-game winner Bill Walker in the nightcap. Lefty went 4-for-4 in the opener, breaking Hornsby's record with a home run off Hubbell, and another 2-for-4 in the nightcap.

O'Doul followed that banner year with another excellent season in 1930, playing in 140 games despite a bout with tonsilitis. He collected 202 hits for a .383 average— good for just fourth in the league. However, the Phillies decided at this point to cash in, selling O'Doul to Brooklyn for three players and $75,000.

The dashing O'Doul was much the same hero in Flatbush as he had been elsewhere. He outfitted a boys team in green uniforms at his own expense and had his section of faithful fans in the stands. Lefty hit .336 in 1931 to finish fifth in the batting race. The next year, he won his second National League batting crown with a .368 average. Even his one-time detractor, John Kieran, was moved to write: "If a great catch is needed to save the game, who comes galloping across the sod to spear the wicked drive? Frank Merriwell O'Doul. If a homer is needed to tie the score, whose big bat hoists the ball over the far-flung wall? Larruping Lefty of San Francisco. With the teams locked in an extra-inning scramble, who slides over the plate in a whirl of dust with the winning run? Fearless Frank, the hero of Flatbush."

Lefty lasted another half-season with the Dodgers, as his age, 36, caught up with him rather quickly. O'Doul started the 1933 season with a string of 27 straight at-bats without a hit (once in Salt Lake City, he'd had 19 hits in 21 at-bats). After he broke the string with a single, he unabashedly got down on his knees and kissed first base. By mid-June he was still hitting only .252, and Brooklyn traded him across town to the New York Giants.

What a gift for Lefty. The Little Napoleon, John McGraw, had been replaced as manager in 1932 by Bill Terry, and O'Doul responded to the trade by hitting .306 as a backup outfielder and pinch-hitter. Lefty was one of the Giants' representatives in the first All-Star game that year and the Giants went on to win the National League pennant and World Series.

This created yet another career moment for Lefty. Behind 1-0 in the pivotal second game of the Series, O'Doul stroked a pinch-hit, bases-loaded single to drive in two runs, single-handedly turning the game around. During his earlier tenure with the Yankees, Lefty was so far down the bench he never got into a World Series game. His one at-bat with the Giants constituted his entire World Series experience.

O'Doul's major league career cruised to a gentle end in 1934. Appearing in 83 games, he hit .316 with nine home runs and 46 RBIs in only 177 at-bats.

His next two careers beckoned.

## AN ASSESSMENT

O'Doul ended his major league career with a lifetime batting average of .349, fourth highest of all-time behind only Ty Cobb, Rogers Hornsby and Shoeless Joe Jackson. But his standing is not listed in *The Baseball Encyclopedia* or any major league record books because he played in only 970 big league games, under the minimum of 1,000, and batted 3,264 times, under the minimum of 4,000. And he's not in the Hall of Fame, probably because four of his 11 major league years were spent as a third-string pitcher. On the other hand, there is no telling whether O'Doul would have developed as he did without the adversity he faced his first decade in professional baseball. Ted Williams expressed his feelings clearly in his autobiography, *My Turn at Bat*, on seeing Lefty for the first time in the PCL. "My first real look at an all-time great," Williams wrote. "The only thing that keeps O'Doul out of the Hall of Fame today is that he didn't play in the big leagues quite long enough. He deserves to be in there."

If not for his brilliant but short career as a player, Lefty O'Doul deserves Hall of Fame recognition at the least for his tremendous development of talent as a PCL manager, and especially for his role as the "American Father of Baseball in Japan."

One of Charlie Graham's smartest moves was immediately hiring O'Doul to manage the Seals in 1935. The investment of $9,000 to buy his release from the Giants paid handsome dividends.

Nobody got more publicity in San Francisco than Lefty. He was loved by everyone, and he came to personify the Seals. This was even true in 1935, 20-year-old Joe DiMaggio's third year with the Seals. DiMaggio easily won the Most Valuable Player trophy, and Lefty's reputation as a manager was instantly secured.

Lefty was versatile in his managerial style. He could be hands off or hands on, depending on the player. This applied to both Joe DiMaggio and a very youthful Ted Williams a year later. With Joe D, Lefty said, "I never taught him anything about hitting. He knew." With Williams, who came to O'Doul for advice in his rookie year with the San Diego Padres in 1936, Lefty simply told him, "Kid, the best advice I can give you is don't let anybody change you." Williams: "I was hitting around .270 in San Diego my first year and I went to O'Doul. All he said was to stay the way that I was, and that advice was invaluable at the time because Lefty knew I could make it, but I didn't until he told me."

Actually, Lefty's impact on DiMaggio was extremely subtle and long-lasting. He predicted in a *Collier's* magazine article in late 1935 that DiMaggio would be a national star within two years, and that he had the best throwing arm Lefty had ever seen. The shy teenager matured in his appearance and in his confidence just by being around the dapper O'Doul. Their friendship lasted many years and sustained them both in 1951 when O'Doul was on the verge of being fired and DiMaggio had just retired.

Without Joe DiMaggio, the 1936 Seals plunged to seventh place. But in 1937 they picked up again and spent the next three seasons in the first division, making the postseason playoffs. Coincidentally, their center fielder those three years was named Dom DiMaggio.

Lefty's talent for nurturing young players was in some ways more important than where the Seals finished in the standings because as the Depression continued, it became essential to sell players to major league clubs just to stay in business. Seals ownership was generally able to sell one player each year to big league clubs from 1936 to 1940, including the younger DiMaggio.

This 1938 portrait shows the personality of a man loved by all baseball fans in San Francisco, around the country, and even in Japan, where he is credited with introducing the game.

Joe DiMaggio gave Lefty O'Doul a great deal of credit for helping advance his career. The two remained friends until O'Doul's death. Below, O'Doul could still hit even as a player-manager with the Seals.

Bespectacled and smaller than his brothers, Dom successfully made the jump from sandlot to PCL. His comments about Lefty as a manager and instructor of young talent are equally generous: "As the 1939 season began I was 21 years old and 20 pounds heavier, at 171, but my weight wasn't necessarily the main reason for my continued improvement. That was due to Lefty O'Doul, the Seals' manager.

"When Joe was playing for the Seals, Lefty helped Joe raise his average 57 points in one season, to .398. I had exactly the same experience with him. He worked on my hitting techniques and philosophy, and my average jumped to .360 in 1939.

"He was far and away the finest hitting instructor that ever put on a baseball uniform. He could spot anything you were doing wrong in a minute and show you how to correct it.

"Lefty's primary emphasis in teaching hitting was to encourage the player to develop strong wrists so he could wait on the pitch better, something Ted Williams has been preaching all his life.

"Another of O'Doul's basics was to look for the fastball on every pitch, a practice now adhered to by most hitters and hitting instructors. If you're ready for the fast ball, you can always adjust your swing and wait a split second longer if you see it's a curve, but the reverse doesn't work.

"Whatever success I had as a batter I owed to Lefty."

Lefty's style as a manager, and particularly as a third base coach, mirrored his personality. Flamboyant and a gambler, one minute he'd be capturing floating suds from the brewery behind Seals Stadium, the next he'd be waving runners around third with his giant white handkerchief. As one jokester said, the path from third base to home plate was piled high with the ghosts of dead Seals who'd been cut down after O'Doul had waved them around. No matter how well the team was doing, the charismatic Lefty entertained the fans.

From 1940 through 1942 the Seals slipped again into the second division, but beginning in 1943 the team began an unparalleled run of success—six straight years in the playoffs and four straight years winning them. Lefty's team won the pennant as well in 1946, and tied for first before losing a playoff to the Los Angeles Angels in 1947. Lefty's second-place 1948 team won 112 games but was aced out by Casey Stengel's "Nine Old Men" on the Oakland Oaks.

Lefty found himself once again thrust into the national spotlight. He became known as a manager who could win by taking a hodgepodge of veterans hanging on for another season, kids just breaking in, run-of-the-mill players not going anywhere and big league rookies back for some seasoning. Sorting out this group each year, creating a winning team, recognizing true talent and polishing it were all attributes which Lefty possessed.

At a 1939 game at Oaks Ball Park, O'Doul shakes hands with Oaks Manager Johnny Vergez. Umpire Babe Pinelli is wearing the chest protector.

O'Doul, named by *The Sporting News* several times as minor league Manager of the Year, was offered a handsome salary plus a portion of the club profits, pushing his income towards the $50,000 level, far in excess of most major league managers. This was enough to keep him in San Francisco despite a series of offers from the Giants, Phillies and Yankees. Indeed, Casey Stengel, upon moving from the Oakland Oaks to the Yankees in 1949, said, "That feller out there in Frisco is the best manager there is. Why isn't he up there in the majors where he belongs?"

O'Doul's second pennant and fourth straight playoff win came in 1946. Larry Jansen became Lefty's second straight 30-game winner as well as the last one in PCL history in that championship season. The next year, Jansen compiled a 21-5 record for the New York Giants.

Jansen is one of a legion of O'Doul's players who credited Lefty with molding his performance: "Although Lefty was criticized for leaving a pitcher in too long, I believe O'Doul's thinking was always to develop and let you work out of a jam. He wanted to see you grow. I always appreciated that he would give you a shot to get out of it. I think he did it to see if you had courage—what kind of a battler you were."

Added Yankees star Gene Woodling, who returned in to the Seals in 1948 and posted a league-leading .385 batting average: "I don't know of anybody who didn't like Lefty or didn't love playing for him. A player doesn't want to go back to the minor leagues, but it turned out to be a heck of a break for me."

Serious events clouded the concluding days of the

1948 season. Lefty's long-time friend Charlie Graham died. Paul Fagan assumed control of daily operations, appointing O'Doul vice president and general manager. It soon became apparent the two had diffferent views of the baseball world.

Attendance nosedived over the next several years as television and suburbanization combined to make serious inroads. Major league owners had no intention of elevating the PCL but put off the league by waffling around the subject for several more years. Fagan grew disillusioned with the failure of his PCL ambitions and O'Doul became bored with the on-field activities of a manager. The "what-have-you-done-for-me-lately?" fans took to calling Lefty by a new nickname, "Marblehead." It was not a happy situation, and after an eighth-place finish in 1951, Lefty's long association with the Seals came to an end.

Lefty now began the second phase of his Pacific Coast League managerial career, taking over the San Diego Padres from 1952 through their pennant-winning season of 1954.

Brought back to the Bay Area as manager of the Oaks in 1955 in a vain attempt to save the Oakland franchise, Lefty migrated north in 1956 as the team was sold and moved to Vancouver. His final year as a PCL manager was 1957 with Seattle.

Major league baseball invaded the West Coast in 1958. Lefty's interest in managing had waned to the point where he was taking separate flights from his players on road trips. He opened "Lefty O'Doul's," a bar and eatery on Geary, and signed on as hitting instructor for the newly arrived San Francisco Giants.

## AMERICA'S GAME COMES TO JAPAN

"O'Doul 'Greatest American' to Japanese." This headline from *The Sporting News* in a 1958 article summed up what many feel is Lefty's greatest accomplishment, bringing baseball to Japan. It began with visits to Japan in 1931 while he was a major league star and included more than a dozen more trips by "O'Dou-San" to his adopted land in the Far East.

The Herb Hunter Major League All-Stars made its third barnstorming tour of Japan in 1931. The personable O'Doul got acquainted with so many Japanese that he decided to return in 1932 with Hunter, Moe Berg and Ted Lyons to coach the leading college baseball league, the Tokyo Big-Six.

Although the Americans had thrashed the Japanese teams in 1931, they were invited to return in 1934. Japan insisted on America's very best as the only way their players could learn the skills necessary to close the gap. As a result, Babe Ruth, Jimmie Foxx and Lou Gehrig were on the team. O'Doul was a member of that group, and after the series he remained to serve as chief advisor to

Matsutaro Shoriki, helping him set up the first professional team in Japan. At Lefty's suggestion the team was named the Tokyo Giants, complete with pinstripes. When the Tokyo Giants came to the U.S. on a barnstorming tour in early 1935, Lefty helped them out despite his new managerial duties with the Seals.

O'Dou-San became a living legend in Japan. Although there was a break of 14 years until he returned in 1949 with the San Francisco Seals for a series of games, Lefty and the team were overwhelmed by their reception, as was a reporter from *The New York Times* covering the event. Under the headline "Tokyo Thousands Cheer Seals Visit," the October 13, 1949 story begins:

"The San Francisco Seals arrived today to a thunderous welcome for their 'bicycle series' with Japanese and GI baseball teams.

"Tens of thousands lined some five miles of city streets to cheer the visiting Pacific Coast Leaguers—first athletes to come here since the war. It was a bigger throng than even Emperor Hirohito has attracted in recent years."

Despite a seventh-place finish in the PCL, a squad of 20 players and various team officials were treated to a month-long, 11-game trip. The team played before crowds approaching 50,000, even including a Lefty O'Doul Kids Day with more than 40,000 schoolchildren watching a game between the Seals and a Big-Six All-Star team. Their contest in Osaka atttracted 106,000 to Koshien Park, which may be the largest crowd ever to see a baseball game.

The team also met with General Douglas MacArthur during the trip. "We met MacArthur at a luncheon just after we arrived," pitcher Con Dempsey said. "He was an amazing man. When we were introduced to him, he knew

After bringing American players to Japan in 1935, 'O'Dou-San' receives a trophy from Japanese baseball officials as a thank you.

came to the plate and hit a long fly to right field for a sacrifice fly and the game-winning RBI.

DiMaggio came to the plate 257 times during his streak and hit safely 104 times for a .405 average. Through the remainder of the season, young Joe batted .307 and wound up with a season average of .340. He led the league with 169 RBIs and led the Seals with 28 home runs. It was Joe's first full season of professional baseball and he was barely 18 years old.

DiMaggio's presence in the lineup had great impact on road attendance. While Seals home attendance picked up less than 10,000 from the year before, attendance rose 130,000 around the league in 1933. It dropped 230,000 in 1934 when DiMaggio was sidelined by a freak injury.

DiMaggio had gotten off to a strong start. In June, he took a jitney cab to his sister's home for dinner. Without realizing it, his foot went to sleep, and when he got out of the cab his knee buckled; he had sustained torn ligaments. Joe tried to play through the injury by coming off the bench as a pinch-hitter. But it was severe and he was too valuable a commodity to risk sustained damage. As a result, Joe was fitted for a full leg cast.

He played 101 games that year and batted .341 with just 12 home runs and 69 RBIs. For Graham, visions of a $100,000 payout for DiMaggio were gone. Scouts still viewed DiMaggio as an exceptional talent, but most backed away from what they considered damaged goods. Not so with the Yankees. They arranged for a discreet knee examination, where the doctor found normal recovery of the knee.

Graham settled for $25,000 and five players, three sent outright to the Seals. DiMaggio was to remain with San Francisco for the 1935 season and report to the Yankees in 1936.

Joe's return to the Seals for the 1935 season became an unforseen blessing for him when Lefty O'Doul signed to manage the team. Joe's statistics for the 1935 season were irrefutable testimony to the full recovery of his knee as well as to O'Doul's teaching. DiMaggio hit .398 with 270 hits, 34 home runs, 173 runs scored and 154 RBIs. Plus, the Seals won the PCL pennant.

DiMaggio's major league career spanned 13 years, with three years lost to the Army during World War II. Joe won three American League Most Valuable Player awards but his greatest accomplishment was his 56-game hitting streak in 1941.

DiMaggio's statistics do not reflect the cult-like devotion that has followed him; none of his statistics place him high on the all-time lists. After a series of painful injuries, Joe wanted to leave the game before his skills were further eroded, so he retired after the 1951 World Series with nine World Championship rings.

## YOUNG DOMINIC

Dominic Paul DiMaggio was the last of the DiMaggio family to sign a professional baseball contract. Dom was not the natural his older brothers were; he was slight of build and wore glasses—the latter usually being enough to turn off the large majority of baseball scouts.

After graduating from Galileo High School, Dom went to work at the Simmons Bed Factory, playing industrial league baseball on the weekends. After a couple of years on the job, Dominic matured, filled out a bit and became a more skilled player.

He attended a tryout camp at Seals Stadium during the winter of 1936 co-sponsored by the Seals and the Cincinnati Reds. In 1937 at age 20, DiMaggio made the Seals out of Spring Training. He played a short center field for the Seals and covered the broad expanses of Seals Stadium gracefully. He led all outfielders with 29 assists in 1938 and 27 the following year. As a hitter, not much was expected from him. In 1937, his rookie season, DiMaggio hit a relatively punchless .306 in 140 games, scoring 109 runs. In 1938, he hit .307 with more than 70 percent of his 202 hits being singles.

After two years of playing for O'Doul, Dom had a big year in 1939. His batting average jumped to .360, second only to San Diego's Dominic Dallesandro at .368. DiMaggio muscled up to hit 14 home runs, 18 triples and 48 doubles. His homers and triples were more than his combined totals from the previous two seasons.

To top things off, DiMaggio was voted the league's Most Valuable Player for 1939 and was sold, along with pitcher Larry Powell, to the Boston Red Sox for $95,000 and some players.

"In 1939 Dominic won at least 40 games for us," O'Doul said in 1941. "He dumped bunts, roped doubles and triples, stole bases, caught drives in the outfield that no human should catch, threw out runners at third and home and in general behaved like a champion.

"For one season, he did more things for his team than any player I know did for his team in a single year . . . Yet not one scout recommended Dominic because he looked frail and wore glasses. Joe Cronin of the Red Sox took him on a gamble."

Dom enjoyed an extremely successful 10-year career with the Red Sox, interrupted by a three-year term in the military during the World War II. Playing in the same outfield with Ted Williams, Dominic continued his unique style of positioning himself at an angle to the hitter while manning center field. He felt this helped him get a better break on a ball hit in his direction.

The DiMaggio brothers never had the opportunity to play together professionally on the same team. Vince and Joe were on the Seals in 1932 and Dominic and Joe were members of several American League All-Star teams in the post-war era. All three brothers came together in 1956 when the Seals Old-Timers traveled to Wrigley Field in Los Angeles to play the Angels Old-Timers. Vince started in left field, Dominic in center and Joe in right. The Angels won the game, but the focus of the crowd was on the brothers in the outfield.

Joe DiMaggio was enshrined in Baseball's Hall of Fame in 1955. Dominic's enshrinement is not expected, but in the early 1950s, a song lyric especially popular in Boston went, "Who is better than his brother, Joe? Dominic DiMaggio."

## OAKLAND'S RAIMONDI CLAN

The Raimondi family was to Oakland what the DiMaggios were to San Francisco. Both families were of Italian background, and both had large numbers; the Raimondi clan totaled seven.

None of the Raimondi brothers played in the major leagues, but their contributions to the Pacific Coast League were huge.

Billy Raimondi was a star catcher for McClymonds High School in West Oakland. This was the same school catcher Ernest Lombardi had attended a few years earlier and the same one Frank Robinson and basketball star Bill Russell would attend in a few more years.

Billy signed with the Oaks while still in school. Where else could a 17-year-old youngster receive a salary of $150 a month during hard times?

Billy was optioned to Phoenix in the Arizona-Texas League for his baptism to professional baseball. His manager there was long-time Oaks player Louie Guisto. Raimondi batted .304, playing against many older players

Al, Ernie and Billy Raimondi.

Billy Raimondi and Walt Raimondi suit up for an Oakland Oaks game.

whom he would face in the Pacific Coast League later on in his career.

In 1932, he was returned with a cut in pay to the A-T League with Bisbee-Douglas. The league folded before the end of its regular season and Raimondi returned to Oakland as a reserve.

Raimondi filled in capably, proving to be a solid field captain and an intelligent handler of pitchers. In 1934, he took command behind the plate for the Oaks and didn't relinquish that role until after the 1948 season.

The closest he got to the majors was in the mid-1930s. After 1935, the Yankees exercised their option on the contracts of Raimondi and outfielder Bernie Uhalt, who had become collateral for a loan made by the Yankees to Cookie Devincenzi. Cookie couldn't make his payment, so the two players became property of New York. Raimondi was sold to Cincinnati and aggravated a sore shoulder during Spring Training, which sidelined him for the season and effectively ended his chance at making the Reds. Billy came home and went to work in a cigar store. With Billy not drawing a baseball salary, the Raimondis again faced financial problems, forcing the family to decide that Ernie, 16, having just finished his junior year at McClymonds, should enter professional baseball.

Ernie, with Billy serving as his advisor and guardian, signed with the Seals in 1936 for 1937 delivery. It was agreed Ernie would be available for night games and weekends only. He was expected to continue attending school and graduate with his class.

Ernie was optioned to Tacoma in 1937 and had a solid year in the field and at the plate, batting .339. He remained with the Seals in 1938-39 but never won the third base job. Ultimately, he was let go and signed with the Oaks for 1940. Again, he was forced to share third

base, this time with manager Johnny Vergez. The same pattern was repeated in 1941. At age 22, in 1942, Ernie Raimondi was a six-year veteran of professional baseball but still not a full-time player.

With mobilization of the war effort in full swing, Ernie was inducted into the Army. He was shipped to Europe where he was killed in action. To memorialize him after the War, Bayview Field in West Oakland was renamed Ernie Raimondi Playground.

## STAR CATCHER OF THE PCL

After staying out of baseball throughout 1936, Billy Raimondi made a complete recovery from his arm problems and was assigned to Oakland for 1937. The following year, Devincenzi acquired his contract from the Yankees and Raimondi was with the Oaks to stay.

Throughout the late 1930s and the early 1940s, Billy was widely acknowledged as the best catcher in the Coast League despite his small stature and the fact he wore glasses. Many scouts felt he would have been an excellent No. 3 catcher in the major leagues, but Devincenzi was always too reluctant to let him go.

Vergez was fired following the 1943 season after five years as manager. He was very popular with the players and the fans but he had only one winning season.

He was replaced by Dolph Camilli, whose relationship with his players was never smooth. After a season and a half, Camilli was let go by Devincenzi, who selected Billy as his replacement. That was a popular choice and the Oaks played well, but it just wasn't right for him. Billy was by no means ready to relinquish his catching duties. At the end of the season, Raimondi informed Devincenzi he would not return as manager in 1946, but wished to continue as a player for the Oaks.

Raimondi continued behind the plate into the 1949 season. He was sharing the backstop duties a little more now with Eddie Kearse, Eddie Fernandes, Gene Lillard or Ernie Lombardi, but Raimondi was still considered the best in the league.

In 1949, Charlie Dressen was hired to replace Casey Stengel as manager. Dressen initiated a housecleaning that sent Raimondi to the Sacramento Solons for catcher Frankie Kerr. In the eyes of Oaks fans, this was unquestionably the worst trade ever made by Oakland. To them, Billy Raimondi personified the Oakland Oaks.

In 1950 with the Solons mired in the cellar, Manager Red Kress and coach Lindsay Brown were fired. Popular veteran Joe Marty was appointed manager and Raimondi became his coach. At the end of the season, Marty returned to player status, which made Raimondi expendable. He was released, but the Los Angeles Angels quickly signed him and Raimondi played another season and a half in Los Angeles before he retired.

For almost two decades Raimondi was the class of the league behind the plate. He was an All-Star 16 times and he caught 100 or more games for 16 years. Offensively, he was a .270 hitter with more than 1,800 Coast League hits. In 1951, he was inducted into the Helms Hall of Fame, the Coast equivalent to Cooperstown.

## MORE RAIMONDI STARS

Al Raimondi pitched and Billy Raimondi caught for the Oaks in 1944 and 1945. Al, a year older than Ernie, had tryouts with the Missions in 1936 and 1937. He moved with the team to Hollywood in 1938, again being optioned out before the season started. In 1939, the Stars released him and he was picked up by Portland. In 1944 Al went 2-4 with a 2.86 ERA in 63 innings. He was used mainly as a reliever in 1945, going 3-2 and posting a 3.21 ERA in 56 innings.

Walt, the youngest of the Raimondi brothers, started out as a shortstop. His career in the Coast League was brief. Walt started for the Oaks in 1943 before he went into the service for the rest of the war. He broke his ankle shortly after the war ended and lost some mobility, so he switched to the mound and was optioned to Phoenix for 1947, where he was a teammate of Billy Martin's. He was fast and a favorite with the fans, but didn't have enough to make it back to the Coast League.

## CHICK AND THE HAFEY COUSINS

At the same time the DiMaggios and the Raimondis were breaking into the Pacific Coast League, the Hafeys of Berkeley were getting a substantial amount of attention. Charles "Chick" Hafey, cousin to the Hafey boys, had broken in with the St. Louis Cardinals in 1924. Chick had an illustrious and sometimes volatile career and was inducted into Baseball's Hall of Fame in 1971.

Daniel, Thomas and Wilbert Hafey would all follow their cousin into professional baseball, and all would have their opportunities in the major leagues.

Chick Hafey's career set a high standard for the boys to aim for, but was not the only baseball career in the family. The boys' uncle, Al, pitched briefly for Walter McCredie's Portland Beavers. A third uncle, Jim, managed the Shattuck Avenue Merchants and other winter league teams, for whom the youngsters served as bat boys.

The Hafey brothers were all born in Berkeley, but the family moved to North Oakland when they were still young and the boys attended Oakland Technical High School. Daniel "Bud" Hafey was an outfielder with a strong arm and power in his bat. When he was 15, Bud started in left field for the Oakland American Legion Juniors, winners of the 1928 World Championship. In

1930, his coach, Roy Sharp, got him a tryout with the Oaks, who released him, saying he was too young.

Bobby Coltrin of the Missions immediately signed him for the 1931 season. Hafey was optioned to Tucson and in mid-July he was recalled to the Reds where he played in 61 games, batting .293 with six home runs and nine doubles.

Hafey was with the Reds for the next three years generally as their regular left fielder, but often playing center field and occasionally filling in at third base and even second base. Bud hit .294 in 1932 and .295 in 1933.

In 1934, with Gabby Street managing the Reds, Hafey blossomed, hitting .322 with 16 home runs. Just 22, Hafey then advanced to the major leagues when the Chicago White Sox acquired his contract.

Bud spent two years in the major leagues before being shipped back to the minors. He played part of the 1938 season with Sacramento before being sold to Knoxville in the Southern Association. At Knoxville he was united with his younger brother, Tom. In 1939, both were in the major leagues.

Tom was a year younger than Bud, but the age difference was enough to separate them from playing together on the same amateur teams. Tom didn't have the youthful successes of his brother. In fact, his growth spurt didn't come until his senior year at Oakland Tech. He only made Coach Al Kyte's varsity team his last year, after Bud left.

Tom used to accompany Bud to San Francisco for Missions games and he would shag balls in the outfield before the game. After he graduated, Tom signed with the Missions and played briefly in the outfield and pinch-hit for the 1934 Reds, batting .182 in 23 games.

In 1935, Oakland released third baseman Eddie Mulligan who was promptly signed by the Reds. This allowed the Reds to shift Harry Rice to left field, making Tom expendable. With Depression economics a consideration, Tom was given his outright release.

Tom was immediately signed by the Cleveland organization with a bonus. During the next four years, Tom played minor league ball east of the Mississippi. He was acquired by the New York Giants for the 1939 season after leading the Southern Association with 24 homers in 1938.

Hafey's career was interrupted by World War II. He was working at the Richmond shipyards in 1944 as part of the war effort when he received a call from Bill DeWitt of the St. Louis Browns. After a few games with the Browns, he was traded to the Washington Senators. He refused to report and was ultimately released under edict from the commissioner's office.

Devincenzi immediately contacted him to play with the Oaks, for whom he played the next five years. During this period, Tom took up pitching. He had pitched a few times earlier in his career, but it was usually in a mop-up capacity. In 1945 Raimondi asked Hafey if he could start a game in order to give the Oaks staff a breather. Tom won, then won three more before getting shelled. It was back to the outfield.

When Stengel came to Oakland in 1946, Hafey was used almost exclusively as a pitcher. Johnny Babich was Stengel's pitching coach and had a good deal of control over Stengel's use of the pitching staff. Hafey was 6-8 with a 2.63 ERA in 1946. The next season Hafey was 7-6, but his game fell apart. He allowed more than a hit per inning and his ERA skyrocketed to 6.15.

Before roster cutdown time in 1948, the Oaks traded Hafey to Sacramento for another veteran, Joe Marty. Marty, a long-time Sacramento resident, refused to go; so did Hafey. The trade was canceled and Hafey was released. The Angels picked him up, and at the end of a 7-11 season, Tom retired from baseball.

But before he retired, he was able to pitch with his brother, Will, for a season. Will Hafey, 10 years Tom's junior, was a star first baseman on Kyte's Oakland Tech team and would sneak into Oaks Ball Park to watch his brother pitch.

After Will was discharged from the Navy, Tom brought the Oaks and Will together. Besides a modest bonus, Will was to receive a percentage of the price if he were sold to a major league club. Of the three brothers,

The Hafeys. Bud (right) was the oldest. He would bring his younger brothers, Tom (below) and Will (bottom right) to the park where they would shag fly balls before the games. Their cousin Chick, a Hall of Famer, set a standard for the boys.

Will was the best hitting prospect even though he was primarily a pitcher by trade.

After spending 1946 at Idaho Falls in the Pioneer League, Will was ready for Oakland. In 1947, Will pitched in 30 games with a 7-5 record and played an additional 57 games as an outfielder and pinch-hitter. Stengel used him sparingly in the early going, but by mid-season Will Hafey and Gene Bearden were the main reasons Oakland remained in contention.

Good things happened to Will in 1948. Stengel showed confidence by choosing Hafey as his Opening Day pitcher. In the first half of the season, Hafey was the workhorse of the staff. And Casey would often bat him in the middle of the lineup rather than in the traditional ninth spot. In May, Brick Laws sold Hafey's contract to the Cleveland Indians for 1949 delivery.

Stengel may have been Will's downfall, however. At mid-season, Hafey pitched a complete-game victory on a Tuesday and was asked to pitch one inning in relief on Thursday. He stayed in and finished the game, but his arm didn't recover from the strain.

When Hafey reported to the Cleveland Spring Training camp in 1949, he faced a series of obstacles; namely, Bob Lemon, Early Wynn, Bob Feller, Mike Garcia, Gene Bearden and Satchel Paige. The Indians were the defending World Champions. However, Hafey's arm still wasn't right and he was optioned to San Diego where he found the Padres brimming with pitching talent. Shortly thereafter, he was sent to Fort Worth in the Texas League.

He retired from baseball during the 1950 season, but tried a comeback as an outfielder with Oakland in 1951 and with the Seals in 1952. Neither trial was successful.

## BROTHERS ALL

In a broad sense, all of the Pacific Coast Leaguer players were brothers. There was a truly unique camaraderie which existed in the PCL. Whether they were the Waners or the DiMaggios going on to big league stardom; a minor league legend like a Jolley, Eckhardt or Boone passing through; or a Billy Raimondi spending his entire career in the league, all of them were bonded forever by playing ball and having fun in the Pacific Coast League. ❖

# CHAPTER 16

# WARTIME BASEBALL

The 1938 season was the nadir of the Oakland Oaks franchise. Under Edward "Dutch" Zwilling, the Oaks finished eighth, winning only 65 games and finishing 50 games behind the champion Angels. The team was terrible. Zwilling lost enthusiasm for his job and, with several weeks remaining in the season, was notified his contract would not be renewed.

Cookie Devincenzi signed Johnny Vergez to a contract to manage and play the infield in 1939. Vergez had been a favorite in Oakland when he played at Oaks Ball Park 10 years earlier and his selection as the new manager was a popular one. Vergez was a good teacher and motivator and the players liked him. When Vergez played the Oaks seemed to perform with more inspiration. At one juncture he was injured and missed a series of games and the Oaks slumped. When he returned the team started winning again.

Vergez hired William "Duke" Kenworthy as his coach. The colorful, scrappy Kenworthy had managed at Portland but was presently in retirement living in Oakland. Kenworthy became Oakland's first official coach—paid only to coach and not to play. He was a good teacher and a strong presence on the bench while Vergez was in the field.

The Oaks still finished seventh, but they were competitive and weren't beaten before the first pitch was thrown, as in 1938. The fans started returning to the park. Attendance for 1939 was 165,000, up more than 71,000 over the previous season.

Devincenzi and Vergez overhauled the pitching staff, the team's most glaring weakness in 1938. Oakland was fortunate to purchase Jack Salveson from the pitching-rich Angels for $1,000. Ben Cantwell was acquired from Baltimore for $1,500. In 1939 Salveson finished at 12-15 with 233 innings pitched, while Cantwell went 13-15 in 227 innings. "Grandpappy" George Darrow and Leroy Herrmann signed with the team as free agents, and Ralph Buxton was obtained from the Philadelphia Athletics in the sale of Bob Joyce.

Joyce had been the only bright spot on the dismal 1938 aggregation. His record was 18-18, but seven of his wins were shutouts. Three of his losses were by 1-0.

Buxton finished the 1939 season at 13-10 with a 2.88 ERA in 200 innings pitched. His was the only winning percentage and the best ERA on the club. All of these pitchers, except Herrmann who was released, were around in 1940.

Smead Jolley joined the Oaks in 1938 after Stars Manager Wade Killefer released Jolley, Oskie Slade and Boom Boom Beck with one sweep of his pen. Jolley had been relegated to occasional pinch-hitting appearances, and it was obvious Killefer felt he was through. Jolley became a fix-

159

ture, literally, in right field for the Oaks. His legs were gone but his bat wasn't. Jolley led the league in hitting at .350, but was 36 at-bats short of the required 450 appearances necessary to qualify for the batting championship. The Stars' Bernie Uhalt was the official batting champion at .332.

In 1939 Jolley's batting average slipped to .309 as he played in 140 games. He was the regular right fielder but was often replaced in late innings for defensive purposes. The loss of his skills was evident to anyone who had seen him in his prime . . . and he never had been a good outfielder.

The Oaks let Jolley go at the end of the 1939 season. He went to the Western International League for 1940 and 1941 and led the league in hitting both years before he retired.

## OAKS RETURN TO PLAYOFFS

Johnny Vergez's second year showed how consistency can have positive effects on productivity. With Vergez's input, Devincenzi made a few changes to bring a deeper team to Oakland in 1940. Along with the departure of Jolley, Joe Abreu was peddled to Fort Worth, allowing Vergez to move from shortstop to third base, his natural position. Reserve outfielder Al Browne was also sold to Portland.

Henry "Cotton" Pippen was purchased from Detroit for $7,500 and Joe Mulligan was acquired from Toronto for $2,500. Both were experienced pitchers with limited time in the major leagues. Devincenzi's final acquisition was Stanley Corbett, a pitcher with Fort Worth in 1939. Corbett was one of several players granted free agency by Judge Landis for having been "stockpiled" in the minor leagues. Devincenzi won the battle to sign him with a $2,500 bonus.

Oakland and San Diego battled for first place over the first two months of the season, but Seattle swept a seven-game series from the Oaks at mid-season and moved steadily away from the field. The Rainiers won their second straight crown while Oakland finished an encouraging third, 94-84, 18 games off the pace.

In the playoffs for the first time since 1936, the Oaks fell to Seattle in the first round, four games to one. Seattle was then taken to seven games before outlasting San Diego in the playoff finals.

## THE SAGGING SEALS

Across the bay, the Seals weren't very competitive in 1940. O'Doul's club was never in the pennant race, finishing seventh at 81-97. The team had sold Dominic DiMaggio and Larry Powell to the Red Sox and had dropped aging pitchers Louie Koupal and Bill Shores along with injury-prone first baseman Harley Boss. The popular Boss had suffered a series of injuries, and his release opened a spot for young Ferris Fain.

As part of the DiMaggio-Powell deal, the Seals received outfielder Johnny Barrett and pitchers Frankie Dasso and Wilfred LeFebvre. The Seals also signed veteran first baseman Jack Burns as insurance at first.

The Chicago Cubs were eager to acquire Seals infielder Harvey Storey and sent pitcher Al Epperly as part-payment. Storey, sold for 1941 delivery, remained with the Seals for more experience.

Storey severely injured his leg early in the campaign and missed the remainder of the season. When he went out, Storey was batting .323 through 63 games. Powell, returned by the Red Sox for more seasoning, was 12-7 and Eddie Stutz had an excellent year at 19-14. The remainder of the staff had disappointing seasons. Even Sam Gibson, the stopper, went 14-14.

Graham was convinced to make changes for 1941. The Seals released Burns after a .270 season, returned outfielder Johnny Barrett to the Red Sox and traded veterans Ted Norbert and Al Wright to Portland for "Cowboy" Ray Harrell. Graham also tried to peddle Eddie Stutz and Ted Jennings, but found no takers.

When the Seals went to Boyes Hot Springs for 1941 Spring Training, O'Doul concentrated on working with the young players. Primary among the crop were pitchers Bob Jensen, Larry Jansen, Hub Kittle and Charlie Schanz; catchers Roy Partee and Wil Leonard; infielders Don Trower and Albert Steele; and outfielders Don White and Joe Brovia.

In somewhat counter-productive moves, Graham spent $10,000 for the contract of Alvin "Jake" Powell, the Yankees' fourth outfielder in 1940, and signed San Franciscan and former major league star Tony Lazzeri as a free agent. Just before camp broke, Graham picked up 10-year major league veteran right-hander Roy Parmelee from Louisville and left-hander Tom Seats from Detroit.

Powell came into camp out of shape and boasting that he wouldn't be on the coast for long. He was right. Powell didn't supply the punch expected of him, was not a positive influence, and was benched in favor of 22-year-old Wally Carroll, who was claimed on waivers from Los Angeles. By mid-season Powell was peddled to Montreal.

Incidentally, Norbert, whose place Powell had taken, batted .278 with 20 home runs for the Beavers in 1941 and led the league in batting at .378 with 28 homers the following season. His home run totals were league highs both seasons.

Lazzeri was a marvelous addition as a teacher, working with Steele, Jennings, Trower and Ed Goorabian in the middle infield. At the start of the season, however, Lazzeri had a bad leg. He managed to play in 102 games but was slowed in the field and batted only .248.

At the 1941 Boosters Day in Oakland, club President Phil Reilly presents gifts to Oaks players Bill Conroy, Billy Raimondi, Ben Cantwell, Marv Gudat and Jack Salveson. In front is Danny Luby, Hugh's son and a future Coast League player.

Fain, entering his second season as a Seals regular, showed real brilliance around first base. Although leading all first basemen with 22 errors, his defensive skills improved greatly. Offensively, Fain persisted in trying to slap the ball to all fields much to O'Doul's consternation. O'Doul continued his efforts to make Fain a pull hitter without much success. Fain only powered five homers, but he waited out 96 bases on balls and scored 122 runs, both league-leading totals. This was done from the sixth spot in the lineup.

Froilan "Nanny" Fernandez, purchased from Yakima of the Western International League in June 1940, played every game for O'Doul at shortstop. He batted .327, second in the league among regulars, with a league-leading 231 hits and 129 RBIs. Fernandez improved greatly in the field but still committed 83 errors, a runaway leader in that statistic. Fernandez led all shortstops in putouts, assists and double plays as well. O'Doul was high on Fernandez because of his winning attitude and tenacious play, and that recommendation encouraged the Boston Braves to purchase him for the 1942 season.

Jennings captured the third base job out of Spring Training and was fielding well and hitting in spectacular fashion when he broke his leg. This marked the second

Ferris Fain, one of the most popular Seals of all time, was an outstanding hitter who spent nine years in the major leagues.

season in a row that a Seals infielder was lost for the season by a June fracture; Harvey Storey was batting .323 in 63 games in 1940 when he was lost. Jennings was hitting .326 in 66 games in 1941. These injuries hampered both players for the rest of their careers.

## BASEBALL MANS THE HOME FRONT

The Seals finished fifth in 1941, and any hopes for improvement were cast aside when the Japanese attacked Pearl Harbor.

Baseball quickly receded as a thought in most Americans' minds. West Coast residents were not sure if there would be an invasion of the mainland or bombings of the major cities by the Japanese. The country geared up for full war-time alert.

On January 14, 1942, Judge Landis asked President Roosevelt in a brief, pointed letter what he wanted organized baseball to do. The President's response was immediate and clear. "I honestly feel that it would be best for the country to keep baseball going," Roosevelt replied. "There will be fewer people unemployed and everybody will work longer hours and harder than before. And that means that they ought to have a chance for recreation and for taking their minds off their work even more than before."

Roosevelt suggested an extension of night games to allow day workers to get to the ballpark. He acknowledged the quality of play might suffer, but the popularity of the game would not be dampened by the use of older players to replace those who were fighting for their country.

Roosevelt concluded, "Here is another way to look at it—if 300 teams use 5,000 or 6,000 players, these players are a definite recreational asset to at least 20 million of their fellow citizens—and that in my judgment is thoroughly worthwhile."

Although Roosevelt had encouraged night games, the PCL situation was complicated because night games had the potential of jeopardizing the safety of coastal residents. It was feared ballpark lights could serve as a beacon for enemy aircraft or submarines. Only San Francisco and San Diego were on or near the ocean. In the case of San Francisco, Seals Stadium was not visible from the sea. San Diego was located on San Diego Bay, but there were many more attractive targets than Lane Field. In fact, a direct hit on Lane Field would have solved one of the league's most nagging problems: the deteriorated condition of the San Diego ballpark.

The military command was slow to deal with this question but eventually approved a limited schedule of night games for 1942.

Individual clubs faced certain obstacles that had to be negotiated with commanders in charge of the local civil

defense. In Seattle, the state commandant ordered that crowds at Sicks Stadium be limited to a maximum of 5,000 people per game. He did not want too many people in one place at the time of an enemy attack. The Rainiers front office countered by planning two single games on Sunday rather than a doubleheader, and by limiting the attendance of women at games.

In Portland, all night games had to be sanctioned by the military commandant of the district. Vaughn Street Ball Park was only three miles from the Union Iron Works where ships for the war effort were being built.

In the Bay Area night games were initially sanctioned. Early in the season before each game, Jack Rice, the Seals' public address announcer, would inform the crowd the guidelines in case there was a blackout. If there was the possibility of an enemy attack, sirens would blow throughout the city and fans at the ballpark would have the option of remaining in their seats or walking to the lighted concourse under the grandstand. The field lights would be shut off one minute after the sirens started. Fans would have to wait it out at the stadium because they would not be allowed to drive during an air raid drill. The game would resume after the "All Clear" call.

Bill Lillard, who had two brief stints with the Seals, had an eerie brush with the Japanese in the early stages of the war. The Lillard boys, Bill and Gene, were the most famous residents of Goleta, near Santa Barbara. During the first winter of hostilities, Bill had just finished walking along Goleta's beach when a Japanese submarine surfaced and fired on the mainland with its deck guns.

## WARTIME UNIFORMS

Shortages existed throughout American life, baseball included, during World War II. Somehow, though, the Oaks and Seals always wore the highest-quality uniforms.

Their uniforms took on a patriotic look during the war. Oakland's colors, normally green and red, became red and blue on white. The Oaks' uniforms of 1942 and 1943 featured a red and blue acorn that also symbolized the American eagle's crest. This was located on both the chest and on the cap.

In 1944, the Oaks went to their popular old English "O" on the chest. Their caps were blue with red brims and the old English "O". The Oaks also experimented with a Sunday-only silken uniform. This jersey had a script "Oaks" across the front.

The Seals' uniforms for 1942-44 featured red and blue lettering on pinstripe, and each uniform featured a "V" on the sleeve. The patriotic crest was featured on their caps. When the war concluded, Seals uniforms featured simple navy blue lettering, a pattern they used into the 1950s.

The Japanese took aim on an oil field but inflicted little damage. Gene Lillard worked this field during the off-season, but was not present at the time. The joke was the Japanese hit two seagulls and a smudge pot, but the attack showed the vulnerability of the West Coast to attack. Anti-aircraft guns were in the hills surrounding the Bay Area, there was a submarine net protecting the entrance to the bay and barrage balloons hovered over the Mare Island Naval Base in Vallejo, just north of the bay.

Midway through the 1942 season, General J.L. DeWitt of the Western Defense Command, stationed in San Francisco, ordered cessation of all night athletic contests as of 12:01 a.m., on August 20, 1942. The edict did not place an undue strain on the league because only 18 night games remained on the schedule throughout the league. Its effect was more serious on community college football schedules and other sports such as auto racing and dog racing. The ban was lifted after the conclusion of the 1943 season.

Baseball's greatest problem created by the war was

---

**WEARING CHEATERS**

"Cheaters" was a pejorative term for glasses. Any baseball prospect who wore glasses had two strikes against him before he took the field. Yet there have been many exemplary players to defy this conventional wisdom.

The 1942 Oaks often played with three players who wore glasses: pitcher Jack Salveson, catcher Billy Raimondi and infielder Billy Rigney. By 1947, the Oaks had three catchers who wore glasses, Raimondi, Eddie Kearse and Gene Lillard.

---

one of manpower. Thousands of players enlisted or were inducted into the military service. For the 1942 season, roster size was cut to 19 players. Normally a team would carry eight pitchers, two catchers and nine field players to fill the seven remaining positions. Pitchers normally filled in as extra field players.

An abundance of dignitaries plus marching units from two branches of the armed forces help the Seals and Oaks commemorate Opening Day at Oaks Ball Park in 1942, less than six months after the United States entered World War II.

The manpower shortage extended the careers of many players in their late 30s or early 40s who were too old to fight in the war. Pard Ballou and Sam Gibson, both in their 40s, just kept rolling along for the Seals. Others, such as Gus Suhr and Harry Rosenberg, came out of retirement to help fill the void. The most graphic examples of careers extended by the war were Seattle pitcher Byron Speece, 48 in 1945, and Herman "Old Folks" Pillette, who played seven games for the 1945 Solons at age 49.

On the other end of the scale, youngsters such as the Oaks' Ernie Raimondi, Wil Leonard and Vic Picetti and the Seals' Ferris Fain, Don White and Joe Brovia were rushed into the lineup. They would play a season or two before receiving their induction notices. If they were lucky, they would continue playing baseball while in the service, entertaining the troops.

Many players had to forego their careers to work in some defense industry. Larry Jansen of the Seals, a farmer in the off-season, became a full-time farmer, pitching bush league games on the weekends. Farming was deemed essential to the war effort, and thus earned Jansen a deferment. Damon Hayes worked in the Seattle shipyards and pitched locally on the weekends. Pitchers Nubs Kleinke of the Oaks and Tom Seats of the Seals worked in the local shipyards and pitched on their days off.

Other defense jobs were located for the players. Emil

Seals right-hander Larry Jansen was forced to abandon his baseball career during the war so he could return to Oregon and raise food for the war effort. He returned to action in 1945 and won 30 games in 1946.

## REPORTING THE GAME—IV

Sportswriters and ballplayers had a unique relationship through the 1940s and 1950s.

The writers assigned to cover the team took the long train rides along with the players. With so many idle hours to fill, writers and players played many games of cards, talked baseball for hours, analyzed the opposite sex—a topic with endless possibilities—and even discussed the philosophy of life.

But these conversations were sacred. A writer wouldn't think of using them in future stories. The writers' job was to report the activities on the field. The player's private life had no place in his reporting.

After a game, the reporters would visit the club room for a little socializing. Here they would be able to talk with the manager to get his slant on the game. Seldom would there be reason for a reporter to enter the clubhouse. He really wasn't welcomed there. Seldom would a reporter attempt to talk with a player about the game. His job was to report what happened, little more.

Mailho, Les Scarsella and Cotton Pippen and several other Oaks players found daytime employment at the Hubbell Galvanizing plant in Emeryville. The players could work a normal shift, then play ball at night.

One of the Coast League's premier war stories was Seats' shutout victories for the Seals over the Solons in both ends of a doubleheader on August 6, 1944. Seats had been unable to get off work during the middle of the week, so he called O'Doul and volunteered to pitch both games on Sunday.

After finishing up his Saturday shift at the shipyards, Seats took a train to Sacramento and arrived early Sunday morning. He threw a five-hit, 6-0 shutout and went 3-for-4 in the first game. Then, in the seven-inning nightcap, he limited the Solons to three hits, winning 3-0.

More than two dozen Oaks and Seals players and employees joined the armed forces. Each franchise lost players in battle, the most well-known being Ernie Raimondi of the Oaks.

Possibly the most curious war story happened to pitcher Rinaldo "Rugger" Ardizoia. Ardizoia was born in Italy but grew up in San Francisco. Red Adams, the Mission Reds' trainer and scout, discovered Ardizoia on the playgrounds. He was signed to a Missions contract out of high school and played briefly with them in 1938. After the team moved to Hollywood, Ardizoia won 14 games for the Stars in each of their first two seasons before he was traded to Newark of the International League.

On his first trip north, the Canadian Government would not allow Ardizoia to accompany the team to Montreal because he did not have his final U.S. citizenship

Oaks outfielder Emil Mailho beats Angels shortstop Billy Schuster's throw to first baseman Eddie Waitkus in a 1942 game in Emeryville. Later in his career, Waitkus was shot by a woman in a hotel room and served as the inspiration for Bernard Malamud's *The Natural*.

papers. A state of war existed between Canada and Italy. Ardizoia's contract had to be transferred to Kansas City in the American Association. Shortly thereafter, Ardizoia was inducted into the service and spent 28 months in the Pacific.

## DEEP IN THE WAR

The 1942 and 1943 baseball seasons were emotionally difficult. The unpredictability of war weighed heavily on everyone. While the draft was not yet in full swing in 1942, players could leave at any time. Owners realized it would become progressively more difficult to put a competitive team on the field.

The Solons and the Angels waged a heated battle for the 1942 pennant while the Seals finished fifth and the Oaks sixth. Sacramento prevailed only to have Seattle win the Shaughnessy-style playoff championship known as the Governor's Cup. The format provided for four first-division clubs to play two rounds of post-season games. Although the playoffs were somewhat anticlimactic, the

winner of the Governor's Cup enjoyed bragging rights for the entire winter.

The 1943 season was probably the most difficult of the war years for supplying Coast League teams with players. Because of the preoccupation with the war, the season was cut to 155 games. Only the abbreviated 1918 war year was shorter. The military draft and the major league draft both sliced deeply into the 1942 rosters. Hollywood had to replace virtually its whole team. Charlie Graham even placed an ad in *The Sporting News* asking free agents to contact him about playing for the Seals.

In addition, there was a scarcity of raw materials needed to produce baseballs, resulting in a brief "Dead Ball" era. Composition of the ball was altered slightly, and they were kept in play longer. Some balls arrived lacking any printing on them, and some split at the seams when hit. The result was a dramatic decline in home run production around the league. Wally Westlake was the Acorn's 1942 home run leader with seven. As a team, Oakland hit only 22. In 1943, Jack Devincenzi, who came to Oakland in a trade sending Marv Gudat to the Padres, led with five out of a team total of only 17.

The Seals' home run production dropped from 53 in 1942 to 22 in 1943 and only 14 in 1944. Outfielder Willie Enos led the team in 1943 with six and 1945 with five. In 1944, Neill Sheridan was the "Home Run King" with four, the Seals' lowest individual total since 1907.

## BUILDING A CHAMPION

War had engulfed the world by 1943. With the many hardships created by the manpower shortage, there were widespread fears that the league might not survive the season. But there was still great interest in baseball, particularly on the Pacific Coast. Although the Angels ran away from the rest of the league to win the pennant by 21 games over the Seals, San Francisco attendance increased; the Seals drew 202,532, just 250 less than in 1942 when the schedule was 23 games longer.

The Oaks sustained a huge attendance drop of 44,000 to 100,493, but its team wasn't very attractive. The Sacramento Solons, after having won the 1942 pennant, lost their association with the St. Louis Cardinals, and the orphaned club drew only 31,694. Only an aggressive campaign by civic-minded leaders saved the team from being turned back to the league.

The Seals made several key player moves for 1943.

Popular Brooks Holder was traded to Hollywood for second baseman Del Young and outfielder Bernie Uhalt. The trade was controversial as Holder was the Seals' most popular player, but Young and Uhalt were proven starters. The Seals also shipped infielder Ollie Bejma to Buffalo for long-time Pacific Coast League outfielder Hank Steinbacher, acquired outfielder George Metkovich from the Boston Braves organization and welcomed pitcher Bill Werle off the Cal campus. Plus, Suhr and Rosenberg were coaxed out of retirement. The result was an experienced club representing the city of San Francisco.

For the Oaks, manpower was at a premium. Salveson was taken in the major league draft by Cleveland. Lost to the military were infielders Cecil Dunn, Bill Rigney and Herm Schulte and outfielders Mel Duezabou and Wally Westlake. There were no adequate replacements for these men.

The manpower shortage eased in 1944. Some men were being discharged from the service and were eligible to play again. Others were coming of age and being inducted. The Oaks took 44 players to Spring Training. Twenty were classified l-C (medical discharges from the armed services), seventeen were 4-F (unfit for military service), two were over 38 years old, and three were 17.

A major coup was pulled off by Devincenzi and Camilli when they signed 17-year-old Vic Picetti of San

A heavy military emphasis permeates Opening Day 1943. This photograph emphasizes the simplicity of Oaks Ball Park, including the light standards—low and at the edge of the field.

Right, Oakland Manager Dolph Camilli and General Manager Cookie Devincenzi prepare for Spring Training 1944. Below, Lefty O'Doul with slugger George 'Catfish' Metkovich.

Francisco. Picetti had drawn substantial interest from several major league teams when he played in a high school all-star game in New York, but he signed with the Oaks to be tutored by Camilli, his boyhood idol. Picetti got into 14 games and batted .208 but showed abundant talent. The San Francisco media criticized Graham and the Seals for allowing a local to escape across the bay, but Picetti had never considered signing with the Seals.

## SEALS BATTLE OAKS FOR GOVERNOR'S CUP

As exciting as the 1944 season would be, it also produced a lesser caliber of play than the previous seasons. Every team had its regulars and stars, but there were fewer of them. The strong players became iron men while job security for reserves was tenuous at best. Dozens of players, filling spots vacated by those who had gone to war, had one-season careers in the PCL.

The general mediocrity created a very competitive league. The Oaks' performance was a good example of the league balance. They remained close to .500 all season but so did every other team. On July 1, San Francisco was in first place at 44-38, four games ahead of seventh-place Oakland.

The Oaks proceeded to win four straight and then swept a July 4 doubleheader from the Seals to take first place as the Seals dropped to third. The race was close through the remainder of July before the Angels, the eventual champions, eased to the top. In August, the Angels compiled a 23-8 record. In the middle of August, the Seals lost 10 of 11. Now the battle was for second, with any of the remaining seven teams having a chance.

The Beavers clinched second on the last day, 12 games behind the Seraphs. The Oaks tied the Seals for third, a game back, setting up an Oaks-Seals matchup in the first round of the Governor's Cup.

A total of 25 pitchers worked for Oakland in 1944. The Seals, meanwhile, carried nine pitchers all season. Seats pitched 320 innings, a league-leading 34 complete games, a 2.36 ERA and had a 25-13 record, one of three 20-game winners for the Seals.

The Seals made short work of the Oaks, winning four games to one in the opening round of the 1944 playoffs. The finals against pennant-winning Los Angeles was considerably more difficult. Gritty pitching performances and a great stroke of baseball fortune pulled it out for O'Doul's team. In the seventh and final game, the Angels were leading 2-1 when Ben Giuntini bunted to advance two baserunners. Angels pitcher Jorge Comellas threw to third for the force just as third baseman Stan Gray slipped. The ball sailed down the line, and all three Seals scored before the stunned Angels could do anything. The 4-2 score became a final and the Seals won their second straight Governor's Cup.


**A YEAR OF GREAT CHANGE**

Lefty O'Doul had been masterful in holding a rather untalented group together in 1944, but nobody could expect the same result in 1945. The war was in its concluding stages, but this had little impact on baseball at any level. Players still had war obligations and players were still being inducted into the military. Les Scarsella was traded to the Philadelphia Phillies for infielder Glen Stewart and pitcher Harry Sherman, but refused to go so he could remain with his family. Also, he would have been drafted if he left his war-industry job in Emeryville. Larry Jansen was denied a deferment from his farming job to play with the Seals. And so it went.

Baseball was jolted by two deaths between the 1944 and 1945 seasons. Commissioner Landis died in November and President Roosevelt died on April 12, 1945, just as the Coast League season opened. These men were single-handedly responsible for the continuation of baseball through the rough times of war.

As a gesture of mourning, the Coast League suspended play on the Saturday following Roosevelt's death. Roosevelt had been working on his welcoming speech to the delegates at the United Nations Conference in San Francisco. That conference had an unexpected impact on the Seals' visiting opponents; it took all available hotel space in San Francisco, forcing teams to bunk out in Seals Stadium for the duration. As Padres trainer Les Cook said, "At least we have ample hot and cold running showers within 10 feet of our beds. We've had worse accommodations."

The Oaks and Seals were both .500 clubs in 1945. The excitement in Oakland centered around the 17-year-old Picetti. Camilli felt Picetti was the best prospect he had ever seen in the league. Picetti manned first base in 142 games, batting .282 but with only one homer. Camilli felt Picetti would develop into a power hitter with experience.

The Oaks also signed pitcher-outfielder Matt Zidich from Sacred Heart High School in San Francisco. This gave Oakland two top San Francisco prospects. Zidich entered 42 games, all but one as an outfielder or pinch-hitter, batting .280. He lost the one game he pitched.

Picetti, Zidich and many other semi-pro players had been given a chance to play in the Coast League out of necessity. In non-war years, all would have been sent to the lower minors for additional experience, but during the war there weren't many minor leagues in operation. They had to train on the job.

O'Doul's Seals finished fourth, 96-87, but won their third straight Governor's Cup. The Seals were comprised of veterans and rookies waiting to be replaced by returning soldiers. The team lacked power but played good defense. Second baseman Del Young and shortstop Roy Nicely formed an acrobatic combination that turned 179 double plays, and Frenchy Uhalt and Emil Mailho were both excellent center fielders.

Bob Joyce, at 31-11 with 35 complete games and a 2.17 ERA, was the league's most dominant pitcher and earned himself a return to the National League in 1946 with New York. He was backed up by Frank Seward (18-13), Elmer Orella (11-11) and Floyd Ehrman (8-4). Ehrman was a typical wartime story. He was hired to throw batting practice for the Seals and was signed to fill in from the bullpen. He was so effective O'Doul gave him several starts near the end of the season, and he completed three games.

World War II ended in August. The Pacific Coast League was on the doorstep of a bright new era. ❖

CHAPTER **17**

# RETURN TO NORMALCY—1946-1948

For the first time in five years, a rich talent pool of players stocked the major and minor leagues. And with the end of the war, entertainment-starved Americans came back to the ballpark in droves. It wasn't immediately a return to normalcy, however. At the park, fans were reminded of the shortages they still faced. They were required to return any baseball hit into the stands in exchange for a ticket to a future game.

Both Bay Area ballclubs anticipated the rush to the turnstiles and made plans for extensive remodeling of their ballparks. Brick Laws oversaw the renovation of Oaks Ball Park and invested more than $250,000 into the ambitious project.

The Seals had a new owner at the end of the war: Paul I. Fagan, a millionaire industrialist from San Francisco who owned thousands of acres in the Hawaiian Islands. He had convinced Charlie Graham to sell him a partial interest, and it was presumed that Fagan would be a silent partner, leaving the business decisions to Graham and his business manager, Damon Miller.

Fagan would be anything but silent.

Between the 1945 and 1946 seasons, Fagan set out to make Seals Stadium once again the finest ballpark in the country. Fagan had the enthusiasm and the financial resources to make the project a success. As a result, Seals

Stadium received its first facelift since it was constructed at the start of the Depression. The previously unpainted facade received a coat of mint and forest green paint that immediately caused a change in nickname from "The Queen of Cement" to "The Queen in Green."

Advertisements on the outfield walls were replaced by solid green. That cost the club thousands of dollars but gave it the non-commercial look Fagan wanted. Flower boxes with real flowers were put in the windowsills of the front office overlooking 16th Street. Out in right field, the cavernous acreage was shortened from 385 feet down the foul line to a more tempting 350 feet. Gone was the 20-foot wall, now replaced by a screen extending only 10 feet up before the bleachers. Still, hitting a home run to right field in Seals Stadium was a major task.

The bleachers were not completed by 1946 Opening Day, so temporary fencing was placed in the outfield until the bleachers were ready for spectators. The completed right field bleachers increased stadium capacity by roughly 2,000, but the grandstand seats down the right field line still remained backless until after the season.

A few years later, Seals Stadium also became the first baseball park in the nation to use Plexiglas instead of a screen or mesh on the backstop. The logic behind using unbreakable glass was to remove the distraction the box-holders faced by having to look through a screen to watch a game. The experiment received less than rave notices; moisture or dirt would often cloud the view of spectators, lights during night games created irritating glares and foul balls lined off the glass created ear-splitting noises.

Fagan instituted a variety of amenities. Uniformed usherettes—undoubtedly the first women employed to do what was heretofore considered men's work—assisted fans to their seats. Ladies' rooms were enlarged and painted in pastel colors. Men's rooms were also improved and even shoeshine stands were installed. Emergency quarters were staffed with a registered nurse, and emergency ambulance service was available. Between innings, a band played music. Indeed, Seals Stadium had become the queen of American baseball parks.

Fagan also constructed a carriage entrance in an effort to encourage the social elite to attend games at Seals Stadium. This circular entrance, located behind home plate, allowed easy access to the park by motor vehicles.

Fagan upgraded the Seals' dressing and training room facilities and stocked them with whirlpools, some-

thing unheard of at the minor league level and virtually nonexistent in the majors. Trainer Leo "Doc" Hughes was instructed to order double sets of home and road uniforms, also unprecedented.

## THE GOAL: MAJOR LEAGUE BASEBALL

Fagan's main objective was to elevate San Francisco and the Pacific Coast League to major league status. His attitude and willingness to spend money to accomplish his goal both gratified and shocked his colleagues. They understood his motives but feared being dragged into a spending spree they might not be able to afford. The other owners also had a greater understanding of the infrastructure of organized baseball and the frustrations in reaching his goal than did Fagan.

Fagan felt if his team were to become "major league," then he must pay the players major league salaries. The minimum salary in the major leagues in 1946 was $5,000, and Fagan made sure every player on the Seals roster was

Paul Fagan, part-owner of the Seals, experimented in 1946 by having the Seals conduct Spring Training in Hawaii. It turned out to be a huge success for the Seals and the islanders. Below, Charlie Graham accepts the key to the city of Honolulu.

making at least that. This attitude created some problems for major league general managers who acquired Coast League stars at season's end. Invariably they offered their new property less than they made the previous season on the Coast. Ferris Fain and Larry Jansen of the Seals and Wally Westlake of the Oaks all found this to be the case. When players heard of the wage structure available in the Coast League, they were provided with another incentive to play and stay on the West Coast.

### SPRING TRAINING IN HAWAII

For 1946, the Seals trained in the Hawaiian Islands, another brainchild of Fagan's. Many feared this junket would backfire by costing the team too much, and that the Hawaiian rains and lack of competition would create an ill-prepared team.

These fears were unfounded. Fagan underwrote the expenses—estimated to be $40,000—but the team actually turned a profit before coming home. Fagan created a training facility and baseball diamond which still exists in remote Hana, using the team to enhance his own status in the islands. Residents and military personnel stationed on the islands flocked to watch the Seals train. Seals players became Hawaiian heroes.

The local organizing committee put together a team of all-stars to play the Seals. A minor labor dispute involving pay for the players had to be resolved before the team would agree to play. To the Seals' surprise, there were a few ringers on the team: major league pitchers Mel Queen and Boots Poffenberger and outfielder Willard Marshall. With this level of competition, the Seals came home prepared to play.

Returning via airplane was not an easy task. Flights to the mainland were irregular and there was competition with returning servicemen for seats. The Seals returned in groups of four, six or eight, taking more than a week for the full complement to arrive home.

### THE 1946 SEALS

Lefty O'Doul's Seals would be a good team but no one expected them to win the pennant. Most observers felt the Angels or the Rainiers were the teams to beat. The Seals may have won the Governor's Cup in 1945, but they finished the regular season in fourth place. Gone was Bob Joyce, who had accounted for nearly one-third of the Seals' 96 victories in 1945. Older players and marginal ones from the 1945 team were replaced by men discharged from the military.

Jansen came back to anchor the Seals' pitching staff. Billy Werle and Al Lien, two left-handed pitchers, returned from military service. "Old Burrhead" Ferris Fain, Ted Jennings and Don Trower strengthened the infield, while Joe Brovia, Don White and Sal Taormina rejoined the outfield.

Above, the 1946 PCL champion Seals. Vince DiMaggio is on the bottom row, second from the right. Lefty O'Doul is in the second row, far left. Pitcher Larry Jansen is in the middle of the top row. Below, O'Doul at the entrance to the dugout.

Doc Hughes felt Fain was the best all-around first baseman in the game. "He possessed soft, quick hands and the instincts to make plays without any hesitation. Fain was a hard worker, taking each practice seriously and refusing to overlook any detail to improve his craft." Nobody questioned Fain's offensive talents.

The New York Giants provided considerable help to the Seals as a consequence of the Joyce deal. Pitchers Cliff Melton and Ray "Chief" Harrell were removed from the New York roster and sent to San Francisco, as was Frank Rosso from Jersey City. When Hugh Luby was discharged from the Army shortly after the season had started, he was sold to San Francisco by the Giants. Melton, Harrell and Rosso would account for 41 Seals victories in 1946, effectively replacing the departed Joyce. Luby would become the Seals' team leader, stabilizing the infield and batting in the .290s.

## THE LEAGUE DEMANDS PARITY

At mid-season, the directors of the league met to handle routine administrative matters, but out of the meeting came some rebellion. The directors unanimously passed a resolution requesting parity with the major leagues at the earliest possible date. Copies of the resolution were sent to Commissioner Happy Chandler and the presidents of the American and National Leagues. While this was just one of many salvos for emancipation, the owners realized it would be difficult to receive any concessions from the major league owners.

## A BAY AREA STRETCH DRIVE

As the season turned into the final month, the race tightened up into a two-team battle between the Seals and the Oaks. At the end of August, San Francisco played the Oaks in a critical series before a string of packed houses in the Emeryville bandbox culminated by a Sunday doubleheader. Traditionally, these local twinbills were divided, with each team hosting one game. This tactic was tremendously successful in attracting thousands of additional fans to watch the rivalry. This particular series began with the Seals holding a three-game lead, but Casey Stengel's Oaks won five of seven and moved into first, .002 percentage points ahead of the Seals. Twice the Oaks defeated Jansen, the Seals' ace who lost just six games all year.

The Oaks immediately traveled to Hollywood to play a Labor Day doubleheader the next day. It was on to the Southern Pacific for the overnight trip to Los Angeles and then to the ballpark upon arrival. There wasn't even time to check into the hotel.

Meanwhile, the Seals hosted the Solons. Jim Tobin and Rosso pitched complete games as the Seals made quick work of the visitors, 3-1 and 5-1. The Oaks weren't as fortunate. The Stars took two, winning 3-2 and 7-3. The Oaks' perch in first place had lasted only 24 hours.

That was it for Oakland. They lost their next four games before salvaging two of the final three games of the series with the Stars. At the same time, the Seals were beating up on the hapless Solons, winning seven of nine in the extended series. At the end of the week, the Seals found themselves with a comfortable five-game lead with only 14 games remaining.

Sunday, September 8 had additional significance for Bay Area sports fans: The San Francisco 49ers played at Kezar Stadium in their first All America Football Conference game. The 49ers lost to the New York Yankees 21-7 to inaugurate major league football in the Bay Area; could major league baseball be far behind?

For their last two opponents, the Seals hosted the Rainiers and then closed at Portland. The Oaks traveled to San Diego and then came home to face the Solons. Logically, the schedule favored the Seals. All four opponents were in the second division, but the Rainiers and Beavers were battling to stay out of the cellar and the Solons had battled the Oaks to a standstill in earlier meetings. In the last week at Portland, the Seals made things more exciting by losing their first three games before Jansen again played the stopper. Jansen squared off against Jack Salveson of the Beavers in a classic duel. Salveson was never one to dally while on the mound, and he went about his business of throwing balls that batters were supposed to hit. One hour and 23 minutes later, Jansen and the Seals prevailed 2-1 as Jansen struck out seven and lowered his league-leading ERA to 1.57. Neither pitcher issued a walk. This was Jansen's 30th win

Top, Larry Jansen was one of the most dominant pitchers in PCL history and was the last one to win 30 games in a season. Above, Roy Nicely was a classic good-field, no-hit shortstop for the Seals in the post-war years.

A warm Sunday afternoon brings a sellout crowd to Seals Stadium in the late 1940s.

Seals second baseman Hugh Luby, 1946.

of the season against six losses; Jansen would go on to be a 21-game winner with the New York Giants as a rookie in 1947.

The Seals gained a tie for the championship on Friday night and won it outright on Saturday, making Sunday's games purely academic. But back in Oakland, the Oaks were playing as if each game meant the championship. Sunday, with the championship already decided, Stengel went into a tirade over an inside pitch to Brooks Holder that was called a strike. The pitcher was Bud Beasley, a Reno schoolteacher who pitched on vacations and weekends. Beasley, not long on talent, seemed to have the Oaks' number. With big, flopping feet and an unorthodox pitching motion, Beasley distracted most batters.

Beasley's antics must have gotten to Stengel because he charged the umpire in frustration, threw his hat into the air and got thrown out of the game. The fans loved it. Even when vanquished, Stengel was a competitor.

The Seals finished with 115 victories and 68 defeats, four games ahead of the Oaks and 20 games in front of the third-place Hollywood Stars. The Seals also won the cross-bay series, 15 games to 14.

Oakland attracted 633,549 paid admissions to Oaks Ball Park for the season. Across the bay, the Seals set an all-time minor league attendance record of 670,563, a record that lasted until the Louisville Cardinals topped the million mark almost 40 years later. Considering the era and the obstacles of the times, the Louisville record pales by comparison.

## REMATCH FOR THE GOVERNOR'S CUP

Although there was $25,000 at stake in the Governor's Cup playoffs—$5,000 each to the winners of the semifinal round and $10,000 to the champions—the excitement generated in the regular season could not be matched.

In the first round, the Seals swept the Hollywood Stars in four games while the Oaks were taken to seven games before defeating the Angels. In the finals, the Oaks jumped off to a 2-1 series lead before the Seals swept a doubleheader and Al Lien threw a 6-0 shutout. For the Seals all was complete; they had won the regular season championship and the playoffs.

Casey Stengel was gracious in defeat. "O'Doul's one of the best managers in the business today," he said. "He beat me fairly and squarely, and I'd like to see him in the big leagues."

Rumors abounded that O'Doul was headed to the New York Giants, but O'Doul immediately squelched them. Stengel reportedly was headed to the Philadelphia Athletics, the Cleveland Indians, the Pittsburgh Pirates or the New York Yankees. In reality, Cookie Devincenzi, now the Oaks' business manager, got a commitment from Stengel during the playoffs that he would return for the 1947 season.

The Seals gloried in their successes. They had been picked to contend, not to win. O'Doul used his players with the aplomb of a chess master. Great pitching, timely hitting and solid defense—all were present.

While the Seals had star-quality players in Jansen and Fain, the beauty of the Seals was their balance and versatility. While O'Doul was often criticized for pulling his starting pitchers one batter too late, he manipulated his pitching staff and his bench with great effectiveness throughout the season.

## THE BOOK OF 1947

The 1947 season had two main chapters. The first was on the field where the regular season ended in a tie between the Los Angeles Angels and the San Francisco Seals. That forced a one-game playoff, won by the Angels. The Angels then defeated the Oaks in the Governor's Cup playoff.

The second chapter was just as intense but much more complicated. It involved the Coast League's effort to be granted major league status for the 1948 season. The major league owners, however, were not ready to share power with some upstarts from out west. Commissioner Chandler's initial response was positive, but it was obvious his authority would not be extended into this domain by the major league owners.

Optimism ran high in the Seals' camp when 1947 Spring Training opened. Gone from the Seals were only two significant contributors to their 1946 successes: Jansen and Fain. Jansen was purchased by the Giants late in the season as part of their working agreement with the Seals. The Giants offered him a raise of less than $1,000 over his 1946 salary, but he negotiated a hefty conditional increase if he proved his worth to the Giants pitching staff. He got his increase.

Fain was drafted by the Philadelphia Athletics, whose contract offer would pay him less than the Seals. Fain balked, then signed when the offer was increased. He became the Athletics' regular first baseman, learned to hit to the opposite field, and won two American League batting championships.

From the Seals' farm club at Salt Lake City came Bob Chesnes, a 26-year-old right-handed pitcher from Oakland. He was the Pioneer League's top pitcher with an 18-6 record, 1.52 ERA and a record 278 strikeouts. He could also field brilliantly, hit well and run the bases intelligently, and he proved to be an excellent replacement for Jansen. By July 4, Chesnes was 15-4. He had a wonderful fastball and a good changeup in addition to a loose spirit.

Fain's replacement was to be Chuck Henson, the Pioneer League's leading batter at .363. Henson earned

Bob Chesnes went 22-8 for the Seals in 1947.

# OLD HOME WEEK

Bay Area baseball fans traditionally looked forward to late October for a very special baseball game. The Elks Club of Alameda sponsored an annual get-together featuring a banquet and a baseball game between local players—the majors vs. the minors.

The Elks initiated the charity contest at Oaks Ball Park after the 1927 season, and it continued until the Oaks left for Vancouver in 1955. The game's driving force was Manuel Duarte, a local clothing salesman who organized the annual affair and encouraged the major and minor league players to participate.

Anyone who was anybody in local baseball waited anxiously to be asked. One year they might play for the minor league team, and hopefully the next for the majors. Casey Stengel even returned to Oakland to manage and players made sure they were in town for the game.

Among the hundreds of players who participated through the years were the DiMaggios, Tony Lazzeri, Joe Cronin, Lew Fonseca, Walter Mails, Lefty O'Doul, George Kelly, Babe Pinelli, Ernest Lombardi, Smead Jolley, Buzz Arlett, Billy Rigney, Cookie Lavagetto, Billy Martin, Bill Wight, Marino Pieretti, Charlie Silvera, Sam Chapman, Ferris Fain, and Eddie Lake.

And while everybody realized the game had no significance, it was competitive and thoroughly enjoyed by players and fans alike. Somehow, the weather cooperated each year. And once in a while, the minor leaguers won.

The 1947 Major League All-Stars at the Alameda Elks Charity Game in 1947 at Oaks Ball Park. Back row (l-r): Manuel Duarte (chairman), Floyd Bevens, Ernie Bonham, Bill Rigney, Cookie Lavagetto, Ernest Lombardi, Ray Lamanno, Wally Westlake, Joe Hatten, Eddie Joost, Joe DiMaggio, Dick Bartell. Front (l-r): Vern Stephens, Sam Chapman, Eddie Lake, Vic Lombardi, Augie Galan, Bruce Edwards, Dom DiMaggio.

Joe Brovia was a fan favorite with the Seals, but on Opening Night 1949 at Seals Stadium he was with the enemy—the Portland Beavers. Brovia was famous for wearing his pants to the ankles, a source of consternation to league President Clarence 'Pants' Rowland.

the job in Spring Training but he was stricken by a migraine condition that defied diagnosis and cure. After hitting .386 in the first 12 games, he fell ill and didn't play again. This was a crushing blow to the Seals.

Another pleasant addition from Salt Lake was Joe Brovia, a left-handed outfielder. Brovia had been farmed out by the Seals in 1946 and responded by batting .339. He would bat .309 for the Seals in 1947 in 114 games. Joe loved to hit, and he had a distinguished Coast League career ahead of him.

The Seals and the Angels ended the season with identical 105-81 records. In a single playoff game at Wrigley Field before close to 23,000 fans, Cliff Chambers, the Angels' 24-game winner, threw a five-hit shutout. The Angels then defeated the Beavers in the Governor's Cup final, four games to one.

At the conclusion of the 1947 season, Graham terminated the working agreement with the Giants in a dispute over player allocation. O'Doul and Graham had pleaded with Horace Stoneham to provide them with an adequate replacement for Fain and the injured Henson at first base.

Gene Woodling won the PCL batting title at .385.

The 1950 Seals get ready to leave on a road trip. PCL teams routinely took flights long before the major leagues considered air travel a safe and economical option.

Because the Giants owed the Seals players from the Jansen deal, and because Jansen had enjoyed great success with the Giants, the Seals expected to be satisfied. O'Doul and Graham wanted Jack Graham, who had hit 34 home runs and 121 RBIs with Jersey City in 1947, but the Giants instead traded Jack Graham to San Diego as part of a package deal.

## ANOTHER WAR WITH THE OAKS

The most intriguing personnel story for the 1948 Seals was the development of pitcher Con Dempsey, who was battling brothers Bob and Dick Drilling for one spot on the staff. Bob Drilling had led the Pioneer League in most categories, including a 23-5 record. Dempsey, a sidearm pitcher, came to camp having won 16 games for Salt Lake.

Dempsey made the squad in unorthodox fashion. "It was my turn to throw batting practice, and all the decision-makers were present. I couldn't get the ball over the plate and was removed. Angry at myself for not performing well, I got a rookie catcher, Harry Eastwood, to play catch with me off to the side of the field. Now, Harry was a Hollywood type, laid back, and it was a leisurely workout until Eastwood started getting into it more, encouraging me to start bearing down. He would put up a target, pound his glove, and demand that I hit it. I couldn't miss!

"Finally, I turned my back to Eastwood to catch my breath and was surprised to see that the coaching staff had come over to watch me. O'Doul, obviously pleased, exclaimed, 'Now that's what we're looking for!'"

O'Doul brought Dempsey along slowly, giving him his first appearance away from home, a relief appearance at Hollywood. In the first six weeks, "Confident Con" pitched in 10 games, winning four and not allowing an earned run in 31⅓ innings. Dempsey got his first start against Oakland on May 23 and shut them out 7-0.

Dempsey wound up with a 16-11 record and led the league in ERA (2.10) and strikeouts (163).

The Seals led the pennant chase most of the way until a string of injuries severely hampered them. The most critical injury was a broken foot sustained by Gene Woodling on May 24. Woodling missed six weeks but came back to lead the league in hitting at .385 and in triples with 14. The 1948 season, which Woodling said was the happiest of his career, propelled him to the major leagues where he went on to play 17 distinguished seasons for the Yankees, Indians, Orioles and Senators.

Meanwhile, the Oaks played .800 ball in the last month to slip past the Seals and win the pennant by two games. The Oaks then captured the Governor's Cup to cap off their greatest season.

The Seals' greatest blow occurred late in the season when Charlie Graham died on August 29. "Uncle Charlie" was an owner ahead of his time. He paid the players well and genuinely looked after their welfare.

Otherwise, the 1948 season had been successful on the field and at the gate for the Seals. Their fans, with thoughts of the war now put aside and life having returned to normal, had to be thrilled. And they were, except for one detail: The Oaks had won the pennant. What could be worse than that? ❖

CHAPTER **18**

# CASEY, BILLY
# & THE NINE OLD MEN

He had a solid 14-year major league career as an outfielder, even hitting .368 for the 1922 Giants in 84 games. He played well in three World Series but was mostly remembered for silly stunts like doffing his cap and having a bird fly out from under it. He became a minor league manager, then spent 10 years managing the Brooklyn Dodgers and Boston Braves and never finished above fifth place. In 1945, with 36 years of organized baseball under his belt, he managed Kansas City of the minor league American Association to a seventh-place finish. But life for Charles Dillon "Casey" Stengel was just beginning.

### NEW OWNERSHIP REJUVENATES THE OAKS

Through the Depression and World War II, all aspects of the Oakland Oaks operation had eroded. Limited finances affected scouting and the signing of prospects, which showed in the team's play. Oaks Ball Park had fallen into a deep state of disrepair and the club itself earned the reputation as a shoestring operation.

By the end of the 1943 season, Cookie Devincenzi announced he would be willing to sell to local qualified buyers. Two local theater-chain operators, Clarence

"Brick" Laws and Joe Blumenfeld, purchased the club, then asked Devincenzi to stay on as business manager.

The new ownership developed a three-point master plan: 1) renovate the ballpark, 2) find a high-profile manager who could mold the available talent into a winning ball club, and 3) search out prospects who could be developed and sold to the majors.

Brick Laws oversaw the $250,000 renovation of the ballpark, which included new light standards, expanded grandstands, new bleachers in right and center field totaling 3,000 additional seats, and a new clubhouse built under the grandstands near home plate. In addition to added comfort and the potential for increased attendance, the new seats moved the distance down the right field line to a very cozy 300 feet.

Although short on space, the new clubhouse was a great improvement over the one that had existed for all of the park's 30-year history. Kids who used to collect autographs or ask for cracked bats now found the connecting walkway from the clubhouse to the dugout a haven for making contact with their local heroes.

Front-office quarters were constructed over the modernized entrance to the ballpark. The large, whitewashed stucco facility in the left field corner afforded an excellent view of the diamond. Famous stars, including Ty Cobb and Lefty Gomez, were invited to watch the game from this forerunner to today's private luxury boxes.

With the physical plant upgraded, the owners turned their attention to on-field leadership and picked Dolph Camilli. A San Francisco native and former National League Most Valuable Player, Camilli—who regularly attended San Francisco Giants games well into the 1990s—had balked at a 1943 trade from the Dodgers to the Giants and returned home. The Oaks then worked out a deal with the Giants and made Camilli their first baseman, pinch-hitter and manager. In return, the Giants got infielder Bill Rigney.

In 1944 the team lifted itself to third, but in June 1945 Camilli left to play for the Boston Red Sox. Under Billy Raimondi, the Oaks slid back to fifth.

## THE STENGEL ERA

The Oaks renewed their search for a manager during the winter of 1945. Among the many candidates was Casey Stengel who, despite his second-division finishes, had gained a reputation as a great motivator and a manager. Both New York Yankees Owner Del Webb and Pacific Coast League President "Pants" Rowland personally recommended Stengel to Brick Laws.

Stengel, with promised access to the owner's checkbook, proposed a three-year plan. The first season, 1946, would be a get-acquainted year. Year Two would be dedicated to obtaining the proper talent. Year Three was to be the payoff year with a pennant and/or a victory in the Governor's Cup.

Casey didn't like what he initially saw at 1946 Spring Training: a dozen leftovers from the 1945 Oaks, a number of players obtained from major league organizations and a growing stream of veterans returning from military service. Soon, only four returnees from 1945 remained: catchers Billy Raimondi and Eddie Kearse, pitcher Tom Hafey and outfielder-first baseman Les Scarsella.

Stengel was most concerned about building a pitching staff to endure the long PCL season. By using his major league contacts, Stengel was able to obtain on option Bryan Stephens from the Cleveland Indians and Gene Bearden, Frank Shea and Rugger Ardizoia from the New York Yankees. Bearden was two years away from a 20-win season for the 1948 World Series-champion Cleveland Indians. Charlie Gassaway came from the Philadelphia Athletics and Floyd Speer from Milwaukee of the American Association. Ralph Buxton and Henry "Cotton" Pippen returned from the military, as did outfielder Wally Westlake and infielder Vic Buccola.

Casey also picked up Mickey Burnett from the Cardinals chain, Billy Hart from the Dodgers and, as the season began, Tony Sabol from the Yankees. About a month into the season the Oaks acquired Ray Hamrick, a talkative, slick-fielding shortstop from Buffalo of the International League. With Scarsella at first, Burnett at second, Hamrick at shortstop and Hart at third, and Sabol and Arky Biggs in reserve, the Oaks had a solid infield.

One of the better acquisitions was Brooks Holder. A member of the Hollywood Stars since 1943, Holder had seen both his playing time and batting average slip and was facing a backup role in 1946. For $2,500, Holder purchased his release from Owner Oscar Reichow and rushed to the Bay Area to see if Stengel and the Oaks would take him on. His Oaks contract included a $2,500 bonus to cover his costs and an added $500 if he made the club.

He not only made the club but provided solid defense as the regular left fielder. He also led the league with 131 walks and was generally considered the most valuable and popular player on the club that year.

Wally Westlake patrolled right field while Hershel Martin, acquired from the Yankees during the winter, was the regular center fielder. Reserve Max Marshall, obtained from the Cincinnati Reds early in the season, still managed to play more than 100 games.

The team roster remained unsettled through the first month of the season. Thirty-seven players passed through the door before Casey finally settled on his 25-man roster.

The Oaks more than got acquainted in 1946. They were in the pennant race all season and finished 111-72, just four games behind the Seals. In the Governor's Cup playoffs they defeated the Los Angeles Angels, then fell in the finals once again to the Seals. In addition, the park renovations created a joyful and well-lit stadium in which to watch baseball.

Postwar fans swarmed to Oaks Ball Park. For their 79 home dates the Oaks drew 634,311 fans, an increase of nearly 300,000 over 1945. In a *San Francisco Chronicle* column, Clyde Giraldo wrote:

### STENGEL NOT FANCY, BUT SOLID

So Casey Stengel lost the playoffs. He lost the pennant. The bum. Persons here and there give voice to sentiments like that today. Other squeaking voices, such as this pillar, think differently. Viewed abstractly, the job Stengel did with the 1946 Oaks—his own hand-picked, personally bought Oaks—stands as a monument to baseball managing.

Not a single team in the Pacific Coast League picked a single Oak on its all-opponent team, yet Stengel had the poor little men in the pennant race running up to the last days and into the finals of the Governor's Cup playoff. He did it himself, and don't let anyone kid you. Brick Laws and Joe Blumenfeld, the moneybags of the Oaks ballclub, gave Casey free hand and free pocketbook to buy men in the spring, and Casey went to town. Casey picked his own team—pets like Hersh Martin of the

Yankees . . . and later Mickey Burnett and Arky Biggs.

Stengel has the best pitching staff in minor league baseball this spring! He had 12 starting pitchers— all experienced. So he picked his own club and had the finest twirlers. Where does managing come in? The roster split at the seams all the way.

Hart developed a sore arm, and never really showed his true self all season. Martin threw his back out of place and although he's one of the gamest guys in the business and for our dough, good, rarely pitched like Stengel expected. Burnett and his blistered finger; this man and that . . . and then the pitchers fell to pieces. The greatest staff that ever lived and flung died by the wayside. Hayes, Vandenberg, Buxton, Hafey, Pippen, name 'em all; at times Stengel, without crying out loud, had a choice of three men for a seven-game series.

The season's over and you can say these things. Did Charles Dillon K.C. Stengel moan? Nay. With due respect to O'Doul, Stengel got as much out of his men as any manager in the game.

And the men liked Stengel. No griping. Down the stretch, with the chips down, Stengel went 12 weeks without the league's leading hitter, Les Scarsella. The team didn't fall apart. In the playoffs Scar chose not to play. The team didn't fall apart. In the last game a third baseman, Biggs, had to play first base where Scar usually perches, and the Oaks looked pretty good. Scar's absence naturally hurt, but Stengel didn't cry.

Joe Devine, veteran scout for the New York Yankees, epitomized Stengel's season: "Casey played smart baseball, the kind they want around the major leagues. He wasn't fancy, but he was solid. Somebody else might have blown up when Scarsella went to the hospital, but Casey came back stronger."

That's the tipoff to his ability.

Casey Stengel was learning to utilize his entire team, a trait that would later bring him greatness as the manager of the New York Yankees. Only one Oaks player batted enough times to qualify for the batting title . . . Mickey Burnett came up 563 times, but batted only .238. No other Oaks player batted the requisite 450 times.

Scarsella would have won the batting crown with an average of .332, but he was 22 at-bats short. But he was named *The Sporting News'* PCL Most Valuable Player, beating out 30-game-winner Larry Jansen of the pennant-wining Seals.

On the mound, it was the same story. There were no 20-game winners, but the overall staff had impressive statistics. Gene Bearden was 15-4, Shea 15-5, while Ardizoia was 15-7.

Before earning immortality as a major league manager, Casey Stengel piloted the Oakland Oaks to the 1948 PCL championship with a group of veterans known as the 'Nine Old Men.' He was never shy about showing his emotions.

Above, a 1947 game brought a capacity crowd of 12,000 to Oaks Ball Park. One of the stars for the Oaks that year was pitcher Gene Bearden (below), who in 1948 pitched the Cleveland Indians to the American League pennant by winning the one-game playoff against Boston. The Oaks briefly led the league that season despite losing the core of their pitching staff to the major leagues, only to finish nine games out.

## NO MAGIC IN 1947

Stengel was unable to sprinkle his brand of magic dust on the 1947 Oaks mainly because the nucleus of the pitching staff advanced to the major leagues. Not that playing in the bigs was that much of a promotion; Oaks outfielder Wally Westlake was sold to the Pittsburgh Pirates after the 1946 season, then complained that his $5,000 contract offered by the Pirates was less than the $850 a month, plus bonuses, he was paid by the Oaks.

The Oaks actually took over first place for a time in mid-June but they eventually slid quietly into fourth place, nine games behind at season's end. They got a bit of satisfaction by defeating the Seals in the first round of the Governor's Cup playoffs but then lost to the Angels in the finals.

One noteworthy acquisition occurred at the end of the season when 19-year-old Billy Martin came to the Oaks. Martin, from Berkeley, was a bright, undersized and scrappy second baseman. With Phoenix of the Class C Arizona-Texas League, Martin played in 130 games, hitting .393, with 230 hits and 174 RBIs in 1947 before his recall to the Oaks.

The 1948 Oakland Oaks, who gained fame as Casey Stengel's 'Nine Old Men.' One youngster, though, was Billy Martin, bottom row, fourth from the left. He's sitting next to batboy Chuck Symonds. Below, Ernie Lombardi.

## THE NINE OLD MEN FLOURISH

Other than Bearden, no significant players were lost from the 1947 Oaks. As the 1948 season neared, Casey began to fine-tune the club by adding major league veterans as they became available. Over the winter the Oaks acquired 37-year-old pitcher Bob Klinger from the Boston Red Sox, who also sent along a third baseman, Merrill Combs, on option for the year. Pitcher Will Hafey was sold to Cleveland for cash and two players. While Hafey remained on option with the Oaks for the 1948 season, the team also received pitcher Les Webber and slugging outfielder George "Catfish" Metkovich, yet another major league veteran who played in the 1946 World Series for the Red Sox. Finally, Mickey Burnett was traded to the Angels for Loyd Christopher.

At the end of Spring Training, Stengel pronounced his club "10 percent" better than 1947. Both the Seals and the Angels were improved as well, so Stengel didn't stop trying to better his team. During the early portion of the season, the Oaks purchased pitcher Earl Jones from Toledo, signed 1947 World Series star Cookie Lavagetto, acquired two 34-year-old pitchers, Lou Tost and Jack Salveson, from the Sacramento Solons and signed catchers Eddie Fernandez and 40-year-old Oakland hero Ernie Lombardi, both of whom had been released by the Solons.

Casey had his "Nine Old Men"—plus teenager Billy Martin—in place. The next youngest player was Will Hafey at 25.

Of this group, easily the most famous in Oakland and around baseball was "The Schnozz," Ernie Lombardi. He

had broken in as a teenaged catcher for the Oaks in the late 1920s, hovering at .370 three years in a row before moving on to the big leagues with Brooklyn and then Cincinnati. Lombardi, a 1986 Hall of Fame inductee, had won two batting titles and a Most Valuable Player award during his 17-year major league career and had played in two World Series. Lombardi also had another unique attribute: He had played on the last Oaks pennant winner, in 1927. Despite his age and reputation as the world's slowest human, Lombardi played in more than 100 games during the 1948 season, hitting a respectable .264. In May he hit a ball out of Sacramento's Edmonds Field that was measured at 578 feet and fans joked that the ball could have been retrieved in time to throw Ernie out at first.

Dario Lodigiani, Metkovich and Lavagetto all had 5-10 major league seasons behind them. Nick Etten had won home run and RBI titles while playing during the war years for the New York Yankees.

Stengel adroitly shuffled and platooned his players, putting them in and taking them out of the lineup as the

Billy Martin learned most of his baseball from Casey Stengel, although his reputation as a scrapper began during his Berkeley schooldays. Below, Martin injects his opinion while Stengel pleads his case with the umpire.

situation dictated. He regularly platooned at second and third; when a left-hander was throwing Lavagetto would play third and Lodigiani would start at second. With a right-hander, Lodigiani would play third and Martin would start at second.

Stengel would innovate further with Will Hafey on the mound. A powerful hitter, Hafey would often bat fifth in the order rather than the usual pitcher's spot of ninth.

This would lead Billy Martin, pushed down to the ninth spot in the order, to complain, "Look at that old bastard. He's got me hitting with the groundskeepers."

Casey would inevitably growl back, 'You're lucky you're even playing.'

Early in the season shortstop Ray Hamrick was on a tear, hitting well and fielding with flair. When Lefty O'Doul suggested to his Seals pitchers they drill Hamrick

## BILLY THE ETERNAL KID

The friendship between Casey Stengel and Billy Martin began in the days when Casey managed the Oakland Oaks and Billy was a feisty rookie infielder who in 1947 had led Phoenix of the Class C Arizona-Texas League with a .393 average, 230 hits and 174 RBIs in 130 games.

But Billy was also a naive, inexperienced athlete, almost devoid of social graces. Oaks pitcher Damon Hayes related a story about Martin's first road trip. The team was staying at the Senator Hotel in Sacramento, and Stengel was holding court in the lobby. Martin entered the lobby from his room dressed in a casual shirt and pants.

Stengel quickly called Martin aside. "Billy," he said, "you have joined a good ballclub, and we stay at good hotels throughout the league. I would like you to dress better than what you're now wearing."

Martin said he was wearing the best clothing he had. At that point, Stengel pulled out $100 and told Martin to go buy some new clothes.

After Casey was promoted to the New York Yankees, he made sure Martin joined him. Martin watched Stengel, and learned well. Traded away from the Yankees against Casey's wishes because he spent too much time teaching Mickey Mantle to carouse, Martin became a baseball nomad. He signed on with a half-dozen teams before retiring from active play to coach.

In 1968 Martin managed the Denver Bears for a season before being promoted to manage the Minnesota Twins. Billy, barely 40 years old, promptly led the Twins to a division title but was fired, initiating a distressing pattern that plagued him throughout his career.

Martin led four different teams to five division championships and the New York Yankees into the World Series in 1976 and 1977. He knew how to win. Martin returned to Oakland to manage the A's in 1980. In Oakland, as in earlier cities, his fiery style would initially inspire his ballplayers, but inevitably his drinking, fighting and acid tongue would lead to his dismissal, often in mid-season.

Controversy shadowed Martin. As a youngster, Billy was bright, but small. Born on the proverbial other side of the tracks—west of San Pablo Avenue in the Berkeley flatlands—Billy had

to learn to protect himself to survive. He soon gained a reputation as a battler and seemed to be the instigator for a lot of the fights, many of which occurred at a recreation center near his home.

At Berkeley High School, Billy took his share of academic courses and came into contact with the more socially active kids from the affluent Berkeley hills. But there was no way he was going to be accepted into their social community.

Martin did find acceptance as an athlete, specifically in basketball and baseball. He was well known around the league. His baseball coach, the legendary Fred Moffett, used to tell of one game in particular when Berkeley played at Hayward High. Several Hayward fans were seated along the third base line, and before long, they picked out Billy as the target for their verbal abuse. Martin didn't react to them initially, but when he came to bat, he lined more than a few foul balls in their direction.

Billy was known to hold grudges large and small. Don Ferrarese, a four-sport athlete at Acalanes High School in nearby Lafayette who played against Martin as a prep and later became his teammate with the Cleveland Indians in 1959, related a summer league experience about Billy. Ferrarese was taking a 1-0 shutout into the last inning when Martin started shouting at him, "I'm going to beat you. I'm going to beat you myself."

Martin came to bat and promptly singled, stole second and third and, with two outs, continued the verbal harangue. Sure enough, Martin headed for home, only to find the flustered batter foul off the pitch. Martin was forced to return to third base, where he was stranded.

The story doesn't end there. Fast-forward to an otherwise nondescript Cleveland Indians game in 1959. Ferrarese had just pitched eight innings and was pulled for a reliever in the ninth. He made his way to the shower, his day's work done. With his face lathered, he suddenly felt a warmness on his leg. Looking down, he found Martin relieving himself.

"That's for the game in high school," Billy said.

Martin was killed in an automobile accident on an icy Christmas night in 1989. It was a violent, sudden end to a turbulent but rich life.

with a pitch, fastballer Manny Perez plunked Hamrick on his bad knee. Casey simply moved Merrill Combs to shortstop, where he developed into a superior player. It was that kind of year, where Casey had all the tools to create a pennant winner.

The Oaks players had learned to trust Casey even though his approach was unique and unpredictable. Periodically, for instance, Casey would announce without notice that it was "Steak Night"—dinner was on him. These meals didn't come as a reward for a winning streak, or as an incentive to break a losing one, they just came.

"Casey—he was outstanding," Lodigiani said. "He'd tell so many stories, he'd keep everybody so loose. He'd put on a show all the time. He was sharp."

One evening in Seattle, for example, during a particularly rough stretch of games, Casey began telling stories in the clubhouse about his career. It came time for the team to take batting practice and Casey kept recalling tales. Infield practice came and went, with the players listening in rapt silence. Just before the game was to start, Casey stopped talking and sent his team out to play. The Oaks scored eight runs in the first inning en route to a lopsided victory and instantly snapped out of the doldrums.

### THE PENNANT RACE

At the end of June the Seals led by a game over the Angels with the Oaks, Seattle and San Diego four games back. But by July the Angels leveled off and the Seals

Nick Etten was the first baseman for the 'Nine Old Men.' He played several years for the New York Yankees.

The fans pour onto the field as pitcher Jim Tobin (5) crosses first base to record the final out against Sacramento, giving Oakland its first pennant in 21 years.

briefly faltered while star Gene Woodling was out with a broken leg.

A crucial six-game series with the Seals seemed to be the turning point for the season. The Seals won the opener 1-0 behind Al Lien's shutout and Woodling's homer. For the next three games Oakland rallied in the late innings for three consecutive come-from-behind victories. After a doubleheader split on Sunday, Oakland had won four of six and was convinced destiny was on its side.

In the season's final month the Seals went 21-10, a .677 pace. The Oaks responded with a 24-6 record, an .800 pace, to finish with 114 wins and the pennant. The Oaks easily captured the Governor's Cup by defeating Seattle four games to one.

Under Casey's leadership, the Oaks won the title without a single league-leader in any of the individual categories. But the Oaks did have the highest team batting

average (.285), the highest team run total (1,022) and most RBIs (931).

Nick Etten led the pennant stretch with a phenomenal second half. On August 1, Etten had played in 105 games, hit 19 home runs and driven in 81 runs. In his last 59 games of the year, he hit 24 more home runs and drove in 74 more. His totals of 43 home runs and 155 RBIs both ranked second in the league.

The rest of the club was extremely consistent. Catfish Metkovich finished the year at .336, fourth best in the league behind Woodling's league-best .385. Christopher hit .321, Lodigiani .301, Lavagetto .304, Maurice Van Robays .313, Holder .297, Martin .275 and Combs .271.

The statistics for the pitching staff also revealed an equal balance as well as Casey's knack for making the right decision. "The thing I appreciated so much about Casey," Lodigiani said, "he knew when a pitcher was

## MIGHTY CASEY AT THE HELM

After leading Oakland to the PCL pennant in 1948, Casey Stengel was hired to manage the legendary New York Yankees beginning in 1949. Over the next 12 years, Casey created a record that probably will never be equaled. John McGraw and Connie Mack managed longer in the major leagues, but even they couldn't match Casey for sustained and brilliant success.

The first five years, 1949-1953, Stengel's Yankees won the American League pennant and the World Series. His 1954 team produced Casey's best record with 103 wins . . . but that was the year Cleveland won the pennant with a 111-43 record.

The Yankees won four more pennants from 1955-1958 to give them nine American League championships in 10 years. All four World Series went seven games, with the Dodgers winning in 1955 and the Braves winning in 1957. New York defeated Brooklyn in 1956 and Milwaukee in 1958.

The 1960 season was Casey's 50th in organized baseball. He lost the Series that year to Pittsburgh and was replaced in 1961 by Ralph Houk.

But Stengel was back at age 72, managing the expansion New York Mets from 1962 into 1965. Given the woeful Mets, Casey was there for entertainment value as well as managerial skills. He kept everyone in stitches, as he had done in Oakland and throughout his career. This was the same Casey Stengel who uttered the memorable line after John McGraw traded him to Boston after Stengel had hit two home runs for the Giants in the 1923 World Series: "Well, maybe I'm lucky. If I'd hit three homers McGraw might have sent me clear out of the country."

Casey Stengel acknowledges the applause of Oaks fans during a 1948 parade celebrating the 1948 championship season.

going to get into trouble, not when he got into trouble."

Casey's two stoppers, Buxton (13-3) and Speer (12-3), had the highest winning percentages, followed by Gassaway (15-8), Jones (13-6), Will Hafey (13-10), Wilkie (11-6) and Salveson (10-8).

Ironically, Cookie Devincenzi resigned as general manager before the season, ending his two-decade association with the Oaks just before their greatest triumph.

This was also the season in which train travel was replaced by airplane flights. Flying was so new and uncertain that league directors required the team to fly on two separate planes, as well as taking out a $1 million insurance policy on the team with Lloyds of London.

Ralph Buxton also become "Mr. Pine Tar" that season. On August 14, during the crucial Seals-Oaks series, Buxton was within one strike of finishing a win over the Seals when umpire Ziggy Sears visited the mound, inspected Buxton's glove, found pine tar and confiscated the glove. Since the umpire allowed Buxton to complete the game, Seals Manager Lefty O'Doul rightly protested to the league offices. PCL President "Pants" Rowland suspended Buxton for 10 days and required that the inning be replayed. After a good deal of arguing, the inning was replayed September 21 with the same result.

Casey, holding a picture of cross-bay counterpart Lefty O'Doul, mugs for the camera in 1948.

A program for the replay of one inning of a Seals-Oaks game that the Seals protested because Oaks pitcher Ralph Buxton was found to have too much pine tar on his glove.

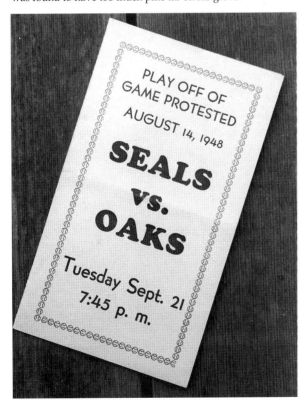

The 1948 championship took on great significance in Oakland and other East Bay communities, which had long felt relegated to second-class citizenship in the Bay Area. Victory parades and banquets were followed by bragging rights, at least for the winter. But fame passed quickly for the Oaks. Casey Stengel began his unprecedented string of American League pennants in 1949 for the New York Yankees. Hafey and Combs were recalled, and most of the "Nine Old Men" retired or were released. Their reign was short, but it was sweet. And memorable. ❖

CHAPTER **19**

# THE PCL'S
# MAJOR LEAGUE EFFORT

Until the post-World War II advent of transcontinental air travel and telecommunications, California never really had a complete perspective of its place in the greater American fabric, particularly when it came to baseball. The Pacific Coast League was an immensely attractive and competitive product, but the better players continued to leave to play in something called the "major" leagues. Why did these young men have to go thousands of miles away to enjoy stardom? Why couldn't they continue to provide their hometown fans with the enjoyment of watching them play?

Like the economy, the league's fortunes rose and fell. But one thing was constant—population was on the increase, creating more baseball fans. With each stage of prosperity on the West Coast, calls mounted for the PCL to declare itself a major league. League directors acknowledged this desire, putting pressure on the owners of the American and National Leagues to grant the Pacific Coast League a more elevated status.

### KEEP OUR BOYS HOME

A number of Pacific Coast League teams, including the San Francisco Seals, outdrew major league clubs in 1945. The Seals' attendance surpassed the Cincinnati Reds, the Philadelphia Phillies and the Boston Braves.

Hollywood's Victor Ford Collins was the champion of the movement in its early stages. At the league's winter meetings in December 1944, Collins presented a resolution calling for cooperation among all members in working together to attain major league status. The resolution, although not carrying any weight of law, also bound all teams together to prevent any major league team from invading their territory. The resolution passed easily but it was not unanimous. Los Angeles cast the lone vote against it.

In 1945, league directors asked Collins to investigate and prepare a resolution for future discussion. The critical problem of solidarity had to be overcome. For the league to have any possibility of success, all eight teams had to be unified.

Los Angeles' Don Stewart was hesitant to commit the Angels too far because of the constant rumors that the National League would expand to 10 teams and locate one of them in Los Angeles. There were also persistent rumors that the St. Louis Browns would transfer to L.A.

The chances that the PCL would elevate to major league status would be effectively doomed if another major league team moved to Los Angeles. In fact, it would necessitate the transfer of two franchises into smaller population areas, disturbing the geographic balance.

These reasons in themselves were the catalyst for Collins' aggressive stand. The Hollywood franchise had

190

much to gain by becoming major league and much to lose if Los Angeles gained a major league franchise.

Thus, the approach Collins advocated and the league accepted was advancement of the league to major league status as a whole. When Paul Fagan became a partner in the San Francisco Seals in 1945, Collins found a vocal ally.

## PROSPERITY INTENSIFIES THE FERVOR

During the 1946 season when the Seals set the minor league attendance record, baseball Commissioner Happy Chandler came west and professed to be impressed with what he saw. While Chandler could not promise anything, he pledged to make a positive report to the major league owners.

Organized baseball's winter meetings were scheduled for Los Angeles in 1946, the first time the meetings had been held so far west. To present a united stand, the PCL directors elected a committee to meet with the American and National Leagues to negotiate elevation of the Coast League to major league status. Chosen were Collins, Charlie Graham and PCL President Clarence Rowland. The committee pressed certain objectives—namely the league's bid for major league status—but more practically the abolition of the major league draft, plus protection of territorial rights from major league invasion.

Previously, any major league club could have acquired a minor league area by purchasing the franchise for a mere $5,000. While the major league owners took no action towards granting major league status to the Coast League or reduction of the draft, they voted the establishment of a seven-man board of arbitration which would determine the amount of compensation to be paid to both the team and to the league upon invasion by any major league team into their territory.

In February 1947, the major league executive council was presented with a formal bid from the Pacific Coast League for elevation to major league status. The executive council tabled any action but scheduled a tour of the league ballparks in early September. An ultimate decision would be made at the next owners meeting.

The decision was a disappointment to the PCL. While the council couldn't argue about recent attendance figures and fan loyalty, it felt several ballparks were inferior to major league standards and had to be improved before any bid could be taken seriously. Three franchises in particular stood out: Sacramento, San Diego and Portland.

The 1947 and 1948 Pacific Coast League seasons showed the wildly successful 1946 season was no fluke. Still, there was no serious movement by the major leagues to grant concessions, let alone parity, to the league. It was obvious major league ownership was not going to give

PCL directors convene to discuss the details of the league's 'open classification' status. Left to right, Sacramento's Charlie Graham Jr., Seattle's Emil Sick, Portland's George Norgan, Oakland's Brick Laws, PCL President Clarence Rowland, Hollywood's Bob Cobb, San Francisco's Damon Miller, San Diego's Bill Starr and Los Angeles' Don Stewart.

SAN FRANCISCO PUBLIC LIBRARY

## SACRAMENTO SAVES ITS FRANCHISE

By far, the weakest PCL franchise in the war years was Sacramento. The St. Louis Cardinals had purchased the franchise in the late 1930s, but their commitment to the city and to the league had been mediocre at best. The Solons took the 1942 pennant by one game over the Angels, but in 1943 they managed to win only 41 games, drawing 31,694 fans for the season.

Sacramento became the major topic at the PCL directors' 1943 winter meetings. The Cardinals had put up the club and the ballpark for sale, asking $110,000 for both. Tacoma, Wash., and Vancouver, B.C., both had delegations present to request a franchise shift. Only an aggressive campaign by *Sacramento Union* Sports Editor Dick Edmonds and Solons General Manager Yubi Separovich saved the team from being turned back to the league.

The pair came to the meeting armed with $50,000 in checks hastily written by Solons supporters, gathered in just two days. This show of support by the citizens of Sacramento saved the franchise from being moved.

The Cardinals were talked into reducing the price of the franchise by $10,000 and the price of Doubleday Park by another $10,000, making the final package $90,000. More than 200 Sacramento citizens pledged in excess of $125,000 to capitalize the franchise.

Edmonds, 31, died unexpectedly after the team was saved, and Doubleday Park was quickly renamed in his memory. The ballpark was as antiquated as San Diego's and Portland's, but Sacramento's problems were solved for them. Following a doubleheader in July 1948, the ballpark burned down, leaving only the covered left field bleacher area, the outfield fences and the center field scoreboard. The Solons became a road team for the remainder of the season.

The 1949 season opened with an attractive cement stadium built on the same site. An exciting team and the return of the nucleus of vocal and knowledgeable fans made Sacramento a good baseball town again.

---

away any of its status, or profits, to the upstarts on the West Coast.

After six years, several PCL owners were ready to advocate desperate steps. Most desperate was withdrawal from the National Association—in effect becoming an outlaw league.

The directors debated their options at meetings in the first half of 1950. There was some sympathy coming from Chandler, but with 1951 the 50th anniversary of the National Association and with a congressional committee about to review baseball's reserve clause, major league officials wanted no incident to mar a unified front by baseball. Additionally, Chandler was up for re-election as commissioner, and his assertive approach to the office had alienated some of the owners. His re-election was not guaranteed, and the Coast League could not count on him to lead their cause.

The PCL directors hired as legal counsel Leslie O'Connor, former secretary to Commissioner Landis, to develop a strategy. O'Connor advised moderation, fearing an assertive approach might antagonize the major league owners into approving the transfer of the Browns to Los Angeles.

Aware that the Major League-Minor League Agreement was up for renewal after the 1951 season, Coast League directors held two volatile meetings during the summer to discuss how they could negotiate concessions. Most team owners felt modification or elimination of the major league draft would substantially ease their financial concerns, so this became a primary target.

The issue came to a head at the meeting in San Francisco on June 22. Aware that by not signing the Major League-Minor League Agreement the league would automatically be dropped from the National Association, the directors felt they were in a position to negotiate with Major League Baseball.

While every club opposed the draft, Damon Miller, serving as Seals Owner Paul Fagan's proxy, represented the most radical viewpoint—withdrawal from the National Association and negotiating a two-party agreement with the major leagues. George Norgan of Portland also strongly advocated this position. San Diego's Bill Starr suggested no ratification of any agreement unless the league was exempted from the draft altogether.

At the conclusion of the June meeting, the directors voted to present two recommendations to the major leagues at their July meeting in Detroit, in conjunction with the All-Star Game. The recommendations would allow players at the Triple-A level the right to accept or reject whether they would be subject to the major league draft. The second recommendation would guarantee that the major leagues would not occupy any territory of any Pacific Coast League club without the consent of all clubs in the Pacific Coast League. Only Miller, consistent with his earlier stand, voted against the plan.

### HOUSE SUB-COMMITTEE HEARINGS

Organized baseball also was receiving a great deal of pressure from Congress. Under the leadership of Congressman Emanuel Celler, a House Judiciary Sub-

Committee was reviewing baseball's exemption from anti-trust legislation. This was a much greater threat to the institution than the toothless threats of a minor league. Baseball had much to lose by these hearings, and it was critical that nothing disrupt the facade of normalcy and peace in the baseball world.

High baseball officials flocked to Washington to urge protection of the reserve clause. Not all witnesses were positive, however. Damon Miller testified to the injustices of the major league draft, using Ferris Fain as an example. Fain, after his excellent year for the Seals in 1946, was drafted by the Philadelphia Athletics for $10,000. Realistically, Fain was worth $100,000.

Miller's point was obvious: The major league draft perpetuated financial exploitation of the minor leagues through their monopoly. But at the hearing's conclusion, the Celler Committee gave organized baseball a pat on the back, virtually ignoring PCL concerns.

## NOW OR NEVER FOR THE PCL

Most owners came to Los Angeles for a second Coast League directors meeting on July 26, 1951 with a much more militant attitude.

Phil Wrigley of the Chicago Cubs and Del Webb of the New York Yankees also attended as emissaries of the majors. Miller initiated the discussion by moving that the league go on record with its intention to resign from the National Association and negotiate separate agreements with each major league.

Wrigley and Webb encouraged an attitude of moderation from the directors, with Webb suggesting, "What do you think of a new classification for the PCL?" After heated discussion, the directors asked O'Connor and Wrigley to outline a proposal to be reviewed at the next day's session. Out of this came the PCL's application for an "open" minor league classification.

Of that day's events, Brick Muller said, "I was ready to go independent when I came to the meeting yesterday, but now I feel different." The next day, O'Connor presented the proposal, and after discussion, Miller again moved that the league announce its intention to resign from the National Association.

In essence, this was a power play to force organized baseball into making concessions to the Coast League. The other alternative was outlaw status and the multitude of problems it could create for all of baseball.

The vote was 4-4, with San Francisco, Oakland, Portland and Sacramento voting in favor. Lacking consensus, Don Stewart of Los Angeles moved the previous motion be tabled until after baseball's winter meetings in December. This motion was carried.

G. Taylor Spink, general manager of *The Sporting News*, editorialized his concerns about the Coast League's aggressive posture. He feared a repeat of the Federal League problem, when a divisive and expensive war erupted over the pirating of players from established teams and competition for territorial rights became fierce.

O'Connor responded to Spink by pointing out that the Federal League was formed by outside forces attempting to go head-to-head against already-established teams in the same cities. The Pacific Coast League, he countered, had been in operation for nearly a half-century, was geographically isolated from the major leagues, and intended to strengthen itself from within. He also felt the major leagues were unduly suppressing the Coast League's chances to grow.

Fagan, who had not attended the meeting, was furious at the outcome of the 4-4 vote. He had grown tired of this kind of meeting and appointed a proxy. The meetings always frustrated him, and he probably realized it was better not to attend because his presence created a backlash against his causes.

The other directors expected an outburst from Fagan, as was his style. Instead, for almost a month there was silence from Fagan's estate in Hana, Maui. Then he came out with a blockbuster, announcing he was leaving baseball effective September 9—the last day of the 1951 season—and would sell the Seals. The inaction in bringing relief from the draft had finally defeated the man. Fagan announced he wanted $350,000 for the franchise and its players and would rent—but not sell—Seals Stadium to the new owners.

Fagan's investment in the San Francisco Baseball Club approximated $1 million. He had purchased the stock in several blocks, costing $645,000, and he had loaned the club substantial amounts of money for stadium improvements and operating costs. Seals Stadium was viewed as prime real estate worth $1-2 million.

Louis Lurie, a prominent real estate investor, and Bill Kyne, operator of Bay Meadows race track, were often mentioned as prospective buyers but neither man was able to work a deal with Fagan.

Over the next four months O'Connor polished the league's application for presentation at the winter meetings in Columbus, Ohio. With the prospect of something positive coming from the meetings, Fagan relented and committed himself to operating the Seals again in 1952.

As a result of O'Connor's presentation and a continued barrage from Rowland and the PCL owners, the major leagues agreed to the establishment of a new open classification, to operate for one year with the option of renewal. This new classification elevated the Pacific Coast League above the Triple-A status of the International League and the American Association. But it fell short of granting major league status.

The new classification gave the league slight relief from the draft. The fee for drafting a player out of the open classification was increased from $10,000 to $15,000.

Additionally, players could waive their right to be drafted from an open classification club.

This option encouraged Coast League teams to sign their own players and make it financially worthwhile for them to stay. In this manner the open classification could gain strength internally, the PCL clubs elevating themselves to major league status.

Incentive seemingly existed for young players to waive the draft clause. They could negotiate better salaries and a percentage of the sales price if their contract was sold to a major league club. But while the concept sounded good, the major leagues increased their pressure by signing local amateurs to bonuses that local teams simply couldn't match.


**READ THE FINE PRINT**

Other stipulations accompanied this new classification. Before major league status could be granted, the league's cities were required to show an aggregate population of 15 million and average attendance of more than 3.5 million over the previous three years. In addition, each ballpark was required to have a potential minimum seating capacity of 25,000. Finally, the league was required to adhere to the minimum salary schedule used at the major league level.

From 1946-49, total attendance had topped 3.5 million each year, dropping to 3,172,718 in 1950. The directors were confident attendance could be pushed back above the minimum requirement. The aggregate population goal could be reached quickly as thousands of Americans were migrating to California each day. Plus, most teams already paid the major league minimum or above. The major problem would be the costs involved with improving or replacing stadium facilities to meet the 25,000 seating capacity.

As a step to becoming more independent, the directors voted to suspend accepting optioned players and negotiating working agreements with major league teams by the 1953 season. To implement this, each team needed to expand its regional scouting network and establish a system of farm clubs, an expensive proposition. Some teams would have more catching up to do than others in this area.

The major leagues were offering concessions with the left hand, but on October 8, 1951, they smacked every minor league in the pocketbook with the right. At a joint meeting of the American and National Leagues, Rule 1 (D) of the Major-Minor League Agreement was repealed. Rule 1 (D) restricted the broadcasting or televising of major league games into areas where minor league home games were being played.

Previously, the rule had been loosely interpreted by some major league clubs, causing severe loss of revenue in some minor league areas. This move virtually guaranteed all minor league teams would feel the penetration of major league baseball into their area.

In an angry letter to the league office dated October 9, Fagan pointed how this action would affect his club in 1952:

"The Seals received for the 1951 season $65,000 for radio rights, and our sponsor paid an additional $60,000 for station time, or a total of $125,000 for the broadcast. How much do you think a sponsor is going to pay for our broadcast in 1952 when they can get the so-called Major or big show for a total of from $30,000 to $40,000?"

Another question could have been asked: "How many fans will come to the local ballpark when they can hear or watch a major league at home?"

The concern regarding a major league franchise shift to Los Angeles was addressed to the presidents of the two major leagues by Rowland on July 2, 1951. Rowland spoke of "the constant gossip about purported intentions to move one or more of your clubs into Pacific Coast League territory."

Rowland asked the two presidents to agree not to move any of their teams into Pacific Coast League territory without the full consent of all clubs of the league. He felt the gossip and rumors had heightened the anticipation of local fans to major league baseball, thus discouraging their attendance at the current games being held.

To complicate this issue further, the *Examiner* newspaper chain had been running an active campaign to bring major league baseball to the West Coast, specifically to Los Angeles and San Francisco.

It is interesting to note that the territorial rights issue was not included as part of the Pacific Coast League's application for open classification. At the league directors meeting on July 27, 1951, Phil Wrigley suggested that the major league owners undoubtedly would allow modifications to the current draft status. But he added that if a request or demand for territorial autonomy were included, both issues would be defeated. The other directors accepted his point.

Soon, word came that Bob Cobb had sold 16 percent of the Hollywood Baseball Club to the Pittsburgh Pirates, shares which had been owned by minority stockholder George Young. This action was looked upon as an infraction of the so-called Buffalo Resolution, which forbade any Pacific Coast League owner from buying stock in a major league club or selling their stock to a major league club. This transaction was completed and couldn't be undone, but it stood as an act reducing the credibility of the whole league.

Realistically speaking, major league baseball never had any intention of giving away the keys to its store. Now, the dramatic shifts created by television and suburbanization would bury the ambitions of the Pacific Coast League.

## THE LONG SLIDE DOWNHILL

In San Francisco, Paul Fagan became less interested in the daily activities of his club, giving more responsibility to Damon Miller. This lack of energy was mirrored at the turnstiles, as Seals' attendance dipped below 200,000 to 199,083 for the first time since 1936. There was little change in attendance in 1952, but a drop of close to 25,000 followed in 1953. Fagan was losing more than $100,000 per year.

Fagan became relatively quiet about the problems of his team and the travails of the league, but he was amazingly prophetic in an interview on the open classification status of the PCL. In the interview, Hal Wood of United Press commented that the only apparent stumbling block to major league status was the size of the league's stadiums. "I can't see that one at all," Fagan responded. "Due to the inroads of television, I believe that the time will come when a park with a seating capacity of 12,000 will be big enough for even major league teams. When that day comes, TV will be paying the bills of ball clubs and millions of people will watch the games from their homes."

The 1953 season was the most critical of the post-war period. The directors had voted not to accept optioned players from, or to negotiate any working agreement with, any major league organization. While the idea seemed logical as a further step towards emancipation, the previous seasons with their poor attendance left virtually every club short of funds to buy players. In the first months of the season, the grumbling started.

Brick Laws of Oakland was one of the most vocal for rescinding the plan. His fans weren't coming to the ballpark because there were no big names to watch. In an emotional 5-3 vote, the directors rescinded their resolution, effective with the 1954 season.

The results of the 1953 season severely dampened any realistic hopes of the league using the open classification status as an avenue to the big leagues. Overall league attendance dropped 400,000 paid admissions to 1,759,795. Oakland's drop was almost 100,000 and San Francisco's was 23,000. Evening television was probably the biggest factor in the decline, but the poor quality of baseball could not be ruled out.

It was at this point that Fagan quit, forcing the league directors to turn the franchise over to Damon Miller and the "Little Corporation."

The directors appointed Eddie Mulligan of Sacramento to meet with Fagan and see what he wanted out of his franchise. Fagan ultimately sold the franchise to the league for $100,000, who turned it over to Damon Miller and his "Little Corporation." Miller's group got two years out of the franchise before they were forced into receivership with the league. Finally, late in the 1955 season, the directors refused to give Miller more time to clear up his massive debt obligations and took the franchise away from him.

Claire Goodwin, now the league president, was charged with finding a new buyer for the Seals. He botched two potential sales, leading ultimately to his own ouster by the directors before a transaction was consummated in December with the Boston Red Sox .

The Oakland franchise also collapsed after the 1955 season. Laws had been an aggressive owner but the fans had not rewarded him with their attendance. Oakland attendance was the league's worst in 1951, 1953 and 1955. It was not unusual for games to be attended by less than 1,000 fans. With cities begging for a Coast League franchise, Laws had no reason to stick with an apparent sinking ship. Vancouver, B.C., outbid Phoenix for the Oaks, making the Pacific Coast League an international circuit for the first time.

While the Bay Area was suffering through a period of low interest and terrible attendance, games in Seattle and in Southern California were drawing large crowds. Although his club was not in trouble, San Diego's Bill Starr decided to sell. Starr had tried to get the San Diego City Council to give him land to build a new ballpark, and when the council refused, Starr sold out to the West Coast Tuna Packing Co. With greater resources, the company set out to construct a new park in Mission Valley.

While the open classification lasted through 1957, it was a foregone conclusion that major league baseball would come to the West Coast before the Pacific Coast League could meet the criteria to qualify as a major league. Throughout the seven years of the open classification, there had been extensive behind-the-scenes activity to seize the league's two major cities, Los Angeles and San Francisco, for the major leagues.

When the grand design succeeded, as it did after the 1957 season, the Coast League was fractured in a manner that would forever remove it as a viable alternative to major league baseball. But in an ironic way, the dreams of Fagan, Collins, Rowland, Laws, Seattle's Emil Sick and others were fulfilled. By 1969, the major leagues had moved into Anaheim, San Diego and Seattle, and the Kansas City franchise transferred to Oakland. ❖

CHAPTER **20**

# 'CHESTY CHET' & OTHER CHARACTERS

Characters and pranksters are as much a part of baseball as the hit-and-run and the stolen base. Stunts such as setting a player's shoelaces on fire, tying his uniform into knots or lining a black toilet seat with black shoe polish are necessary to provide release from the mounting tensions over a long, arduous season. Characters and pranks are not in any way monopolized by the major leagues; in fact, the old Pacific Coast League was notorious for having its share.

### "CHESTY CHET"—KING OF THEM ALL

King of the modern characters, without a doubt, was "Chesty Chet." Chester Lillis Johnson was an above-average left-handed pitcher who toiled for five different Coast League teams during the 1940s and 1950s. Johnson was generally in double figures each year for both wins and losses. His career peaked in 1950 with the Seals when he went 22-13 for a fifth-place team.

Johnson tended to play it pretty straight and serious during the earlier years of his career, but after 1950, when his career was going nowhere, he discovered that humor added to his appeal and undoubtedly extended his career. As his reputation around the league grew, fans flocked to the park to watch him pitch. Attendance would double or triple on the dates when Johnson was scheduled to pitch.

Seals play-by-play announcer Don Klein remembered Johnson as "a good person, quiet and unassuming. Johnson would play it straight for five or six innings, then he would pull some trick from his act. He wouldn't take any chances. He had to be a talented pitcher to get away with it."

Klein admitted he usually was unable to describe Chesty Chet's antics on the air. "I couldn't," Klein said. "He would get me laughing, and I couldn't describe it."

Johnson's antics had a purpose, of course—they were a weapon against the most dangerous or temperamental opposing batters. Johnson became a master of the pantomime, using over-exaggerated movements and facial expressions to amuse fans and confuse batters. He developed a standard routine and varied it on occasion. His pitching style featured a two-armed windup featuring lots of circling with his arms, a thrown glove, a blooper pitch, and occasionally, an adequate fastball and a better-than-average curve.

### THE LITTLE BLACK BOOK

His major prop was a little black book which he would take from his back pocket as a batter stepped up to the plate. After thumbing through the pages, he would stop, study one page assiduously, finally nodding in

Chester 'Chesty Chet' Johnson was one of the great characters in Pacific Coast League history, constantly drawing laughter from crowds during the game. Left, Chesty Chet displays his double-windmill windup, one of the ploys he used to distract the batter. Right, Johnson demonstrates how to pitch and hit at the same time. Johnson resorted to comic tactics after his career peaked in 1950.

agreement. Then he would prepare to pitch. If he got the batter out, he would repeat the routine on the next batter. Ultimately, someone would get a hit, and Johnson would pull the book out of his pocket, find the offending page and rip it into tiny pieces, throwing them to the wind.

During night games, Johnson frequently would feign difficulty seeing the catcher's signal. Then he would move closer to home plate and peer in again. Still no luck, and Johnson would move even closer. Ultimately, Johnson would end up crawling across the plate, lighting a match before getting the catcher's signal. Feeling confident he had the signal right, he would stride back to the mound and shake the signal off, to the huge delight of the crowd.

In 1954, although not having one of his greatest years, Johnson was included on the league All-Star team selected to play the first-place Hollywood Stars at Gilmore Field.

To boost attendance for the game, Chesty Chet was announced as the starting pitcher. Before the game, Johnson pulled catcher Al Evans aside and gave him some

specific instructions. Johnson wanted Evans to return the first three pitches to him hard, harder and blistering, in that order.

The first batter stepped in and Johnson pitched. Evans threw the ball back as instructed. Johnson caught the throw and winced slightly, looking strangely at Evans. After the second pitch, Evans fired the ball back to Johnson who yelped, shook his glove hand and looked at Evans as if to say, "What are you doing?" With the third and hardest return, Johnson caught the ball, let out an enormous howl, falling to his knees while grabbing his pitching hand. The crowd fell silent. Johnson's teammates rushed to his assistance, and after several moments of milking the situation, Johnson gestured the players to back away from the mound. He struggled to his feet, held his glove hand out from his body, and gingerly removed the glove from his hand.

Holding his hand out for the crowd to see, there was an oversized, rubber thumb, dripping a red substance to the ground. Chesty Chet stood there, grinning. The crowd had been taken, and they wanted more.

Portland's Vaughn Street Park had an iron foundry located behind the right field fence. Occasionally, the foundry would belch out a thick, black smoke that would drift over the diamond, causing a delay in the game. This happened during one of Johnson's pitching assignments.

Johnson pantomimed an inability to see or breathe, staggered around the mound and waved his hands in the air. When the cloud finally dissipated, Johnson gathered his composure, climbed on to the mound and looked in for the catcher's sign. The only problem: he was facing second base.

Late in the 1952 season, neither Johnson nor his Sacramento teammates were going anywhere. The Solons were mired deeply in the cellar when they played the Oaks in the last series of the season. Catcher-coach Vinnie Smith had earlier vowed to grow a beard which he would cut off only when the Solons won a doubleheader or the season concluded, whichever came first. By now the beard was full, with little prospect of being shorn. Johnson pitched the second Sunday game and was in great form. Smith was coaching third base when Johnson led off an inning. Johnson concealed himself from Smith and put on a fake beard. He then strode out to the third base coaching box to confer with Smith. Johnson proceeded to carry on an animated conversation while Smith could do nothing but break up in laughter. Vinnie should have known he would be a target for Chesty Chet.

This was the same game that Oaks shortstop Roy Nicely, a batter who scared no one, caught a Johnson blooper pitch in his hand, tossed it into the air before him, and fungoed it against the left field wall. The umpire called it "no pitch," undoubtedly saddening Nicely, who needed all the help he could get.

Finally, in July 1956, the Solons weighed Johnson's gate appeal against his pitching effectiveness and optioned him out of the league. Shortly thereafter, he was out of baseball. In an 18-year career, Johnson both won and lost more than 200 games. In 1946, he had no decisions in five games as a major leaguer with the St. Louis Browns.

## "TWO GUN" GETTEL

In 1951, Johnson split the season between San Francisco and Oakland. One of his teammates with the Oaks was another character: Allen "Two Gun" Gettel. Despite his reputation, he was all business on the mound. From 1949 through August 1955, when his contract was sold to the St. Louis Cardinals, Gettel was considered the best right-hander in the league. He won 23 games in 1950 and 24 in 1953.

Gettel acquired his nickname because he wanted to be a cowboy actor. He apparently had been encouraged by a few Hollywood studios but nothing came of it. Nevertheless, Gettel played the part both at the ballpark and away from it.

On road trips, for example, Gettel boarded airplanes wearing his loaded six-guns and his 10-gallon hat. No big deal; it was just "Two Gun" Gettel. At Oaks Ball Park, he would entertain the fans before the game by riding his horse around the outfield and swinging his lasso.

Lefty O'Doul managed Gettel in 1955 and used to signal Gettel in from the bullpen by standing on the mound and pantomiming the gallop of a horse. When managing against Gettel, O'Doul quickly learned that his attempts to rattle the pitcher guaranteed the next batter would likely hit the dirt.

## JACKIE PRICE AND HIS PINK CADILLAC

Gettel wasn't the only member of the Oakland Oaks who liked to ride around the Oakland outfield. But Jackie Price would drive a World War II Jeep. Price was a smallish, light-hitting infielder who spent much of the time riding the bench as a member of Casey Stengel's 1946 Oaks. His contributions to the team were minimal. He was a poor hitter and only an average fielder. And at 34, he was not a prospect.

But Price would get the fans into the stands early with a series of amazing and amusing tricks. He could throw three balls to three players at three distances all at the same time. He could throw between his legs while standing on his head. He could hit a ball while hanging upside down from an apparatus.

He would use either a Jeep or his lavish pink Cadillac convertible as part of his act, getting a teammate to fungo baseballs high into the outfield, first to left field, then to right field and back again. All the time, Price would drive around, catching the balls. Then he would hop out of the vehicle, loosen his belt and catch thrown balls in his pants. Often, when reaching into his pants to retrieve the ball, he would extract a five-foot snake instead. Stengel eventually made Price get rid of the snake act, though, because the slithery creatures unnerved him.

One of Price's foils for his act was popular batboy Chuck Symonds, who traveled with the team primarily to help Price with his act. Price was so popular, in fact, he was allowed to leave the team to perform his act at neighboring ballparks while the Oaks were on the road. Even in the middle of a pennant race, this was not a hardship for the Oaks.

Bill Veeck, the showman owner of the Cleveland Indians, was so impressed with Price that he purchased his contract from the Oaks in the latter part of the season. The Indians' Lou Boudreau was not pleased when Price was purchased and placed on the active roster, but the

Jackie Price wasn't much of a hitter and didn't play extensively, but he was a master of baseball tricks. Over the years he developed more than 100 gags, including catching baseballs in his pants and throwing three balls to three players in three different locations. Brick Laws eventually sold Price to Bill Veeck.

fans enjoyed his pre-game act. Price actually did get into seven games for the Indians, collecting three hits for a .231 batting average. But that was it for his major league career. Price worked for Veeck and the Indians in 1947, but after that, he drifted out of baseball.

## "SEACAP" CHRISTENSEN'S SOMERSAULTS

Walter "Seacap" Christensen was a diminutive outfielder for the Mission Reds in 1929-30. Christensen was also known as "Cuckoo." He enjoyed doing somersaults in the outfield, normally when the ball wasn't in play. The fans enjoyed Christensen's antics, but his manager, Wade "Red" Killefer, was never pleased by them.

Occasionally, Christensen would do a somersault while getting in position to catch a lazy fly ball, but on one occasion, his flippancy got the best of him. With the Reds leading by one run in the bottom of the ninth

inning and runners on base, Christensen went after a fly ball, did a somersault, then dropped the ball. The Reds lost the game, and an angry Killefer chased Christensen all the way into the center field clubhouse.

Christensen served as a Coast League umpire in the 1930s and 1940s after his playing days were over.

## THE GREAT MAILS

Probably the most immodest player to grace the Pacific Coast was Walter Mails. Mails, who referred to himself as "The Great," was actually a pretty good pitcher.

He had a spotty, seven-year major league career disrupted by stints with Sacramento in 1919-20 and Oakland in 1923-24. He finished by playing for the Seals twice and then the Beavers before retiring to work in promotions for the Seals. When the Giants came to San Francisco in 1958, Mails remained in that capacity well into his 70s before he died in 1974.

A 1927 photograph of the Missions' Walter Christensen, who was known as 'Seacap' and 'Cuckoo.' He would do somersaults while waiting for lazy fly balls.

Mails was acquired from Sacramento by Cleveland during the latter stages of the 1920 season. The Indians were in a ferocious pennant race with the White Sox and the Yankees when Mails arrived. He was thrust into the starting rotation and went undefeated in eight starts, winning seven games and compiling a 1.85 ERA. The Indians won the pennant over the Sox by only two games.

In Game Three of the World Series, Mails entered as a reliever with one out in the first and promptly shut down a rally. Mails pitched shutout ball the rest of the way in a losing cause to the Dodgers. In Game Six, Mails blanked Brooklyn on a three-hitter, 1-0. Stan Coveleski won three games for the eventual World Champion Indians to be the Series hero, but Cleveland wouldn't have reached the post-season without Mails.

Mails won 14 games for the 1921 Indians before a bout of wildness prompted his return to Oakland in 1923.

Besides "The Great," Mails' other nickname was "Duster." Mails was a burly, left-handed pitcher who fit the southpaw stereotype—fast and wild. He consistently led his team in walks, wild pitches and hit batsmen. In 1920, an opposing catcher suggested to Mails that his sidearm style of pitching was not in his best interests. By throwing overhand, Mails could take advantage of his natural speed while reducing his wildness. Mails tried the suggestion and had an immediate reversal in his performance. The nickname, however, remained.

Mails was arrogant on the mound. He used to talk to the batters, challenging them to hit his pitches. The only problem was batters started talking back to him, and it was Mails who got flustered. In the first month of the 1924 season, Mails got into two separate fights on days he was pitching. At Salt Lake City, he and Bees Manager Duffy Lewis went at each other to no decision. Within three weeks, back in Oakland, Mails challenged "Bim" Meyers of the Angels to a fight after the game because Meyers had been insulting Mails all afternoon while he pitched. Meyers showed up, and Mails whipped him, claiming victory in that one.

On at least one occasion, Mails' ego got the better of him. In a 1926 game, Mails was pitching to Mickey Finn of the Missions, bantering at him between every pitch. Finn had taken enough and uttered some menacing comments back to the mound. At that point, Mails challenged him to a fight right then and there. Finn accepted and decked him with a single right to the jaw. Little did Mails know that Finn was a fairly successful boxer in the Navy. From that point, players knew they could get to Mails by calling him "Canvasback."

In 1935, with Mails' career winding down, he faced Missions third baseman George McDermott at Seals Stadium. Both Mails and McDermott had played baseball at St. Mary's College in Moraga. When McDermott lined a single, Mails, in a voice expressing mock anger and hurt, said, "That's a hell of a thing to do to an alum."

Although Mails seemed to have an answer for every challenge, at least one fan left him speechless as Mails left the park following a Sunday afternoon loss in 1924. A fan approached Mails and asked to shake his hand. "Why do you want to shake my hand?" Mails asked. The fan responded, "I came 100 miles to see you get your ears dented by the Seals sluggers, and I want to congratulate you for my good time."

In retirement, Mails served as the Seals' official greeter and promoter, enjoying the chance to remain in the spotlight even though he wasn't the most popular man in town—a product of his arrogance and frequent insensitivity. For special occasions, he would dress up in his formal attire, complete with top hat, tails and cane. He was an impressive figure. Occasionally, he would help out Lefty O'Doul by coaching at first base. The number on the back of his uniform was "?".

Carl "Buzz" Sawyer was a good infielder for the Vernon Tigers in the early 1920s, but he is primarily remembered for his pre-game antics more than his game heroics. Sawyer had no shame. He would try any trick and use any prop for a laugh. One of his favorites was playing chimpanzee by climbing up the backstop screen. He would also dance with an oversized rag doll or knock the bottom out of an apple basket, dressing up as a young damsel with the inverted basket serving as his dress. His baseball cap was always turned askew, and his use of facial expressions would make Charlie Chaplin or Lucille Ball proud.

Happy Hogan, a native of San Francisco who managed the Vernon Tigers in the 1910s, would pull off any stunt imaginable on an umpire to get a laugh.

## CHARACTERS UP AND DOWN THE COAST

Happy Hogan of the Vernon Tigers was one of the league's greatest assets during the first decade of its existence. A San Franciscan, Hogan was a genuine "flake," but he was also a solid baseball man. In a particular series at Recreation Park, "Hap" felt his team was not getting a fair shake from the umpiring staff. So Hogan organized a glee club on the bench. They began to sing the tune of "London Bridge." "All the umpires: they are blind, they are blind . . ."

The umpires did not take kindly to the chorus and ordered Hogan and the players to the clubhouse in center field. Hogan lined his men up, marched them off, lock step, singing again as they went.

Carl 'Buzz' Sawyer of the Mission Bells dances with a rag doll prior to 1926 Opening Day at Recreations Park. Sawyer was a master of the pantomime and became a crowd favorite.

Bud Beasley was a left-handed pitcher for the Solons and Rainiers in the war years. On the mound, Beasley played it straight until one day he heard Lefty O'Doul comment on his philosophy of hitting: "Hitting is 90 percent mental." Beasley thought about the comment and said, "If 90 percent of hitting is in the head, then you've got to destroy that 90 percent. You've got to get them thinking about something besides hitting."

Soon thereafter, during a pepper game, the ball was hit past the fielders and was picked up by a player's young son. Beasley noticed how each of the players tensed up as the boy wound up to throw the ball back. They didn't know exactly when it would be released or where it would be thrown. Beasley realized the unorthodox style of his motion could accomplish the same result with batters. Beasley developed a herky-jerky style, involving unorthodox motions with his arms to throw off the batter's concentration. "They either think you're crazy, or you're a nut, or they are mad at you, or they're laughing at you, but they're thinking about everything but hitting," Beasley said. "Break their concentration, anything to keep them from getting into timing with me. If you let them get in timing with you, you're at a great disadvantage. That's what developed the windup."

Beasley was especially effective against better hitters. Joe Brovia and Les Scarsella both acknowledged in retirement how much they were bothered by Beasley's style. A slap hitter had better success against Beasley. "It was tough to break the concentration of a 'Punch-and-Judy' hitter because he wasn't a consistent hitter," Beasley said.

"JoJo White and Gene Handley hit me pretty good," Beasley said. "Neither were power hitters. Believe it or not, it worked pretty good against Billy Martin. He was a great competitor, but he was temperamental, and if I could get him mad at me, then it was a big help, and it was easy to get Billy mad at anybody, including his mother.

"When I started this whole thing, my idea was [to annoy] the batter, but this had such an appeal to the fans that I really started to capitalize on it because it drew people into the ballpark. Chet Johnson told me he got the idea [to pitch that way] from me."

Beasley's motion was responsible for the rule that limits the "pump," or the multiple windup; Beasley would rock his arms over his head many times before pitching, but the new rule limited the pumping action to two. "They put that one in to stop me," Beasley said with pride.

Beasley's managers generally supported his unorthodox pitching because they knew what his objective was. But he was a thorn in the side to Dick Bartell, Beasley's manager with the Solons in 1947. Bartell tried to dump him, but Yubi Separovich, the Solons' business manager, wouldn't have it. Beasley was a major gate attraction. Still, their relationship was tenuous at best and led to some humorous conflicts.

Bartell liked to take batting practice before the Solons games. On one occasion, pitcher Tony Freitas brought a small, painted grapefruit to the park and dared Beasley to throw it to Bartell. Beasley took the dare, served it up to Bartell and, as could be expected, the grapefruit splattered juice everywhere. Bartell did not appreciate the prank.

During a 1947 game against the Angels at Edmonds Field, Angels outfielder Lou Novikoff was hitting everything. Bartell warned his pitchers, "Anybody who pitches above his belt is going to be fined $100." Early in the game Solons pitcher Guy Fletcher slipped and "the Mad Russian" hit the ball out of the park.

Bartell charged to the mound, took the ball from Fletcher, sent him to the showers and fined him. Later in the game, Beasley entered and faced Novikoff. "Bartell gets up and is standing on the steps of the dugout, and he's motioning 'down, down,' and he's glaring at me," Beasley recalled. "I wind up and roll the ball on the ground all the way to the plate. He comes charging to the mound and says, 'What the hell are you doing?', and I says, 'Protecting my $100.' The next day I was sold to Seattle."

"Broadway" Billy Schuster played for the Rainiers and the Angels during the 1940s, but fans from every city loved to see him. It was not unusual for Schuster, when sacrificing down the first base line, to stop short of the first baseman's tag, turn around and sprint towards home plate, sliding "safely" across the plate. It was equally not unusual to see the first baseman sprinting after him rather than routinely throwing the ball to first base for the out.

In a game at Wrigley Field against the Oaks in 1943, Schuster was responsible for an Angels victory. Schuster was on third with two outs in the bottom of the ninth of a tie game. The Oaks brought in a relief pitcher and

## JOE BROVIA AND 'PANTS' ROWLAND

In an era when all baseball players wore their pants at the knees, Joe Brovia was an exception. Brovia, long-time slugger for the Seals, Beavers, Oaks and Solons, was used to wearing his pants down to his ankles . . . much to the disdain of league President Clarence "Pants" Rowland.

Brovia broke into baseball with his pants at the ankle length and saw no reason to change. "I used to hate going to Hollywood or Los Angeles because I knew Rowland was going to bother hell out of me from the start of the series to the morning of the doubleheader," Brovia said. "So it looks sloppy [to him]. I thought that funny little hat Rowland always wore was a little ridiculous too."

When Rowland retired from the game in 1954, Brovia said, "Now he's gone, and I'm not a bit sorry about it."

## GAME CALLED ON ACCOUNT OF . . .

Over the course of baseball history, hundreds of baseball games have been postponed. The most common cause has been weather—rain, lightning or wind storms.

Before the advent of lighted parks, games were often called on account of darkness. Games usually started on a spring or summer afternoon at 2:45 p.m. A game taking the normal 1½ hours would be over shortly after 4 p.m. If the game went into extra innings, there could be a problem with visibility. A pitcher with a slight streak of wildness, throwing a well-used ball out of the twilight, would encourage any umpire to send the players and the fans home.

Of course, many Coast League parks were located along the Pacific Coast where fog was the problem. Fog cost the Padres' many games at Lane Field, located at the edge of San Diego Bay. When Cal Ewing built Ewing Field in the center of San Francisco's fog belt, it was not unusual to lose sight of the outfielders in the fog. Because of these opaque afternoons, Ewing Field was the Seals' home for only part of the 1914 season.

In 1911, a 24-inning game between Sacramento and Portland ended in a 1-1 tie when smoke from a pile of burning trash indundated the field, making further play impossible. Technically, this was the league's longest game and it had the potential of being longer, but it was called on account of smoke.

In the 1930s, Coast League umpire Bill Bedford was forced to halt a PCL exhibition game in Ventura because of mid-day darkness: A full eclipse of the sun took place!

But there have been other reasons for postponement, some verging on the bizarre. Games have been called because they ran out of baseballs, because during the first decades of the league, the home team had to provide only two baseballs.

Seattle's Frank Brazill hit an interesting home run in Recreation Park in 1925. As he was rounding third base, fans started running onto the field. They were not venting their anger against him for homering against their heros. They were leaving the bleachers because of an earthquake.

In 1937, a game was called because a ball dropped foul. The Missions were tied with the Seals 4-4 in the top of the ninth at Seals Stadium. Harry Longacre represented the go-ahead run at third base with one out for the Seals. With a long fly ball hit down the left field line, Max West settled under the ball, then let it drop when he saw it was going to be a foul ball.

Umpire Harry Fanning saw it differently and called it a hit and Longacre scored from third. West and Reds shortstop Joe Vitter immediately challenged Fanning's decision and his judgment, leading to their prompt removal from the game.

Reds Manager Willie Kamm charged out past third base to dispute the call, at which point Fanning gave him one minute to get replacements for the ejected players. Kamm walked back to the first base dugout, but not fast enough. Fanning wasn't satisfied with Kamm's nonchalance and forfeited the game to the Seals. The score reverted from 5-4 to 9-0.

In 1940, the Oaks and Stars lost two games from their schedule because the U.S. Army practiced at Oaks Ball Park for a holiday parade. Their horses damaged the park so much that it took almost two days to make the field playable again.

Undoubtedly, the most bizarre cancellation of a ballgame came at the end of the third inning Vaughn Street Park, Portland in 1942. Oaks outfielder Emil Mailho had just caught a fly ball to end the inning. He was jogging in from the outfield when he disappeared!

Mailho's weight caused the ground to collapse under him into a sinkhole. The only thing visible was the top of Mailho's cap.

Game called on account of sinkhole.

---

Schuster whispered to Manager Bill Sweeney, who was coaching at third, "I'm going to make him balk."

On the first pitch, Schuster ran 20 feet down the line, turned around and sprinted back. The flustered pitcher halted his motion for the balk, and the Angels won.

The Seals' Con Dempsey also experienced the Schuster lunacy after striking out a Los Angeles player to end an inning. Schuster, on deck, dropped his bat and sprinted directly at Dempsey, stopping just inches before him. Dempsey, not knowing what to expect, prepared to defend himself. Schuster looked at him, said, "Nice pitch!", and jogged off to his defensive position.

In the twilight of Schuster's career he managed in the Western International League. One of his pitchers was Bud Beasley. "Did we put it on," Beasley said.

"With the two of us, whether there was any baseball played or not, we got a crowd."

Sometimes, players ganged up against an umpire. Oaks Manager Ivan Howard and Missions Manager Wade Killefer put one over on the umpiring crew on Opening Day 1929. When the umpires gathered for their meeting at home plate, Killefer came storming out, demanding the flower pots be removed from the area in front of the center field fence. Howard was unsympathetic, and the two managers' voices were raised.

Serving as the true peacekeepers they were, the umpires ordered the managers to accompany them to center field to determine the best resolution to the problem. When the group got to within 75 feet of the fence, the umpires realized they had been made butts of a joke: The pots were painted on the fence.

Final score: Managers 1, Umpires 0. ❖

CHAPTER **21**

# AND IN THIS CORNER . . .

acific Coast League history is dotted with legendary fights. Some were confrontations between individuals, others were full-fledged donnybrooks. At least one famous brawl, the culmination of a series of beanball incidents, was racially motivated.

It is impossible to chronicle all the fights that took place on the local diamonds. For some of the participants, this was their only moment of glory. For others, a fight might have been nothing more than a chapter in an already colorful career. Some of the fights were truly spectacular.

In 1917, a season-long feud developed between Oaks catcher Dan Murray and Seals pitcher Casey Smith. Smith was a Native American, proud of his heritage and tired of the rash of comments directed at him about it. On June 17, Smith came to bat with Murray catching. Murray attempted to rile Smith by calling him a Negro. Smith told Murray not to repeat the comment. Murray came back with something stronger. At that point, Smith swung his bat at Murray, missing him. Murray initiated a hasty retreat with Smith in pursuit.

Players from both sides restrained the two men, but Murray took an ongoing kidding from fans and players alike. He vowed this was not the last of the incident. So it wasn't surprising that Murray, on the last day of the season, challenged Smith to combat.

Murray was waiting for Smith when he came out of the visiting locker room. Smith said he wanted no trouble but was flattened by a right to the jaw. When Smith arose after several moments, he pulled out a blackjack but was quickly disarmed. He grabbed a bat, but was prevented from using it, so the two men fought with their fists. The fight was intense and eventually was broken up by players from both sides. Murray had been vindicated.

## BLOOD ON JAKE WADE DAY

Bad blood can develop quickly as the result of one player's successes against another. During the 1935 season, the Mission Reds were playing a series in Portland's Vaughn Street Park. It was "Jake Wade Day," with Wade pitching the first game of the Sunday doubleheader. Reds center fielder Lou Almada was having a field day against Wade. Anything Wade tossed up to the plate, Almada hit out of reach of the Beavers' defenders. The two began jawing at each other. Wade became more angry with each Almada success, and by the end of the game, he was angry and embarrassed.

Between games, both teams retired to their respective clubhouses. After a few minutes, there was a knock on the Reds' clubhouse door. Outside stood John "Moose" Clabaugh, the burly Portland outfielder. Clabaugh was there as Wade's second for a showdown with Almada. Manager Gabby Street told both players to take off their cleats and go out to settle their differences. Almada made quick work of Wade as Clabaugh passively stood by.

Beavers pitcher Sailor Bill Posedel later told the Missions' George McDermott that Clabaugh had urged Wade to challenge Almada. Clabaugh didn't care at all for Wade and was confident Almada could beat him. Ah, teammates.

## SEALS FRUSTRATION LEADS TO BATTLE

The Seals fell victim to similar emotions near the end of the 1921 season. On September 1, the Seals held a 6½-game lead over a closely bunched group of three other teams. By October 1, the Seals had lost nine games in the standings and were struggling to prevent themselves from sliding into fourth place.

The Seals were in Seattle and had already lost three of four. In Saturday's game, just one day before season's end, frustration caught up with both teams. The game was a slugfest with the Seals leading in the sixth and threatening to add to their lead. Plate umpire Jake Croter angered Seals batter Dee Walsh with a called third strike. Walsh countered by throwing his bat against the backstop and was summarily ejected from the game. Walsh reportedly threw a punch at Croter and the benches emptied.

Fights broke out all over the diamond and upwards of 1,000 fans left the grandstands to enter the melee. A humorous aspect of the fight developed when Croter somehow ended up sitting on first baseman Jimmy O'Connell's head, thus effectively removing him from the fray. Police were called to quell the riot, whereupon the game continued.

Croter sent his report to league President Bill McCarthy, naming Manager Charlie Graham and Seals players Walsh, O'Connell, Sam Agnew and Ernie Shore as the instigators. With the season concluding the next day, no action was taken and the incident died without any players being punished.

When Graham was met by reporters on his return to San Francisco, he stated the riot was exaggerated. O'Connell and Croter had been pushed by a police officer and fell, Graham claimed. Graham insisted no blows had been thrown. He also said that Seattle fans were angry at the Indians players for having lost nine out of 15 games to the Portland Beavers before the Seals came to town. That could have added to the fan involvement.

Often, an umpire's actions can instigate a reaction leading to a violent response. Such was the case involving umpire William Byron, known either as "Billy" or "Lord."

Byron was a flamboyant, argumentative umpire who practiced his trade during the 1920s. Byron, by his mannerisms, could complicate a simple umpiring decision, angering one side or the other as a result. Many observers felt he wasn't a strong umpire and others felt he showed certain biases.

In 1923, the Seals assembled one of the finest minor league teams ever and left the rest of the league behind. The Sacramento Senators dogged the Seals during much of the race, making a valiant but futile attempt to catch them. A critical series took place in Sacramento between the two teams in late September. Byron and Jim Ward were assigned to umpire the series. Lew Moreing, owner of the Senators, asked McCarthy for a replacement for Byron. For such a critical series, Moreing felt a better umpire could be found. But Moreing was turned down.

In the second game of the series, the Seals' Eddie Mulligan hit a long fly to left field. Senators left fielder Harry Brown raced back and either caught or trapped the ball off the wall. Byron ruled it was a trap and Mulligan steamed into second base. After the argument abated, the Seals rallied for two runs and held on for a 4-2 victory.

The Sacramento fans, well known as the most volatile in the league, blamed Byron for the loss, and nearly 500 of them were waiting for the umpires after the game. When Byron and Ward appeared, the mob showered them with rocks and fruit. Ward was felled by a rock and the umpires retreated to the clubhouse.

Flanked by policemen and several members of the Seals squad, the umpires tried again, this time reaching the safety of a streetcar. Several players and policemen were hit by flying objects. The motorman on the streetcar was unable to depart because angry fans continued to pull the trolley line away from the electric wire.

Finally, the umpires made their escape to the hotel only to be besieged again. Police and city officials stepped in to prevent further violence. When President McCarthy received the report of the incident, he contacted Moreing, the chief of police and the president of the Chamber of Commerce, warning them to control the situation or he would order the series switched to San Francisco.

While it was an uncomfortable week for the two umpires, the series continued without incident. The crowds were vocal but controlled. To make things worse for Sacramento, the Seals won seven of the eight games, the eighth ending in a tie, eliminating any hopes the Senators had of closing the gap.

## BUZZ ARLETT TAKES THE NIGHT OFF

In 1930, Buzz Arlett came out second in a confrontation with an umpire. Arlett was sitting out a close battle in Sacramento when umpire Chester Chadbourne ejected him in the eighth inning from the bench for abusive language. As Chadbourne was going to the dressing room after the game, Arlett accosted him. Chadbourne claimed Arlett hit him in the side, at which point Chadbourne swung his mask and connected with Arlett's face. Arlett went down with a gash over his eye.

Chadbourne claimed Arlett was drunk on the field, a contention given some credibility by the fact that Ray Brubaker subbed for him in right field that evening. Manager Carl Zamloch insisted Chadbourne reached over three players to deliver his blow.

Pearl Casey, Chadbourne's partner, witnessed the skirmish, as did several players and a police officer. After all the reports were received by Harry Williams at the league office, Williams suspended both men.

## A "DAVID VS. GOLIATH" MISMATCH

The art of intimidation is practiced effectively by some, especially those who can be intimidating, like Max Surkont, a muscular right-handed pitcher who had a marginal major league career. On the mound, Surkont was an imposing feature. Few saw him smile.

In a game at Sacramento's Edmonds Field in 1950, Surkont threw a couple of intimidating pitches to Oaks pitcher Frank Nelson, who was nothing close to a physical match for Surkont. Several Oaks started getting on Surkont for his actions, foremost among them being Mel Duezabou. Duezabou, no heavyweight himself, had been on the boxing team at Cal. Surkont looked menacingly into the dugout to see who was yelling at him. Duezabou

Billy Martin and Mel Duezabou were local products and popular among Oaks fans. Both of them were free-swingers with their bats as well as their fists.

picked up the pace and then turned his back, pointing to his uniform number—3—so there would be no question who the culprit was.

Two weeks later, the Solons came to Emeryville. Before the game, Duezabou was playing catch along the sidelines and Surkont was running with the pitchers in the outfield. Surkont yelled from the outfield, "You little shit. Let's see you do something about it now."

At that point Surkont and Duezabou started walking towards each other as if it were a cowboy movie. Before Duezabou started walking, he called over batboy Chuck Symonds and gave him his false teeth.

When the two met, Surkont said, "What are you going to do now?" Duezabou landed a quick punch to the jaw and Surkont went down. The stunned Surkont held on to Duezabou's legs and a harmless wrestling match followed before teammates pulled the players apart.

Duezabou, the victor, had to retreat to the clubhouse to get his hand iced by trainer Red Adams. A few minutes later, the door to the clubhouse opened and there was Surkont once again. Duezabou didn't know what to expect, so he again prepared for battle. But Surkont stuck his hand out to Duezabou and said, "I deserved it. Let's shake hands."

The next night, Charlie Dressen called a team meeting. He singled out Duezabou before the team and handed him $50. "This is for sticking up for one of your teammates," he said. "Go buy your kid a bike."

Oaks announcer Bud Foster mentioned the fight in his game broadcast, and when Duezabou came home that afternoon, his 6-year-old son, Johnny, asked if he could hold his daddy's teeth for the next fight.

One other thing: Duezabou broke a bone in his hand when he hit Surkont and was out of action for awhile.

## DUKE KENWORTHY GETS HIS REVENGE

Not all differences are settled as simply as the Duezabou-Surkont battle. In 1924, a grudge developed between Seals third baseman Eddie Mulligan and Duke Kenworthy, player-manager of the Portland Ducks. Mulligan slid into second base with Kenworthy covering. Mulligan's cleats caught Kenworthy on the leg and he reacted by swatting Mulligan on the ear. Mulligan jumped up and landed a right cross to Kenworthy's jaw and Kenworthy went down like a rock. Kenworthy was embarrassed by this incident and vowed his revenge, but not on Mulligan.

Mulligan was fined and suspended for one day. Dee Walsh was a teammate of Mulligan's, and the two had grown up together in "the Patch," a neighborhood in St. Louis. Walsh had apparently rushed to Mulligan's support during the action. Kenworthy was told Walsh had hit him while he was down. Kenworthy didn't forget it.

Eddie Mulligan played for all three Bay Area PCL teams and is remembered for his on-field battle with Duke Kenworthy.

In 1925, Kenworthy was out of baseball living in Oakland, and Walsh had been transferred from San Francisco to Portland. When the Ducks came to Oakland, Kenworthy was waiting for Walsh outside the clubhouse. Upon Walsh's arrival, Kenworthy challenged him and punched Walsh in the face. Walsh retreated to the clubhouse and came out with a bat. The bat was wrestled away by bystanders and a scuffle ensued. Kenworthy had regained his dignity.

Walter Mails was the other "brawler" of the 1924 season. Mails was proud of his fights with Duffy Lewis of Salt Lake City and Bim Myers of the Angels. After Mulligan beat Kenworthy in their fight, Mails challenged Mulligan to a fight for the "league championship." His challenge was in jest, but several of Mails' Oakland teammates would have enjoyed seeing Mails taken down. And of course, Mails was taken down by Mickey Finn in 1926. That was a fight he never did live down.

## "BATTLING BILLY" MARTIN

One of Duezabou's teammates in 1948 and 1949 was another fighter, Billy Martin. While Duezabou's boxing style was patterned after the Marquis of Queensberry, Billy was a street brawler. He had a short fuse and needed only the slightest spark to be ignited.

On August 2, 1948, in the thick of the pennant race, the Oaks played the Hollywood Stars in a doubleheader. In the first game, Lou Stringer, the Stars' volatile second baseman, slid hard into second with Martin covering.

The two collided and Stringer, not knowing yet if he

Mickey Finn (left) was an ex-Navy boxer and used his skills to flatten Walter 'The Great' Mails. From then on, Mails was known as 'Canvasback.'

was safe or out, held his base. But his foot was on Martin's hand, much to Billy's displeasure. Stringer didn't move his foot quickly enough. Billy pushed him and the fight began.

Martin slipped Stringer's first punch and landed a counter punch. Both benches cleared and satellite fights broke out everywhere. Somehow in the melee, Casey Stengel got decked by an unidentified Stars player. When order was restored, Martin and Stringer were thrown out of the game and later fined, and Stengel came back to the Oaks bench wearing a Stars cap.

## SEALS VS. OAKS—RACIAL SCORES SETTLED

Black players were forced to endure taunts and actions from their white counterparts. One of the most effective and dangerous injustices was the knockdown pitch. Several black players had been hurt this way.

A day of reckoning was presented to one black athlete, Piper Davis of the Oaks, on July 27, 1952 in a Sunday doubleheader against the Seals. By taking six of the previous seven games, the Oaks had slipped into first place over the Stars, while the Seals were going nowhere.

Bill Boemler, a huge left-hander, was on the mound for the Seals. Several times in previous series between the teams, Boemler had dusted off Davis and Rafael Noble, the Oaks' two black regulars. In the fourth inning of the first game, Davis came to bat, and down he went again. On the next pitch, Davis singled. The next Oaks batter, Johnny Ostrowski, bunted down third, and first baseman Joe Grace bobbled Reno Cheso's throw. Davis rounded second and continued on to third. Second baseman Jim Moran ran the ball down and threw wildly past third. Davis continued towards home as Cheso retrieved the ball and threw a strike to Boemler covering the plate.

Boemler caught the ball in ample time and waited, bracing himself for the collision with Davis. Davis hit him high and hard and the brawl erupted. Both dugouts cleared quickly. The Oaks' Augie Galan said, "It was the biggest and wildest brawl I've seen in my 20 years of baseball."

Noble was the most aggressive player on the field, swinging at opponents and teammates without discrimination. "If I could have sneaked my Seals back to the dugout," said Seals Manager Tommy Heath, "I think Noble would have decked the entire Oakland team."

Heath was hit on the side of the jaw by an unknown

Sandy Koufax (top) attempts to keep his battery-mate, John Roseboro, from a bat-wielding Tito Fuentes as Giants pitcher Juan Marichal, also holding a bat, approaches the Dodgers' catcher.

assailant. "The only thing I'm positive of," Heath said, "is that it wasn't Paul Fagan because he's in Hawaii."

Surprisingly, there were no ejections by plate umpire Roman Bentz, and there were no serious injuries. Players were bruised and had toes stepped on, but nobody was forced to leave the game. Boemler went on to register a 4-2 victory over the Oaks, tiring after eight innings, and Al Lien repeated Boemler's effort with an identical 4-2 effort in the second game. The Seals knocked the Oaks out of first place and the brawl knocked the Summer Olympics off the front page of Monday's sport section.

## A FRONT-OFFICE BRAWL

The most peculiar fight in PCL history did not involve players. It occurred during the 1920 winter meeting in Sacramento.

The meetings were already emotionally charged over the issue of Bill McCarthy's tenure as league president. John P. Cook, secretary of the Salt Lake City club, had long fought for McCarthy's removal, and Angels President John F. Powers had supported McCarthy's presidency. The two men had disliked each other for at least two years, and it didn't take much to start them off.

Cook landed the first punch, staggering Powers who clutched at Cook while regaining his equilibrium. Powers recovered and proceeded to take the fight to Cook when it was broken up. The men continued to dislike each other, but no further battles were fought.

The following morning, a bellhop raised a laugh by paging "Johnny Powers, the lightweight champion." Powers was still in bed and couldn't share in the joke. Cook didn't share in the humor, either.

## THE GREAT SLUGFEST OF 1965

One of the most significant fights in major league history came August 22, 1965. In an emotion-charged series against the Dodgers at Candlestick Park, Juan Marichal, reacting to taunts from Dodgers catcher John Roseboro, hit him with a bat. With Sandy Koufax on the mound and Marichal batting, Roseboro returned a throw to Koufax that whistled by Marichal's ear. When Marichal questioned Roseboro's motives, Roseboro reacted by advancing towards Marichal.

Marichal hit Roseboro on the side of the head and both benches cleared. Roseboro, bloodied, was taken to the clubhouse and Marichal was thrown out of the game. He was later suspended and fined.

The incident was yet another small sign of the changing, turbulent times, an example of the continuing loss of innocence. Of greater significance to the Giants was the loss of Marichal in a tight pennant race. Marichal incurred a nine-day suspension and lost at least two pitching opportunities. The Giants finished in second place that season, two games behind the Dodgers, who went on to a World Series victory over the Minnesota Twins.

Roseboro sued Marichal and the Giants and later settled out of court. To this day, memories of the incident heighten the emotions of Giants and Dodgers fans. ❖

# CHAPTER 22

# BREAKING THE PCL COLOR BARRIER

In 1916 Herb McFarlin, secretary of the Oakland club, signed a pitcher named George "Jimmy" Claxton to play with the Oaks. Claxton made his debut on May 28 by starting the first game of the Memorial Day double-header at Oakland. He was batted out of the box but came back to finish the second game. That was the extent of his career in organized baseball.

Claxton had been promoted as a fine Native American pitcher from a reservation in Nebraska, but stories that he was "colored" began circulating shortly after he signed his contract. The Oaks quickly and quietly released him. Claxton was around long enough to have his photo taken for the Zeenut baseball cards. His card was printed that year, gaining him a certain degree of immortality.

It was naive to assume the Oaks could have kept Claxton for any length of time without being discovered because Claxton had pitched for a local "colored" team the year before. Nevertheless, Claxton had a fairly long career in baseball. Born near Vancouver, B.C., of black, Indian and Scandinavian descent, he pitched for several semi-pro teams in the Pacific Northwest before coming to the Bay Area. Later, in 1920, he pitched for the Shasta Limiteds, a "colored" team sponsored by the Southern Pacific Company, which won the state semi-pro championship

that year. Still later, in 1932, he was a teammate of Luis Tiant Sr., on the New York Black Yankees. Little else is known about his career.

## PLAYERS NO, TRAINERS YES

Of greater longevity and equal interest was William Harrison Garrison "Shine" Scott. Scott, an African American, served as trainer for the Vernon Tigers in the early 1920s, coming to San Francisco when that franchise became the Missions in 1926.

As legend has it, Scott was plowing a field with a mule outside the Vernon ballpark when the Vernon trainer quit. Tigers Manager Bill Essick needed an immediate replacement. He saw and approached Scott, inquiring what he was doing. Scott responded he was plowing the field. Essick asked him if he would like a different job. "Is it better than what I'm doing now?" asked Scott. "Much better," was the reply. "I'll take it," exclaimed Scott, as he kicked the mule in the butt and told him to go home.

During this era, a trainer was in charge of the club-house. He administered basic physical therapy, probably using the same bottle of salve for all problems. Scott became a legend at his task, not because of a fine skill in

ZEE-NUT
SERIES
1916
CLAXTON
OAKS

The Oaks released Jimmy Claxton (above) in 1916 after discovering he was black. Below, trainer 'Shine' Scott had to endure clubhouse 'jokes.' Buzz Sawyer is holding the cape.

solving the medical woes of his players, but because of his ability in dealing with their psychological ills.

Scott was a combination psychologist, doctor and comedian; his lighthearted approach kept the clubhouse at ease. Despite his popularity, he frequently took the brunt of clubhouse jokes.

Eddie Joost, a Missions player during the early 1930s, told a story about how Scott didn't like to make the train trips to Southern California because he knew his wife would be at the railway station waiting for him, wanting money. He would devise several elaborate plans to avoid her but usually failed in the effort, much to the amusement of the players.

## A SLAP IN THE FACE

Skin color itself served as judge and jury for many aspiring professional ballplayers. Countless players were not offered contracts because their skin was too dark. Of particular note was the case of a fine young infielder from San Francisco named Tony Gomez.

Gomez grew up on the city's sandlots in the early 1930s along with Joost, Dario Lodigiani and Joe DiMaggio. Gomez played alongside Joost on youth teams and the two formed a spectacular double-play combination. As a professional, Joost was later shifted to shortstop, but at this early stage, Gomez was the better fielder.

Gomez and DiMaggio often attended the same tryout camps and would compete for the same position, short-

stop. Before the tryouts were concluded, DiMaggio would have been shifted to first base to take the throws of the far more talented Gomez.

Seals Manager Ike Caveney once pulled Gomez aside and said, "Kid, why don't you quit playing ball? You're just too black."

For a 16-year-old to receive such a message was devastating. For several years, Gomez's life became a roller coaster before he pulled himself together. He played baseball in Mexico along with many Cubans who had faced a similar fate. But for many "bushers" and some players who signed professional contracts, Tony Gomez's theatrics at shortstop will always be legendary.

## STRIKE TWO

The war years produced, among many other things, a great shortage of quality baseball players. But there was an abundant and available supply of black players . . . if only someone would take the risk and sign one of them.

League President Clarence Rowland decided it was time in July 1943, proposing to the Los Angeles Angels that they sign two black players. The Angels were making a shambles of the pennant race, but they still could use pitching and defensive help. Rowland had two players in mind. Chet Brewer had a reputation as one of the finest pitchers in the Negro Leagues and had been eminently successful against Coast League players in post-season barnstorming tours. Lou Dials had graduated from Cal with a degree in engineering but found greater success playing baseball than finding a suitable job. Both lived in Southern California and were willing and eager to give the Coast League a try.

The Angels considered, then declined, Rowland's offer. Phil Wrigley, owner of both the Angels and their parent Chicago Cubs, feared too much criticism from his major league colleagues if he allowed the players to sign. Dials quoted Wrigley as saying, "I know how good you are, but I don't have a place for you."

Rowland then made the same proposal to Cookie Devincenzi, whose Oaks were in L.A. for a series against the Angels. Devincenzi grew up in an integrated neighborhood in Oakland and had an understanding of the problems facing blacks in the community. He was also under some pressure from the local media to challenge the existing color barriers. Devincenzi soon accepted Rowland's offer.

Brewer and Dials presented themselves to the visitors' clubhouse at Wrigley Field and asked for uniforms. Spotting them, Oaks Manager Johnny Vergez ordered them to leave. The players told him they were present on Devincenzi's instructions. Vergez called Devincenzi to confirm the players' assertion, finding it was accurate. The manager still refused to admit the players.

THE OAKLAND LARKS—
BARNSTORMING SPECIALISTS

The Oakland Larks won the championship of the 1946 West Coast Baseball Association, the equivalent to the Coast League for black players. When the league folded, the Larks, with a record of 36-12, weren't ready to quit. Eddie Harris, the team's business manager, arranged a barnstorming schedule up the Pacific Coast and the Larks strengthened themselves by signing some of the better players off the defunct clubs.

The Larks had five talented pitchers. Marion "Sugar" Cain was the staff leader with a 10-1 record. Charles "Speck" Roberts was 7-3, Willie Jones was 5-2 and Wade James was 4-4. These four were right-handers. Lionel "Lefty" Wilson, later mayor of Oakland, was 8-2, but decided against barnstorming.

The catcher was Smiley Clayton, a rangy player with a great throwing arm and good hitting instincts. Johnny Allen was a slick-fielding shortstop who often batted cleanup for Larks Manager Jim West. The club's left fielder, Mel Reid, doubled as a professional football player with the Oakland Giants.

The Larks barnstormed again in 1947. During May and June, the Larks reeled off 29 straight victories before losing a 2-1, 13-inning squeaker in Lincoln, Nebraska.

Vergez knew Dials well, having played against him in college; Dials at Cal, Vergez at St. Mary's. The manager's statement to Dials was, "They'll crucify me. I'll quit before I [allow blacks on the team]."

The Oaks finished the season tied for fifth place and Devincenzi fired Vergez immediately after the final game.

While the need to fill depleted rosters continued, white owners and players continued to resist breaking the color line.

During 1944 Spring Training, Hollywood Stars Manager Charlie Root wrote to his son. "I almost forgot to tell you about yesterday at the park. There were five Negroes who came out to the park and wanted me to sign them up as players," Root wrote. "They really gave me some good arguments. I told them to go see Judge Landis as I had nothing to do with hiring colored players, and that I would not be the first manager to start hiring them."

## THE OAKLAND LARKS

In 1946, black players along the West Coast attempted to establish a professional baseball league similar to the Negro Leagues. While black semi-pro teams had flour-

The West Coast Baseball Association was a 'Negro League' formed at the end of World War II. The teams played in PCL ballparks when Coast League teams were on the road. When the WCBA failed, the Oakland Larks continued to be a successful barnstorming club. Their pitching staff included (l-r) Wade James, 'Wee' Jones, Charles 'Speck' Roberts and Marion 'Sugar' Cain.

ished throughout the Bay Area for decades, this was the first attempt at expanding into a professional circuit. The West Coast Baseball Association was formed with six teams spanning the West Coast from Los Angeles to Seattle. In the Bay Area, the teams were the Oakland Larks and the San Francisco Sea Lions. The teams used Oaks Ball Park and Seals Stadium when the locals were on the road. These two teams were very popular in the black community and drew large crowds. The same couldn't be said about the other four teams in the league, and after four months the league folded due to lack of finances and poor management.

The Larks and the Sea Lions became barnstorming teams, but the necessity to travel, and later, the acceptance of black players into organized baseball, caused their collapse. Like the league itself, their history and their records have disappeared into obscurity.

Two of their number deserve special mention. Lionel Wilson, a young lefty pitcher, toiled for the Larks. This is the same Judge Lionel Wilson who later became mayor of Oakland, serving three distinguished terms. Jesse Alexander was a Sea Lions pitcher. His distinction came from the fact he had no left arm.

## JOHNNY RITCHEY LEADS THE WAY

Organized baseball, with all of its preparation time and knowing it was important to move ahead as quickly as possible with integration, was still unprepared for the breaking of the color barrier. It was essential to find the right players—players who could help the ballclub, who could deal with the anticipated backlash and who would fit in with his new teammates and with the community.

Jackie Robinson integrated the major leagues in 1947 and Johnny Ritchey integrated the Coast League one year later, playing for the San Diego Padres.

Ritchey was a young catcher who had grown up in San Diego. In his senior year of high school he was named to the All-Southern California Baseball team. He attended San Diego State College, playing both football and baseball before the start of World War II. Ritchey served 32 months with the Army Engineers, most of them in Europe. Before signing with the Padres, he played with the Chicago American Giants of the Negro League and led the league in hitting.

Ritchey was 23 when he signed with the Padres, playing two years there and sharing the catching duties with

World War II hero Johnny Ritchey was the first full-time black player in the PCL. Ritchey joined the 1948 Padres and later played with Seattle, San Francisco and Sacramento.

Lennie Rice. He later played with Portland, Sacramento and San Francisco before concluding his professional career. Ritchey's presence with the Padres in 1948 undoubtedly helped attendance wherever the club went, but this would be nothing compared to the impact black players had in 1949.

## LUKE EASTER PUTS ON A SHOW

Two of the most popular players ever to grace the Coast League came to San Diego in 1949 when Luke Easter and Artie Wilson signed with the Cleveland Indians and were optioned to the Padres.

Easter, an agile 240-pound first baseman with a reputation for hitting prodigious home runs, had been acquired from the Homestead Grays by Cleveland's Bill Veeck. In two seasons as Josh Gibson's replacement as the Grays' power hitter, Easter hit .336 and .376.

In 1949, Easter combined with Max West, Al Rosen, Orestes "Minnie" Minoso and Buster Adams to pound out 187 home runs, the highest number hit by one team since 1929. West was the PCL home run leader with 48. Easter had broken his kneecap in Spring Training but kept playing. By mid-season, after Easter had already hit 25 homers, the pain had become too great and Easter was

sidelined. At the time, the Padres were well on the way to breaking the league home run record of 204 set in the rarified air of Salt Lake City in 1923. When Easter was healthy later that season, he was recalled by the Indians and played in 21 games.

Easter played in 80 games for the Padres that season, batting a robust .363 on 99 hits, including 23 doubles. He also accounted for 92 runs batted in. Easter returned to the Padres in 1954 to only moderate success, but his legacy had already been guaranteed by his fabulous rookie season in 1949.

Easter's abbreviated Coast League career was important in many respects. He was an enormous draw at the gate and he gave instant credibility to black players' abilities to compete in the PCL and at higher levels.

## ARTIE WILSON JOINS THE OAKS

Joining Ritchey and Easter on the 1949 Padres was the flamboyant Wilson. Wilson had played shortstop for the Birmingham Black Barons where he evoked considerable major league interest for his marvelous defensive skills,

Luke Easter was one of the greatest power hitters in the old Negro Leagues. Towards the end of his career, Easter signed on with the San Diego Padres of the PCL.

Orestes 'Minnie' Minoso was a versatile star for San Diego. He would later gain fame by becoming the first 'five-decade' player in the major leagues.

was the only negative teammate reaction Wilson faced while he played for the Oaks.

Wilson was something special. He immediately became Oaks fans' most popular player. Not only did he lead the league in hitting (.348) and stolen bases (46), but he charmed fans with a ready smile and a willingness to chat and sign autographs. He would often sign an official PCL ball, made by Wilson Sporting Goods, by writing, "Artie," and then circling the "Wilson" logo on the ball.

Wilson said he encountered few problems in being one of the first black players in the Coast League: "It was a great experience," he said. "It was really nice—no problems whatsoever."

A possible exception was Sacramento, where fans could be somewhat hostile. He recalled one fan in particular who sat behind the visitor's dugout. He had a foghorn voice and could be unmerciful on his targets. In 1949,

Artie Wilson became the Oaks' first full-time black player in 1949. He won the batting championship his first season and became the most popular player on the team.

outstanding speed and slap-hitting style. In his five years with the Black Barons—where one of his teammates was Willie Mays—he never batted below .300. The New York Yankees ultimately purchased Wilson's contract and assigned him to the Newark club in the International League, but he refused to report because he would have taken a cut in salary over what the Black Barons had been paying him. Wilson independently negotiated a contract with Veeck and was optioned to the Padres at the start of the 1949 season.

The Yankees appealed the case to Commissioner Chandler, who ruled in their favor. Wilson consequently was ordered off the Padres' roster and immediately sold to the Oakland Oaks, where he became the first black player since Claxton.

Wilson reported to Manager Charlie Dressen and was inserted into the lineup at shortstop, batting leadoff. First baseman Les Scarsella objected to a black man's presence on the team and Scarsella was immediately released. That

Ray Dandridge closed out his legendary professional career with the Oakland Oaks in 1953.

Wilson and Jackie Jensen got most of this fan's attention. On one occasion Jensen grabbed a bat and started into the stands after his provocateur, and on another Wilson's female landlord, who traveled to the game from Berkeley, had to be restrained from clubbing the man with her high heeled shoe. Ironically, when Wilson later played with the Solons in 1957, he and his antagonist became friends.

There were other pioneers in 1949. Pitcher Alonzo Perry and infielder Parnell Woods joined Wilson at Oakland during mid-season, although they provided minimal help. Perry had won 14 games as Wilson's teammate at Birmingham the year before, but arm trouble had taken the fire out of his fastball. Woods, from the Kansas City Monarchs, was with the Oaks for only a short time when he was beaned, something black players constantly had to be wary of. This ended his season.

The Seals finally broke the color line in 1951 by signing Barney Serrell and later taking slugger Bob Thurman from the Yankees on option. While Serrell was limited to coming off the bench, Thurman's solid batting earned him a respectable major league career.

Cuba-born catcher Rafael Noble earned a spot on the New York Giants after a .316 season with the 1950 Oaks. He returned to the Oaks in 1952. In 1951, the Oaks acquired a long-time Negro League veteran, Lorenzo "Piper" Davis. Davis had played with the Black Barons, had managed Artie Wilson and Willie Mays and could play any position. He was also a leader. Don Ferrarese recounted how he once saw Davis giving teammate Dave Mann both a verbal and a physical lashing for getting out of line. The respect for Piper Davis transcended racial boundaries.

Davis played with the Oaks for the better parts of five seasons and, although more quiet and reserved than Artie Wilson, was still immensely popular with the fans and with his teammates.

## THE UMPIRES BREAK THE BARRIER

Finding a qualified black umpire was not as easy as finding players. In the Coast League, Emmett Ashford became the first black umpire when President Rowland signed him for 1954.

Ashford was a highly personable individual with a flair for the dramatic and a need to work hard and hustle. He was 5-feet-6, stocky, and an impeccable dresser.

Ashford had 3½ years of experience in the lower minor leagues and several additional years of umpiring semi-pro ball in the Los Angeles area. His contract was purchased from the Western International League after the 1953 season. For the start of the season, Ashford was instructed to report, along with Mickey Hanich, to veteran Cece Carlucci to form one of the four umpiring teams.

Carlucci's job was to mold the trio into a smooth unit. This meant reviewing and coordinating mechanics, determining positions for different play situations and setting a philosophy for how an umpire should act on and off the field. This team developed several umpiring techniques common to umpiring today.

When not umpiring behind the plate, Ashford would sprint down the first or third base line to his position. The fans loved it. When making calls, whether at home plate or on the bases, there was never any question what his signal was. However, on more complicated or close calls, Ashford would sometimes confuse the issue by hesitating or giving an unclear signal. His penchant for flamboyance would interfere with his effectiveness, leaving himself open for criticism.

Carlucci, who worked with Ashford for four years, felt Ashford was a good umpire. Some players, though, were not as complimentary, feeling Ashford's strike zone was not consistent and believing his need to be noticed on the field affected his calls during the game.

That Ashford was an umpire left himself open for the typical criticism umpires have always received. The fact he was black left himself open for racial slurs and barbs from a few fans, players and managers. References to "watermelon" and "stovepipe"—referring to his portly appearance—were regularly used. That he was flamboyant added more fuel for the antagonists.

Tommy Heath, longtime manager of the Seals and later manager of the Solons and the Beavers, was possibly Ashford's greatest antagonist in the Pacific Coast League. Their battles were continuous. Heath, generally a kind man, had little good to say about Ashford.

Things were so bad that Heath had a nickname for him—"Vomit." Heath had perfected a barb used when he felt Ashford had missed a call: "You missed another one, Vomit. You make me Emmett."

Bobby Bragan, the Hollywood Stars' manager during the middle 1950s, told of a run-in Heath had with Ashford in 1954. Hollywood was playing in San Francisco and Ashford had thrown Heath out of the game the previous night. Heath was still angry the following day. Ashford was to be the umpire behind the plate, and when the umpires appeared to accept the lineup cards, nobody came out from the Seals' dugout. Heath was in the dugout, gesturing and mumbling, but out of the umpires' earshot. Finally, Ashford yelled over to Heath, "Are you going to play or pass?" Heath slowly approached the gathering at home plate, still mumbling angrily. Ashford asked Heath if he had anything he wanted to say, to which Heath responded, "Yes. God damn Branch Rickey, and God damn Abraham Lincoln."

Heath missed that game, too, thumbed before a single pitch had been thrown.

## OTHER MINORITIES

Often overlooked in the discussion of integration and discrimination in baseball has been the treatment faced by players of other minorities. Mexican-Americans, Hispanics, Native Americans and Asians were deemed inferior and faced the brunt of continued discrimination and racial slurs.

Although they were allowed to play the game, Hispanics and Indians faced obstacles beyond their ability to pitch or hit the ball. If two players of equal abilities were fighting for the same position on the roster, the white player would win it without question. Upon retirement from active playing, Mexicans or other minorities could count on being totally discarded, not having any chance to scout, coach or work in the front office.

There were some very talented Mexican-American players with the Seals. Manny Perez was a fastballing right-hander who started regularly in the late 1940s and early 1950s for the Seals. Nanny Fernandez, of Spanish

Kenso Nushida (above) pitched one game for Sacramento in 1932. Masanori Murakami (top) pitched for the Giants in 1964 -1965 as the first Japanese national to play in the big leagues.

extraction, was one of Lefty O'Doul's favorites during the early 1940s.

With a month left in the 1953 season, the Seals purchased the contracts of Jose Perez and Tony Ponce from Ventura of the California League. Perez had won the league batting championship and he never batted under .300 in the lower minors. Ponce had won 15 games, losing 20, but had 25 complete games at Ventura. Ponce put together a string of eight victories without a defeat for the Seals. He remained a starter for two years before being released. Perez was unable to break into the Seals lineup and didn't return in 1954.

The non-presence of Asian players in organized baseball rivaled that of blacks before Jackie Robinson. There was one heralded exception to the dearth of Asians, in 1932. Sacramento had signed Kenso Nushida out of the local semi-pro leagues in July. Nushida, of Japanese descent, was slightly taller than 5-feet and was signed to boost sagging attendance in the capital city.

The Oaks then signed Lee Gum Hong, a 19-year-old from Oakland High School. Lee, of Chinese descent, stood 5-foot-11 and weighed 170 pounds.

The two pitchers started against each other on Wednesday evening, September 28, and met again on Sunday in the last game of the season. The games were well publicized, and brought large Asian contingents to the games. Lee pitched well for the Oaks, losing the first game on unearned runs. In the Sunday contest, Lee pitched a complete seven-inning game, winning 7-1. Nushida received no decision in the first contest and lost the second. Neither pitcher would ever play professional baseball again.

In 1935, Fumito "Jimmy" Horio, a former Tokyo Giants player, was a reserve outfielder with the Solons, but he was rarely used. In succeeding years, almost no players of Asian descent would enter organized baseball.

One obvious exception was Masanori Murakami, who in 1964 became the first Japanese national to play in the major leagues. A young left-handed pitcher, "Mashi" was one of several Japanese players to train with the Giants in Spring Training during the mid-1960s. Murakami pitched successfully at Fresno and was a late-season call-up to the Giants. In 1965, as a 21-year-old, Murakami was an integral player on the Giants' relief corps. He finished with a 4-1 record with eight saves and a strikeout rate of better than one per inning.

He was soon "recalled" to Japan where he had a solid career. In 1982, Murakami attempted an unsuccessful comeback with the Giants and returned to Japan.

Murakami spoke no English when he arrived in the United States and, naturally, his Giants teammates had some fun with him while teaching him the language. Once, when the corpulent Manager Herman Franks came to the mound to lift Murakami, the pitcher greeted him, in all seriousness, with, "Take a hike, Fatso." ❖

CHAPTER **23**

# THE DRESSEN YEARS

Casey Stengel and the "Nine Old Men" had been a wonderful fantasy-turned-reality for baseball fans in Oakland. But just as fabulous dreams rarely recur, 1948's magic couldn't be duplicated in 1949.

The 1948 Oakland team had been built for the moment. The 1949 Oaks would need a massive infusion of players to remain competitive, and roster changes came at a furious pace. Also, because Stengel had left for greater fortune with the New York Yankees, Laws needed a new manager.

Laws searched extensively before finally settling on Charlie Dressen. Dressen had been a coach for the Yankees and was a colorful character as well. He was an excellent teacher and had a reputation as a motivator who engendered self-confidence. In Oakland he quickly gained a reputation as an umpire baiter and one of the most effective sign-stealers the league had ever seen.

Molding the team in Dressen's style was a difficult transition for Oaks traditionalists. Nobody realized how massive the change would be. Even the traditional red and blue caps and the uniforms with the classic old English "O" were discarded. In their place came clean white jerseys with royal blue script "Oaks" across the front and royal hats with an open, cursive "O."

Dressen was just as successful as Stengel, bringing a pennant and a second-place finish to the Oaks in two seasons. But he wasn't Casey. It didn't help that the 1948 team was practically gutted by the time 1949 rolled around. Oakland's fans found it hard to warm up to Dressen. The ballplayers felt like a family under Casey, but ultimately they came to respect Dressen as the superior tactician. In fact, the majority of ballplayers who played under both managers consider Dressen to be the better manager. Several of his players eventually would agree: "He was my best manager."

Dressen hired George L. "Highpockets" Kelly, the great Hall of Fame infielder, as coach. The two had a long association with the Cincinnati Reds as players. Later, when Dressen managed the Reds, Kelly was his coach. Kelly was a patient, effective teacher.

## A TEAM IN TRANSITION

Coming out of 1949 Spring Training, the Oaks were a blend of veterans from the 1948 team, players acquired over the winter and a handful of rookies. But from April to the beginning of June, the Oaks played bad baseball.

Pitching was shoddy and the infield was porous. Young players fell short of expectations and were sent elsewhere. Laws and Dressen ran up costly telephone bills searching for qualified replacements.

Then the pieces started coming together. The Oaks needed a shortstop and leadoff batter and Artie Wilson, Oakland's first black player, was transferred from San Diego in May. His arrival allowed Billy Martin to shift back to second base, his natural position.

As May ended, Laws and Dressen concluded a series of deals that sent shock waves throughout the East Bay. In a two-day period, the front office reported the sale of outfielder George Metkovich to the Chicago White Sox and southpaw Lloyd Hittle to the Washington Senators, both for immediate delivery. Just a few days later, Dario Lodigiani was waived to the Seals—the PCL's worst team at the time—for $4,000. "Lodi" had signed a bonus contract with the Oaks in 1947 and his placement on waivers was irrevocable.

The fourth move topped the previous three. The Oaks traded 17-year veteran Billy Raimondi to Sacramento straight up for catcher Frankie Kerr. This deal convinced Oakland fans of Charlie Dressen's intention to dismantle Casey Stengel's team and rebuild it his way.

Charlie Dressen and his coach, Highpockets Kelly, came to Oakland in 1949, one year after Casey Stengel's 'Nine Old Men' won the PCL crown. The 1949 Oaks were the franchise's first fully integrated team.

**OAKLAND'S 1949 BASEBALL CLUB OF THE PACIFIC COAST LEAGUE**

Back row: Red Adams, Trainer; Keith Simon, P; Lou Tost, P; Billy Martin, 2B; Earl Toolson, P; Rex Cecil, P; Jim Tote, P; Alonzo Perry, P; Milo Candini, P. Middle row: Dick Kryhoski, IF; Walt Pocekay, OF; Frank Nelson, P; Loyd Christopher, OF; Maurice Van Robays, OF; Frank Kerr, C; Don Padgett, C; Allan Gettel, P; Earl Rapp, OF; Earl Harrist, P. Front row: Jack Jensen, OF; Charley Gassaway, P; Artie Wilson, IF; Cookie Lavagetto, Player-Coach; George Kelly, Coach; Charles (Chuck) Dressen, Manager; Forrest Thomson, P; Parnel Woods, 3B; Earl Jones, P; Mel Deuzabou, P. Sitting (left): Ed Marseth, Bat Boy; (right) Chuckie Symm, Bat Boy.

## GROUND RULES CHANGE

Brick Laws and Charlie Dressen realized new ground rules in the post-war period made team rebuilding much more difficult. An era of specialization in athletics was beginning. Superior athletes found greater discouragement in attempting to diversify themselves. Organized baseball faced tremendous competition for talented athletes, and they were shocked to be losing out to other professional sports.

The story of two local football stars shows just how much things had changed. In the post-war period, two of the nation's top collegiate running backs played football in the East Bay: Herman Wedemeyer at St. Mary's and Jackie Jensen at Cal. Both were excellent baseball players, but conventional wisdom dictated each would cast his future with professional football, especially with the formation of the new All American Football Conference.

Wedemeyer left St. Mary's to sign with the Los Angeles Dons of the AAFC. During the spring of 1948, Laws and Cookie Devincenzi met with Wedemeyer to discuss the possibility of his playing baseball as well. Wedemeyer presumed the Dons were amenable to his signing with the Oaks, but when the Oaks made a specific request to Dons' General Manager Harry Thayer, he invoked a clause in Wedemeyer's contract that forbade his playing a second sport. The issue was dead, and Wedemeyer pursued a moderately successful football career.

Jensen's case was less complicated but more spectacular. A graduate of Oakland High School, Jensen was a consensus All-American who led Cal to an undefeated season before the Bears lost to Northwestern in the Rose Bowl. Jensen had also helped pitch and bat the Bears to the NCAA baseball championship in 1947, twice being selected to the All-Pacific Coast Team. All this in his junior year.

Abandoning his final year of football eligibility, Jensen signed a contract in 1949 to play for the Oaks, rejecting many offers from major league teams. This not only infuriated university administration and alumni but it also brought to a head the philosophical conflict over the early signing of baseball prospects. Jensen's contract was for $75,000 divided equally over a three-year period, and it was reported he received a $6,000 bonus payment which made him eligible for the major league draft after the season. The Oaks also presented him with a Cadillac convertible.

The major leagues' approach to acquire players had gradually changed over the years. Major league teams had always attempted to sign budding prospects in the past, but they usually let minor league teams search out, sign and train local prospects. Normally, the majority of players on the Seals and Oaks rosters were local players, and major league teams would send scouts west to watch and acquire their best players.

As Branch Rickey developed the concept of the farm system, other major league franchises were forced to follow his lead to remain competitive. Bonus payments enlarged as enticement for prospects, and the whole system of scouting and signing players changed. Even the most prosperous minor league franchises couldn't compete with the bonus signings from major league teams.

Jensen's signing by the Oaks was a clever ploy that brought an immediate reaction from major league owners. The signing of a marquee player like Jensen indicated Oakland's intention to be competitive. Fans would throng to Oaks Ball Park to see him play and major league teams would compete to purchase his contract.

Laws had little worry he would have to pay Jensen the full $75,000. He figured a major league team would purchase him and be obligated for the remainder of the contract. As it was, the Yankees were that team. At Casey Stengel's suggestion, George Weiss negotiated the acquisition of both Jensen and Billy Martin in October 1949 for 1950 delivery.

Major league club owners then asked Commissioner Chandler whether the receiving team must honor the obligations of the long-term contract. Laws had received approval from George Trautman, head of the National Association of Minor Leagues, for such a contract. Trautman felt confident that such a document would hold up in the courts. Naturally, major league owners felt threatened by this new innovation.

While the Jensen contract provided a balanced sum for each of the three years, there was a legitimate fear long-term contracts could be negotiated with the player receiving minimal pay in the first year and a staggering sum in the final year of the agreement. This would allow the minor league team to incur minimal financial obligation before the player advanced to the major leagues.

Laws' strategy ultimately backfired. Major league clubs intensified their efforts to outbid minor league teams for the better prospects, leaving fewer hometown players within reach of local teams.

The 1949 season ushered in the era of greater dependency for the Coast League as the Hollywood Stars signed a close working agreement with Branch Rickey's Brooklyn Dodgers. The Stars received an immediate infusion of talented young players, elevating them to the class of the league. The Seals, trying to retain their independence, continued their loose agreement with the Pirates, while the Oaks established closer ties with the Yankees.

Earl Rapp was a power-hitting outfielder for Dressen's Oaks teams, usually leading the league in most categories.

Brick Laws justified the moves. "We intend bringing Oakland a pennant contender this season," he said. "Other players will go if we feel we can do better."

Indeed, the Oakland roster featured 58 different players in 1949.

Metkovich had been enjoying a spectacular season in center field and it was obvious he belonged in the majors. He brought $40,000 to the Oaks and the option of young first baseman Gordy Goldsberry and powerful outfielder Earl Rapp. In announcing the sale, Laws acknowledged the reality of the situation. "I hate to lose Metkovich, but we've been lucky to keep him this long. He'd certainly be drafted next fall, so why not forfeit him now for a season's use of two outstanding youngsters?"

The Washington Senators' Clark Griffith must have seen something special in Lloyd Hittle, a rookie pitcher from Stockton who was 5-4 when the deal was made. As part of the transaction, Oakland acquired a bullpen with this deal: pitchers Milo Candini and Forrest Thompson. Hittle, who undoubtedly could have benefited from more minor league experience, was a losing pitcher for two seasons with the Senators before being returned to Oakland in 1951. Candini went 15-9 and Thompson was 11-8 with a 3.16 ERA. Candini was drafted by the Phillies at the end of the season.

Metkovich was hitting .337 when he left, but Rapp filled the gap by finishing at .344 with 15 home runs. Goldsberry, one of the finest defensive players of the era, took over first base when Les Scarsella was released for

---

## STENGEL VS. DRESSEN

Because of their success in Oakland, Casey Stengel and Charlie Dressen both were rewarded with major league managerial positions. Stengel became one of baseball's most successful managers ever. Dressen used his Oakland experience to return to Brooklyn where, after two years, he left over contractual differences, returning to manage the Oaks in 1954. His return was a short-lived breath of fresh air for the franchise. The Washington Senators hired him to manage for 1955, and over the next decade he held various major league manager's jobs until he died.

Former Oaks veteran Mel Duezabou and his wife, Jackie, described the differences between these two managers. Jackie Duezabou described Dressen as "a very different manager to play for than Stengel. I think he knew more about baseball than Casey, but Casey knew more about men. Casey was lovable. Dressen could be admirable because of his baseball knowledge."

Mel added, "Stengel was loved by his players. He knew how to treat us as individuals and to get the best out of each. There was an attitude of family surrounding the ballclub. Dressen was respected but feared by his players. There was no question who was in charge. Things were done Dressen's way."

Stengel wanted to manage a finished product. He did not have much patience for rookies. He was not a teacher, but a motivator. Dressen was patient with younger players and under him they learned and improved, but he remained rather aloof. A number of ballplayers who played under both managers expressed their feeling that Dressen was the better manager.

"Stengel's signals to batters and runners were old fashioned—simple," Duezabou said. "The first time I ever saw multiple signs was under Charlie Dressen. I never saw that from Casey Stengel. I played for him for three years—never saw that from Stengel. We had signs, but they were very simple.

"Charlie Dressen had a lot of signs. I said, 'How the hell am I going to remember that?' But we did. As far as I know, Charlie Dressen started that. And Charlie could really read pitchers and steal their signs. Some of the guys really liked to be told whether it was going to be a fastball or a curve. I didn't want to know, but others did."

refusing to play with black teammates. With Cookie Lavagetto and newly acquired Parnell Woods holding down third base, the infield—considered a liability at the beginning of the season—became a team strong point. Later in the season, Goldsberry was replaced at first base by Dick Kryhoski, on loan from the Yankees. Although giving up some defense, Kryhoski batted .328 for the Oaks, some 80 points better than Goldsberry.

The Raimondi trade was the ultimate insult for Oakland fans. Raimondi was unquestionably the most popular of the Oaks and he was generally regarded as the best catcher in the league. But Kerr was seven years younger and more agile. Kerr shared the catching responsibilities with Don Padgett, a seasoned veteran with a solid bat.

Frank Nelson, acquired from Spokane where he won 24 games in 1948, went 14-11 as a starter. Charlie Gassaway was 15-9 to earn a spot on the All-Star team. Reliever Ralph Buxton, 38, earned a well-deserved promotion to the Yankees at mid-season. In 1950, he would pitch for the Seals.

Familiar faces still roamed the outfield. Mel Duezabou finished at .308, Loyd Christopher hit 21 home runs and played solid defense, and veteran Maurice Van Robays batted .298, mostly in a pinch-hitting role.

Two rookie outfielders commanded attention that year. Bill Taylor was a robust left-handed batter. Although optioned out early in the season, his potential was so obvious that the Giants purchased his contract early in 1950 for 1951 delivery. The Giants also sent the Oaks three players for use during the 1950 season as part of the deal.

The other rookie outfielder was Jackie Jensen. Jensen joined the Oaks on May 26 amid a publicity onslaught seldom viewed in the Bay Area. Jensen came in and fell flat on his face; after one month his batting average was in the low .220s. The fans gave him no relief. Unaware of how insecure and sensitive Jensen was, their reception probably compounded his slump.

But Dressen and Kelly saw Jensen's potential and worked with him. Jensen admitted he had never learned how to play the game properly in college, where he could get by on his superior talents. With Oakland, Jensen learned the basics: How to be patient at the plate, how to hit the cutoff man from the outfield and how to prevent runners from taking an extra base.

Jensen's average and confidence climbed as the season progressed and he finished with a .261 average and nine homers in 125 games. The statistics belied his gifts, and the Yankees bought him.

Mel Duezabou (left) was a speedy outfielder and Dario Lodigiani a versatile infielder for the Oaks.

## ANATOMY OF A ROOKIE

Tommy Munoz was one of the most highly scouted prep ballplayers in the East Bay in 1952. With a flock of major league scouts following him, Munoz signed a three-year, $30,000 contract with Brick Laws of Oakland. An Oaks fan, Tommy was just as happy to stay at home. The day after signing with the Oaks, Cleveland offered him $80,000.

Munoz was a mid-semester graduate from San Leandro High, signing with the Oaks after graduation in February 1952. In March, he went to Spring Training with the Oaks. "When I entered the Oaks' clubhouse, (trainer) Red Adams was real nice to me. He asked me what number I wanted on my uniform and introduced me to the players as they started coming in. One can't imagine what a thrill it was to be in the same locker room."

On meeting Manager Mel Ott for the first time, Munoz said, "Ott was very helpful to me. I was only 17 when I signed and he was only 16 when he reached the majors. He knew I would be nervous so he picked me up and helped me alot to build my confidence.

"In an exhibition game against the Giants at Oakland, (Sal) Maglie has a perfect game after six. Ott tells me to bat for the pitcher and break up the no-hitter, and I got a hit. That was my biggest thrill."

Munoz faced a continuing problem in making the Oaks' lineup: Jim Marshall. Also a first baseman, Marshall was a couple of years older than Munoz and the Oaks felt they had a big payoff with him. By playing Marshall, there was no room on the roster for Munoz and he was optioned to Albuquerque in 1952 and Wenatchee in 1953-54.

"A person can't explain the thrill of signing a contract, then going out there with the players," Munoz said. "In Spring Training, the players were great. They knew I wasn't going to take their job away. Piper (Davis) was a wonderful person. He helped me and every other youngster any way he could. There are ballplayers who won't help rookies, but Piper wasn't one of them.

"Bill Howerton and Sam Chapman were also great. Part of being away from home . . . they could sense it and they could pick you up. 'Let's go to dinner. Let's go to a show.' Eddie Lake was my roommate. He was from San Leandro and I already knew him. He kept an eye on me."

Munoz's career with the Oaks spanned parts of 1952-54. He was an excellent example of how luck can affect a career. One day's hesitation and Munoz might have signed with another team for more money, and he may have found less competition at his position. Still, Tommy never expressed regret.

---

If any one of the first three months of the season could have been deleted from the Oaks record, the Oaks would have been repeat champions. On July 9, the Stars held their greatest lead, 10½ games ahead of the pack. The Oaks were able to reduce the deficit at one point to only two games, but the Stars won the pennant by five.

By the end of the season, the Oaks were the best team in the league but they just ran out of time. Unfortunately, there was no Governor's Cup playoff that year.

### RETURN TO THE TOP

Early season favorites Hollywood and San Diego jumped ahead of the field to start the 1950 season while the Oaks and Seals hovered around .500. By the end of May, the Oaks started closing on the Stars. From June 1 through July 12, the date the Oaks caught the Stars, the Oaks played .692 baseball (29-13). They kept a comfortable lead of 4-6 games the rest of the race and finished four games ahead of the Padres. The Stars faded to a distant third, 14 games behind.

The stalwarts of the 1949 pitching staff—Gassaway, Nelson, Thompson, Tost and Jones—all returned. But Allen Gettel and Earl Harrist, both acquired late in 1949, were the staff leaders. Gettel was 23-7, effective in both

Don Padgett gave the Oaks solid defense behind the backstop and consistent power at the plate.

The 1950 Oaks returned to championship form under Charlie Dressen, who was promptly hired to manage the Brooklyn Dodgers the following season. As usual, Artie Wilson helped lead the Oaks, batting .311 while playing good defense at shortstop.

starting and relief roles and pinch-hitting on days that he didn't pitch. Harrist was 18-8. Hank Behrman and George Bamberger, both provided by the Giants, were 17-8 and 17-13, respectively. Clyde Shoun, the only lefty of the big five, brought 15 years of major league experience to the Oaks and was 16-10 in his last year as a professional baseball player.

Artie Wilson again anchored the infield at shortstop, batting .311 while playing in 196 of the Oaks' 200 games. Wilson teamed up with Bobby Hofman, another Giants optionee, to form a solid double-play combination. Hofman batted .296 in 166 games. The Oaks' infield also featured three veterans who alternated between first and third base. Augie Galan spent much of his time at first base while Lavagetto played third. Hall of Famer Billy Herman came out of retirement for one last fling and served as a strong utility player, batting .307 in 71 games. Metkovich returned to the Oaks to hit .315 in 184 games.

The Oaks also benefited from a player-management dispute that led to the acquisition of a proven major league outfielder. During the winter of 1949, the Yankees traded Dick Kryhoski to Detroit for former bonus baby

## DICK WAKEFIELD: DOLLAR-A-YEAR MAN

Outfielder Dick Wakefield played parts of the 1950 and 1951 seasons with Oakland. Wakefield, who skirted the fine line between character and eccentric, came to town like a lion and left like a lamb. While he was in Oakland, he got more publicity in 1½ seasons than better players received in their career.

Wakefield, one of the early bonus babies, played several years with the Detroit Tigers after leaving the University of Michigan. Wakefield was making $17,000 a year when he was traded to the Yankees.

When it came time to negotiate a contract with the Yankees, Wakefield felt he deserved the same salary, plus cigar money. Wakefield, who always had a cigar in his mouth when not playing, settled for $17,100. He made the big club out of Spring Training but was almost immediately sent to Oakland on option.

As the Oaks' fourth outfielder, Wakefield played in 87 games with a .293 batting average, seven home runs and 38 RBIs. Wakefield knew he had not put up enough numbers to warrant a return to the majors, so one day late in 1950 he went to the front office to visit Owner Brick Laws. From this meeting came one of the more curious contract negotiations in league history.

"I went up to Brick Laws and told him I was one guy he wouldn't have trouble signing for 1951—that I hadn't been given a real chance in 1950, but knew I could play ball," Wakefield said. "I said I would play for exactly $1 this season. He was surprised, but we shook hands on it.

"If I have a good year and he wants to give me a Cadillac or something like that—OK."

When contract time rolled around, Laws sent a $1 contract to Ann Arbor for Wakefield to sign. "Actually, I was only offering Dick his own terms. Dick said he would be willing to play this year for

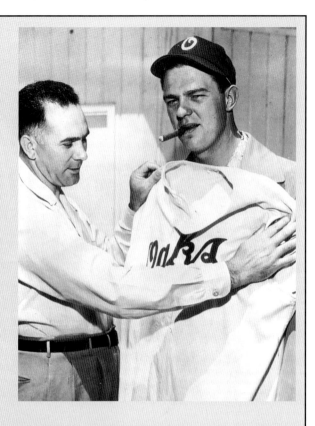

$1 and expenses, and that's the contract I sent him," Laws said.

Wakefield accepted the contract and reported to camp. While record books listed his weight at 210 pounds, Wakefield actually checked in at 237. By the time the regular season rolled around Wakefield was still overweight. His manager, Mel Ott, used him in pinch-hitting situations, but never allowed the pudgy Wakefield to take the field defensively. After a couple of weeks, the Oaks released him.

As a consolation, Wakefield received his full salary when he was released. No Cadillac, though.

---

Dick Wakefield. Wakefield didn't fit into the Yankees' plans and was sold to the Oaks in late May. He refused to report but finally relented. When Wakefield arrived in Oakland, he told reporters he didn't think he would be good enough to make the team.

For three years, Oakland was the top franchise in the league—two pennants and a near miss. More than 500,000 fans watched the Oaks in their quaint little park each year. No other PCL team drew more.

After his championship year with the Oaks, Dressen was hired by Walter O'Malley to pilot the Brooklyn Dodgers for the 1951 season. Guiding the Dodgers turned from joy to nightmare as the Giants made their miracle run and Bobby Thomson hit the "Shot Heard 'Round the World" to win one of the most famous post-season play-offs of all time. Dressen continued in 1952-53, winning pennants both seasons, but falling to Stengel's Yankee Express in the World Series. ❖

CHAPTER **24**

# FROM CHAMPS
# TO VANCOUVER

After Charlie Dressen left to manage the "Boys of Summer," Brick Laws brought in a string of big names: Mel Ott, Augie Galan, Dressen again and finally Lefty O'Doul. Laws' list of coaches was equally impressive. These included "Highpockets" Kelly and Billy Herman, both future inductees into the Hall of Fame, as well as Cookie Lavagetto, Galan and Eddie Taylor, a giant among coaches even though he was only 5-6.

Laws negotiated a working agreement with the New York Giants, signed a continuing flow of high-profile major league veterans and competed with the major leagues for the best local prospects. With all these factors in place, the Oakland franchise should have been prosperous, but it wasn't.

The problems were not Oakland's. They were the problems of minor league baseball—the phenomenon of a television set in every living room, saturation of major league radio broadcasts into minor league territory, five-figure bonus payments to untried prospects and the enforced dependency of every minor league to their eastern patriarchs. Laws' finest efforts were doomed to failure, even the hiring of "Mr. Giant," Mel Ott, to manage. Ott had been working in the Giants' front office and yearned to return to the coaching lines.

Ott's signing with Oakland represented his first experience in baseball with any club other than the Giants. Ott broke into organized baseball at the age of 17 with New York and played continuously through 1942 when he was player-manager. He stepped down as manager midway through the 1948 season, whereupon he moved into the front office as assistant director of the Giants' minor league operations.

Ott was a gentle person from Louisiana, truly liked by his players but not always respected. His personality did not allow him to discipline players when they needed it and as a result, his players sometimes took advantage of his loose leadership.

Ott was a natural attraction and Acorn attendance was even more stimulated by his presence in 1951 when he was inducted into the Hall of Fame.

Like Dressen before him, Ott had to rebuild the team because the Oaks' 1950 championship caused several of the best players to advance to the majors. Gone were pitchers Allen Gettel and George Bamberger, catcher Rafael Noble, infielder Artie Wilson and outfielder George Metkovich—more than 20 percent of the 23-player roster. By the end of the season, though, Gettel and Wilson were back in Oakland.

## PRE-GAME ENTERTAINMENT

Oaks fans who came to the park early during the 1949 and 1950 seasons were treated to some special entertainment. After both teams had taken their infield practice, coach George Kelly would put the batboys through their paces on the infield, hitting grounders to the kids. The youngsters were enthusiastic, attacking the ball, diving for balls hit into the hole, making accurate throws to turn a double play—in short, they played great baseball. They never erred . . . and if one of them did drop a ball, he'd scoop it up in time to successfully complete the play.

And the most amazing part of their whole act . . . they did it all without a baseball.

Oaks Manager Mel Ott welcomes outfielder Sam Chapman to his team (above). Chapman had told the Athletics he wanted to return to the West Coast to be with his family. Below, Ott and Augie Galan (right) confer with Owner Brick Laws.

The Giants provided several players to Oakland, either as compensation for the Oaks stars or as part of the working agreement. Most of the players Oakland received came from the Giants' Triple-A Minneapolis farm club. Most successful was rugged right-handed pitcher Bill Ayers, who finished at 20-13 with 17 complete games

and a 3.85 ERA for the 1951 Oaks. Pitchers Charlie Bishop, Francis "Red" Hardy and Wes Bailey, third baseman Bert Haas, shortstop Bill Jennings, second baseman Pete Pavlick and first baseman-outfielder Joe Lafata also joined the Oaks.

Haas hit .331 with 10 homers in 86 games and was sold in mid-season to the White Sox as a pinch-hitter. Jennings was transferred to San Diego when Artie Wilson's contract was returned to Oakland. Wilson, with little chance of breaking up the Giants' double-play combination of Eddie Stanky and Alvin Dark, was sent out to Ottawa and later transferred to Minneapolis. Lafata, a disappointment, was sold to Portland.

Long-time major leaguer Sam Chapman, now 36, decided he had been away from home long enough. Chapman had gone from Cal directly to the Philadelphia Athletics' outfield in 1938. After 11 years in the American League and three in the military, Chapman wanted to finish his professional career closer to his home in San Rafael. In the spring of 1951, he refused to report to the Cleveland Indians and negotiated his transfer to Oakland.

Chapman immediately found himself in center field where he was forced to work himself into shape by playing. Chapman played in 173 games, hitting 16 home runs, batting in 98 and hitting .263.

Reacquiring Wilson was another blessing for Oaks attendance. Laws had pestered the Giants' front office for

Sam Chapman gets a hero's welcome from Eddie Lake after hitting a home run at San Diego.

his return when he was optioned out. But the Giants were short of middle infielders in their farm system and before the Giants would acquiesce, Laws had to ship Piper Davis, on option, to Ottawa as compensation.

Trainer Red Adams was delighted with Wilson's return. "Wilson is a natural leader," Adams said. "He sets the pace. He is the fellow who moves faster than the others—and the others are willing to follow him. He has a fine disposition. He can make his teammates laugh, but he isn't a clown. There's a happy atmosphere when Artie is around. I'm confident Wilson personally will add between 500 and 1,000 spectators to every Oakland ball game from now until the end of the season."

Indeed, Oakland drew 8,640 to Oaks Ball Park in Wilson's first game back, roughly 6,000 above normal attendance for a weeknight.

The Oaks were anything but a pre-season favorite coming out of Spring Training. That honor was bestowed upon the Stars and the Rainiers. And as it turned out, the Oaks, with a thin outfield and mediocre pitching—despite the presence of former Seals star Chet Johnson and consecutive no-hit pitcher Johnny Vander Meer—completed the season in fifth place.

The season was a financial disaster for Oakland. Attendance was off almost 300,000, dropping to 193,822, the worst in the league. Over the winter Laws shopped Artie Wilson. The Seals were reportedly offered Wilson for $25,000 but declined. Ultimately, Wilson was sold to Seattle for 1952.

## SAM CHAPMAN ON THE COAST LEAGUE

After 11 years in the major leagues, Sam Chapman decided he would not return in 1952. Chapman sat out Spring Training, negotiated his release from the Cleveland Indians and immediately signed with Oakland.

Chapman got off to a slow start but wound up hitting .263 with 98 RBIs and 16 home runs. He played one more season with the Oaks before retiring.

The gray-haired Chapman was a fatherly figure to many of the Oaks youngsters, and it came as little surprise that he was made player-coach for the Oaks.

"The PCL surprised me," Chapman said. "The quality of baseball is a lot better than I was led to expect. What has surprised me most of all is the pitching. I thought you'd see a good pitcher one day, then so-so pitching the next couple of days. Instead, you see good pitching every day.

"The difference between this and the majors is that back there you see good pitching a couple of days, then excellent pitching the third day. You can't really make a comparison, but I would say the PCL standard is 75 percent as good as the majors."

Allen 'Two-Gun' Gettel was the best pitcher in the PCL in the early 1950s, but he was better known as one of the league's funniest characters.

Wilson had been a disappointment in 1951. His batting average had slipped to .255 in 81 games, and it was a rather soft average. Only nine of his 89 hits were for extra bases, eight doubles and one triple. And he walked only 14 times. Laws had to assume Wilson was through.

## PIPER DAVIS—MOST VERSATILE PLAYER

Piper Davis opened the 1951 season behind the plate but played a total of 122 games filling in wherever he was needed. He was the team's top batter at .306, but his versatility was his true value. Early in the season, Manager Mel Ott said, "I've got a great idea. Let's play a nine-inning game some day and have Piper play a different position every inning."

To which the stadium concessions manager reportedly replied, "Let's make it a 10-inning game and have Piper sell popcorn."

Ott's whimsical suggestion materialized. On the last day of the season, September 21, Piper was awarded a $500 bond by the boosters and headed out to the mound to start the game. After retiring three batters, Davis played each of the remaining eight positions. Easily, Piper Davis was the team's most valuable—and versatile—player.

## MOVING UP IN 1952

After a thorough housecleaning, Ott guided the 1952 Oaks to a second-place finish, 104-76, five games behind the Stars. The pitching staff was rebuilt, with only Ayers, Gettel, Hittle and Jay Ragni returning. Gettel was the staff workhorse, toiling 273 innings and recording a 17-14 record with a 3.43 ERA. Ayers was 13-12, and Hittle, now a starter, was 11-10.

The most significant winter acquisitions for the pitching staff were Hal Gregg and John Van Cuyk. Gregg came out of retirement to post an 11-2 record, including a 3-0 seven-inning no-hitter over the Beavers, before he was sold to the Giants. Gregg's no-hitter was the first at Emeryville since 1944, and his sale brought two solid young pitchers to the Oaks for the remainder of the season. Van Cuyk finished with a 9-3 record and a 2.75 ERA in 61 appearances.

Early and mid-season acquisitions made the difference in Oakland's successes, however. Reliever Milo Candini returned to Oakland from the Phillies and set a league appearance record—69 games—while going 9-6 with a 2.56 ERA. With the left-hander Van Cuyk and the right-hander Candini, Ott had the Coast League's most effective bullpen.

As compensation for Gregg, the Giants sent George Bamberger and Roger Bowman to the Oaks on option. In half a season, "Bambi" went 14-6 with a 2.88 ERA. Bamberger was Ott's most effective starter. Bowman was 7-5 with a 3.29 ERA and a no-hitter.

That no-hitter occurred on July 3 when he beat the Hollywood Stars 3-0. "To throw a no-hitter, you've got to be lucky," he said. "Most of their players knew my style of pitching, but what they didn't know was my arm was hurting. The first time through [the lineup] I kept them off balance with breaking pitches. They were expecting more fastballs. By the middle innings, my arm had loosened up some."

The Stars began looking for Bowman's breaking pitches but he was starting to throw fastballs by them. "By their third at-bats, I'm tiring. Now they're looking for the fastball."

Bowman, out of necessity, went back to his breaking pitches, once again fooling the Stars batters.

Hollywood Manager Fred Haney had loaded his batting order with right-handed batters. Still, Bowman retired the first 15 before giving up a walk. The walk was followed by a double play. Hank Schenz and Spider Jorgensen made spectacular diving plays in the field, taking away sure hits and ensuring Bowman's place in Coast League history.

While any pitcher would be content to throw a no-hitter, Bowman repeated the feat two years later with a perfect seven-inning game, 10-0, against the Beavers. By then he was pitching for the Hollywood Stars.

## AUGIE GALAN TAKES THE HELM IN 1953

Whether Ott, with his high salary, would return in 1953 was in doubt at the end of the 1952 season. Laws acknowledged Ott did a solid job but said, "We can't afford to pay $20,000 a year for a manager and $10,000 for a coach." For Laws, the season had resulted in more financial losses. Although attendance was up to 234,952, the payroll was also higher. Marquee players like Chapman, Ostrowski, Jorgensen and Gettel weren't cheap.

Finally, Ott decided to stay in New Orleans and not return to Oakland. Laws subsequently appointed Augie Galan, Ott's coach, to manage the 1953 team. Galan's tenure in Oakland was not a happy one. The team made a couple of poor trades that weakened it and the pitching staff was plagued by a series of maladies. The Oaks ended up seventh, 29 games out of first at 77-103. The only plus was in winning a season-long battle with Sacramento to stay out of the cellar.

Other than Gettel (24-14, 3.20 ERA), the pitching staff was weak. What appeared to be a good staff on paper disintegrated in a flurry of injuries and poor trades. Hal

Don Ferrarese, an East Bay product, was a highly touted left-handed pitching prospect.

Gregg, back in an Oakland uniform, pitched two innings and retired with a chronic sore arm. Con Dempsey, signed as a free agent out of Spring Training, found he was unable to recover from arm injuries and was released. Bill Ayers, a 20-game winner two years earlier, couldn't locate the plate and was sold to Wenatchee. The same fate befell Jay Ragni. John Van Cuyk, equally ineffective, was sold to the Padres.

With the Oaks getting off to a poor start, the front office made some trades. The Oaks shipped Lloyd Hittle to Hollywood for pitcher Billy Joe Waters and shortstop Johnny O'Neil. Waters finished at 5-11 while Hittle went 8-11 at Hollywood. The Oaks already had two shortstops and O'Neil was ultimately released.

Laws quickly negotiated another trade, sending veteran reliever Milo Candini and second baseman Hank Schenz to Sacramento for veteran starter Jess Flores and former Negro Leagues star Ray Dandridge. The whole purpose of the trade was to acquire another starter, but Flores arrived with a sore shoulder and was released. Laws protested the trade, but Flores had sufficiently recovered and Laws re-signed him. Flores finished with an 8-7 record at Oakland. Candini, ineffective at Oakland, found his groove in Sacramento and went 9-4 in 57 games.

Dandridge, who listed himself as 36—which nobody believed—had lost his Hall of Fame skills. He hit .268 in 86 games but was released before the season ended.

## LOOKING TO THE FUTURE

Three young Oaks attracted considerable attention around the league: Don Ferrarese, Bob Murphy and Ernie Broglio. Ferrarese, the diminutive lefty, was back from military service. Much was expected of him but he was used sparingly because of a tender arm and wound up with a 4-4 record. Bob Murphy was a highly touted prospect who led his Stanford teammates to the 1953 California Intercollegiate Baseball Championship with an 8-1 record. He debuted with a complete-game, 3-2 victory over Portland. Murphy went 4-5 with a 4.17 ERA but failed to match his first year's record later in his career.

Law's biggest coup was the signing of 17-year-old prep phenom Ernie Broglio from El Cerrito High. Broglio was easily the top prospect in the Bay Area and he rejected a dozen major league offers to sign with the Oaks. Broglio trained with the team and watched them play for a month before he made his debut. On July 10, Broglio pitched an impressive complete game against the Portland Beavers, losing 5-0. He allowed 10 hits with six walks and four strikeouts, but showed an excellent fastball and an effective curveball.

Broglio's second game was another complete-game loss, this time to Sacramento. In three additional starts and six relief outings, Broglio was 2-4 with a 6.71 ERA. He needed seasoning and would get it in the California League the next year.

The Oaks signed another El Cerrito High graduate, Elijah "Pumpsie" Green, who had played two stellar seasons at West Contra Costa Junior College. Green was sent to Wenatchee and soon drifted out of the Oaks organization, later playing with the Seals before becoming the first black player with the Boston Red Sox—the last all-white major league team—in 1959.

Catcher Len Neal was an iron man in 1953, playing in 174 of the Oaks' 180 games. In one stretch he caught 130 consecutive games, including 27 doubleheaders, while setting a league record of 100 consecutive games catching without an error. Art Cuitti and Harry Bartolomei were his seldom-used backups.

The 1953 season was another financial disaster. Only 135,784 fans came to Oaks Ball Park, a league low and the lowest attendance mark of any team since the 1943 Sacramento "orphans" drew barely 31,000. Laws fired Galan and looked for other activities to generate revenues from the use of the Oaks Ball Park. Could rodeo and auto racing be far behind?

## CHARLIE DRESSEN RETURNS

After his second pennant in Brooklyn, Charlie Dressen made a tactical blunder by demanding a three-year contract from Walter O'Malley, who promptly fired him. Laws jumped at the chance of rehiring Dressen.

The 1954 Oaks were a veteran group as Dressen used his contacts to bring replacements to Oakland on option and moving veterans who had lost their skills. He guided the Oaks to third place, 16 games behind the Padres.

League directors reintroduced an abbreviated Governor's Cup playoff to conclude the season with an initial best-of-three series leading to a single-game championship. The Oaks downed the Padres 2-0 while the fourth-place Seals took the second-place Stars in three games. In the best-of-three championship series, the Oaks won the first two games for the Governor's Cup title.

That ended Dressen's tenure in the Coast League. The Washington Senators hired him, but he wasn't able to break their long-standing losing tradition. Dressen went on to manage three major league teams over nine years. In 1966, as manager of the Tigers, he suffered two heart attacks. The second was fatal.

## O'DOUL COMES TO OAKLAND

Replacing Dressen was a major challenge for Laws, but when the job opened up Lefty O'Doul, now manager of San Diego, expressed an interest in it. Lefty had brought a pennant winner to San Diego in 1954.

Padres Owner Bill Starr did not particularly want to lose Lefty because of his fan appeal. But Starr had gotten tired of some of O'Doul's habits, such as Lefty's penchant for playing golf on company time. Starr ultimately granted Lefty's request to be released.

For Laws and the people of Oakland, O'Doul's hiring seemed like a major coup. But it would not take long for them to discover this was not the same fiery manager who used to torment and tease them while wearing the pinstripes of the San Francisco Seals.

Lefty made one good move, however, by hiring Eddie Taylor as coach. Taylor played briefly with the Boston Braves in 1926 but was more well-known as the long-time coach for the Seattle Rainiers. As a player, Taylor was a scrappy shortstop who had broken both legs, severely dislocated an ankle, almost died in a beaning incident and had several broken noses and countless broken fingers. That was the way he played the game and was the way he coached it. Eddie was always there for the Oaks even when Lefty wasn't.

The Oaks were a 1955 pre-season favorite along with the Stars and Padres. Oakland had experienced players at every field position.

During the winter of 1954, Laws sold Ferrarese and Marshall to the White Sox. The Sox optioned Marshall back to Oakland so first base was in the same excellent defensive hands as before. The situation around second base was cemented when the Oaks acquired Billy Consolo, who had been cut by the Red Sox. The left side of the infield was solid with Russ Rose at shortstop and veteran Spider Jorgensen returning at third.

But the infield's offensive contributions were part of the reason for Oakland's dismal finish. Consolo batted a respectable .278 with 14 home runs in 160 games. Rose and Jorgensen both hit .244. Marshall hit .239 with 30 homers in 169 games.

During the previous winter, Laws outbid several other Coast League teams to purchase the contract of George Metkovich from Milwaukee. He also acquired Joe Brovia from Sacramento and Eric Rodin from the Giants organization. Art Cuitti, the fourth outfielder in 1954, was the only holdover. Metkovich, 33, returned to lead the league in hitting at .335 with 17 home runs and 80 RBIs. Brovia hit .326 with 18 homers and 73 RBIs before he was sold to the Cincinnati Reds in late June. After waiting 15 years for his call, Brovia shed tears of joy as he bade farewell to his teammates and to O'Doul, one of his staunchest supporters. But he stayed in the majors only a few months before he was returned to the Oaks. He appeared in 21 games as a pinch-hitter, going 2-for-18 for a .111 lifetime major league average.

Pitching was supposed to be the Oaks' strength, but it turned out to be their major disappointment. They kept Gettel, Bamberger and Van Cuyk and acquired veteran Karl Drews. The front office was also high on two local

(continued on page 241)

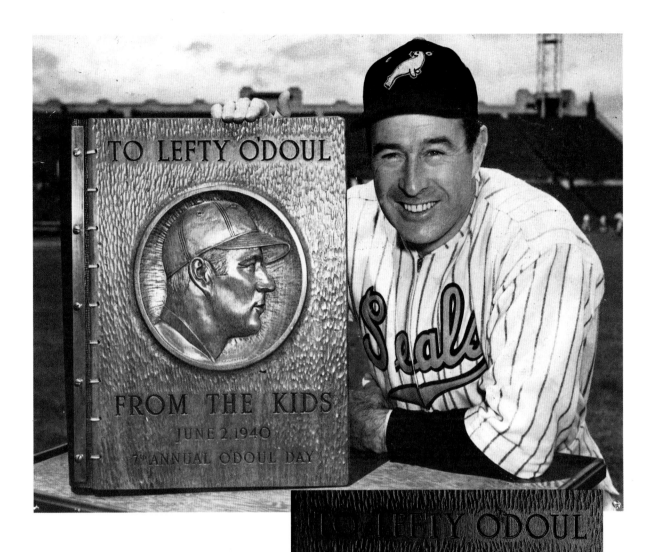

On one of the several "Lefty O'Doul Days" to celebrate San Francisco's most popular baseball player, the pitcher-outfielder-manager was presented with a scrapbook signed by hundreds of fans. It also included a letter from Commissioner Kenesaw Mountain Landis.

This 1936 Oaks uniform was worn by the batboy.

Oaks infielder Joe Abreu's jersey, 1939.

Outfielder Mike Christoff's 1942 Oaks jersey.

Even Lefty O'Doul wore an Oaks uniform, 1955.

Seals road uniform, 1921, worn by infielder Dee Walsh.

A 1933 Seals uniform. Player unknown.

A 1943 Seals uniform. 'V' for victory.

Larry Jansen wore this 1946 Seals jersey and went 30-6.

# CONTRACT

CLASS AAA

### APPROVED BY THE

# NATIONAL ASSOCIATION
## OF
# PROFESSIONAL BASEBALL LEAGUES

## UNIFORM PLAYER'S CONTRACT

### IMPORTANT NOTICES

The attention of both Club and Player is specifically directed to the following excerpt from Rule 3(a), of the Major-Minor League Rules:

"No Club shall make a contract different from the uniform contract and no club shall make a contract containing a non-reserve clause, except permission first be secured from the Executive Committee or the Advisory Council. The making of any agreement between a Club and Player not embodied in the contract shall subject both parties to discipline by the Commissioner or the Executive Committee."

A copy of this contract when executed must be delivered to player either in person or by registered mail, return receipt requested.

**Parties**      The_____ OAKLAND ASSOCIATION

herein called the Club and_____ ALFRED M. MARTIN

of_____ BERKELEY, CALIF._____ herein called the

**Recital**      The Club is a member of the National Association of Professional Baseball Leagues. As such, and joint the other members of the National Association of Professional Baseball Leagues, it is a party to the National tion Agreement, and to the Major-Minor League Agreement and Rules with the American League of Professiona ball Clubs and its constituent clubs and with the National League of Professional Baseball Clubs and its cons clubs, and is a party to the Constitution and By-Laws of the league of which the club is a member. The purpo these agreements, rules, Constitutions and By-Laws is to insure to the public wholesome and high-class professiona ball by defining the relations between club and player, between club and club, between league and league an in a designated Commissioner, Executive Committee and President of the National Association, broad po and discipline and decision in cases of disputes.

**Agreement**      In view of the facts above recited the parties agree as follows:

**Employment**      1. The Club hereby employs the Player to render skilled service as a baseball player in connectio the Club during the year 1946 including the Club's training season, the Club's exhibition game season, and any official series in which the Club may participate and in any games or series of of which the Player may be entitled to share; and the Player covenants that he is capable of and expertness, diligence and fidelity the service stated and such duties as may be required of him in such

**Salary**      2. For the service aforesaid the Club will pay the Player an aggregate salary of $ 200.00

**per month**_____, as follows:

In semi-monthly installments after the commencement of the playing season covered by this con Player is "abroad" with the Club for the purpose of playing games, in which event the amount then d on the first week day after the return "home" of the Club, the terms "home" and "abroad" meaning, resp away from the city in which the Club has its baseball field.

If a monthly salary is stipulated above, it shall begin with the commencement of the Club's playing subsequent date as the player's service may commence) and end with the termination of the Club's sc season, including split-season play-off series, and shall be payable in semi-monthly installments as abov

If the player is in the service of the Club for part of the playing season only he shall receive such salary above mentioned, as the number of days of his actual employment in the Club's playing sea number of days in said season.

**Loyalty**      3. (a) The Player during said season will faithfully serve the Club or any other Club to which the agreements above, or hereinafter recited, this contract may be assigned, and pledges himself to the conform to high standards of personal conduct, fair play and good sportsmanship.

(b) The Player represents that he does not, directly or indirectly, own stock or have any fin ownership or earnings of any club, except as herein expressly set forth, and covenants that he wil connected with any club, acquire or hold any such stock or interest except in accordance with the Rules.

**Service**      4. (a) The Player agrees that, for the purpose of avoiding injuries and to remain in physica the services he has contracted with the club to perform, while under contract or reservation he otherwise than for the Club or for such other Clubs, as may become assignees of this contrac said agreements; that he will not engage in professional boxing or wrestling; and that, except sent of the Club or its assignee he will not engage in any game or exhibition of football, bas athletic sport.

(b) The Player agrees that while under contract or reservation he will not play in any except in conformity with the National Association Agreement and Major-Minor League Rul in any such baseball game after October 31st of any year until the following spring traini any ineligible player, or team.

Billy Martin's first professional baseball contract. Martin, from West Berkeley, was signed by the Oaks but was sent to Arizona for some much needed seasoning. When he was recalled to Oakland, he played under Casey Stengel. This contract had to be countersigned by Billy's mother, Joan Downey.

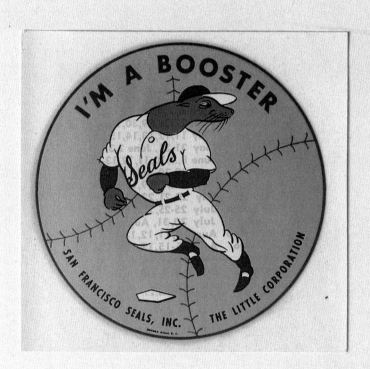

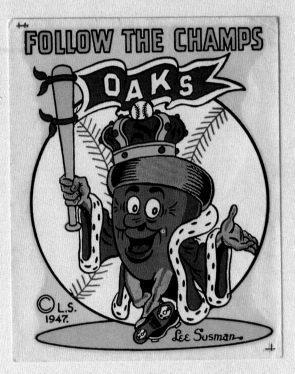

In a precursor to bumper stickers, fans of the Oaks and Seals could attach these decals to their car windows. The design on the Oaks decals was created by prominent *Oakland Tribune* cartoonist Lee Susman.

Left, Lefty O'Doul's uniform, 1950-1951. Below, a painting of O'Doul that was used on the cover of a Japanese sports magazine. Bottom left, a strip of Japanese baseball cards. Bottom, a 1949 Japanese tour program and Seals yearbook.

Left, Tommy Heath's Seals uniform from the Little Corporation days. Below, a stock certificate and decal showing ownership shares in the Seals.

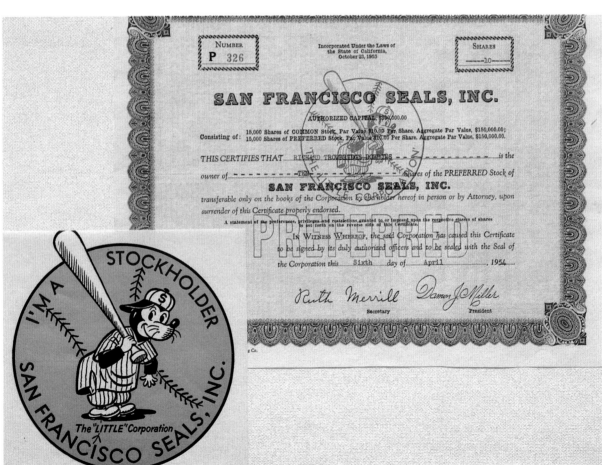

Home plate, Oaks Ball Park, Emeryville.

Brick Laws signed Lefty O'Doul to manage the Oaks in 1955 in an effort to boost attendance, but the move didn't work.

**(continued from page 232)**

prospects, Charlie Beamon from McClymonds High and Bob Murphy.

Gettel, Bamberger and Drews were regular starters, but each had losing seasons with ERAs above 4.00. Gettel was 12-13, Bamberger concluded at 12-14, and Drews was 9-13. Beamon and Murphy were early season disappointments. Both had been given chances to prove themselves, but both were optioned to Stockton at cut-down time.

At Stockton, Beamon was unbeatable. He went 16-0 with a 1.36 ERA, then came back to Oakland where his record was 2-8, 4.79. Murphy was a respectable 11-7 with a 3.35 ERA, but he never fulfilled his promise.

## FAREWELL

As the Oaks' fortunes on the field slipped, so did their revenues at the box office. Attendance slipped to 141,397, again the worst in the league and a drop of 60,000 from 1954. Laws had now suffered through three consecutive seasons of fairly substantial losses.

Several growing communities coveted a PCL ballclub. Most prominent among them were Phoenix, Salt Lake City and Vancouver, B.C. The best prospects for franchise shifts were Hollywood—whose situation was complicated by a territorial rights dispute with the Angels—and Oakland.

During the season, Vancouver representatives presented Laws with a sweetheart, practically rent-free, deal. Laws countered with a few modifications, primarily adding seats and amenities to Capilano Stadium, and then committed the Oaks to Vancouver for 1956. It would be the first PCL franchise move since 1938.

Poor daily attendance dropped even further. On the last day of the season, September 4, 1955, the Oaks hosted their hated rivals, the Seals. As Bob Stevens reported in the *San Francisco Chronicle*, "It was a dreadfully disappointing day from every conceivable angle. A crowd of 2,941 that came to bury Oakland, not praise it, sat restlessly and glumly in the sunswept seats as San Francisco climaxed forever its tradition-rich rivalry with the Oaks by sweeping the doubleheader, 9-5 and 3-0.

"The incidents of the contest now seem unimportant. It was more than 20 minutes after that last catch that some of the fans straggled out, peeking unhappily every so often at the lifeless diamond as they threaded their way home, never again to come back to the ball park that for 53 years produced heartaches, thrills, champions and never a bum."

## A POSTSCRIPT

On April 6, 1992, the Alameda County Historical Society and the Native Daughters of the Golden West staged a brief ceremony at the site of the Oaks Ball Park, now a soft drink distributorship, to lay a plaque. Imbedded in a bench, it read: "This plaque marks the site of OAKLAND BALL PARK from 1913 to 1955 the home of four-time Pacific Coast League Champions THE OAKLAND OAKS whose ranks included Baseball Legends Casey Stengel and Billy Martin." ❖

The original home plate from Oaks Ball Park. Author Dick Dobbins recovered and restored the relic, which had been rototilled into three pieces before the park was demolished.

CHAPTER **25**

# PRINCE FAGAN— A GREEK TRAGEDY

Paul Fagan's tenure as owner of the Seals spanned more than eight years and was filled with enormous drama. It was, in fact, analogous to a Greek tragedy in three acts.

In Act One, Fagan enters the scene in 1945 as a savior and protector against the powerful baseball lords east of the Mississippi River. He and his league of allies earn several hard-fought victories, leading to great prosperity on the Pacific Coast. Fagan's ambitions rise mightily.

Those ambitions are stymied in Act Two. Economic conditions deteriorate beginning in 1948 and league strength wanes. The major leagues, with its greater resources, weakens the resolve of Fagan and his followers.

Act Three begins after the 1951 season. Fagan threatens to stop leading if he doesn't receive more support from his colleagues. After it becomes evident over the next two seasons that he will not receive that support, Fagan resigns. His former allies disparage him, his loyal followers mourn him. His battle has been lost.

### THE CURTAIN OPENS

Paul I. Fagan's dream was to bring major league baseball to San Francisco, his home. Fagan married into money

and increased his fortune in ranching and real estate in the Hawaiian Islands. He was a very successful businessman used to having his own way; when he purchased one-third ownership of the Seals in 1945, close followers of the team presumed he would be a silent partner. He was anything but.

Under Fagan's direction, Seals Stadium became the finest ballpark in the land, the Seals stepped forward as one of the best franchises in all of baseball and their manager, Lefty O'Doul, was recognized as one of the great managers in the game. Fagan's great desire was for the Seals and the Pacific Coast League to be recognized as a third major league. He made sure his players were treated in a first-class manner by paying them at or above major league levels.

Charlie Graham died towards the end of the 1948 season, his insight lost forever. Graham had breathed life and vitality into the San Francisco franchise for more than 30 years and Fagan had added financial resources Graham never had. Fagan acquired Graham's stock holdings and assumed an even more active role in the Seals. But he was not a baseball man.

Young Charlie Graham, the old man's son, assumed many of his father's duties, but his leadership fell short of Fagan's expectations. Fagan made Lefty O'Doul vice pres-

After receiving a face-lift supervised by Paul Fagan, Seals stadium regained its stature as one of the finest baseball stadiums in the land.

ident in charge of player transactions while he still managed the team. This did not work out either.

Fagan's aspirations for elevating the Pacific Coast League to major league status frightened some of the other owners. While each wanted the same success as Fagan, several did not have the financial resources or the courage required to battle the major league baseball moguls. Fagan's approach was confrontational. He demanded immediate action. He was frustrated regularly by the more tentative, thoughtful actions of his colleagues, the club owners. Additionally, some of the owners had been down this road before and knew the wounds that Fagan's approach could inflict. Disagreement became a running theme through Fagan's reign.

## FADE INTO DIFFICULT TIMES

The boom days following the war created a false sense of security, a belief that prosperity would continue unabated for years to come. But with the 1949 season came signs that the days of prosperity were ending. Also, the major leagues successfully continued to dance around the subject of granting major league status to the PCL.

On the playing field, the Seals lost the nucleus of their dynamic post-war contingent to the major leagues or to advancing age. Their replacements in the early 1950s were not as talented. With the development of major league farm systems, independent operators such as the Seals and Oaks were no longer able to compete with their wealthier

The 1949 San Francisco Seals tried going with youngsters to start the season, but most weren't ready. Switching to a lineup heavy with tired veterans, the Seals finished in seventh place, 25 games behind league-leading Hollywood.

adversaries for local talent. The independents were forced to settle for inferior players or wait until major league cutdown time to acquire respectable players. This normally occurred up to 30 days into the regular season.

It is the nature of a minor league franchise to start fresh each year, since their superior ballplayers will inevitably be promoted. But Fagan, in a decision showing his naivete in personnel development, instructed O'Doul to fill the roster with rookies rather than continue to search for proven veterans. The Seals had signed a large crop of local high school prospects and all were given a chance to make the team. Only Reno Cheso, who batted .248 in a utility role, survived the camp. Among the youngsters optioned were catchers Anthony "Nini" Tornay and Will Tiesiera, pitchers Lloyd Dickey, Bob Greenwood and Dick Larner, infielders Jim Westlake and Mike Baxes and outfielder Jack Bacciocco. Most would return to the Seals in the future, but in 1949 none were ready to help the big club.

The 1949 Seals finished in seventh place, 25 games behind the pennant-winning Stars. This represented a 38-game drop-off from the club's 1948 finish.

It was apparent O'Doul and Fagan had to spend more money to get some offense for 1950. Les Fleming, a burly first baseman, was acquired from Indianapolis. He provided the power with 25 home runs and 138 RBIs, batting .292. Outfielder Joe Grace, acquired from Sacramento for pitcher Jack Brewer, batted .335. Don White, reacquired from the Athletics, batted .300, as did rookie catcher Ray Orteig and third baseman Dario Lodigiani, who rebounded from his sub-par year in 1950.

Chet Johnson, acquired from Indianapolis, made a

grand return to the Coast League by posting a 22-13 record, while Lien was 20-13. The aging Ralph Buxton, acquired from the Yankees, was 6-3 in relief. His presence in a Seals uniform aggravated many Oakland fans.

O'Doul's Seals established a modern record by ending the season with 100 victories and 100 losses, in fifth place at .500.

One noteworthy game that season took place at Seals Stadium on Sunday afternoon, September 10, when Al Lien pitched a 17-inning shutout over the Hollywood Stars. Gordy Maltzberger started for the Stars and pitched 14 innings before being lifted for a pinch-hitter.

In the 17th inning, the Stars loaded the bases with one out but didn't score. What the box score didn't show was a stellar non-catch by left fielder Brooks Holder to save the day. With a runner on third base, a long fly was lifted down the left field line. When the ball drifted into foul territory, Holder let it drop, forcing the runner at third to hold. Had Holder caught it—which he easily could have done—the runner would have tagged up and probably scored. Lien then retired the side without further damage.

The Seals had been held hitless over the last eight innings but Tobin opened the bottom of the 17th with a double, advanced to third, then scored when Harry Eastwood hit a short sacrifice fly to right field. The speedy Tobin, using a fadeaway slide into foul territory to avoid catcher Mike Sandlock's tag, was probably the only Seal who could have beaten the throw to the plate.

A popular joke was used to explain the type of team San Francisco had in 1951. The Seals were actually three teams: The one you saw today, the one they just replaced from yesterday, and the team that arrives tomorrow.

## PLAYING AT SEALS STADIUM

"There's a towering pop foul ball hit towards the first base stands! George Vico is positioning himself over by the rail. Uh-oh! The ball is drifting back onto the playing field! Jim Moran has come over from his second base position, and he makes the catch near the foul line behind first base."

This re-creation of a Don Klein play-by-play report was a frequent occurrence at Seals Stadium. The weather could be pleasant or it could be cold and windy. The winds would often blow from behind the first base grandstand and carry out to left field.

The winds, coupled with a 350-foot distance down the foul line, meant home runs to right field were scarce. And hitting a ball over the back fence, 385 feet away and 20 feet up, brought gasps of wonderment from fans and players alike. The Padres' Jack Graham and the Angels' Chuck Connors—he of "Rifleman" fame—were two strongmen able to accomplish that feat.

When they could, the Seals orchestrated their roster towards right-handed batters. The prevailing winds added distance to the loping fly balls hit out towards the left field wall. Little Eddie Lake came to the Seals in 1951 and hit a career high 27 homers, better than his more powerful, left-handed teammates, Bob Thurman, Jack Graham and Joe Grace. In his previous 11 major league seasons, Lake hit a total of only 39 homers.

San Francisco's cool air helped Seals players retain their energy especially as the season droned on into September, but it also made for some uncomfortable evenings. Vico, the Seals' first baseman in 1953 and 1954, related how it was impossible to work up a sweat during a night game. "You'd have a sweatshirt on, but you wouldn't start sweating until you were in the clubhouse 10 minutes after the game," he said.

For pitchers, the problem was more acute. A starting pitcher had to warm up longer than normal for a game at Seals Stadium. Jack Brewer would use Capsolin, a balm, on his pitching arm to keep it warm. "Still," he said, "the fog just blew right through you."

Between innings, Brewer wore a jacket with heating filaments plugged into an electrical socket. He was the only player to have such a luxury.

Seattle knuckleball pitcher Jim Davis used to love pitching at Seals Stadium. Davis felt there were extra wind currents between home plate and the pitcher's mound. Davis chuckled when he recalled throwing an 0-2 knuckler to the Seals' Bill McCawley. "McCawley swung, and the ball hit him in the stomach!"

Except for the quirkish weather, Seals Stadium was a wonderful place to play. Players enjoyed the atmosphere as much as the fans. The field was impeccably manicured and bad hops were a rarity.

Gene Woodling echoed the sentiments of many teammates when he said 1948—his only year in the Coast League—was his happiest year in professional baseball.

The expanse of Seals Stadium should have made it a pitcher's park, although lefty Al Lien often complained about all the bloop hits that would drop at a charging outfielder's feet. And there were balls that frequently sailed into the gaps in the outfield. During the 1938 season, young Dominic DiMaggio patrolled center field for the Seals. In a game against Seattle, Indians batter Mike Hunt hit a ball headed for the ivy. DiMaggio ran it down and made a spectacular catch. As Hunt rounded second base, he yelled out, "While you're out there, look for Amelia Earhart's airplane."

Two former Seals, Larry Jansen and Lefty O'Doul, were involved in one of the more humorous home run blasts. In 1957, Jansen, a good-hitting pitcher for the Seattle Rainiers, hit a ball over the deep right center field wall for a home run. As he rounded third base, O'Doul, then managing the Rainiers, fell backwards in a faint. The only person who didn't think O'Doul's act was funny was the pitcher.

Willie Mays played center field at Seals Stadium for the Giants in 1958 and 1959. For him, after playing in the Polo Grounds in New York, Seals Stadium was frustrating. After chasing balls that slammed against the walls, Mays would come in and say to Giants Manager Bill Rigney, "Skip, I would have had that ball in New York."

The year represented a turning point for Fagan, who spent most of the season brooding in exile at his Maui ranch. Daily operations were turned over to his staff. Joe Orengo was hired as general manager, relieving O'Doul of the burden of player transactions, and Damon Miller assumed more executive powers.

By 1951, the PCL's confrontation with organized baseball had produced the open classification, but it also created a battery of questions regarding administration of the league and its players. Changes in the drafting of players, new salary structures for a more advanced league and accepting players on option were among the many issues to face and problems to solve.

Along with the open classification—a fiction created to keep the PCL a minor league without really calling it one—the major leagues sent along a series of stipulations the PCL had to meet in order to be considered for elevation to the majors. The most difficult hurdle was the requirement that every team had to have a stadium seating at least 25,000.

## FAGAN: PORCHES AND PEANUTS

As an owner, Paul Fagan was always willing to try new ideas, some of which proved to be embarrassing. Fagan had spurned thousands of dollars annually by rejecting advertising on the outfield walls because he didn't think it looked classy. He also used Plexiglas for the backstop at Seals Stadium so the fans could see more clearly. Neither idea lasted.

One of his better ideas was shortening the left field fence from 365 feet to 347 feet and lowering it from 20 feet to 10 feet for 1951. Bleachers erected behind the fence were quickly named "Paul's Porch." The Seals clubbed 126 home runs that season, the all-time stadium record. Diminutive Eddie Lake hit 27, while Bill McCawley, Ray Orteig and Eddie Sauer slugged 16 each. All were right-handed batters. Left-hander Bob Thurman, a true power hitter, hit only 13. Jack Graham, the other lefty, couldn't take advantage of the shortened fence and was traded.

Fagan's most embarrassing incident was "The Great Peanut Controversy." It started when the park janitors had complained that peanut shells, swept into piles for collection, would get caught up in the Seals Stadium breezes and blow away. Fagan figured he could make substantial savings by outlawing peanuts there, so he banned the peanut at Seals Stadium.

He leaked the idea to *Call-Bulletin* columnist Jack McDonald. Other reporters, irritated they weren't let in on the scoop, proceeded to write a series of negative articles about Fagan and his idea.

The public became incensed and the caper nearly became an international incident when a foreign ambassador from a South American peanut-producing country called Fagan to com-

plain. The reaction was so vocal, Fagan had to make a hasty retreat and ordered the peanut back to Seals Stadium.

Don Klein recalled how he almost lost his broadcasting job because Fagan decided game broadcasts weren't essential. Regal Pale Brewery indicated it wouldn't renew its sponsorship of the broadcasts for 1952, so Fagan unilaterally decided not to broadcast the games. "This way more people will come out to the ballpark," he reasoned.

Klein, Miller and others discreetly tried to reason with him, but Fagan found no reason to compromise. He finally settled on the idea of allowing a quick recap of the highlights immediately following the game's conclusion. He suggested to Klein that he leave at the end of the eighth inning to drive to the radio station for the broadcast. When Klein asked how he would receive results of the ninth inning, Fagan responded, "Well, you can hear it on the radio." Rainier Beer was contacted and they picked up the sponsorship for the following year.

Although Lefty O'Doul had assumed responsibility for player transactions, Fagan insisted on being involved. Fagan's thoughts were not always based on good baseball sense. For example, he didn't like Joe Brovia because Brovia wore his pants down to his ankles. He didn't like slugger Les Fleming, feeling he was brutish. He insisted on both being moved, so Brovia was sold to Portland after hitting .322 with 89 RBIs in 1948, and Fleming took 138 RBIs, 25 home runs and 184 games played in 1950 when he left. O'Doul must have been terribly and understandably frustrated. For almost two decades Lefty had been the public personality of the Seals while the quiet Graham ran the business operations. Now the combative and baseball-ignorant Fagan ran the show and grabbed the headlines.

Paul Fagan eats peanuts with a couple of young Seals fans and General Manager Joe Orengo. Fagan banned first baseman Les Fleming (left), simply because he didn't like him.

The Seals' starting rotation for 1950 (l-r): Billy Werle, Cliff Melton, Manny Perez, Jack Brewer and Chet Johnson. 'Chesty Chet' won only five of 20 decisions at mid-season and was sent to Oakland.

Hoping some of the Yankees' magic would rub off in the West, Orengo negotiated a working agreement with them. The Yankees promised substantial help but they sent a group of has-beens and never-will-bes to San Francisco. The agreement was so distasteful the Seals terminated it in early August.

In the off-season, Orengo consummated one major trade to increase the firepower in the middle of the lineup, sending outfielders Jackie Tobin and Don White to San Diego for outfielder-first baseman Jack Graham and pitcher Bob Savage. Graham had clouted 33 homers and 136 RBIs while batting .293 in 1950.

The team O'Doul put on the field for the opener was old and weak. The vaunted Seals rookies of the previous year still needed more seasoning. Ominous signs of impending doom came early when the Seals started the season by losing 13 straight. O'Doul used 17 different players in the opening three-game series at San Diego. By August 1, 13 of them were gone. Only nine players lasted the full season in San Francisco.

Chet Johnson, the 22-game winner in 1950, won only five of his 20 decisions and was shipped off to Oakland at mid-season.

The biggest disappointment was Graham. He got off to a terrible start, barely raised his average to .243 in 45 games, then was traded back to San Diego for outfielder Eddie Sauer.

The Yankees optioned some viable players to the Seals. Foremost among them was Lew Burdette, Jim Brideweser and Ed Cereghino. Burdette, a slightly wild and crazy right-hander from Nitro, West Virginia, was the Seals' most reliable pitcher, recording a 14-12 mark with a 3.21 ERA in 210 innings. He was recalled at the end of the season and traded to the Braves along with $50,000, for Johnny Sain. He enjoyed an excellent major league career, winning 203 games over the span of 18 years.

Brideweser, from USC, was a fixture at shortstop after his arrival, batting .283 in 146 games. Brideweser played seven years in the American League as a utility infielder after leaving the Coast League.

Cereghino was the 17-year-old "prep phenom" from Daly City who signed with the Yankees and was optioned back home. He ended the season 4-6 with a 5.64 ERA in 13 games. Cereghino moved on to Kansas City in 1952. In 1955 he was sold to Sacramento, never having pitched for the Yankees.

Among those finishing the season on option from New York was Joe Page, who had been the Yankees' top relief pitcher. Page was at the end of his career and didn't perform particularly well for the Seals, but he made significant contributions to San Francisco's economy via the city's night life. Before Page would go out for the evening, he often asked his roommate, Bill McCawley to "mess up my bed, roomie."

Orengo worked tirelessly to acquire players to improve the team, but nothing stopped the team from slipping deeper into the cellar.

In another interesting acquisition, Dale Long was optioned to San Francisco by the St. Louis Browns. Long was sent to work with O'Doul on his hitting and to learn how to be a catcher despite the fact Long was left-handed. The project didn't work but Long played 36 games in left field and at first base, batting .266.

After the early losing streak, the Seals spent most of the season mired in the cellar. In late August, the Seals put together a seven-game winning streak, placing themselves in sixth place, a game out of last—for one day. The Padres, Solons and Seals shared the cellar at one time or another during the concluding days of the campaign.

Overall league talent was down in 1951 from previous seasons. Seattle, under Rogers Hornsby, was the class of the PCL, finishing six games ahead of the Stars.

## A FRUSTRATED FAGAN CLEANS HOUSE

Fagan had been conspicuous in his absence from San Francisco. Ten days before the end of the season, Fagan ordered Orengo and O'Doul to clean out their desks.

San Francisco Manager Lefty O'Doul kisses his pitcher, Manny Perez, for snapping the Seals' 13-game losing streak. Joe Sprinz and Dario Lodigiani look on.

Although they weren't officially fired, no one was sure baseball would even be played in San Francisco in 1952.

The last day of the season was hurriedly organized as "Lefty O'Doul Day." It wasn't much of a celebration as the Seals lost two to Sacramento to clinch last place, one game behind the Solons and 25 games out of first. This was the first cellar finish since Nick Williams' 1926 Seals.

As to his immediate future, O'Doul said, "My mother and father were born in San Francisco and lived their lives in San Francisco. Even when I was in the big leagues I couldn't wait for the season to end so I could return to San Francisco. This is my home and I expect to stay here."

After the World Series was concluded, O'Doul took a group of major league all-stars to Japan. It was at this point that Fagan fired O'Doul, long distance. Fagan demanded 100 percent effort and had been unhappy with O'Doul's work habits. All too often Lefty—the best-paid manager in baseball—arrived just before game time. Lefty was spending too much time at his downtown bar and on the golf links.

## FAREWELL, PRINCE

Fagan genuinely did not understand what it took to run a successful baseball franchise but tried to impose his ego on everyone anyway. As with all situations of this nature, his refusal to accept and deal with reality doomed his efforts to failure.

The events of 1951 had soured Fagan so much that he threatened to padlock Seals Stadium for 1952. Although he relented before the winter meetings, it was apparent Fagan was deeply upset with his situation.

An underlying frustration still nagged at him. He knew the major league executive council was toying with the Pacific Coast League directors and he knew his colleagues were not totally dedicated to the fight. Fagan now sent Miller to the directors meetings as his proxy, undoubtedly to the relief of all.

After firing O'Doul, Fagan hoped for a new beginning. His new manager for the 1952 season was Tommy Heath, who was virtually unknown on the Pacific Coast. As a player or manager, the farthest west he had ever been in a uniform was San Antonio in 1933 and 1934. As manager of the Minneapolis Millers of the American Association, he helped develop several future Giants including Willie Mays.

As a step towards strengthening their open classification, the PCL directors agreed to reject any working agreements with major league teams and to refuse players sent on option. This practice was to kick in with the 1953 season but several clubs, including the Seals, started in 1952.

Heath's first roster was woeful, filled with veterans whose better days had passed them and youngsters of marginal abilities and little experience. Gone was any ves-

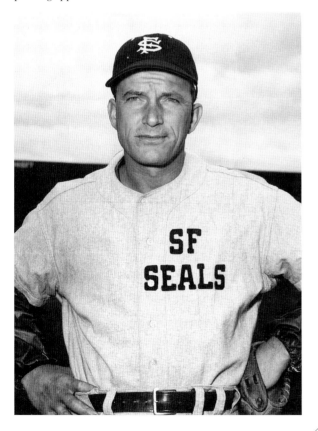

Tommy Heath (above) became Seals manager when Paul Fagan fired Lefty O'Doul after the 1951 season. Bob Muncrief (below) set a team record for pitching appearances with 65 in 1952.

tige of the Yankees. The Seals pinned their hopes on two winter acquisitions. Because they had finished last in 1951, they drafted first and chose 16-game winner Frank Biscan from Memphis. The Seals also purchased the contract of Arcado "Hank" Biasatti, a slick-fielding first baseman from Buffalo.

Biscan arrived in San Francisco complaining about the cold weather and the unfamiliar circumstances. He performed so poorly and was such a negative influence in the clubhouse that the Seals were relieved to return him to Memphis.

Biasatti was purchased to shore up first base. He did not work out and was released after 43 games and a soft .273 batting average.

Although the Seals' pitching staff wasn't the most talented, it had the prospect of being the tallest in baseball. Newcomer Bill Boemler, up from Yakima, stood 6-6, while veteran newcomer Bill Reeder and rookie Jack Thompson were each 6-5. Floyd "Bill" Bevens, back from a 20-victory season at Salem in the Western International League, was 6-3. Elmer Singleton, Lien, Bill Bradford and Bob Muncrief were all over 6-feet.

Reeder was the Opening Day pitcher and blanked the Portland Beavers on one hit. But he lost his control from that point on, lost his next nine decisions, and was unconditionally released.

Singleton anchored the staff with a 17-15 record and 2.67 ERA. But his luck was awful. On April 24, pitching on only three days' rest in a night game at Seals Stadium, Singleton set the Solons down without a hit for 12⅓ innings before allowing three hits and a run to lose the game in the 13th. Only 790 fans were on hand to witness Singleton's masterpiece.

Traditionally, the Seals had balanced their books by selling a player or two to some major league club. The 1952 aggregation had no chance of advancing a player. The team finished in seventh place and attendance dipped to 198,778.

The 1953 Seals put together a winning season, 91-89, for fifth place, but attendance fell to 175,000. Fagan did little to improve the club and lost even more interest when the league directors voted to rescind the no-option clause at season's end. Still, Heath put together a spirited group that generally played together and was fun to watch.

During Spring Training, the Seals acquired pitcher John "Windy" McCall from Birmingham of the Southern Association and Leo Righetti from Charleston of the American Association. Both were raised in San Francisco, finding circuitous ways of returning home. McCall, a Balboa High product, was rejuvenated under Heath's tutelage, ending at 12-7 with a 3.05 ERA. He was sold to the New York Giants in 1954.

Righetti, the father of future major league star Dave Righetti, had proved at Sacramento in 1951 that he could field with the best of them, but his .202 average with the

Tony Ponce, not a bad-hitting pitcher, went 8-0 for the Seals after arriving in September 1953. He pitched and won both games of a season-ending doubleheader against the Angels.

Solons carried a different message about his hitting talents. At Charleston his batting average declined to .199. In San Francisco, though, Leo hit .258 with 61 RBIs, his best offensive statistics as a professional. "Rags" had a busy day on August 5, setting a league record for accepting 19 chances at shortstop in a 22-inning game the Seals finally lost to the Beavers 4-2.

The Seals were playing near-.500 ball into September when they acquired two players from Ventura in the California League. Jose Perez was league batting champion at .373 and capable of playing all eight field positions. Almost as an afterthought, pitcher Tony Ponce came north with Perez. While Perez had difficulty finding a position to play, Ponce had an immediate impact on the tired pitching staff. In just 16 days, Ponce won eight times without a setback, capping his streak by beating the Angels in the season-finale doubleheader, 4-2 and 1-0.

Fagan put the Seals up for sale at the end of the 1953

season, and for the second time in three years threatened to padlock Seals Stadium. This time he would not relent.

The league appointed Solons President Eddie Mulligan to negotiate a settlement with Fagan. Most directors were happy to see Fagan pull out. As a tactical matter, the league determined the same eight teams would play in 1954, with the possibility of San Francisco playing its games in Oakland if Fagan followed through on his threat to padlock Seals Stadium.

In late September, Mulligan and Fagan worked out a plan in which Fagan would sell the Seals to the league for $100,000—10 percent of his asking price two years earlier. Fagan also agreed to lease Seals Stadium to the new owner for five years with an option to buy back the Seals back for $100,000 if San Francisco were awarded a major league franchise.

Fagan's years as owner of the Seals were over. Fade to black. ❖

CHAPTER **26**

# THE LITTLE CORPORATION

On September 23, 1953, the league appointed Damon Miller, Fagan's secretary and general manager, as president/conservator of the Seals and transferred the franchise to Miller at no cost. Miller agreed to form a corporation to raise the necessary cash to operate in 1954.

Miller approached the Seals' few remaining employees about buying into the franchise. Everybody wanted to participate and Miller raised $20,000. Miller incorporated his group for $100,000, and on October 29, league directors turned the franchise over to Miller's syndicate. The corporation was officially called San Francisco Seals, Inc., but it was known as the Little Corporation.

The league directors carefully watched the Little Corporation's development over the next month. Several directors believed the group didn't have sufficient financial resources. They feared the league would be liable for any debts incurred by the new group.

### A LAST-MINUTE CLIFFHANGER

On December 2 the league revoked the franchise but gave Miller until December 11 to accumulate enough capital to convince the directors the Little Corporation could operate independently.

Over the course of the next week, local newspapers published details about the public offering of stock in the Seals, and checks poured in. Even pitcher Al Lien invested $1,000 in the Little Corporation—but only after he received permission from the commissioner's office. When the offering was concluded, the Little Corporation had sold $91,000 worth of stock. Many subscribers had bought single shares at $10 apiece.

As the deadline approached, Miller worried about the directors' upcoming decision, particularly since a $50,000 indemnity bond was required on Seals Stadium. At the last minute, Earle H. LeMasters of the Pacific National Bank covered the bond, and H.S. Patterson of UHF television station KSAN committed approximately $75,000 for the television rights to Seals evening games. These two last-minute deals put the Little Corporation over the top.

A good feeling pervaded the city and the franchise, but there was hard work ahead for Miller and his colleagues. They had to develop an austere budget, sell enough stock to guarantee them working capital, provide a competitive team and convince people to come to games. Seasonal attendance of anything below 300,000 would put the team in the red.

Manager Tommy Heath was a member of Miller's small investor group, so the Seals had a bit of continuity. Still, by Opening Day, the roster remained unsettled largely because of the Seals' tenuous financial position coupled with the league-wide agreement to develop its own and not accept any more optioned players. One curious acquisition was the purchase for $10,000 of center fielder Teddy

Beard from Hollywood, which raised some eyebrows because of the price.

Miller and Heath had sold Windy McCall to the Giants, receiving cash and pitchers Adrian Zabala and Frank Hiller, then acquired castoff pitcher Ken Holcombe and outfielders Bob DiPietro and Gordy Brunswick. The Seals also picked up on waivers first baseman Chuck Stevens from Hollywood and pitcher Eddie Chandler from Los Angeles and then dropped several players from their roster.

As the season played itself through, the Seals proved to be more exciting than good and finished at 84-84, in fourth place right behind the Oaks. Each of the pitchers finished close to .500, Ponce the workhorse with 237 innings and a 14-16 record. Dave Melton hit .301 in 82 games, Beard was an even .300 and first baseman Jimmy Westlake hit .285. The Padres won a one-game playoff to win the league championship after the Pads and the Stars ended the regular season tied at 101-67.

With all the publicity, the fans returned to Seals Stadium. The Seals led the league in attendance with 298,908 and exceeded their break-even goal when a single Governor's Cup playoff game was included.

For the year, they netted $464. League attendance figures continued to spiral downward, however. While there was real pleasure at the Little Corporation's success in their first season, more realistic observers were concerned. Miller's group had not been able to defray any of its major obligations, and even the salaries they had declared for themselves had not been paid in full.

Nevertheless, the Little Corporation plunged into 1955 hoping to build on its successes. Heath returned to manage, and both he and Miller worked diligently to strengthen the team.

Heath decided to try something new with his pitchers. He concluded his staff was versatile enough that each pitcher could start, pitch in middle relief or be a closer. The result was a staff with the game decisions fairly evenly divided among them.

The Seals were a veteran team, adequate at every position. Gene Bearden, acquired in a trade with Seattle, went 18-12 with a 3.52 ERA and was an exciting pitcher to watch. Ponce had a great following in San Francisco. The two youngsters on the team, shortstop Mike Baxes and Melton, both had good years, Melton hitting .299 with 19 homers and 116 RBIs.

Melton, Baxes and pitcher Bill Bradford were sold to the Kansas City Athletics for approximately $75,000 and one player. This was important cash to have on hand before the directors meeting, which would determine the fate of the Seals' franchise.

After languishing in the depths of the second division for most of the season, the Seals claimed sixth place, 15 games out at 80-92. League attendance increased slightly but Bay Area figures spelled impending doom. Seals attendance dropped more than 140,000 to 158,476, seventh in the league. Only Oakland's 141,397 was worse.

The poor attendance in San Francisco killed the Little Corporation. As the Seals limped to the finish line, the officials of the Little Corporation knew they had lost their battle. They were broke. The *Chronicle's* headline for the last day of the season was: "'Little Corp' is now the 'Little Corpse'".

The league directors met two days after the season's conclusion. The Seals' situation was their top priority. A few days earlier, the Patterson family, which owned the TV rights to Seals games, exercised an option to buy out the preferred stockholders—specifically, Miller and his colleagues. By taking such action, they would become responsible for the outstanding debts of the corporation, estimated to be $284,000.

Many of the directors doubted the Pattersons' willingness to incur such a large debt. In fact, on the day before the meeting, the Pattersons pulled out. Another investor, an acquaintance of Tommy Heath's, stepped forward but then backed off as well.

While the San Francisco franchise was very attractive to potential investors, the shadow of Paul Fagan scared them off. Fagan still owned Seals Stadium and his lease commitment to the Seals had only three years to run. After that he planned to tear the stadium down and use it for more financially beneficial projects. Prospective buyers were also afraid of Fagan's buy-out clause if major league baseball came to San Francisco. While Fagan announced the cancellation of his buy-back clause, investors still feared its existence.


**REVOKED**

With no serious prospects of a sale, the league revoked the franchise. Through California League President Jerry Donovan—who would become Seals president in 1957—the league ultimately sold the San Francisco franchise to the Boston Red Sox. Sox General Manager Joe Cronin engineered the deal, guaranteeing baseball for San Francisco in 1956.

The Little Corporation had extended the life of the San Francisco Seals by two years but at an enormous personal expense. Eight Fagan employees had each put up $20,000 of their hard-earned reserves to convince the league directors to give them a chance.

"There was a lot of heartbreak connected with this," said Kay Miller, Damon Miller's wife. "They stuck their necks out and gambled their financial assets. It was a very brave thing they did. I knew in my heart they could never [succeed], but I'd never say it. You can't shoot down a man's dream." ❖

CHAPTER **27**

# ENDINGS & OTHER BEGINNINGS

Even though they were saddened by the passing of the Little Corporation, Seals fans were gratified that their team would play in 1956 and that people with San Francisco roots controlled the team. Although now a resident of Boston, Joe Cronin could not have forgotten his Mission District background. And Jerry Donovan, another product of the Mission District, was appointed president of the Seals.

Cronin chose another native San Franciscan, veteran infielder Eddie Joost, as his first manager. Joost had honed his baseball skills on the city's sandlots 25 years earlier and played his first professional baseball with the 1933 Mission Reds. Joost had managed the 1954 Philadelphia A's but was cut loose when the team moved to Kansas City. He signed on with the Red Sox as a utility infielder for the 1955 season, so he remained fresh in Cronin's mind.

Cronin promised the fans of San Francisco "the best minor league baseball the game affords. They deserve the best." Those were soothing words for emotionally battered Seals followers.

But their travails with the ball club weren't over yet.

The Seals' 1956 Spring Training took place at the Red Sox's Florida base. This was the first time the Seals had trained east of California. And the team was a group of

unknowns such as Mahoney, Casale, Tanner, Sadowski, Grba. Who were these people?

By the time the April 10 opener rolled around, several excellent prospects had been sent to the Seals from the Red Sox camp. The Seals held their first home workout two days before the opener against Vancouver, the former Oakland Oaks. They sported bright new uniforms that resembled the traditional Red Sox style, but with "SEALS" across the front in red. Several of the players had traveled through the Sox's farm club at San Jose, but this was most of the players' first experience with Northern California's moderate coastal climate.

### OPENING DAY

On Opening Day, 14,401 curious fans ventured to Seals Stadium where the Seals took a crisp 6-3 decision from the Mounties. The Seals' lineup featured tiny Albie Pearson leading off in center field, Ken Aspromonte at second, Joe Tanner at third, veteran major leaguer Don Lenhardt in left field, Bob DiPietro at first, Tommy Umphlett, a three-year major leaguer, in right field, Eddie Sadowski catching, Jim Maloney at shortstop and speedballing Jerry Casale on the mound.

Joe Gordon (above) managed the Seals to the PCL crown in 1957, their last year in San Francisco. Ken Aspromonte (below) led the league in hitting that season with .334.

The Mounties prepared for the new season as if they were a newly granted franchise. Lefty O'Doul, who had said he wouldn't go with the team, did. Six former Oaks made the initial Mounties roster: pitchers George Bamberger, Charlie Beamon and Chris Van Cuyk, catcher Lennie Neal, infielder Spider Jorgensen and outfielder George Metkovich.

The remainder of the Mounties were free agents and Baltimore Orioles farm hands. Like the Seals, there were many names to learn, but unlike the Seals the Mounties were short on talent.

The Seals were confined to the middle of the pack through the first few months. By late June they were 38-37 before going on a nine-game losing streak. The Red Sox had underestimated the caliber of the league. As a result, many of the players ticketed for a full season in San Francisco were demoted to Double-A Oklahoma City in the Texas League.

Joost was having a rough time in San Francisco. He had been suspended twice, and on one occasion visited the mound a second time in an inning even though nobody was warming up in the bullpen. But his real problems were centered in Boston. "Joe [Cronin] and I were good friends," Joost related, "and he asked me [to manage]. They were picking up this franchise in San Francisco and they expected the American League to pick up the city, and they would have the franchise."

Johnny Murphy was the minor league director for the Red Sox—the man responsible for sending players out to Joost. "Johnny Murphy didn't hire me," Joost said, "and I didn't know he resented my being hired.

"When I first met him there was animosity, and during the season he started criticizing my moves, calling me late in the evenings, telling me what I did wrong. He wouldn't send me the players I was supposed to get, so he made it tough for me."

Shortly after the losing streak ended, Joost was playing third base when he had a run-in with an umpire. Joost felt he had an advancing runner tagged out by several feet, but the umpire didn't see it that way and called him safe. Joost argued and was thumbed. "I still had the ball in my hand, so I threw it out," Joost said. "They told me it went over the back fence."

Joost's spectacular feat of throwing the ball out of Seals Stadium got everybody's attention, including Murphy's. Joost finally had it out with Murphy and was fired. Donovan issued a statement to the press stating, "Eddie wasn't getting the best potential out of the club."

Joe Gordon took over and directed the team to sixth place, 24½ games behind the league-leading Angels. As the season progressed, the Seals played better baseball, but the season was a disappointment for the Red Sox.

Of the starters, Casale was the most consistent of a young and talented group and went 19-11 with 16 complete games and a 4.10 ERA. The majority of the staff would have benefited from another year of experience at the Double-A level.

Eddie Sadowski started the season as the regular catcher but was relegated to the bench when the Red Sox sent Haywood Sullivan out for seasoning. Sullivan was one of Boston's top prospects, so he got most of the work. In 136 games, Sullivan batted .299 with 11 home runs and 77 RBIs.

The infield was strengthened with the arrival of Ken Aspromonte at second and Frank Malzone at third. Aspromonte hit .281 and Malzone hit .296 in 83 games. Marty Keough, another of the Red Sox's prime rookies, came to San Francisco early in the season but damaged his ankle after 79 games.

Seals fans weren't overly impressed by Boston's inaugural season in San Francisco. Attendance was 183,241, about 24,000 higher than the 1955 figures. A substantial number of the 1956 Seals would advance to the major leagues, but they generally weren't ready for Triple-A ball at this time.

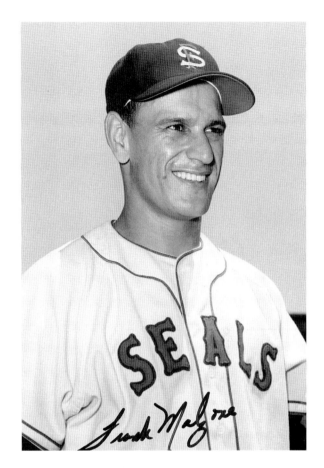

First baseman Bob DiPietro (above) was leading the Coast League in hitting at .371 in 1955 when he broke his ankle. The injury affected the rest of his career. Frank Malzone (top) and Marty Keough (right) both graduated to the Red Sox after outstanding seasons in the late 1950s.

The 1957 PCL-champion Seals (above). The Seals' starting
infield that season consisted of (below) Frank Kellert, Grady
Hatton, Elijah 'Pumpsie' Green and Harry Malmberg.

## MAJOR LEAGUE RUMORS FLY

The 1957 Seals won the pennant and attendance
increased by more than 100,000. But of greater impact
were the rumors of major league expansion into PCL territory. Rumors of an existing franchise moving to Southern
California were not new; only World War II prevented the
St. Louis Browns from moving to Los Angeles. The same
Browns were rumored to be headed to San Francisco
before they relocated in Baltimore in 1954.

Other challenges to the very existence of the league

were issued. In 1954, Francis McCarty, a San Francisco
supervisor and chairman of Mayor George Christopher's
Major League Baseball Committee, initiated a $5 million
bond issue to finance a major league stadium. The money
would be available for use as soon as a major league team
committed to moving to San Francisco. The voters passed
the issue, which provided Mayor Christopher with a valuable negotiating tool.

In New York, Brooklyn Dodgers Owner Walter
O'Malley had been rebuffed by Flatbush politicians in his
attempt to have a modern ballpark built downtown. Even
with recent successes on the field, O'Malley's Dodgers had
lost money in 1956. Ebbets Field was outmoded and
small. With the prospect of continued losses in 1957 and
beyond, O'Malley was looking into the possibility of relocating his team.

The shrewd O'Malley had taken several calculated
steps to give himself leverage. He sold Ebbets Field and
negotiated the purchase of the Los Angeles Angels and
their Wrigley Field home from the Chicago Cubs. The
1957 Los Angeles Angels presented a roster of new faces
to their fans, faces owned by the Dodgers, not the Cubs.

O'Malley's moves were not ignored by Los Angeles
Mayor Norris Paulson or George Christopher in San
Francisco. In May, O'Malley came to Los Angeles to meet
with Mayor Paulson. On May 9, Christopher and
McCarty flew to New York to promote San Francisco's

candidacy to O'Malley. The following day, Christopher and McCarty had lunch with O'Malley and Giants President Horace Stoneham.

## GIANT STRIDES

At this lunch, all parties agreed to pursue the concept of Brooklyn transferring its franchise to Los Angeles while the New York Giants would move to San Francisco. Christopher invited Stoneham to visit San Francisco within the next few weeks. The Saturday, May 11, 1957, edition of the *San Francisco Chronicle* sported the following headline: "N.Y. GIANTS 'SURE' FOR S.F. IN 1958."

Although Commissioner Ford Frick admonished all parties to keep quiet about their plans, the story was too big to be silenced. The *Chronicle* story talked about the Giants playing in Seals Stadium in 1958 before moving "into a 70,000-seat stadium at South Basin, near Hunters Point in 1959."

The implications of the New York meeting caused shock waves up and down the Pacific Coast. The directors of the Pacific Coast League convened in special session to determine a course of action. In previous invasions of minor league territory by the major leagues, indemnification of the affected parties had been held to a minimum. The remaining Coast League team owners stood to lose hundreds of thousands of dollars each if they didn't present a strong and unified front.

In an impassioned letter to Stoneham dated May 17, 1957, Pacific Coast League President Leslie O'Conner wrote, "I am writing to ask that you not visit San Francisco at this time. Such a visit would add greatly to the mess of propaganda being put out in this town and to its destructive effect."

Stoneham respected the request and discussions regarding the Giants' transfer to San Francisco continued under great secrecy.

O'Conner continued, "I hope, also, that this request will not be misunderstood as indicating any hostility to your club's moving out here if and when you may decide to do so. Actually, if and when Los Angeles is taken out of this league, I personally hope San Francisco will be taken also, as I do not believe that either it or the league could operate properly with our two clubs in Los Angeles eliminated."

It was critical for the Dodgers and the Giants to be marketed as a package. If only one team were to leave New York, the natural rivalry would be lost and travel expenses to the league would be exorbitant. If only one team came, the effect on the Coast League would have been just as grave. It was important for the Dodgers and Giants to work together. On May 28, 1957, the Dodgers and Giants received unanimous approval from the National League to move their franchises to California.

## NEGOTIATING THE DEAL

Over the next three months, representatives of San Francisco and the New York Giants exchanged proposals. Finally, on August 6, the city's proposal to the Giants was ready. It called for the construction of a new stadium with a seating capacity of 40,000-45,000 with room for expansion if necessary, and a parking area with a capacity of 10,000-12,000 cars.

The lease would run for 35 years at a rate of $125,000 per year or five percent of the gross receipts after certain deductions, whichever was greater. The lease also mentioned the availability of a 90-acre site, namely Bay View Park, for construction of the ballpark. This was the land owned by Charles Harney, who later constructed the baseball stadium he called "Harney Stadium." That choice was disregarded by everybody but himself.

Christopher attached a memorandum to the city's offer stating that it had not been made public and that he felt "it would be best if we kept it confidential until your Board of Directors acted upon it." On August 19, the board of directors of the National Exhibition Company—the parent company of the New York Giants—accepted San Francisco's offer by an 8-1 vote. Only Donald Grant, a minority stockholder and later chairman of the expansion New York Mets, voted against it.

## SEALS GO OUT IN STYLE

With the distractions caused by the arrival of the Giants in San Francisco in 1958, it was easy to overlook the successes of the San Francisco Seals in 1957. The Seals won the pennant in a tight race in a fitting conclusion to Pacific Coast League baseball in San Francisco.

The season opened with the normal excitement of a new year. Lefty O'Doul had signed to manage the Seattle Rainiers for the 1957 season. This would be his fifth managerial assignment in the Coast League, and his last.

Sadness struck early when popular Portland Manager Bill Sweeney died of a perforated ulcer. Sweeney had a career as distinguished as O'Doul's, having managed at Los Angeles, Hollywood and Seattle. He was replaced by San Leandro's Sailor Bill Posedel, but the Beavers, who should have been a competitive group, never got untracked and finished last.

Seals President Jerry Donovan and the Red Sox signed several veteran free-agents over the winter and during Spring Training acquired many of Boston's top young prospects. Of the veterans, pitchers Jim Konstanty, Walter Masterson and Duane Pillette and infielder Grady Hatton were signed as free agents.

A significant acquisition was first baseman Frank Kellert from the Angels for pitcher Bill Henry and cash. The Red Sox also obtained outfielder Bill Renna from the

## OFFICIAL VOTE

## Directors Approve Shift Next Year

By Art Rosenbaum

The most "impossible" move in baseball history—a departure from the world's largest city—was sealed yesterday when the New York Giants' board of directors agreed to shift to San Francisco in 1958.

The Coast-to-Coast hop was voted, 8 to 1, at a 1-hour 48-minute session of the board in New York. President Horace Stoneham then announced the shift was

> Mayor Christopher explains what the Giants' arrival will mean to the "economic well being" of the community. See Page 1H, Main News.

official up to the point of signing contracts, and that he planned to visit San Francisco next week.

The team will be known as the San Francisco Giants, according to Stoneham in New York. He discarded sugges-

## Chronicle Sporting Green

BILL LEISER, EDITOR     ART ROSENBAUM, EXECUTIVE EDITOR

FHE ★     SAN FRANCISCO, TUESDAY, AUGUST 20, 1957     PAGE 1H

### Major League Baseball in S. F.

## Man (and Woman) in the Street Calm but Enthusiastic

The "man on the street"—the guy who will buy the tickets when the San Francisco Giants play here next season—was enthusiastic but relatively calm about it all yesterday.

The general impression that the deal was already sewed up before the New York board of directors met, snuffed all the surprise from the official announcement.

If there was spontaneous dancing and shouting and

The *San Francisco Chronicle* Sporting Green trumpets the arrival of major league baseball to the city.

Yankees for pitcher Eli Grba and outfielder Gordy Windhorn off the Seals' roster. Renna was then sent to San Francisco.

During Spring Training, Ken Aspromonte and Marty Keough were returned to San Francisco, followed by pitchers Leo Kiely, Tommy Hurd, Bert Thiel and outfielder Tommy Umphlett.

Through the first six weeks of the season the Angels and Stars battled for the league lead while the surprising Vancouver Mounties remained close behind. The Seals played through an extended power shortage—they hit only eight home runs in their first 32 games—but they did lead the league in batting average.

Through the next 35 games the Seals found their collective power stroke, clubbing 26 homers, many of them in the clutch. In early June the Seals took over the league lead and held it to the end of the season.

Gordon received pitching help in early May when the Red Sox optioned lefty Jack Spring to the Seals. Then the club purchased John "Windy" McCall from the Giants.

The Seals released Masterson, Konstanty and Pillette and shifted Leo Kiely to the bullpen.

The Pillette release was a curious one. When released on May 21, Pillette was 4-1 with four complete games and a 2.91 ERA. He was picked up by Seattle where he finished the season 16-8 and a 3.15 ERA in 205 innings. But Pillette was 35 and he was taking a roster spot from one of the Red Sox's younger prospects.

Kiely won 14 straight in relief and ended the season at 21-6 with a 2.20 ERA in 59 games. He led the league in pitching wins. Kiely would have won the Most Valuable Player award were it not for the Angels' Steve Bilko, who won the honor for the third straight season.

Kiely teamed up with Bill Abernathie to give the Seals a dominant bullpen. Abernathie was 13-2 with a 4.23 ERA in 45 games. Bert Thiel served as the middle man in relief, pitching in 41 games with a 5-4 record and 2.78 ERA.

Around the infield, Kellert played in 164 of the team's 168 games, batting .308 with 22 homers and 107 RBI. The infield jelled when Gordon switched Aspromonte and

Leo Kiely was a Seals relief pitcher in 1957 and finished second in the league MVP vote to Los Angeles' Steve Bilko.

Malmberg, Aspromonte taking over second and Malmberg occupying short. Although called up by the Red Sox in September, Aspromonte's .334 batting average in 143 games was good enough to pace the league in hitting. Malmberg hit a respectable .277 in 150 games, providing solid defense in the process.

Batting cleanup, left fielder Renna hit .281 with 29 homers and 104 RBIs. He was slowed by a bruised leg early in the campaign, but his recovery coincided with the Seals' surge to the top of the standings in May and June.

Albie Pearson came of age with the 1957 Seals. He played in 158 games as the starting right fielder and leadoff batter, compiling a .298 average with 99 runs scored. In January 1958 Pearson was traded to Washington for Pete Runnels and spent the next nine years in the American League.

As the race continued into September, only the Mounties kept the pressure on the Seals. The Seals won their 100th game on Friday night, September 13, and clinched the pennant.

## A BITTERSWEET FINALE

The Seals' final day in San Francisco was bittersweet. They lost both ends of a doubleheader to Sacramento in front of 15,484. But the nightcap provided some laughs.

Albie Pearson was the starting pitcher, yielding four runs before retiring the side in the first. He proceeded to play each infield position. Gordon, not officially on the active roster, inserted himself at second base. Solons Manager Tommy Heath at first protested Gordon's presence in the lineup then relented; when Gordon came to bat the first time, all four members of the Solon infield lay down. Still, Gordon roped a hit into center field, out of the reach of any legitimate fielder.

Gordon even pitched, leading to more hilarity. On an offering to Jimmy Westlake, umpire Chris Pelekoudas called it a ball and Gordon stormed the plate in protest. Pelekoudas responded that he could do better and took the mound while Gordon put on the umpire's gear. After one slow pitch by the umpire, the men returned to their original places.

Between games, the Seals players were presented mementos of the championship season. At that point Sal Taormina stepped to the microphone and announced that Coach Glenn Wright was not present because he was receiving treatment for cancer. Taormina told the crowd that each Seals player had contributed a day's pay to help defray Wright's medical expenses and asked the fans to contribute to the fund. All the players—Seals and Solons alike—plus the umpires circulated through the stands and collected more than $7,000 in their caps.

After the slapstick second game, players embraced players, saluted the crowd and slowly worked their way up the ramp to the clubhouse. Fifty-five years of minor league baseball had concluded in San Francisco.

An era had died, but another was soon to begin.

## ANOTHER DEAL

On September 27, two days before the New York Giants' last game at the Polo Grounds, Paul Fagan and the National Exhibition Company agreed to terms for the Giants' use of Seals Stadium for 1958.

Four days later, the Giants filed notice of their intention to acquire the territory of San Francisco for transfer of the franchise. In a letter to the San Francisco Bay Area Baseball Club, dated October 15, 1957, the Giants offered to trade their Minneapolis franchise in the American Association for the San Francisco franchise.

The Red Sox's Joe Cronin had repeatedly stated the Red Sox were willing to cooperate to bring major league baseball to San Francisco. He and Stoneham finally signed an agreement on February 14, 1958, completing the transfer of the San Francisco franchise to the Giants and the Minneapolis franchise to the Red Sox. The Giants also paid $57,000 to the Red Sox.

Indemnification of the Coast League by both the Dodgers and the Giants was complicated because the Pacific Coast League moved its evicted franchises into ter-

Beginnings and endings: Ruben Gomez tosses the first major league pitch in San Francisco history to the Dodgers' Gino Cimoli. Valmy Thomas is the catcher, Jocko Conlan the umpire. Below, the razing of Seals Stadium in 1959.

ritories occupied by other leagues. The San Francisco franchise was transferred to Phoenix and the Los Angeles franchise was moved to Spokane, Washington. Bob Cobb sold his Hollywood franchise to business interests in Salt Lake City.

The Coast League indemnified the Pioneer League with $30,000 and the Arizona-Mexico League with $16,000. These monies were paid by the Dodgers and Giants to the Pacific Coast League, which passed it on to the lower leagues.

Indemnification of the six remaining Coast League teams was set at $25,000 a year for 1958, 1959 and 1960 per team from the Dodgers and the Giants. In return, the league and its teams released the Dodgers, the Giants and the National League from all claims of damage created by the move. The document was completed on February 24, 1958. Total indemnification was $900,000 plus $46,000 passed on to other leagues.

The San Francisco Giants signed Bill Rigney to a two-year contract to manage the team on October 16, 1957. Many key office members came with the team from New York and several members of the Seals' front office were kept on. Most notable were Jerry Donovan and Walter Mails. Donovan was appointed business manager and Mails headed up the speakers bureau.

Every baseball fan in the Bay Area wanted tickets to Opening Day in April. Bleachers were added behind the left field fence—a cyclone fence replacing the former tall wooden barrier. Press facilities were expanded to meet the increased demands for media credentials.

Black and orange baseball caps swept through the Bay Area by the time the Giants broke Spring Training in Arizona. Tickets to the first game were impossible to get at any price.

The city of San Francisco was electrified with antici-pation the morning of April 15, 1958. It was sunny and warm and the crowd arrived early.

It was finally time to play major league ball.

San Francisco-born Gino Cimoli, playing for the Los Angeles Dodgers, was the game's first batter. Giants right-hander Ruben Gomez took the mound and looked for the sign from catcher Valmy Thomas. Future Hall of Fame umpire Jocko Conlan crouched behind Thomas. At 1:34 p.m., Gomez threw the first pitch and major league baseball was inaugurated on the West Coast.

The Giants won 8-0. It was a good day in San Francisco. ❖

CHAPTER **28**

# WHEN THE GIANTS COME TO TOWN

The first San Francisco Giants team was a blend of New York and San Francisco. The Opening Day lineup included four players—Willie Mays, Daryl Spencer, Valmy Thomas and pitcher Ruben Gomez—who had been with the Giants in 1957. Third baseman Jim Davenport, first baseman Orlando Cepeda and right fielder Willie Kirkland were appearing in their first major league game. Left fielder Jim King and second baseman Danny O'Connell were major league veterans, new to the Giants. Alameda-born Bill Rigney, a veteran of Pacific Coast and National League play, was the manager.

The season was all the transplanted management could have wished for. Cozy Seals Stadium offered the hottest ticket in town and local socialites who previously didn't know the difference between a baseball and a beach ball began asking how many hits Cepeda got each game.

San Franciscans took to the rookies. Cepeda, Davenport, Kirkland, catcher Bob Schmidt and outfielder Felipe Alou—these were true San Francisco Giants. The city took tremendous pride in Cepeda's selection as Rookie of the Year.

With the rookies playing an integral role, the Giants surprised the National League by a strong third-place standing, 80-74. The Giants drew 1,272,625 fans to Seals Stadium, compared to the 653,923 they drew at the Polo Grounds in 1957.

## TRADING FOR PITCHERS IN 1959

The Giants' biggest weakness in the inaugural season was pitching. During the winter of 1958 Giants' General Manager Chub Feeney sent the inaugural battery of Gomez and Thomas to the Phillies for Jack Sanford, a solid right-hander. Then in Spring Training, popular Ray Jablonski and first baseman Bill White—the future National League president—were sent to the Cardinals for pitchers "Toothpick" Sam Jones and Don Choate.

In a winter trade he would live to regret, Feeney sent pitchers Ernie Broglio and Marv Grissom to the Cardinals for pitcher Billy Muffett, catcher Hobie Landrith and a minor leaguer. Grissom was at the end of his career but Broglio, an East Bay product, had several good years ahead of him, including 21 victories in 1960. The contributions of Muffett and Landrith were minimal.

The presence of Sanford and Jones made the Giants pre-season favorites to win the pennant, and with eight games remaining, the Giants held a tenuous two-game lead over the Los Angeles Dodgers and Milwaukee Braves. Candlestick Park wasn't quite ready, but officials began theorizing how it could be used to accommodate the 1959 World Series.

Then the Dodgers came to Seals Stadium and swept three games. The Giants proceeded to lose four of their

## SAN FRANCISCO'S FIRST MAJOR LEAGUE GAME
### April 15, 1958 - Seals Stadium

| DODGERS | AB | R | H | BI | GIANTS | AB | R | H | BI |
|---|---|---|---|---|---|---|---|---|---|
| Cimoli, cf | 5 | 0 | 1 | 0 | Davenport, 3b | 4 | 1 | 2 | 1 |
| Reese, ss | 3 | 0 | 0 | 0 | King, lf | 3 | 1 | 2 | 1 |
| Snider, lf | 2 | 0 | 0 | 0 | Mays, cf | 5 | 2 | 2 | 2 |
| Hodges, 1b | 4 | 0 | 0 | 0 | Kirkland, lf | 5 | 0 | 1 | 1 |
| Neal, 2b | 4 | 0 | 2 | 0 | Cepeda, 1b | 5 | 1 | 1 | 1 |
| Gray, 3b | 4 | 0 | 2 | 0 | Spencer, ss | 4 | 1 | 1 | 1 |
| Furillo, rf | 3 | 0 | 0 | 0 | O'Connell, 2b | 2 | 1 | 0 | 0 |
| Walker, c | 3 | 0 | 1 | 0 | Thomas, c | 1 | 2 | 0 | 0 |
| Roseboro, pr, c | 1 | 0 | 0 | 0 | Gomez, p | 4 | 1 | 2 | 1 |
| Drysdale, p | 1 | 0 | 0 | 0 | | | | | |
| Bessent, p | 0 | 0 | 0 | 0 | | | | | |
| Larker, ph | 1 | 0 | 0 | 0 | | | | | |
| Negray, p | 0 | 0 | 0 | 0 | | | | | |
| Gilliam, ph | 0 | 0 | 0 | 0 | | | | | |
| TOTALS | 31 | 0 | 6 | 0 | TOTALS | 33 | 8 | 11 | 8 |

| | | | | R | H | E |
|---|---|---|---|---|---|---|
| LOS ANGELES | 000 | 000 | 000— | 0 | 6 | 1 |
| SAN FRANCISCO | 002 | 410 | 01x— | 8 | 11 | 0 |

E—Hodges. DP—SF 1. LOB—LA 10, SF 9. HR—Spencer, Cepeda. SF—Davenport.

### PITCHING SUMMARY

| DODGERS | IP | H | R | ER | BB | SO |
|---|---|---|---|---|---|---|
| Drysdale (0-1) | 3.2 | 5 | 6 | 6 | 3 | 1 |
| Bessent | 2.1 | 4 | 1 | 1 | 1 | 0 |
| Negray | 2 | 2 | 1 | 1 | 3 | 1 |
| GIANTS | | | | | | |
| Gomez (1-0) | 9 | 6 | 0 | 0 | 6 | 6 |

Balk—Negray. PB—Walker. Umpires—Conlon, Secory, Dixon and Venzon. Time—2:29. Attendance—23,448.

next five to the Cubs and Cardinals and were out of the race. For the second straight year, they finished third.

But 1959 marked the arrival of Willie McCovey. McCovey was promoted from Phoenix at the end of July and immediately went 4-for-4 against future Hall of Fame pitcher Robin Roberts and the Phillies. McCovey created a real dilemma for Rigney, because both Cepeda and McCovey were true first basemen. Rigney tried Cepeda at third and then left field, but Cepeda resisted. In the end, although McCovey followed Cepeda by winning the 1959 Rookie of the Year award, one of the two had to remain on the bench.

In mid-1960, with the Giants dogging the Pirates' heels, Stoneham replaced Rigney as manager with Tom Sheehan, the Giants' advance scout who also happened to be Stoneham's drinking buddy. At best, the move could be called questionable. The Giants took a nosedive from which they wouldn't recover for a couple of years. But one redeeming blessing from 1960 was the arrival of pitcher Juan Marichal. Marichal, called up in mid-July, debuted with a 2-0, one-hit victory over the Phillies. He immediately became the ace of the pitching staff.

Stoneham's search for a new manager for the 1961 season was resolved by a trade. The Giants acquired infielder Alvin Dark from the Milwaukee Braves in exchange for utility shortstop Andre Rodgers. Dark was quickly named manager while Stoneham finally acknow-

The early San Francisco Giants boasted a fearsome hitting lineup, including (l-r): Willie Mays, former American League batting champion Harvey Kuenn, Mateo Alou and Felipe Alou.

A sellout crowd greeted the Giants on Opening Day 1960 (above) for the first game at Candlestick Park. Although the team boasted stars such as Willie Mays, the fans instantly took to Orlando Cepeda (below left) and Willie McCovey, back-to-back Rookies of the Year in 1959-1960.

San Francisco Giants
1962 National League Champions

The 1962 Giants brought the National League pennant to San Francisco after defeating the Dodgers in a playoff.

ledged failure of his pet project—to transform the Bahamas-born Rodgers, who was primarily a cricket player, into a baseball star.

Dark came to an extremely talented team that nevertheless was missing a spark. He quickly took care of that, trading for infielder Harvey Kuenn and catcher Ed Bailey. Still, Dark had to resolve several lineup matters. How could he play Cepeda, McCovey, Alou, Kuenn and Mays in the lineup at the same time? And, in what would become a yearly problem, was there enough pitching?

Cepeda became an All-Star left fielder in 1961 but was back on first base in 1962, with Willie Mac moving to left field. Catcher Tom Haller and second baseman Chuck Hiller both arrived in 1961 and became regulars the next season. During the winter, Feeney acquired pitchers Billy Pierce and Don Larsen from the White Sox. The puzzle was about to be solved.

## THE GIANTS WIN THE PENNANT

The Giants, Dodgers and Reds embarked on a furious race for the 1962 pennant. At the end, the Giants and Dodgers were tied for first place, 3½ games ahead of Cincinnati.

The clubs split the first two games of a three-game playoff series to determine the National League champion. Pierce won the first game 8-0 and Sanford was leading 5-0 in Game Two before the Dodgers scored seven runs in the sixth en route to an 8-7 win.

In Game Three, Marichal left after seven innings, trailing 4-2. Larsen—who had thrown the only perfect game in World Series history for the Yankees against the Dodgers in the 1956 World Series—came on to pitch the

eighth. When the Giants scored four in the ninth inning, he was credited with the victory.

The San Francisco Giants, just five years removed from New York, were in the World Series. Against the Yankees, yet.

The 1962 Fall Classic opened at Candlestick with Whitey Ford beating Billy O'Dell 6-2. In Game Two, Sanford tossed a 2-0 shutout. In Yankee Stadium for Game Three, Bill Stafford beat Pierce 3-2, and Larsen won Game Four in relief as Chuck Hiller crushed a grand slam to break a 2-2 tie—the first-ever National League grand slam in the World Series.

Ralph Terry beat Sanford 5-3 in a seesaw Game Five, sending the Series back to San Francisco. Then the rains came. Three straight days of rainouts helped a rested Pierce defeat Ford 5-2, setting up the climactic seventh game—Sanford against Terry.

Sanford surrendered a single run in the fifth while Terry allowed the Giants but two hits through eight innings. In the bottom of the ninth trailing 1-0, the Giants' Mateo Alou led off with a pinch-hit single. Two outs later, Mays laced a two-out double, putting runners on second and third.

McCovey came to the plate. Manager Ralph Houk elected to have Terry pitch to him even though McCovey had homered off Terry in Game Two and had tripled earlier in this game. Terry's first pitch to McCovey was lined foul. McCovey then smashed Terry's second offering on a searing line to the right side of the infield.

*And now the pitcher holds the ball and now he lets it go,*
*And now the air is shattered by the force of Willie's blow . . .*

As quickly as the hearts of Giants fans went soaring

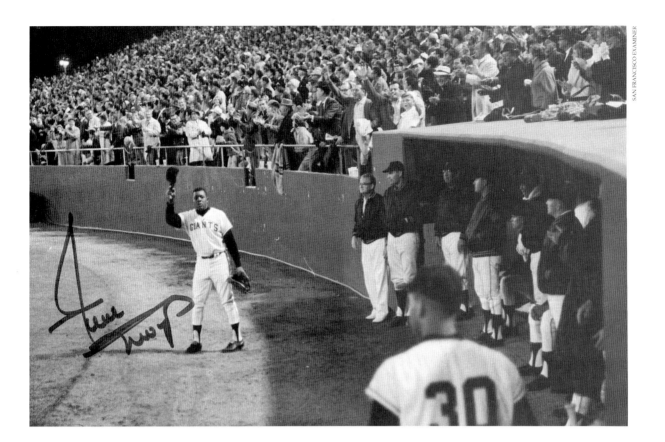

at the sound of the crack of the bat they went crashing down. Second baseman Bobby Richardson snared the ball, ending the game and the World Series.

## ALWAYS A BRIDESMAID

Throughout the remainder of the 1960s, the Giants won more games than any other National League team but finished second five straight times. Dark left after the 1964 season. He was followed by Herman Franks through 1968 and then by Clyde King.

Most of the players on the 1962 championship team were gradually traded away. The most controversial one sent Cepeda to the Cardinals for lefty pitcher Ray Sadecki in May 1966. Cepeda went on to become MVP in 1967 while Sadecki became a symbol of the Giants' failures.

Gaylord Perry came through the Giants' farm system and joined the big club in the early 1960s, emerging as a dominant pitching force along with Marichal. Jim Ray Hart, a third baseman, looked like a future star who could complement Mays and McCovey until he was hit by a Bob Gibson fastball. Hart would never be the same and he became a reserve before being sold to the Yankees in 1973. Mike McCormick was reacquired from the Washington Senators during the winter of 1966 and promptly won a Cy Young award the following year, but was traded again three years later.

Willie Mays (top) tips his cap in recognition of the crowd's reaction after he hit his 512th home run on May 5, 1966 to break Mel Ott's National League record. Below, Mike McCormick pitches en route to his 20th victory of 1967.

Bobby Bonds (top) scored a league-leading 120 runs in 1969. Above, Juan Marichal was famous for his big-kick delivery. He was elected to the Hall of Fame in 1983.

In the middle of 1970, King was fired and replaced by coach Charlie Fox. The "Three Ms"—Mays, McCovey and Marichal—remained, but their supporting cast continued to change.

## THE YEAR OF THE FOX

San Francisco returned to the top of the National League West in 1971, which became known as "The Year of the Fox."

Chris Speier jumped from Double-A ball to start at shortstop and formed an almost magical combination with second baseman Tito Fuentes. Bobby Bonds led the Giants in virtually every offensive category and Dave Kingman, a gangling newcomer from USC, gave the Giants additional offensive punch. This was a great ballclub for coming from behind.

The Giants clinched the Western Division on the last game of the regular season by one game over the Dodgers when Marichal beat the Padres 5-1. But the Eastern Division-champion Pirates defeated the exhausted Giants in four games to win the National League pennant.

Perry was traded to the Cleveland Indians along with infielder Frank Duffy for pitcher "Sudden Sam" McDowell over the winter. In 1972, Mays was dealt to the Mets for pitcher Charlie Williams and much-needed cash. During the winter of 1973, McCovey was sent to the Padres and

Marichal was sold to the Red Sox. After 1974, Bonds was traded to the Yankees for outfielder Bobby Murcer.

What appeared to be unwise trades were necessary because the club was in serious financial straits. Stoneham could no longer afford to pay market rates.

From 1972 through the end of the decade, the Giants wound up in the middle of the Western Division standings. Charlie Fox survived 2½ seasons before being replaced by Wes Westrum, who managed through 1975 when the Giants finished a game under .500. Financially, the franchise was in serious condition.

When the Kansas City franchise was transferred to Oakland in 1968, attendance at Candlestick dropped nearly 500,000, the first time the San Francisco Giants drew less than a million. The 1971 pennant race pushed attendance back over the million mark to 1,088,083, but as the Giants traded away their stars, interest waned even more, pushing the franchise to the verge of bankruptcy.

A disheartened Stoneham initiated the search for buyers. The only legitimate offer was from the Labatts Group, a Canadian brewery that planned to move the team to Toronto. After obtaining an injunction against moving the team, Mayor George Moscone convinced San Francisco businessman Bob Lurie and Arizona cattleman Bud Herseth to buy the Giants, thus saving it for San Francisco. Two years later Lurie bought out Herseth.

Lurie, somewhat of a traditionalist, convinced Bill Rigney to return and manage the ballclub in 1976. In 1977,

Only 3,774 fans watched the Giants and Padres play on July 3, 1974 (top). Poor teams and an inhospitable ballpark compelled Owner Bob Lurie to search for out-of-town buyers.

John 'The Count' Montefusco was as well-known for his personality as his hard throwing during his seven seasons in San Francisco. He pitched a league-leading six shutouts in 1976.

Vida Blue began his career with the Oakland A's but came to the Giants in a famous 1978 trade and won 18 games.

McCovey was signed as a free agent to play again for the Giants. Joe Altobelli, a long-time minor league manager, replaced Rigney after the 1976 season and led the 1978 contingent to a surprising finish, rekindling interest in the Giants. After leading the division in mid-August, the Giants slumped to third but continued to play an active role in the outcome of the pennant race.

Rawboned Jack Clark was the team's legitimate hitting star. He was complemented by McCovey, Mike Ivie, Darrell Evans, Bill Madlock and Terry Whitfield. The latter four all came to San Francisco via trades made by General Manager Spec Richardson. This was the first legitimate offense since the 1971 days of Mays, McCovey, Bonds and Kingman.

On the mound, the undisputed star was lefty Vida Blue, acquired from Oakland during Spring Training for seven players and cash. Unlike the offense, the pitching staff mostly was home-grown. Starters Bob Knepper, Ed Halicki, Jim Barr and John "The Count" Montefusco, plus relievers Gary Lavelle and Greg Minton, had worked their ways up through the Giants farm system.

As in 1971, the 1978 Giants had the ability and temperament to come from behind in the later innings. Ivie was particularly effective off the bench. As a pinch-hitter, he clubbed four homers—two of which were grand slams—and drove in 20 runs. McCovey hit his 500th home run on June 30. For the first time in seven years, the Giants regained fan support, drawing 1,740,480—an increase from 1977 in excess of one million. It was also the largest attendance in San Francisco since 1960.

Jack Clark, lining one past the Dodgers' Ron Cey, was one of the many Giants ballplayers who disliked playing at Candlestick Park.

The emotional high didn't last. With much the same team as in 1978, the Giants played near .500 ball into August before the team collapsed and fell to fourth. Altobelli was fired and replaced by coach Dave Bristol. Bristol's 1980 team was never in the running and he was removed after the season. McCovey retired in late June. In his last at-bat on July 6 in Los Angeles, Willie Mac came off the bench to drive in the tying run in a game the Giants ultimately won. Even the hated Dodgers fans gave Willie a standing ovation in his swan song.

## FRANK ROBINSON, MANAGER

Frank Robinson, a Giants nemesis in his playing days with Cincinnati, became San Francisco's first black manager when he was hired for 1981. Robby's first season was interrupted in June by a player strike that lasted almost two months. The Giants were five games under .500 when the strike hit but went 29-23 in the post-strike period to help salvage the season.

That cohesiveness was evident in the latter stages of 1982. The Giants carried a 42-46 record out of the All-Star break, 12 games out of first place, but they played the best ball in the National League during the second half to close in on the Dodgers and Braves. With 10 games remaining, the Giants went into Los Angeles and swept three from the Dodgers to move into second. With three games remaining, all against the Dodgers at Candlestick, the Giants were one game behind the Dodgers and Braves.

The Dodgers won the first two games, eliminating the Giants from contention. On Sunday, the Dodgers needed the win to tie for the championship because the Braves had swept San Diego. The Dodgers led 3-2 in the seventh when, in one of the most dramatic hits in San Francisco history, Joe Morgan hit a three-run home run into the right field bleachers to win the game.

The Giants stumbled in 1983 and 1984 and Robinson was fired. Jim Davenport took over in 1985 but was fired at mid-season as Lurie decided drastic changes were needed. The woeful Giants stumbled to a 100-loss season, the first in franchise history. ❖

CHAPTER **29**

# MULES
# & MOUSTACHES

At first glance, the Kansas City Athletics team that moved to Oakland in 1968 was not very good. But experienced baseball men could see that the team was on the verge of flowering into baseball's most dominant franchise.

Only four men had owned the Athletics since the Mack family helped inaugurate the American League in 1901. Connie Mack, the long-time family patriarch and team manager, ran a frugal ship when the franchise was located in Philadelphia and more than once had to sell the team's stars to pay his bills.

By 1954, a year in which franchise moving was acceptable, the Macks sold out to industrialist Arnold Johnson, who transferred the team to Kansas City for the 1955 season. Johnson, with high hopes of elevating the fortunes of a talent-poor franchise, became impatient when his efforts didn't bring immediate results in the standings or at the turnstiles.

With a quick-fix mentality, the Athletics consummated a series of trades for major league veterans in exchange for young, untried prospects. Sadly, the veterans were nearing the ends of their careers while many of the youngsters were on the doorsteps of greatness. Among the players traded away—all to the New York Yankees—were Roger Maris, Clete Boyer, Ralph Terry and Ryne Duren. The Yankees and Kansas City Athletics completed so many trades the A's were called a Yankees' farm club.

### FINLEY BUYS THE FRANCHISE

Insurance executive Charles O. Finley acquired controlling interest in the club from Johnson's estate after the 1960 season. Johnson's impatience was nothing compared to Finley's. During his first season, Finley fired both Manager Joe Gordon and General Manager Frank Lane, whom he had recently signed to an eight-year contract. These were the first of a continuous line of managerial departures under Finley's controversial ownership.

Finley, the quintessential salesman and self-promoter, correctly evaluated the needs of his team and established a plan. Although not a baseball man, he had confidence in his abilities to compete. Probably his greatest strength was his willingness to listen to experienced men and act on their advice. Finley was convinced of the need to have an effective scouting system, and he set it into place.

The timing of Finley's entry into baseball was provident. He would not have been willing to pay the exorbitant bonuses necessary to sign the most talented amateurs during the 1950s. But other owners started to feel the same way, and by 1965 the amateur draft was created. As major league baseball's worst team, the Kansas City A's were granted the first draft choice, which they used to pick Rick Monday from Arizona State University.

Over the next three years, with the A's continuing to finish on or near the bottom of the standings, they were able to draft Arizona State stars Reggie Jackson and Sal Bando plus Jim Hunter, Rollie Fingers, John Odom, Gene Tenace and, later, Vida Blue.

Finley, with his bent for promotion, added something extra to a player's signing bonus if he would accept a nickname. Thus, Hunter became known as "Catfish" and Odom, "Blue Moon." Finley tried and failed in changing Blue's first name to "True," however.

At Kansas City's Municipal Stadium, mules became mascots, players wore white alligator shoes, greased pigs were chased and caught, cows were milked, and the Beatles performed at bargain prices. But Finley wasn't happy with his midwestern farm town, so he began looking for a more attractive market.

## THE A'S COME TO OAKLAND

From the start, Finley acted in ways that alienated the other owners, his own players and the city fathers of Kansas City. As early as 1963, he stated his intentions to move the team out of Kansas City. He looked at Oakland and Dallas, and settled on the former. But there were problems: He had a contract with Kansas City, the league owners hadn't approved any relocation of his team and Oakland didn't have a stadium.

Finley attempted to solve the stadium concern by asking Horace Stoneham of the Giants if the Athletics could play their games in Candlestick Park while a new park was constructed in Oakland. Rebuffed by Stoneham and turned down by the owners, Finley signed a four-year contract to remain at Kansas City's Municipal Stadium. After four years of haggling with everybody in Kansas City, Finley was given permission to move his team to Oakland, but only after A.L. President Joe Cronin promised Kansas City an expansion team for the 1969 season. Kansas Senator Stuart Symington, in a swipe at Finley, called Oakland "the luckiest city since Hiroshima."

The new Oakland A's opened the 1968 season against Baltimore. California Governor Ronald Reagan delivered

Charlie Finley, the A's colorful and iconoclastic owner, welcomes the crowd to his team's first game at Oakland Coliseum. Note then-Governor Ronald Reagan at lower left.

Bob Kennedy (top left) was the Oakland A's first manager and led them to an 82-80 record and sixth-place finish in 1968. Lew Krausse (above) throws the first pitch for the A's in Oakland, April 17, 1968 against Baltimore.

the ceremonial first pitch and Lew Krausse pitched the home season-opener. Opening Night was a sellout as was the August 18 game honoring the 1948 Oaks and Seals. But crowds were sparse in between. On May 8, Hunter tossed a perfect game before 6,298 fans, a figure more representative of game attendance than the 47,233 who attended Opening Night.

Under Manager Bob Kennedy, the A's finished the season 82-80, showing early signs of future greatness.

## FINLEY'S M.O.

Finley's temperament was a combination of patience and impatience, tolerance and intolerance. He knew he had to be patient to allow his players to develop, but his record in Kansas City of seven different managers in seven years spoke to his expectations of the leaders in the dugout. Even after a winning season—the franchise's first since 1952—Kennedy was fired and replaced by Hank Bauer for 1969.

Finley generally was feared and disliked by his players. He used every device available to him to keep his players' salaries down at contract time. He was not above using coercion to get a player to sign on his terms. Finley's unwillingness to award Blue with a legitimate raise after his MVP/Cy Young year in 1971 almost forced Blue into retirement and contributed to his sub-par 6-10 record in 1972.

While Finley was tolerant of his players' dress and appearance, he was intolerant of their criticism and their ineptitude. The Oakland A's gained an identity by growing moustaches in 1972 because Finley payed bonuses to all players who grew them. Yet in 1967, when first baseman Ken Harrelson had criticized Finley's interference with his manager's decisions, Finley became so angry that he released Harrelson outright. This allowed Harrelson to sign a contract containing a handsome signing bonus with the Boston Red Sox.

In Game Two of the 1973 World Series, Finley's actions reached a nadir after second baseman Mike Andrews made two errors in a loss to the New York Mets. Finley forced Andrews to write a statement that he was injured, and Finley placed him on the disabled list. The media and players were openly critical, and Commissioner Bowie Kuhn reinstated Andrews for the third game. When Andrews appeared as a pinch-hitter in Game Three, he was greeted with a standing ovation from the fans.

## THE DICK WILLIAMS REIGN

Finley fired Johnny McNamara after a disappointing second-place finish in 1970 and hired Dick Williams. Williams was the right man for the Oakland. As a player

Jim Hunter, given the nickname of 'Catfish' by Charlie Finley, threw a perfect game against Minnesota on May 8, 1968. Only 6,298 fans were on hand to watch.

During the championship years of 1972-74, first base was unsettled. Mike Epstein, Tenace and Mike Hegan all played there. Second baseman Green and shortstop Campaneris, both A's products in Kansas City, were outstanding up the middle. Bando, known as "Captain Sal," was a steady influence at third base. Left fielder Joe Rudi wasn't spectacular, but 23 other teams would have loved to see him in their outfield. Monday, a solid player, went to the Chicago Cubs for pitcher Ken Holtzman after the 1971 season in one of Finley's most significant trades. Center field was ultimately filled by Bill North in a trade with the Cubs for Locker.

Jackson owned right field. As a young player, Reggie was strikeout-prone and a defensive liability. Still, he became the darling of Oakland's fans, especially those in the right field bleachers who became members of "Reggie's Regiment."

Tenace was the regular catcher, but Dave Duncan, Larry Haney and then Ray Fosse also contributed.

In an era when a starting pitcher was still expected to pitch a full nine innings, Williams could call upon his four aces, Hunter, Holtzman, Odom and Blue. That kind of poker hand that won everywhere.

Reggie Jackson hit 29 home runs in his first season in Oakland. Jackson played 10 of his 21 seasons for the A's.

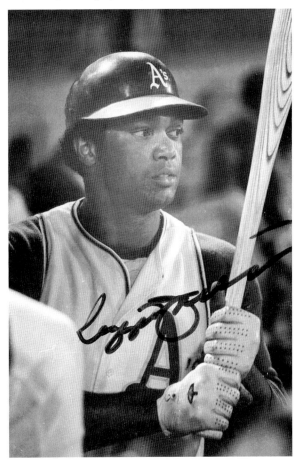

Williams was nothing more than a journeyman; as a manager he was a combination of teacher, friend, disciplinarian and referee.

Analyzing the A's position-by-position, it was apparent this was a team of talented players. Three made the Hall of Fame: Hunter, Fingers and Jackson. Collectively, it was a terrific lineup.

Clutch hitting compensated for the weak bat of defensive marvel Dick Green. Gene Tenace's versatility and leadership skills made up for his low batting average, and Jackson's strong arm and potent bat allowed critics to overlook his fielding deficiencies. And a suffocating bullpen of Fingers, Paul Lindblad, Bob Locker and Darold Knowles made everybody look good.

Williams ruled with an iron fist but instilled the attitude of winning. While players fought among themselves in the clubhouse, they played as a unit on the field. And Finley made the necessary trades that brought key players to fill the holes.

## FIVE YEARS OF DOMINATION

The A's dominated the American League West for five years. In 1971, Williams' first year, the A's lost three straight to the powerful Eastern Division champions, Baltimore.

In 1972, the A's met the Detroit Tigers in a volatile championship series. With the feisty Billy Martin managing the Tigers, fans witnessed a true cat-and-mouse series.

The series took a violent turn in the sixth inning of Game Two at Oakland when reliever Lerrin LaGrow hit Campaneris in the ankle with a pitch. Campaneris, the catalyst of the A's running game, had little doubt the pitch was thrown to injure him, and instinctively threw his bat at LaGrow. Both benches emptied, and Martin and Tiger outfielder Willie Horton had to be restrained from attacking Campaneris.

After peace was restored, Campaneris was thrown out of the game and fined and suspended from the remaining playoffs and the first week of the 1973 season. The series remained tense, with the A's finally emerging victorious by taking Game Five, 2-1, in Detroit. Jackson scored the winning run but pulled a hamstring and was lost for the World Series.

In a World Series full of heroes, the upstart A's defeated Cincinnati's Big Red Machine in a seven-game series, giving Oakland its first of three consecutive World Championships.

In 1973, the A's defeated the New York Mets in seven games in a World Series that concluded the distinguished career of Willie Mays. Knowles set a World Series record by entering all seven games as a pitcher.

The baseball world was shocked when Dick Williams resigned as manager immediately after that World Series. For Williams, the Andrews incident was the last straw in a string of what he complained was constant meddling and inappropriate actions by Finley.

Veteran Alvin Dark returned for his second tour as a Finley manager in 1974 and guided the A's to the World Series for the third straight time. After taking the Orioles in four games, the A's defeated the Los Angeles Dodgers in five, securing the title of "The Team Of The Decade." After winning the 1975 Western Division crown by five games, the wheels came off the wagon as the Red Sox swept the A's in four ALCS games to win the American League pennant.

## FINLEY OUTRAGES THE PLAYERS

By the 1974 season, events in baseball were starting to spin out of control. Although Oakland-raised Curt Flood lost his 1972 suit to be declared a free agent, the Players Association won concessions allowing arbitration of salary disputes with owners starting in 1974. Finley was the big

Bert 'Campy' Campaneris (top) and Sal Bando were both original members of the Oakland A's who became integral members of the team's three straight World Championships from 1972-74.

loser in the first round, having to pay the arbitrator's rate to Jackson, Bando, Holtzman, Knowles and Fingers.

Hunter claimed Finley had not abided by stipulations in his 1974 contract and filed for free agency. Arbitrator Peter Seitz agreed with Hunter, setting him free of any obligations to Oakland. Free agency was now a factor in dealing with players, and the frugal A's owner could envision the loss of all his stars.

Seeing the inevitability of the situation, Finley traded Jackson and Holtzman to the Orioles for Don Baylor, Paul Mitchell and Mike Torrez before the 1976 season opener. But Finley wasn't finished. Early in the season he sold Blue, Fingers and Rudi to the Red Sox, only to have Commissioner Bowie Kuhn cancel the deals as not being "in the best interests of baseball." Finley sued and lost in federal court. Then he proceeded to lose Rudi and Fingers, along with Tenace, Campaneris, Bando and Baylor, to free agency at the end of the season. He also sold Haney and Lindblad, still under contract, and was rebuffed in his effort to sell Blue to the Reds.

With this utter turmoil, it was surprising to see the 1976 A's, now managed by Chuck Tanner, finish only 2½ games behind Kansas City in the A.L. West. Then in a move unusual even for Finley, he traded Tanner to Pittsburgh for catcher Manny Sanguillen and $100,000 after the 1976 season.

In 1978, Finley finally traded Blue to the Giants for $300,000 and seven players: pitchers Dave Heaverlo, Phil Huffman, John Henry Johnson and Alan Wirth, catcher Gary Alexander, infielder Mario Guerrero and outfielder Gary Thomasson. Finley ultimately moved each of his new players, making sure some cash was included in the deal when they left.

It was apparent Finley's days as owner of the A's were numbered. He refused to accept conditions restricting him from doing business "his" way. He warned the baseball establishment of the pitfalls of free agency and blamed Kuhn for allowing it to happen.

## BILLY MARTIN RETURNS

One of Finley's last strokes of genius was hiring Billy Martin to manage a tattered group of Oakland A's in 1980. Martin took a team that had won only one of every three games in 1979 and made them a contender in 1980. The

Rickey Henderson, a graduate of Oakland Technical High School, served as the main catalyst of the Athletics' offense in three separate stints with the team.

1980 season also marked Rickey Henderson's first full season in the majors.

Martin's main strategy was to use Henderson as the catalyst to play for the single run. Henderson, playing as if he were on a mission, stole 100 bases. Two years later, Rickey stole 130 bases, eclipsing Hall of Famer Lou Brock's major league record of 118.

The A's stole home seven times during the season, another Martin influence. With runners on first and third base, Martin instructed the runner on first to stray away from the base, enticing catchers to throw behind the runner at first base. At the instant the throw was made, the runner on third broke for the plate. Henderson and Dwayne Murphy, both speedsters, each stole home twice . . . but so did the lumbering Wayne Gross.

Another key Martin strategy involved his pitching staff. He had little strength in his bullpen but had strong starters, so he adopted a five-pitcher rotation of Rick Langford, Mike Norris, Matt Keough, Steve McCatty and Brian Kingman. Martin rationalized that pitchers in previous eras were expected to complete their starts.

The result was an amazing 159 starts and 94 complete games from his five iron men—the latter figure twice the total of any other major league team. Langford's 28 complete games were more than the total of many teams' pitching staffs. Incidentally, the A's registered a major league low of 13 saves.

## FINLEY SELLS TO THE HAAS FAMILY

Finley had actively searched for a buyer for several years. For a time it appeared the buyer would be wealthy Denver oilman Marvin Davis. Faced with losing the team to Colorado, Oakland civic leader Cornell Maier negotiated the mid-summer 1980 sale of the A's to the Haas family, operators of Levi Strauss.

The Haas family, represented by Roy Eisenhardt and Walter J. Haas, pledged to make the A's an integral part of the community, something Finley failed to do. One of Finley's biggest weaknesses was failing to promote his team. Somehow, the publicity focused on the owner and his mule, not on his fine young players. The new management determined to promote the team by encouraging families to enjoy an affordable time at the ballpark.

In one of their more imaginative marketing promotions, new Business Manager Andy Dolich unveiled "Billy Ball," a phrase coined by *Oakland Tribune* sports columnist Ralph Wiley.

As the Oakland A's opened the 1981 season, Martin's touch seemed magical. The A's started with an 11-game win streak and finished April at 18-3. But the season was interrupted by a players' strike, and although Oakland was the overall statistical leader, Kansas City won the post-strike portion and forced a best-of-five playoff.

The A's defeated the Royals in three games but were swept by the Yankees in three games for the American League championship. Thus the dream evaporated, but for the new ownership, it had been a wonderful inauguration. A total of 1,311,761 fans attended, 235,000 more than ever before.

"Billy Ball" continued into the 1982 season but Martin's pitching strategy backfired as his starters, one after another, came up with arm trouble and their ERAs skyrocketed.

Martin's opponents were no longer surprised by his style and the A's started losing. As Martin had done in other towns, he allowed himself to self-destruct. He became more volatile towards umpires and less tolerant of his players' mistakes. Soon, it became obvious Martin would have to leave.

For the next five years, the club was mired in the second division. Managers came and went. Steve Boros replaced Martin for 1983 and he in turn was replaced by Jackie Moore, who lasted parts of two seasons. General Manager Sandy Alderson needed an established and respected manager. Tony La Russa was that man. ❖

The Oakland A's floundered in the standings and at the turnstiles until Walter A. Haas Jr., and his family purchased the team, then hired Tony La Russa as manager.

MICHAEL ZAGARIS

CHAPTER **30**

# THE CRAIG AND LA RUSSA YEARS

Bay Area baseball was generally mediocre in the first half of the 1980s. This changed with the arrival of two new managers: Roger Craig in San Francisco and Tony La Russa in Oakland.

In San Francisco, Bob Lurie set in motion the rejuvenation of the Giants by hiring Al Rosen as his new president and general manager. Rosen, a former American League Most Valuable Player with Cleveland and major league executive, enjoyed a reputation as a "no-nonsense" general manager and a tough negotiator. He was willing to take risks as well.

Roger Craig was hired out of semi-retirement on September 18, 1985 and quickly established a new direction for the discouraged Giants. During the last few weeks of the 1985 season, he began teaching pitchers his pet pitch, the split-fingered fastball.

Spring Training 1986 opened to an unusual display of enthusiasm in the Giants' camp. When camp was over, two rookies, first baseman Will Clark and second baseman Robbie Thompson, were in the starting lineup. Clark showed he was going to be something special by cracking a home run off Nolan Ryan in his first major league at-bat. Thompson's contributions were more subtle, but he nevertheless was honored as *The Sporting News'* National League Rookie of the Year.

## GIANTS HIT THE TOP

The 1986 season was supposed to be a rebuilding year but the Giants finished a surprising third with an 83-79 record. They got off to a great start in 1987 before faltering in May and June, at which point Rosen went to work. On July 4 he engineered a massive trade with San Diego for pitchers Dave Dravecky and Craig Lefferts and third baseman Kevin Mitchell.

When it was apparent the Giants needed even more pitching, Rosen worked two separate deals with Pittsburgh, acquiring Don Robinson and Rick Reuschel for prospects. These three trades stabilized the team, allowing the Giants to catch Cincinnati on August 12 before pulling away from the field to win the Western Division by six games. The four new pitchers contributed 20 wins and only 12 losses. Mitchell hit .306 with 15 homers.

In the National League Championship Series, the Giants and Cardinals split the first two games played in St. Louis. At Candlestick, Robinson lost in relief 6-5, but Mike Krukow and Joe Price, in relief of Reuschel, took Giants victories, 4-2 and 6-3. The Giants were now ahead three games to two—one game away from their first World Series appearance in 25 years.

At Busch Stadium, however, Cardinals pitchers John

Roger Craig came out of retirement to manage the Giants at the end of the 1985 season and led them to two division flags.

Cubs split a pair. Will Clark was the hero in the fourth inning of Game One when he launched a ball over the right center field wall for a grand slam to lead the Giants to an 11-3 victory. Reuschel was knocked out of the box in the first inning of Game Two as the Cubs scored six times on route to a 9-5 victory. The Giants won the series at Candlestick by sweeping three games. With 13 hits in 20 at-bats (.650) and eight RBIs, Clark was an overwhelming selection as NLCS MVP.

For Giants fans, the World Series proved to be a terrible climax to an exciting baseball season. After scoring only one run in 18 innings and losing both games to the A's in Oakland, the Giants returned to Candlestick Park. At 5:04 p.m., on October 17—just minutes before the Series was to resume—the 7.1-magnitude Loma Prieta earthquake hit Northern California.

At first, the temblor began as a loud rumbling, growing louder and shaking stronger until the entire structure began undulating. Profound silence filled the stadium for a few seconds and then the crowd, finally realizing what had just taken place, roared in a deafening cheer. And then, confusion. Many were frightened, others wanted to settle down and play ball. Because the power was out, there could be no announcements on the public address system or the message board. Spectators then began to notice a black cloud of smoke coming from downtown.

Tudor and Danny Cox tossed back-to-back shutouts, 1-0 and 6-0, to clinch the league pennant. Jeffrey Leonard, with a .417 batting average and home runs in each of the first four games, was selected as playoff MVP.

The 1988 Giants slipped back to fourth place at 83-79. Center fielder Brett Butler was a significant free agent signing and utility player Ernest Riles came over in an early season trade. Riles hit the franchise's 10,000th home run on July 9.

During the off-season, Rosen signed free agent pitcher Goose Gossage and traded for catcher Terry Kennedy. Rosen kept busy during the season, picking up infielder Ken Oberkfell and outfielder Pat Sheridan, then negotiating a blockbuster trade to acquire premier relief pitcher Steve Bedrosian from Philadelphia. In early August, the Giants signed free agent pitcher Bob Knepper, who won three crucial games down the stretch. Rookie pitcher Jeff Brantley made the Opening Day roster as a non-roster player and wound up with a 7-1 record in 59 games out of the bullpen.

### SHADES OF 1906

The 1989 Giants built up a seven-game lead thanks to a strong September and won the division by three games. It was on to the NLCS at Chicago where the Giants and

Will Clark was the Giants' first-round selection in the 1985 draft and hit a homer in his first major league at-bat in 1986.

Preliminary, error-filled reports announced that the Bay Bridge had collapsed and cars were in the water.

Within the next hour, fans calmly began making the uncertain trek home. Those living in the East Bay faced having to cross the Bay without benefit of the Bay Bridge. Many reported journeys lasting more than five hours over alternate, gridlocked roads.

Many citizens felt the World Series should have been canceled. But after 10 days, during which the people of Northern California had a chance to put their lives back in order, the Series resumed.

Baseball strategies had changed when the teams returned to Candlestick. A's Manager Tony La Russa modified his pitching rotation, passing over 17-game winner Bob Welch in favor of his earlier starters, Dave Stewart and Mike Moore. Craig started Garrelts in Game Three and switched from Rick Reuschel to Don Robinson for Game Four. Although the Giants found their batting stroke, their pitching was ineffective. Oakland defeated the Giants 13-7 and 9-6 and won the World Championship in a World Series that had captured the attention of a country for reasons having nothing to do with baseball.

Meanwhile, Candlestick Park's deficiencies were a serious concern for Bob Lurie during the 1980s. Players and officials both acknowledged Candlestick was probably the worst baseball facility in the major leagues.

Kevin Mitchell led the league with 47 home runs in 1989 but his off-field activities compelled management to trade him.

Robby Thompson became the spiritual anchor of the Giants' infield during the late 1980s and into the 1990s after being named National League Rookie of the Year in 1986.

Willie Mays felt the winds sweeping in from left field cost him more than 10 home runs a season but said nothing when he played there. Outfielders ran in circles to corral fly balls, while infielders and batters were pelted by swirling dust and trash. Pitcher Stu Miller was blown off the mound by a gust of wind in the 1961 All-Star Game.

Even Ewing Field was abandoned after just one season in the fog and wind. Not Candlestick. Lefty O'Doul told Lawrence Ritter, "This is the most ridiculous site for a ball park I've ever seen. When I was a child, the wind would blow the sheep I was herding off Candlestick hill."

During the 1970s it became popular among Giants players to bash the park, but when the Rosen-Craig team arrived in San Francisco, they instructed their players to use the park's idiosyncrasies to their advantage. Still, Lurie knew the frigid climate at the park hurt attendance, and early in his ownership he started posturing for the construction of a new downtown baseball stadium.

Matt Williams was a sturdy force at third base for the Giants and also provided power at the plate.

Mayor Dianne Feinstein effectively sidestepped the issue until she was out of office, something the next mayor, Art Agnos, couldn't do.

## BOND ISSUE DEFEATED BY EARTHQUAKE

A bond issue that would have placed a new stadium near the Southern Pacific train yards, south of Market Street, was defeated after adjacent neighborhoods protest-

Bob Brenly provided dependable catching and a solid bat during the mid-1980s.

ed loudly against it. The bond issue had been hastily prepared and left many questions unanswered regarding the source of funding.

The Mayor's Office tried again in 1989. Proposition W was more balanced and answered the concerns raised

### THE DRAVECKY DRAMA

The saga of left-hander Dave Dravecky was a portrait of courage and tragedy. During the 1988 off-season, a cancerous growth was discovered in Dravecky's pitching arm. After treatment, his goal was to pitch again and his rehabilitation sent him to San Jose in the California League. After a couple of successful outings in the minors, Dravecky was recalled to the Giants.

Dravecky returned on August 10, 1989, in front of more than 35,000 emotional fans at Candlestick. He pitched eight innings in a 4-3 victory over Cincinnati. Five days later, Dravecky started against the Expos at Olympic Stadium. Pitching into the sixth inning with a 3-2 lead, Dravecky started his delivery to the plate when the whip-action of the throw broke his upper arm. He went down in pain as a deathly silence fell over the crowd.

Dravecky's therapy had included freezing the bone during surgery, causing it to become more brittle. The stress proved to be too much. Dravecky was credited with the victory, but his career was over.

He continued to travel with the team through the season and into the Championship Series. In an awful twist, Dravecky refractured his arm during the post-championship celebration.

A few months later the malignancy returned and Dravecky's left arm was amputated.

The Oakland Coliseum (top) was usually a comfortable place to watch a game at night. The A's began setting attendance marks when Tony La Russa came to Oakland.

by the earlier bond issue. Proposition W proposed to construct a stadium at China Basin in the southern section of the city. Mayor Agnos and a host of volunteers had worked hard to bring support to the proposition, and it seemed likely it would pass until the earthquake hit. At that point the proposition lost its support as voters felt the money could be better spent elsewhere. Proposition W received the endorsement from every major newspaper and from many political groups, but still it was defeated on election day. At the last moment negative mailers were distributed to San Francisco voters. Additionally, the silence of State Senator Quentin Kopp, a noted San Francisco sports booster but a long-time adversary of Agnos', contributed to the defeat.

Lurie then turned his efforts to find a new home park. After two more stadium measures were defeated by Santa Clara County voters, Lurie put the club up for sale. On August 7, 1992, Lurie sold the San Francisco Giants to a group in Tampa, Florida.

## THE TONY LA RUSSA ERA

The 1986 season was pivotal for the A's. By early July, they were already out of the race. Manager Jackie Moore was fired and replaced by coach Jeff Newman on an interim basis. On July 14, Sandy Alderson hired Tony La Russa to manage the ballclub. It was a homecoming of sorts, as La Russa had signed with the Kansas City A's out of high school and broke in with them a year later in 1963.

After a spotty minor league career, he made it to Oakland in 1968, the A's first year on the West Coast. But nobody would ever call Tony a great major league player.

His hiring as manager was met with great enthusiasm, however. His six-plus seasons at the helm of the Chicago White Sox had earned him a reputation as an intelligent and cool manager, one who could get the most out of his players. Knowledgeable observers felt La Russa had his White Sox playing above their ability.

La Russa's presence had immediate impact as the team, stuck in the cellar, elevated itself to third place by season's end.

The return trip from mediocrity to contender started early in 1986 when General Manager Sandy Alderson signed free agent Dave Stewart to a contract. The Oakland-born pitcher had been beset with personal and physical problems over the previous two seasons and Alderson felt Stewart could rehabilitate himself. After a short stay at Tacoma, Stewart was recalled and put in the starting rotation where he became the heart of the Oakland A's and a 20-game winner in each of the next four seasons.

Over the winter of 1986, Alderson signed Reggie Jackson as a free agent and traded for Ron Cey. While both players were past their prime, they helped re-establish a winning attitude in Oakland. Just a few days before the 1987 season opener, Dennis Eckersley was acquired in

Mike Bordick took over at shortstop for the A's in the early 1990s after Walt Weiss fell victim to a string of leg injuries.

Dennis Eckersley (top) and Dave Stewart came to Oakland and revived their careers. Eckersley became the game's top reliever and Stewart won 20 games four years in a row.

a trade from the Chicago Cubs. Eckersley, a starter throughout his career, was turned into a reliever by La Russa and became the most dominant closer of his era.

The 1987 A's closed at 81-81, in third place. At mid-season Alderson acquired pitchers Storm Davis and Rick Honeycutt. During the winter he traded for pitcher Bob

Welch and outfielder Dave Parker, and signed catcher Ron Hassey, infielder Glenn Hubbard and outfielders Dave Henderson and Don Baylor as free agents. During the winter of 1988 the A's signed pitcher Mike Moore, and in June 1989 Rickey Henderson returned to Oakland via a trade with the Yankees.

While Alderson was making critical player transactions, the farm system produced three straight Rookies of the Year starting in 1986: Jose Canseco, Mark McGwire and Walt Weiss. Other home-grown products included All-Star catcher Terry Steinbach and infielders Lance Blankenship, Mike Bordick and Brent Gates.

The 1988 Athletics were a complete team. Winners of 104 games, the A's quickly made a shambles of their division. The club built up a commanding lead through April and May before slumping slightly in June. Picking up momentum in July, the A's concluded by winning 40 of their last 57 games before sweeping the Eastern Division-champion Red Sox in four games.

La Russa was selected American League Manager of the Year and Jose Canseco, the major league leader with 42 home runs and 124 RBIs, was a unanimous American League Most Valuable Player and Major League Player of the Year. Terry Steinbach was selected All-Star Game MVP, Walter Weiss was Rookie of the Year and Dave Henderson was named Comeback Player of the Year.

Dennis Eckersley was everybody's Fireman of the Year with 45 saves. In the ALCS against Boston, Eckersley recorded four saves, a record that can never be broken. Dave Stewart got the ball whenever La Russa needed a win, and he won 21 for his second 20-win season in a row.

After such a marvelous season, the World Series was a horrible disappointment. The A's traveled to Los Angeles for the first two games and in the first game went into the bottom of the ninth inning with a lead, courtesy of a grand slam by Canseco. What occurred next was probably the biggest momentum shift in World Series history. With Eckersley on the mound, Kirk Gibson—barely able to walk because of bad knees—unloaded a home run to right field, giving the Dodgers a 5-4 victory.

An unexplainable power outage then hit the A's for the duration. Canseco's grand slam would be his only hit and Mark McGwire's winning homer in the ninth inning of Game Three was his only contribution. With Orel Hershiser pitching two complete-game victories, the Dodgers won four of five games to win the World Championship.

La Russa's 1989 A's won 99 games during the regular season before defeating the Blue Jays in the ALCS in five games. The Loma Prieta earthquake interrupted the "Battle of the Bay" World Series against the Giants, allowing Stewart and free-agent signee Mike Moore to win two games apiece in the A's romp.

The 1989 record was more of a team effort, accelerated by the re-acquisition of Rickey Henderson. Rickey bat-

The 'Bash Brothers,' Mark McGwire and Jose Canseco (above), made the A's the most feared hitting team in the American League. Brent Gates (top) was part of the new wave of A's infielders as the team moved into the austere 1990s.

Rickey Henderson holds aloft the third base bag after breaking Lou Brock's career stolen bases mark with his 940th theft on May 1, 1991.

ted leadoff, played left field and served as a catalyst for the offense, stealing 52 bases after his arrival in mid-June. Canseco missed half the season; Weiss tore cartilage in his knee and McGwire and Dave Henderson slumped at the plate. Carney Lansford hit .336 as the only consistent bat in the lineup.

On the mound, Stewart went 21-9 with Moore winning 19 and Welch 17. Eckersley missed more than a month with a strained shoulder and dropped off to 33 saves. The slack was taken up by Rick Honeycutt, Todd Burns and Gene Nelson.

In 1990, the A's were blessed with better health and they won 103 games to win the division by nine games. The signing of free agent Scott Sanderson (17-11) complemented Stewart's fourth straight 20-win season (22-11) and Bob Welch's marvelous Cy Young year (27-6). Ironically, Stewart had complained the past three seasons

that he had been unfairly overlooked in Cy Young voting, particularly since he had won 64 games in that span. But Welch's record, combined with a 2.95 ERA, was impossible to vote against.

Meanwhile, Eckersley turned in 48 saves and a 0.61 ERA, walking only four batters all season. The A's team ERA was 3.18.

McGwire hit 39 homers while batting .235. Canseco, the other half of the "Bash Brothers," added 37 homers. Rickey Henderson hit .325 with 28 homers and 65 stolen bases—closing to within three of Lou Brock's career major league record—and was named league MVP.

As in 1988, the A's swept the Red Sox in the ALCS. Stewart and Roger Clemens hooked up in a pitchers' duel in Boston before the A's scored seven in the ninth to blow the game open. Welch won the second game. Back in Oakland, Moore won Game Three before Stewart and Clemens hooked up for a rematch. In this game, home plate umpire Terry Cooney took exception to comments from Clemens and ran him from the game in the second inning. The A's went on to win 3-1.

But the A's fortunes again went south. The Cincinnati Reds, huge underdogs, scored a decisive 7-0 win in Game One, then won the second game in extra innings, 5-4. Back in Oakland, Cincinnati scored seven in the third to coast to an 8-3 Game Three win. Finally, in

A's catcher Terry Steinbach's career took off after he was named All-Star Game Most Valuable Player in 1988.

The A's 'Dream Team.' Top row (l-r): D. Parker, B. Welch, D. Stewart, R. Henderson, D. Eckersley, R. Jackson, J. Canseco, C. Lansford, M. McGwire, T. Steinbach. Seated (l-r): V. Blue, R. Fingers, T. La Russa, C. Hunter, C. Campaneris.

Game Four, Cincinnati completed the totally unexpected sweep and was crowned World Champions.

Reds pitching limited the A's to eight runs and a .207 batting average in the four games, while A's pitchers allowed 22 runs.

The next season was disappointing to the organization. Stewart tailed off to 11-11 and Welch dropped to 12-13. Moore won 17 and Eckersley saved 43, but the staff was not sharp.

It was also a strange season at the plate. Lansford was lost due to a ski-mobile accident in the off-season and McGwire lost his batting eye, hitting .201 with 22 home runs. Canseco led the team with 44 homers, however.

The 1992 season was one of La Russa's most rewarding. The A's overcame a rash of injuries to hold off the defending World Champion Twins by six games. Eckersley converted 51 of 54 save opportunities to win the Cy Young and MVP awards.

The big news was the trade of Canseco to Texas for a package that brought Ruben Sierra and Bobby Witt to the A's. Also, Rickey Henderson finally broke Brock's stolen base record. McGwire bounced back to hit .268 with 42 home runs, while Lansford's .262 average and continued great defense was an asset to a team in transition.

In the ALCS, though, the Blue Jays began their own little dynasty by simply wearing down the emotionally and physically drained Athletics. After splitting two games in Toronto, the A's lost the first two in Oakland before Stewart pitched a complete-game victory to force a return to Toronto. But in Canada, the Jays made quick

work of Mike Moore and advanced to the World Series against Atlanta.

With the season concluded and the front office facing budgetary constraints, the A's decided to pursue potential free agents Steinbach, McGwire, Sierra and pitcher Ron Darling. They watched Stewart and Moore sign elsewhere, then lost Weiss in expansion maneuvering and Lansford to retirement.

The 1993 season showed the effect of age and critical personnel losses. When McGwire went down early with a heel injury and Dave Henderson hobbled by chronic leg problems, La Russa was forced to improvise with his line-up, using several untried players in daily roles.

On the field, Brent Gates earned raves at second base and Craig Paquette gained experience at third. Gates and designated hitter Troy Neel hit .290 apiece, and Sierra drove in 101 runs.

Then, during the winter, Rickey Henderson—dealt to Toronto during the Jays' 1993 stretch drive—signed a free agent agreement to return to Oakland for 1994.

The 1994 season brought to the major leagues a three-division alignment per league. The Giants and A's prepared as usual at their respective Spring Training camps in Arizona before returning to the Bay Area for their traditional "Bay Bridge" exhibition series. To honor the area's past, both teams "turned back the clock," the A's wearing the uniforms of the Oakland Oaks and the Giants adorning themselves in old-time Seals uniforms.

The memory of the Bay Area's rich baseball tradition had come alive again. ❖

CHAPTER **31**

# AN IMPROBABLE DREAM

The 1992 announcement of the pending sale of the Giants to an investor group in Florida sent shock waves throughout the Bay Area, Northern California and the rest of the United States. The announcement prompted several groups to mobilize efforts to keep the Giants in San Francisco.

Tampa Bay's offer caught new Mayor Frank Jordan flat-footed, and Jordan quickly responded by initiating a campaign that combined City Hall's resources with the Giants' fan base in Northern California. Giants fans wrote thousands of letters to influential owners and officials. The sale appeared headed for completion but National League officials were seriously concerned about giving up Northern California to the American League. American League officials were equally concerned over the possibility of a second National League team placed in the lucrative Florida market.

With local sports agent Leigh Steinberg and CBS executive Larry Baer working to locate investors, hope remained for San Francisco. Several votes by the club owners that would have confirmed the sale were delayed, which gave local interests more time to put together a counter-offer.

The period between August 7 and November 10, 1992 seemed like an eternity for local fans. And it was another month before the local group, headed by Safeway CEO Peter Magowan and local investor Walter Shorenstein, came to an agreement with Lurie and the National League on the purchase of the Giants.

Even before the National League granted final approval to the new group, Magowan, as managing partner, selected Bob Quinn as general manager. Dusty Baker was then hired to manage the team. Together, Magowan and Quinn pulled off the coup of the winter by signing free agent outfielder Barry Bonds to a multi-year contract.

The new owners also developed plans to make Candlestick Park a better place to watch a game. A full scoreboard in right field, padded outfield fences, bleachers right behind the left field fence and a variety of food choices were the most notable changes made at the ballpark.

Coming out of Spring Training, most experts predicted the Giants would finish in the bottom half of the division. Pitching was expected to be the major weakness, but the staff got excellent early season results from John Burkett, Bill Swift and Bud Black. The bullpen usually was able to finish when the starters could not. Middle

Dusty Baker played most of his career with the Dodgers but quickly became a favorite of Giants fans when he managed San Francisco to the brink of the N.L. West pennant in 1993.

Padres. McGriff came to Atlanta and immediately put on a display of home run hitting. His teammates picked up the pace and the Braves started winning.

The Giants endured a string of injuries. Black and Wilson were both disabled with arm woes, while Jackson was lost temporarily with a bruised knee. The remainder of the staff started to show the strain of overwork.

From the All-Star break to August 22, the Braves played .722 ball, winning 26 of 36, but only reduced the Giants' lead by 1½ games. Entering a crucial three-game series with the Giants on August 23, the Braves had to sweep to keep any hopes alive of catching the Giants.

The Braves did sweep at Candlestick, closing to 4½ games and sending chills of apprehension up the backs of Giants faithful. In a week, the Giants would play three more against the Braves in Atlanta, their last head-to-head meetings of the season.

To reinforce the tired and injured pitching staff, Quinn signed free agent Scott Sanderson and traded for

Rod Beck, a hard-throwing right-hander, became the stopper in Dusty Baker's bullpen in 1993, consistently putting out fires as the Giants challenged for the division title.

relief work by Dave Burba and Bryan Hickerson set the table for Mike Jackson to shoot fastballs by weary batters before giving way to closer Rod Beck, who mixed a wicked splitter with menacing glowers from the mound.

At bat, Bonds and Williams got off to exceptional starts and led the league in run production and batting average. Will Clark suffered through a horrendous early season slump but found his batting stroke again in June. Willie McGee and Robby Thompson soon climbed into the top 10 in batting average, and unexpected support came from Kirt Manwaring and Royce Clayton. Darren Lewis established himself as a Gold Glove performer, setting a major league record for errorless games.

## A COMMANDING LEAD

The Giants held a 9½-game lead over the favored Atlanta Braves at the All-Star break. But as the August trading deadline approached, the Braves acquired first baseman Fred McGriff in a trade with the San Diego

Barry Bonds' magnificent 1993 season, which produced his third MVP award in four seasons, prompted many experts to call him the greatest left fielder of all time.

Jim DeShaies from the Twins. The long-awaited debut of Salomon Torres was at hand as the young right-hander was recalled from Phoenix just before the September roster deadline. Torres got his inaugural start on Sunday, August 29, against the Florida Marlins. Torres did not disappoint as he defeated Florida and came back five days later to defeat St. Louis on the road.

The second Atlanta series was sandwiched between the Florida and St. Louis series. After the Braves took the first game, pinch-hitter John Patterson, in his first major league at-bat of the season, hit a dramatic home run to win the second game. The Braves took the final game to slice an additional game off the Giants' lead. After the St. Louis series, the Giants returned to Candlestick Park where the Giants experienced their only slump of the season, losing eight straight.

The slump ended against Cincinnati when the Giants won 13-0. But the damage had been done. Over a 21-game span, the Braves gained 11½ games in the standings, climbing from 7½ games out to a four-game lead.

Only 16 games remained for the Giants to regroup and make up four games in the standings . . . and they did it in 11. In the 158th game of the season, the Giants won their 100th game by defeating the Rockies 6-4. But the next afternoon, the Braves beat the Astros and the Giants lost to Colorado 5-3, putting San Francisco one game back with four games to play.

In the last series of the regular season, San Francisco traveled south to play Los Angeles, while the Braves had one more game against the Astros before concluding with three games against Colorado at home. Both teams needed to sweep their remaining games.

Houston dumped the Braves to win their series, 2-1, while at Chavez Ravine, Swift won his 21st, making the race a tie again. The Giants and Braves each won their next two games, keeping themselves dead even at 103-58 going into the Sunday finale.

The Giants and Braves had slugged it out over 161 games to no advantage. The Braves sent Cy Young winner Tom Glavine, shooting for his 22nd win, against the Rockies. From his weary staff, Baker selected Torres.

After his two initial starts, Torres had gone 1-4. Greg Gross, 0-2 against the Giants in 1993, was the Dodgers' starter. The Giants soon knew they had to win because Atlanta had just beaten the Rockies for a 13-0 record against the new franchise. However, the Dodgers poured it on throughout the day and eliminated their rivals 12-1.

Predicted to be a .500 team, the Giants had won 44 more games than they had lost. Predicted to have a poor pitching staff, there were two 20-game winners and possibly the most dominant closer in the league. Predicted to have a weak bench, the reserves played a critical part in replacing the regulars who went down.

Despite the ultimate failure to win the division, there was a great deal of pride and satisfaction with the 1993 Giants. In one year the city of San Francisco had saved its franchise and had rewarded its baseball fans with an improbable season it would long remember. It wasn't a dream season, but the season was still a dream come true, offering much hope for 1994—even without Will Clark, who signed a free agent contract with Texas.

The long-term prospects of the franchise remained in doubt as Giants ownership and San Francisco politicians continued to look for possible stadium sites within and adjacent to the city limits.

Yet while the future is always uncertain, there can be no doubt about the major roles San Francisco, Oakland and the greater Bay Area have played in the history of professional baseball. From Van Haltren and Arlett to DiMaggio and Henderson, from the San Francisco Seals' dynasty of the 1920s to the Oakland A's in the 1970s and 1980s, no other region in the United States can match the Bay Area's rich legacy. ❖

# APPENDIX

# THE BAY AREA BASEBALL TEAMS

## OAKLAND—PACIFIC COAST LEAGUE

| YEAR | MANAGER | POS | RECORD | PCT. |
|------|---------|-----|--------|------|
| 1903 | Pete Lohman | 6 | 89-126 | .414 |
| 1904 | Pete Lohman | 4 | 116-109 | .516 |
| 1905 | Pete Lohman/Geo. Van Haltren | 4 | 103-119 | .464 |
| 1906 | George Van Haltren | 5 | 77-110 | .411 |
| 1907 | George Van Haltren | 3 | 97-101 | .489 |
| 1908 | George Van Haltren | 4 | 83-116 | .417 |
| 1909 | Geo. Van Haltren/Bill Reidy | 5 | 88-125 | .413 |
| 1910 | Harry Wolverton | 2 | 122-98 | .555 |
| 1911 | Harry Wolverton | 3 | 111-99 | .528 |
| 1912 | BAYARD "BUD" SHARPE | 1 | 120-83 | .591 |
| 1913 | Carl Mitze/Art Devlin | 6 | 90-120 | .429 |
| 1914 | Art Devlin/Tyler Christian | 6 | 79-133 | .372 |
| 1915 | Tyler Christian/Rowdy Elliott | 5 | 93-113 | .451 |
| 1916 | Rowdy Elliott/Del Howard | 6 | 72-136 | .346 |
| 1917 | Del Howard | 5 | 103-108 | .488 |
| 1918 | Del Howard | 6 | 40-63* | .388 |
| 1919 | Del Howard | 5 | 86-96 | .473 |
| 1920 | Del Howard | 6 | 95-103 | .480 |
| 1921 | Del Howard | 5 | 101-85 | .543 |
| 1922 | Del Howard | 6 | 88-112 | .440 |
| 1923 | Ivan Howard | 7 | 91-111 | .450 |
| 1924 | Ivan Howard | 4 | 103-99 | .510 |
| 1925 | Ivan Howard | 6 | 88-112 | .440 |
| 1926 | Ivan Howard | 2 | 111-92 | .547 |
| 1927 | IVAN HOWARD | 1 | 120-75 | .615 |
| 1928 | Ivan Howard | 5 | 91-100 | .476 |
| 1929 | Ivan Howard | 4 | 111-91 | .549 |
| 1930 | Carl Zamloch | 5 | 97-103 | .485 |
| 1931 | Carl Zamloch | 5 | 86-101 | .460 |
| 1932 | Carl Zamloch | 7 | 80-107 | .428 |
| 1933 | Ray Brubaker | 5 | 93-92 | .502 |
| 1934 | Ray Brubaker/Art Veltman | 5 | 90-98 | .479 |
| 1935 | Oscar Vitt | 3 | 91-83 | .523 |
| 1936 | Bill Meyer | 3T | 95-81 | .540 |
| 1937 | Bill Meyer | 7 | 79-98 | .446 |
| 1938 | Dutch Zwilling | 8 | 65-113 | .410 |
| 1939 | Johnny Vergez | 7 | 78-98 | .443 |
| 1940 | Johnny Vergez | 3 | 94-84 | .528 |
| 1941 | Johnny Vergez | 5T | 81-95 | .460 |
| 1942 | Johnny Vergez | 6 | 85-92 | .480 |
| 1943 | Johnny Vergez | 5T | 73-82 | .471 |
| 1944 | Dolph Camilli | 3T | 86-83 | .509 |
| 1945 | Dolph Camilli/Bill Raimondi | 5 | 90-93 | .492 |
| 1946 | Casey Stengel | 2 | 111-72 | .607 |
| 1947 | Casey Stengel | 4 | 96-90 | .516 |
| 1948 | CASEY STENGEL | 1 | 114-74 | .606 |
| 1949 | Charlie Dressen | 2 | 104-83 | .556 |
| 1950 | CHARLIE DRESSEN | 1 | 118-82 | .590 |
| 1951 | Mel Ott | 5 | 80-88 | .476 |
| 1952 | Mel Ott | 2 | 104-76 | .578 |
| 1953 | Augie Galan | 7 | 77-103 | .428 |
| 1954 | Charlie Dressen | 3 | 85-82 | .509 |
| 1955 | Lefty O'Doul | 7 | 77-95 | .448 |

* Season shortened by World War I.

## MISSION—PACIFIC COAST LEAGUE

| YEAR | MANAGER | POS | RECORD | PCT. |
|------|---------|-----|--------|------|
| 1914 | | 5 | 90-121# | .426 |
| 1926 | Walter McCredie/Walter Schmidt/ Bill Leard | 3 | 106-94 | .530 |
| 1927 | Bill Leard/Al Walters/ Harry Hooper | 7 | 86-110 | .439 |
| 1928 | Wade Killefer | 4 | 99-92 | .586 |
| 1929 | WADE KILLEFER | 1 | 123-78@ | .612 |
| 1930 | Wade Killefer | 7 | 91-110 | .453 |
| 1931 | George H. Burns/Joe Devine | 7 | 84-103 | .449 |
| 1932 | Joe Devine/Fred Hofmann | 8 | 71-117 | .378 |
| 1933 | Fred Hofmann | 7 | 79-108 | .422 |
| 1934 | Gabby Street | 2 | 101-85 | .543 |
| 1935 | Gabby Street | 5 | 87-87 | .500 |
| 1936 | Willie Kamm | 6 | 88-88 | .500 |
| 1937 | Willie Kamm | 8 | 73-105 | .410 |

\# The Sacramento team vacated Sacramento in mid-September, relocating in San Francisco as the Missions. At the end of the season, the franchise was sold to William Lane who moved the team to Salt Lake City.

@ The 1929 Missions had the best overall record, but lost a split season playoff series to the Hollywood Sheiks.

## SAN FRANCISCO—PACIFIC COAST LEAGUE

| YEAR | MANAGER | POS | RECORD | PCT. |
|------|---------|-----|--------|------|
| 1903 | Charles Irwin | 4 | 107-110 | .493 |
| 1904 | Charles Irwin | 5 | 101-117 | .463 |
| 1905 | Parke Wilson | 2 | 125-110 | .556 |
| 1906 | Parke Wilson/Jack Gleason | 4 | 91-84 | .520 |
| 1907 | Danny Long | 2 | 104-99 | .515 |
| 1908 | Danny Long | 3 | 100-104 | .490 |
| 1909 | DANNY LONG/JACK GLEASON | 1 | 132-80 | .623 |
| 1910 | Danny Long | 3 | 114-106 | .518 |
| 1911 | Danny Long | 5 | 95-112 | .459 |
| 1912 | Danny Long | 5 | 89-115 | .436 |
| 1913 | Danny Long | 4 | 104-103 | .502 |
| 1914 | Del Howard | 3 | 115-96 | .545 |
| 1915 | HARRY WOLVERTON | 1 | 118-89 | .570 |
| 1916 | Harry Wolverton | 4 | 104-102 | .504 |
| 1917 | HARRY WOLVERTON/JERRY DOWNS | 1 | 119-93 | .561 |
| 1918 | Charlie Graham | 3 | 51-51* | .500 |
| 1919 | Charlie Graham | 4 | 84-94 | .472 |
| 1920 | Charlie Graham | 4 | 103-96 | .517 |
| 1921 | Charlie Graham | 3 | 106-82 | .564 |
| 1922 | JOHN "DOTS" MILLER | 1 | 127-72 | .538 |
| 1923 | JOHN "DOTS" MILLER/BERT ELLISON | 1 | 124-77 | .617 |
| 1924 | Bert Ellison | 3 | 108-93 | .537 |
| 1925 | BERT ELLISON | 1 | 128-71 | .643 |
| 1926 | Richard "Nick" Williams | 8 | 84-116 | .420 |
| 1927 | Richard "Nick" Williams | 2 | 106-90 | .541 |
| 1928 | RICHARD "NICK" WILLIAMS | 1 | 120-71 | .628 |
| 1929 | Richard "Nick" Williams | 2 | 114-87 | .567 |
| 1930 | Richard "Nick" Williams | 4 | 101-98 | .508 |
| 1931 | RICHARD "NICK" WILLIAMS | 1 | 107-80 | .572 |
| 1932 | James "Ike" Caveney | 4 | 96-90 | .516 |
| 1933 | James "Ike" Caveney | 6 | 81-106 | .433 |
| 1934 | James "Ike" Caveney | 4 | 93-95 | .495 |
| 1935 | FRANK "LEFTY" O'DOUL | 1 | 103-70 | .595 |
| 1936 | Frank "Lefty" O'Doul | 7 | 83-93 | .472 |
| 1937 | Frank "Lefty" O'Doul | 2 | 98-80 | .551 |
| 1938 | Frank "Lefty" O'Doul | 4 | 93-85 | .522 |
| 1939 | Frank "Lefty" O'Doul | 2 | 97-78 | .554 |
| 1940 | Frank "Lefty" O'Doul | 7 | 81-97 | .455 |
| 1941 | Frank "Lefty" O'Doul | 5 | 81-95 | .460 |
| 1942 | Frank "Lefty" O'Doul | 5 | 88-90 | .494 |
| 1943 | Frank "Lefty" O'Doul | 2 | 89-66 | .574 |
| 1944 | Frank "Lefty" O'Doul | 3 | 86-83 | .509 |
| 1945 | Frank "Lefty" O'Doul | 4 | 96-87 | .525 |
| 1946 | FRANK "LEFTY" O'DOUL | 1 | 115-68 | .628 |
| 1947 | Frank "Lefty" O'Doul | 2 | 105-82 | .561 |
| 1948 | Frank "Lefty" O'Doul | 2 | 112-76 | .596 |
| 1949 | Frank "Lefty" O'Doul | 8 | 84-103 | .449 |
| 1950 | Frank "Lefty" O'Doul | 5 | 100-100 | .500 |
| 1951 | Frank "Lefty" O'Doul | 8 | 74-93 | .443 |
| 1952 | Tommy Heath | 7 | 78-102 | .433 |
| 1953 | Tommy Heath | 5 | 91-89 | .506 |
| 1954 | Tommy Heath | 4 | 84-84 | .500 |
| 1955 | Tommy Heath | 6 | 80-92 | .465 |
| 1956 | Eddie Joost/Joe Gordon | 6 | 77-88 | .467 |
| 1957 | JOE GORDON | 1 | 101-67 | .601 |

## OAKLAND ATHLETICS—AMERICAN LEAGUE

| YEAR | MANAGER | POS | RECORD | PCT. |
|------|---------|-----|--------|------|
| 1968 | Bob Kennedy | 6 | 82-80 | .506 |
| 1969 | Hank Bauer/John McNamara | 2 | 88-74 | .543 |
| 1970 | John McNamara | 2 | 89-73 | .549 |
| 1971 | Dick Williams | *1 | 101-60 | .627 |
| 1972 | Dick Williams | ***1 | 93-62 | .600 |
| 1973 | Dick Williams | ***1 | 94-68 | .580 |
| 1974 | Alvin Dark | ***1 | 90-72 | .556 |
| 1975 | Alvin Dark | *1 | 98-64 | .605 |
| 1976 | Chuck Tanner | 2 | 87-74 | .540 |
| 1977 | Jack McKeon/Bob Winkles | 7 | 63-98 | .391 |
| 1978 | Bob Winkles/Jack McKeon | 6 | 69-93 | .426 |
| 1979 | Jim Marshall | 7 | 54-108 | .333 |
| 1980 | Billy Martin | 2 | 83-79 | .512 |
| 1981 | Billy Martin | *1 | 64-45 | .587 |
| 1982 | Billy Martin | 5 | 68-94 | .420 |
| 1983 | Steve Boros | 4 | 74-88 | .457 |
| 1984 | Steve Boros/Jackie Moore | 4 | 77-85 | .475 |
| 1985 | Jackie Moore | 4 | 77-85 | .475 |
| 1986 | Jackie Moore/Jeff Newman/ | | | |
|      | Tony La Russa | 3T | 76-86 | .469 |
| 1987 | Tony La Russa | 3 | 81-81 | .500 |
| 1988 | Tony La Russa | **1 | 104-58 | 642 |
| 1989 | Tony La Russa | ***1 | 99-63 | .611 |
| 1990 | Tony La Russa | **1 | 103-59 | .635 |
| 1991 | Tony La Russa | 4 | 84-78 | .519 |
| 1992 | Tony La Russa | *1 | 96-66 | .593 |
| 1993 | Tony La Russa | 7 | 68-94 | .420 |

\* American League Western Division Champion
\*\* American League Champion
\*\*\* World Champion

## SAN FRANCISCO GIANTS—NATIONAL LEAGUE

| YEAR | MANAGER | POS | RECORD | PCT. |
|------|---------|-----|--------|------|
| 1958 | Bill Rigney | 3 | 80-74 | .519 |
| 1959 | Bill Rigney | 3 | 83-71 | .539 |
| 1960 | Bill Rigney/Tom Sheehan | 5 | 79-75 | .513 |
| 1961 | Alvin Dark | 3 | 85-69 | .552 |
| 1962 | Alvin Dark | **1 | 103-62 | .624 |
| 1963 | Alvin Dark | 3 | 88-74 | .543 |
| 1964 | Alvin Dark | 4 | 90-72 | .556 |
| 1965 | Herman Franks | 2 | 95-67 | .586 |
| 1966 | Herman Franks | 2 | 93-68 | .578 |
| 1967 | Herman Franks | 2 | 91-71 | .652 |
| 1968 | Herman Franks | 2 | 88-74 | .543 |
| 1969 | Clyde King | 2 | 90-72 | .556 |
| 1970 | Clyde King/Charlie Fox | 3 | 86-76 | .531 |
| 1971 | Charlie Fox | *1 | 90-72 | .556 |
| 1972 | Charlie Fox | 5 | 69-86 | .445 |
| 1973 | Charlie Fox | 3 | 88-74 | .543 |
| 1974 | Charlie Fox/Wes Westrum | 5 | 72-90 | .444 |
| 1975 | Wes Westrum | 3 | 80-81 | .497 |
| 1976 | Bill Rigney | 4 | 74-88 | .457 |
| 1977 | Joe Altobelli | 4 | 75-87 | .463 |
| 1978 | Joe Altobelli | 3 | 89-73 | .549 |
| 1979 | Joe Altobelli/Dave Bristol | 4 | 71-91 | .438 |
| 1980 | Dave Bristol | 5 | 75-86 | .466 |
| 1981 | Frank Robinson | 4 | 56-55 | .505 |
| 1982 | Frank Robinson | 3 | 87-75 | .537 |
| 1983 | Frank Robinson | 5 | 79-83 | .488 |
| 1984 | Frank Robinson/Danny Ozark | 6 | 66-96 | .407 |
| 1985 | Jim Davenport/Roger Craig | 6 | 62-100 | .383 |
| 1986 | Roger Craig | 3 | 83-79 | .512 |
| 1987 | Roger Craig | *1 | 90-72 | .556 |
| 1988 | Roger Craig | 4 | 83-79 | .512 |
| 1989 | Roger Craig | **1 | 92-70 | .568 |
| 1990 | Roger Craig | 3 | 85-77 | .525 |
| 1991 | Roger Craig | 4 | 75-87 | .463 |
| 1992 | Roger Craig | 5 | 72-90 | .444 |
| 1993 | Dusty Baker | 2 | 103-59 | .636 |

\* National League Western Division Champion
\*\* National League Champion

# ROSTERS OF PENNANT WINNERS

## PACIFIC COAST LEAGUE

1909 SAN FRANCISCO SEALS. Managers: Danny Long, Jack Gleason. Catchers: Claude Berry, Nick Williams. Pitchers: Rex Ames, Berger, Pete Browning, Carmen, Cooper, Joe Corbett, Jim Durham, Frank Eastley, Ed Griffin, Cack Henley, Mielke, Harry Stewart, Ralph Willis. Infielders: Roy McArdle, Kid Mohler, Howard Mundorff, Tom Tennant, Rollie Zeider. Outfielders: Ping Bodie, George Davis, Henry Melchior, Jimmy Lewis, R. Miller, John Williams. Trainer: Denny Carroll.

1912 OAKLAND OAKS. Manager: Bayard "Bud" Sharpe. Catchers: Carl Mitze, Bill Rohrer, John Tiedemann. Pitchers: Harry Ables, W.F. Barrenkamp, Tyler Christian, Blaine Durbin, Howard Gregory, Hamilton, Jack Killilay, Al Loomis, Bill Malarkey, Elmer Martinoni, Henry Olmstead, Cy Parkin, Henry Pernoll, Ashley Pope, Lloyd Ramsey. Infielders: Albert Cook, Jimmy Frick, Gus Hetling, Bill Leard, Bud Sharpe. Outfielders: Ody Abbott, Bert Coy, Bert Delmas, Claire Patterson, Elmer Zacher. Trainer: Denny Carroll.

1915 SAN FRANCISCO SEALS. Manager: Harry Wolverton. Catchers: Cy Block, Walter Schmidt, Louis Sepulveda. Pitchers: Harry Ables, Spider Baum, Curley Brown, Pug Cavet, Johnny Couch, Tyler Christian, Dent, Charlie Fanning, Jack Killilay, W. Reisigel, Chief Smith, Bill Steen. Infielders: Chick Autrey, Beatty, Sammy Bohne, Roy Corhan, Jerry Downs, Harry Heilmann, Bobby Jones, Bill Leard. Outfielders: Allen, Ping Bodie, Justin Fitzgerald, Biff Schaller, Paul Meloan. Trainer: Denny Carroll.

1917 SAN FRANCISCO SEALS. Managers: Harry Wolverton, Jerry Downs. Catchers: Del Baker, Ray McKee, Louis Sepulveda, Tom Stevens. Pitchers: Spider Baum, Frank Decanniere, Red Erickson, Chief Johnson, Rudy Kallio, Lefty O'Doul, Red Oldham, Chief Smith, Bill Steen. Infielders: Roy Corhan, Jerry Downs, Herb Hunter, Phil Koerner, Charlie Pick. Outfielders: Jacinto Calvo, Justin Fitzgerald, George Maisel, Biff Schaller. Trainer: Denny Carroll.

1922 SAN FRANCISCO SEALS. Manager: John "Dots" Miller. Catchers: Sam Agnew, Archie Yelle. Pitchers: Ernie Alten, Harry Courtney, Fritz Coumbe, Daka Davis, Carl Gillenwater, Bob Geary, Shovel Hodge, Herb McQuaid, Doug McWeeney, Oliver Mitchell, Pat Shea, Jim Scott. Infielders: Bert Ellison, Willie Kamm, Pete Kilduff, Dots Miller, Ralph Miller, Jimmy O'Connell, Hal Rhyne, Dee Walsh. Outfielders: Pete Compton, Justin Fitzgerald, Joe Kelley, Charlie See, Gene Valla. Trainer: Denny Carroll.

1923 SAN FRANCISCO SEALS. Managers: John "Dots" Miller, Bert Ellison. Catchers: Sam Agnew, Pete Ritchie, Archie Yelle, Andy Vargas. Pitchers: Ernie Alten, Tim Buckley, Harry Courtney, Bob Geary, Marty Griffin, Shovel Hodge, Oliver Mitchell, Doug McWeeney, Jim Scott, Pat Shea, George Stanton. Infielders: Bert Ellison, Ray Flashkamper, Pete Kilduff, Eddie Montague, Eddie Mulligan, Hal Rhyne, Dee Walsh. Outfielders: Pete Compton, Erich, Tim Hendryx, Joe Kelley, Phil Tanner, Paul Waner, Gene Valla. Trainer: Denny Carroll.

1925 SAN FRANCISCO SEALS. Manager: Bert Ellison. Catchers: Andy Vargas, Pete Ritchie, Archie Yelle. Pitchers: Jim Crockett, Bud DeMeyer, Bob Geary, Marty Griffin, Oliver Mitchell, Dick Moudy, Doug McWeeney, Ed Pfeffer, Guy Williams. Infielders: Bert Ellison, Ray Flashkamper, Joe Kelley, Pete Kilduff, Eddie Mulligan, Norbie Paynter, Hal Rhyne, Vern Stivers, Gus Suhr. Outfielders: Frank Brower, Smead Jolley, Tim Hendryx, Gene Valla, Paul Waner, Lloyd Waner, George McKnew. Trainer: Denny Carroll.

1927 OAKLAND OAKS. Manager: Ivan Howard. Catchers: Del Baker, Al Bool, Ernest Lombardi, Addison Read. Pitchers: George Boehler, Wilbur Cooper, Howard Craghead, Pete Daglia, Art Delaney, Leo Dickerman, Pudgy Gold, Bob Hasty, Harry Krause, Herm Sparks. Infielders: Ray Brubaker, Jimmy Caveney, Jack Fenton, Louie Guisto, Lyn Lary, Leo Metz, Art Murphy, Jimmie Reese. Outfielders: Buzz Arlett, Joe Bratcher, Tony Governor, Ralph Shinners, Gene Valla.

1928 SAN FRANCISCO SEALS. Manager: Richard "Nick" Williams. Catchers: Bob Reed, Joe Sprinz, Andy Vargas. Pitchers: Les Ferguson, Val Glynn, Elmer Jacobs, Gordon Jones, Walter Mails, Oliver Mitchell, Dick Moudy, Herb May, Dutch Ruether, Hollis Thurston, Junk Walters. Infielders: Jimmy Caveney, Frankie Crosetti, Jerry Donovan, Solly Mishkin, Babe Pinelli, Hal Rhyne, Gus Suhr. Outfielders: Earl Averill, Ping Bodie, Smead Jolley, Roy Johnson, Bill Jones, Frank Welch. Trainer: Denny Carroll.

1929 MISSION REDS. The Missions won the first half, but lost the second half by one game to Hollywood, and then lost the playoff series. Mission had the best overall record. Manager: Wade "Red" Killefer. Catchers: Red Baldwin, Bill Brenzel, Freddie Hofmann. Pitchers: Charlie Biggs, George Caster, Bert Cole, Wilbur Hubbell, Jack Knott, Harry Krause, Dutch Leiber, C.A. Lockwood, Herb McQuaid, Clyde Nance, Mert Nelson, Ernie Nevers, Herm Pillette, Dutch Ruether, Don Weaver. Infielders: Mickey Finn, Eddie Mulligan, Bill Rodda, Jack Sherlock, Gordy Slade. Outfielders: Fred Berger, Ike Boone, Seacap Christensen, Fuzzy Hufft, Pete Scott, Newell Morse. Trainer: William "Shine" Scott.

1931 SAN FRANCISCO SEALS. The Seals, winners of the second half, defeated Hollywood in the playoff series. The Seals also had the best overall record. Manager: Richard "Nick" Williams. Catchers: Red Baldwin, Chief Mealy, Pop Penebsky, Joe Ward, Bill Wilson. Pitchers: Johnny Babich, Billings, Curtis Davis, Art Delaney, Ken Douglas, Sam Gibson, Bill Henderson, Art Jacobs, Art McDougal, Guido Simoni, Hal Turpin, Claude Willoughby, Jimmy Zinn. Infielders: Jimmy Caveney, Frankie Crosetti, Art Garibaldi, Jimmy Keesey, Babe Pinelli, Julie Wera. Outfielders: Jerry Donovan, Roy Frazier, Nelson Hawkes, Mike Hunt, Prince Oana, Ernie Sulik, Red Wingo. Trainer: Denny Carroll.

1935 SAN FRANCISCO SEALS. Manager: Francis J. "Lefty" O'Doul. Coach: Larry Woodall. Catchers: Joe Becker, Neil Clifford, Vince Monzo, Larry Woodall. Pitchers: Win Ballou, Bert Cole, Bob Cole, Jimmy Densmore, Sam Gibson, Roy Joiner, Walter Mails, Minietti, Floyd Newkirk, Ken Sheehan, Eddie Stutz, Hal Stitzel, Jimmy Zinn. Infielders: Lenny Backer, Steve Barath, Art Garibaldi, Frank Gira, Brooks Holder, Les Powers, Hal Rhyne. Outfielders: Joe DiMaggio, Roy Lamphere, Joe Marty, Ted Norbert, Lefty O'Doul, John Thomas. Trainer: Bobby Johnson.

1946 SAN FRANCISCO SEALS. Manager: Lefty O'Doul. Coaches: Joe Sprinz, Del Young. Catchers: Mel Ivy, Bruce Ogrodowski, Norm Schleuter, Joe Sprinz. Pitchers: Ray Harrell, Larry Jansen, Bob Jensen, Al Lien, Dale Mathewson, Cliff Melton, Emmett O'Neill, Elmer Orella, Larry Powell, Frank Rosso, Frank Seward, Eddie Stutz, Jim Tobin, Bill Werle. Infielders: Willie Enos, Ferris Fain, Ray Perry, Harry Goorabian, Joe Hoover, Ted Jennings, Hugh Luby, Roy Nicely, Bones Sanders, Del Young. Outfielders: Joe Brovia, Vince DiMaggio, Kermit Lewis, Doug Loane, Charlie Peterson, Sal Taormina, Neill Sheridan, Dino Restelli, Don White, Bernie Uhalt. Trainer: Leo Hughes.

1948 OAKLAND OAKS. Manager: Charles D. "Casey" Stengel. Coach: Johnny Babich. Catchers: Eddie Fernandes, Gene Lillard, Ernie Lombardi, Billy Raimondi. Pitchers: Lee Alton, Ralph Buxton, John Conant, Charlie Gassaway, Eddie Graham, Tom Hafey, Will Hafey, Damon Hayes, Lloyd Hittle, Earl Jones, Bob Klinger, Thornton Lee, Tony Ponce, Jack Salveson, Jim Tobin, Lou Tost, Les Webber, Aldon Wilkie. Infielders: Merrill Combs, Nick Etten, Norm Grabar, Ray Hamrick, Dario Lodigiani, Cookie Lavagetto, Billy Martin, Allen Maul, Les Scarsella, Maurice Van Robays. Outfielders: Loyd Christopher, Mel Duezabou, Eddie Graham, Brooks Holder, Cliff McClain, George Metkovich, Eddie Murphy, Walt Pocekay, Eddie Samcoff, Les Scarsella, Bernie Uhalt. Trainer: Jesse "Red" Adams.

1950 OAKLAND OAKS. Manager: Charles Dressen. Coaches: Augie Galan, George L. Kelly. Catchers: Jim Fiscalini, Eddie Malone, Rafael Noble, Don Padgett, Bud Sheely. Pitchers: George Bamberger, Hank Behrman, Dave Dahle, Bill Dietrich, Charlie Gassaway, Allen Gettel, Ernie Groth, Earl Harrist, Earl Jones, Frank Nelson, Jay Ragni, Clyde Shoun, George Stanich, Bill Tanner, Forrest Thompson, Lou Tost, Jim Tote. Infielders: Lil Arnerich, Don Fracchia, Augie Galan, Ray Hamrick, Billy Herman, Bobby Hofman, Al Kozar, Cookie Lavagetto, Jim Marshall, Allan Maul, Mike McCormick, Eddie Samcoff, Artie Wilson, Roy Zimmerman. Outfielders: Loyd Christopher, Mel Duezabou, George Metkovich, Jay Ragni, Earl Rapp, Bill Tanner, Bill Taylor, Dick Wakefield, Roy Weatherly. Trainer: Jesse "Red" Adams.

1957 SAN FRANCISCO SEALS. Manager: Joe Gordon. Coach: Glenn "Cap" Wright. Catchers: Nini Tornay, Eddie Sadowski, Haywood Sullivan. Pitchers: Bill Abernathie, Bob Chakales, Harry Dorish, Tom Hurd, Leo Kiely, Jim Konstanty, Walter Masterson, John McCall, Walter Payne, Duane Pillette, Bill Prout, Al Schroll, Bob Smith, Jack Spring, Bert Thiel, Bob Thollander, Roy Tinney. Infielders: Ken Aspromonte, Bob DiPietro, Joe Gordon, Pumpsie Green, Grady Hatton, Doug Hubacek, Curt Jensen, Frank Kellert, Harry Malmberg, Jack Phillips, Lou Stringer, Joe Tanner, Sal Taormina. Outfielders: Hal Grote, Marty Keough, Albie Pearson, Bill Renna, Tom Umphlett. Trainer: Leo Hughes.

1962 SAN FRANCISCO GIANTS—National League Champions. Manager: Alvin Dark. Coaches: Larry Jansen, Whitey Lockman, Wes Westrum. Catchers: Ed Bailey, Tom Haller, John Orsino, Joe Pignatano. Pitchers: Bob Bolin, Jim Duffalo, Bob Garibaldi, Don Larsen, Dick LeMay, Juan Marichal, Mike McCormick, Stu Miller, Billy O'Dell, Gaylord Perry, Billy Pierce, Jack Sanford. Infielders: Ernie Bowman, Orlando Cepeda, Jim Davenport, Chuck Hiller, Jose Pagan, Cap Peterson, Dick Phillips. Outfielders: Felipe Alou, Matty Alou, Carl Boles, Harvey Kuenn, Willie Mays, Willie McCovey, Manny Mota, Bob Nieman. Trainer: Frank Bowman.

1971 SAN FRANCISCO GIANTS—Western Division Champions. Manager: Charlie Fox. Coaches: Larry Jansen, John McNamara, Ozzie Virgil, Wes Westrum. Catchers: Dick Dietz, Russ Gibson, Fran Healy, Dave Rader. Pitchers: Jim Barr, Ron Bryant, Don Carrithers, John Cumberland, Steve Hamilton, Jerry Johnson, Juan Marichal, Don McMahon, Gaylord Perry, Frank Reberger, Rich Robertson, Steve Stone, Jim Willoughby. Infielders: Jim Arnold, Frank Duffy, Tito Fuentes, Al Gallagher, Ed Goodson, Jim Ray Hart, Bob Heise, Frank Johnson, Hal Lanier, Willie McCovey, Chris Speier. Outfielders: Bobby Bonds, George Foster, Ken Henderson, Jimmy Howarth, Dave Kingman, Willie Mays, Jimmie Rosario, Floyd Wicker, Bernie Williams. Trainers: Leo Hughes, Al Wylder.

1971 OAKLAND A's:—Western Division Champions. Manager: Dick Williams. Coaches: Vern Hoscheit, Jerry Lumpe, Irv Noren, Bill Posedel. Catchers: Curt Blefary, Dave Duncan, Frank Fernandez, Gene Tenace. Pitchers: Vida Blue, Chuck Dobson, Rollie Fingers, Rob Gardner, Mudcat Grant, Catfish Hunter, Ron Klimkowski, Darold Knowles, Marcel Lachemann, Paul Lindblad, Bob Locker, Blue Moon Odom, Jim Panther, Daryl Patterson, Jim Roland, Diego Segui. Infielders: Dwain Anderson, Sal Bando, Larry Brown, Bert Campaneris, Ron Clark, Tommy Davis, Mike Epstein, Dick Green, Mike Hegan, Tony La Russa, Don Mincher. Outfielders: Felipe Alou, Adrian Garrett, George Hendrick, Steve Hovely, Reggie Jackson, Angel Mangual, Rick Monday, Joe Rudi, Ramon Webster. Trainer: Bill Jones.

1972 OAKLAND A's—World Champions. Manager: Dick Williams. Coaches: Jerry Adair, Vern Hoscheit, Irv Noren, Bill Posedel. Catchers: Dave Duncan, Larry Haney, Gene Tenace. Pitchers: Vida Blue, Chuck Dobson (DL), Rollie Fingers, Dave Hamilton, Ken Holtzman, Joel Horlen, Catfish Hunter, Mike Kilkenny, Darold Knowles, Bob Locker, Denny McLain, Blue Moon Odom, Jim Roland, Diego Segui, Don Shaw, Gary Waslewski. Infielders: Dwain Anderson, Sal Bando, Curt Blefary, Larry Brown, Bert Campaneris, Orlando Cepeda, Ron Clark, Tim Cullen, Mike Epstein, Dick Green, Mike Hegan, Ted Kubiak, Gonzalo Marquez, Marty Martinez, Dal Maxville, Bill McNulty, Don Mincher. Outfielders: Matty Alou, Brant Alyea, Bobby Brooks, Ollie Brown, Adrian Garrett, George Hendrick, Reggie Jackson, Allen Lewis, Angel Mangual, Joe Rudi, Art Shamsky, Bill Voss. Trainer: Joe Romo.

1973 OAKLAND A's—World Champions. Manager: Dick Williams. Coaches: Jerry Adair, Vern Hoscheit, Irv Noren, Wes Stock. Catchers: Ray Fosse, Larry Haney, Tom Hosley. Pitchers: Glenn Abbott, Vida Blue, Chuck Dobson, Rollie Fingers, Rob Gardner, Dave Hamilton, Ken Holtzman, Catfish Hunter, Darold Knowles, Paul Lindblad, Blue Moon Odom, Horacio Pina. Infielders: Mike Andrews, Sal Bando, Pat Bourque, Bert Campaneris, Phil Garner, Dick Green, Mike Hegan, Ted Kubiak, Dal Maxville, Rich McKinney, Gene Tenace, Manny Trillo. Outfielders: Jesus Alou, Rico Carty, Billy Conigliaro, Vic Davalillo, Reggie Jackson, Deron Johnson, Jay Johnstone, Allen Lewis, Angel Mangual, Jose Morales, Billy North, Joe Rudi. Trainer: Joe Romo.

1974 OAKLAND A's—World Champions. Manager: Alvin Dark. Coaches: Jerry Adair, Vern Hoscheit, Irv Noren, Wes Stock. Catchers: Ray Fosse, Larry Haney, Tim Hosley. Pitchers: Glenn Abbott, Vida

Blue, Rollie Fingers, Dave Hamilton, Ken Holtzman, Leon Hooten, Catfish Hunter, Darold Knowles, Paul Lindblad, Bob Locker (DL), Blue Moon Odom, Bill Parsons. Infielders: Sal Bando, Pat Bourque, Bert Campaneris, John Donaldson, Phil Garner, Dick Green, Jim Holt, Ted Kubiak, Dal Maxvill, Rich McKinney, Gaylen Pitts, Gene Tenace, Manny Trillo. Outfielders: Jesus Alou, Vic Davalillo, Reggie Jackson, Deron Johnson, Angel Mangual, Billy North, Joe Rudi, Champ Summers, Claudell Washington, Herb Washington. Trainer: Joe Romo.

1975 OAKLAND A's—Western Division Champions. Manager: Alvin Dark. Coaches: Bobby Hofman, Wes Stock, Bobby Winkles. Catchers: Ray Fosse, Larry Haney, Gene Tenace. Pitchers: Glenn Abbott, Stan Bahnsen, Vida Blue, Dick Bosman, Rollie Fingers, Dave Hamilton, Ken Holtzman, Paul Lindblad, Craig Mitchell, Mike Norris, Blue Moon Odom, Jim Perry, Sonny Siebert, Jim Todd. Infielders: Sal Bando, Bert Campaneris, Charlie Chant, Phil Garner, Billy Grabarkewitz, Tommy Harper, Jim Holt, Ted Kubiak, Ted Martinez, Dal Maxvill, Rich McKinney, Gaylen Pitts, Joe Rudi, Tommy Sandt, Cesar Tovar, Denny Walling. Outfielders: Matt Alexander, Don Hopkins, Reggie Jackson, Angel Mangual, Billy North, Claudell Washington, Herb Washington, Billy Williams. Trainer: Joe Romo.

1981 OAKLAND A's—Western Division Champions. Manager: Billy Martin. Coaches: Clete Boyer, Art Fowler, George Mitterwald, Jackie Moore. Catchers: Mike Heath, Bob Kearney, Jeff Newman. Pitchers: Dave Beard, Rich Bordi, Ed Figueroa, Dave Heaverlo, Jeff Jones, Matt Keough, Brian Kingman, Rick Langford, Steve McCatty, Bo McLaughlin, Craig Minetto, Mike Norris, Bob Owchinko, Tom Underwood. Infielders: Shooty Babbit, Mark Budaska, Jeff Cox, Bryan Doyle, Keith Drumright, Wayne Gross, Tim Hosley, Cliff Johnson, Mickey Kluttz, Dave McKay, Kelvin Moore, Jim Nettles, Rob Picciolo, Dave Revering, Jim Sexton, Jim Spencer, Fred Stanley. Outfielders: Tony Armas, Rick Bosetti, Mike Davis, Rickey Henderson, Dwayne Murphy, Mitchell Page, Mike Patterson. Trainers: Jack Homel, Barry Weinberg.

1987 SAN FRANCISCO GIANTS—Western Division Champions. Manager: Roger Craig. Coaches: Bill Fahey, Bob Lillis, Gordon MacKenzie, Jose Morales, Norm Sherry, Don Zimmer. Catchers: Bob Brenly, Kirt Manwaring, Bob Melvin, Mackey Sasser. Pitchers: Randy Bockus, John Burkett, Keith Comstock, Mark Davis, Kelly Downs, Dave Dravecky, Scott Garrelts, Jim Gott, Mark Grant, Atlee Hammaker, Mike LaCoss, Craig Lefferts, Mike Krukow, Roger Mason, Greg Minton, Jon Perlman, Joe Price, Rick Reuschel, Don Robinson, Jeff Robinson. Infielders: Mike Aldrete, Chris Brown, Will Clark, Ivan DeJesus, Francisco Melendez, Kevin Mitchell, Chris Speier, Harry Spilman, Robby Thompson, Jose Uribe, Mark Wasinger, Rob Wilfong, Matt Williams, Mike Woodard. Outfielders: Chili Davis, Dave Henderson, Randy Kutcher, Jeffrey Leonard, Candy Maldonado, Eddie Milner, Jessie Reid, Joel Youngblood. Trainers: Mark Letendre, Greg Lynn.

1988 OAKLAND A's—American League Champions. Manager: Tony La Russa. Coaches: Dave Duncan, Rene Lachemann, Jim Lefebvre, Dave McKay, Mike Paul, Bob Watson. Catchers: Ron Hassey, Orlando Mercado, Matt Sinatro, Terry Steinbach. Pitchers: Rich Bordi, Todd Burns, Greg Cadaret, Jim Corsi, Storm Davis, Dennis Eckersley, Rick Honeycutt, Gene Nelson, Steve Ontiveros, Dave Otto, Eric Plunk, Jeff Shaver, Dave Stewart, Bob Welch, Curt Young, Matt Young. Infielders: Lance Blankenship, Mike Gallego, Glenn Hubbard, Doug Jennings, Ed Jurak, Carney Lansford, Mark McGwire, Tony Phillips, Walter Weiss. Outfielders: Don Baylor, Jose Canseco, Dave Henderson, Stan Javier, Felix Jose, Dave Parker, Luis Polonia. Trainers: Barry Weinberg, Larry Davis.

1989 OAKLAND A's—World Champions. Manager: Tony La Russa. Coaches: Dave Duncan, Art Kuysner, Rene Lachemann, Dave McKay, Merv Rettenmund, Tommie Reynolds. Catchers: Chris Bando, Scott Hemond, Ron Hassey, Terry Steinbach. Pitchers: Todd Burns, Greg Cadaret, Jim Corsi, Storm Davis, Bill Dawley, Dennis Eckersley, Rick Honeycutt, Mike Moore, Gene Nelson, Dave Otto, Eric Plunk, Brian Snyder, Dave Stewart, Bob Welch, Curt Young, Matt Young. Infielders: Larry Arndt, Lance Blankenship, Mike Gallego, Glenn Hubbard, Carney Lansford, Mark McGwire, Ken Phelps, Tony Phillips, Jamie Quirk, Dick Scott, Walter Weiss. Outfielders: Billy Beane, Jose Canseco, Dave Henderson, Rickey Henderson, Dean Howitt, Stan Javier, Doug Jennings, Felix Jose, Dave Parker, Luis Polonia. Trainers: Barry Weinberg, Larry Davis.

1989 SAN FRANCISCO GIANTS—National League Champions. Manager: Roger Craig. Coaches: Dusty Baker, Marty DeMerritt, Bill Fahey, Wendell Kim, Bob Lillis, Norm Sherry. Catchers: Bill Bathe, Bob Brenly, Terry Kennedy, Kirt Manwaring. Pitchers: Steve Bedrosian, Jeff Brantley, Ernie Camacho, Dennis Cook, Kelly Downs, Dave Dravecky, Scott Garrelts, Goose Gossage, Atlee Hammaker, Bob Knepper, Mike Krukow, Mike LaCoss, Craig Lefferts, Randy McCament, Terry Mulholland, Joe Price, Rick Reuschel, Don Robinson, Stu Tate, Russ Swan, Trevor Wilson. Infielders: Mike Benjamin, Will Clark, Charlie Hayes, Ed Jurak, Mike Laga, Greg Litton, Ken Oberkfell, Ernest Riles, Chris Speier, Robby Thompson, Jose Uribe, Matt Williams. Outfielders: Brett Butler, Tracy Jones, Candy Maldonado, Kevin Mitchell, Donell Nixon, Pat Sheridan, James Steels, Jim Weaver. Trainers: Mark Letendre, Greg Lynn.

1990 OAKLAND A's—American League Champions. Manager: Tony La Russa. Coaches: Dave Duncan, Art Kusnyer, Rene Lachemann, Dave McKay, Merv Rettenmund, Tommie Reynolds. Catchers: Troy Afenir, Ron Hassey, Jamie Quirk, Terry Steinbach. Pitchers: Joe Bitker, Todd Burns, Steve Chitren, Dennis Eckersley, Reggie Harris, Rick Honeycutt, Joe Klink, Mike Moore, Gene Nelson, Mike Norris, Dave Otto, Scott Sanderson, Dave Stewart, Bob Welch, Curt Young. Infielders: Lance Blankenship, Mike Bordick, Mike Gallego, Scott Hemond, Carney Lansford, Mark McGwire, Ken Phelps, Willie Randolph, Walter Weiss. Outfielders: Harold Baines, Jose Canseco, Ozzie Canseco, Dave Henderson, Rickey Henderson, Steve Howard, Dann Howitt, Stan Javier, Doug Jennings, Felix Jose, Darren Lewis, Willie McGee. Trainers: Barry Weinberg, Larry Davis.

1992 OAKLAND A's—Western Division Champions. Manager: Tony La Russa. Coaches: Dave Duncan, Art Kusnyer, Rene Lachemann, Dave McKay, Tommie Reynolds. Catchers: Scott Hemond, Henry Mercedes, Jamie Quirk, Terry Steinbach. Pitchers: Kevin Campbell, Jim Corsi, Ron Darling, Jim Deshaies, Kelly Downs, Dennis Eckersley, Rich Gossage, Johnny Guzman, Shawn Hillegas, Vince Horsman, Mike Moore, Jeff Parrett, Jeff Russell, Todd Revenig, Joe Slusarski, Dave Stewart, Bob Welch, Bobby Witt. Infielders: Lance Blankenship, Mike Bordick, Scott Brosius, Jerry Browne, Carney Lansford, Mark McGwire. Randy Ready, Walter Weiss. Outfielders: Harold Baines, Jose Canseco, Eric Fox, Dave Henderson, Rickey Henderson, Dann Howitt, Mike Kingery, Troy Neel, Ruben Sierra. Willie Wilson. Trainers: Barry Weinberg, Larry Davis.

# LEADING BATTERS

## OAKLAND—PACIFIC COAST LEAGUE

| YEAR | PLAYER | GAMES | HITS | PCT. | PLAYER | RUNS |
|------|--------|-------|------|------|--------|------|
| 1903 | Bill Moskiman | 117 | 141 | .313 | Bill Murdock | 109 |
| 1904 | Oscar Graham | 70 | n/a | .310 | John Ganley | 100 |
| 1905 | Bill Moskiman | 138 | 114 | .257 | no record | |
| 1906 | Art Krueger | 161 | 211 | .316 | Art Krueger | 116 |
| 1907 | Truck Eagan | 194 | 237 | .335 | Walter Smith | 103 |
| 1908 | John Slattery | 99 | 119 | .331 | Heinie Heitmuller | 104 |
| 1909 | Howard Murphy | 112 | 125 | .285 | Willie Hogan | 95 |
| 1910 | Willie Hogan | 200 | 193 | .261 | Willie Hogan | 99 |
| 1911 | Harl Maggart | 114 | 137 | .314 | Izzy Hoffman | 110 |
| 1912 | Claire Patterson | 138 | 157 | .305 | Bill Leard | 122 |
| 1913 | Rube Gardner | 134 | 115 | .285 | Bill Leard | 101 |
| 1914 | Rube Gardner | 153 | 156 | .306 | Jack Ness | 90 |
| 1915 | Jimmy Johnston | 206 | 274 | .348 | Jimmy Johnston | 140 |
| 1916 | Duke Kenworthy | 200 | 231 | .314 | Duke Kenworthy | 99 |
| 1917 | Rod Murphy | 207 | 227 | .303 | Eddie Mensor | 100 |
| 1918 | Hack Miller | 102 | 131 | .316 | R.H.Middleton | 47 |
| 1919 | Dennis Wilie | 153 | 170 | .326 | Bill Lane | 122 |
| 1920 | Hack Miller | 199 | 280 | .347 | Dennis Wilie | 135 |
| 1921 | Hack Miller | 184 | 252 | .347 | Claude Cooper | 148 |
| 1922 | George LaFayette | 182 | 205 | .310 | Dennis Wilie | 113 |
| 1923 | Ted Cather | 191 | 269 | .344 | Ted Cather | 139 |
| 1924 | Buzz Arlett | 193 | 229 | .328 | Buzz Arlett | 122 |
| 1925 | Buzz Arlett | 190 | 244 | .344 | Buzz Arlett | 121 |
| 1926 | Buzz Arlett | 194 | 255 | .382 | Buzz Arlett | 140 |
| 1927 | Buzz Arlett | 187 | 321 | .351 | Lyn Lary | 124 |

| 1928 | Ernest Lombardi | 120 | 120 | .377 | Buzz Arlett | 111 |
|---|---|---|---|---|---|---|
| 1929 | Buzz Arlett | 200 | 270 | .374 | Buzz Arlett | 146 |
| 1930 | Ernest Lombardi | 146 | 175 | .370 | Johnny Vergez | 138 |
| 1931 | Ray Brubaker | 147 | 154 | .349 | Leroy Anton | 95 |
| 1932 | Greg Mulleavy | 132 | 162 | .321 | Leroy Anton | 100 |
| 1933 | Bernie Uhalt | 171 | 221 | .350 | Emil Mailho | 142 |
| 1934 | Leroy Anton | 175 | 204 | .312 | Eddie Mulligan | 118 |
| 1935 | Emil Mailho | 172 | 230 | .353 | Emil Mailho | 117 |
| 1936 | Leroy Anton | 153 | 176 | .317 | Jack Glynn | 107 |
| 1937 | Dario Lodigiani | 162 | 176 | .327 | Walt Judnich | 107 |
| 1938 | Smead Jolley | 119 | 145 | .350 | Jess Hill | 77 |
| 1939 | Marv Gudat | 153 | 167 | .324 | Hugh Luby | 84 |
| 1940 | Mike Christoff | 165 | 180 | .321 | Hugh Luby | 94 |
| 1941 | Hugh Luby | 178 | 204 | .301 | Mel Duezabou | 103 |
| 1942 | Hugh Luby | 177 | 207 | .310 | Emil Mailho | 91 |
| 1943 | Les Scarsella | 157 | 192 | .326 | Emil Mailho | 100 |
| 1944 | Les Scarsella | 156 | 196 | .329 | Chet Rosenlund | 88 |
| 1945 | Frankie Hawkins | 114 | 136 | .341 | Les Scarsella | 95 |
| 1946 | Les Scarsella | 121 | 142 | .332 | Brooks Holder | 88 |
| 1947 | Hershel Martin | 116 | 106 | .361 | Brooks Holder | 137 |
| 1948 | Geo. Metkovich | 134 | 168 | .336 | Geo. Metkovich | 116 |
| 1949 | Artie Wilson | 165 | 211 | .348 | Artie Wilson | 116 |
| 1950 | Geo. Metkovich | 184 | 233 | .315 | Artie Wilson | 168 |
| 1951 | Earl Rapp | 97 | 115 | .322 | Pete Pavlick | 97 |
| 1952 | Piper Davis | 122 | 122 | .306 | Tookie Gilbert | 95 |
| 1953 | Pete Milne | 175 | 210 | .323 | Pete Milne | 110 |
| 1954 | Sam Chapman | 129 | 137 | .290 | Spider Jorgensen | 102 |
| 1955 | Geo. Metkovich | 150 | 178 | .335 | Geo. Metkovich | 94 |
| | | | | | Billy Consolo | 94 |

## MISSION—PACIFIC COAST LEAGUE

| YEAR | PLAYER | GAMES | HITS | PCT. | PLAYER | RUNS |
|---|---|---|---|---|---|---|
| 1926 | Ike Boone | 172 | 238 | .380 | Evar Swanson | 157 |
| 1927 | Eddie Rose | 182 | 226 | .334 | Eddie Rose | 115 |
| 1928 | Evar Swanson | 180 | 256 | .346 | Evar Swanson | 151 |
| 1929 | Ike Boone | 198 | 323 | .407 | Ike Boone | 195 |
| 1930 | Fuzzy Hufft | 187 | 257 | .356 | Johnny Monroe | 158 |
| 1931 | Oscar Eckhardt | 185 | 275 | .369 | Oscar Eckhardt | 129 |
| 1932 | Oscar Eckhardt | 134 | 200 | .354 | Louie Almada | 95 |
| 1933 | Oscar Eckhardt | 189 | 315 | .414 | Oscar Eckhardt | 145 |
| 1934 | Oscar Eckhardt | 184 | 267 | .378 | Louie Almada | 148 |
| 1935 | Oscar Eckhardt | 172 | 283 | .399 | Oscar Eckhardt | 149 |
| 1936 | Harry Rosenberg | 172 | 233 | .334 | Eddie Joost | 120 |
| 1937 | Harry Rosenberg | 162 | 202 | .330 | Harry Rosenberg | 92 |
| | Max West | 151 | 183 | .330 | | |

## SAN FRANCISCO—PACIFIC COAST LEAGUE

| YEAR | PLAYER | GAMES | HITS | PCT. | PLAYER | RUNS |
|---|---|---|---|---|---|---|
| 1903 | Patrick Meaney | 219 | 251 | .309 | Danny Shay | 146 |
| 1904 | Geo. Hildebrand | 204 | 239 | .284 | Geo. Hildebrand | 134 |
| 1905 | Jimmie Nealon | 207 | 208 | .286 | no record | |
| 1906 | Nick Williams | 142 | 146 | .309 | Henry Spencer | 133 |
| 1907 | Nick Williams | 189 | 175 | .257 | Charlie Irwin | 80 |
| 1908 | Nick Williams | 198 | 200 | .270 | Kid Mohler | 118 |
| 1909 | Henry Melchior | 195 | 206 | .298 | Rollie Zeider | 141 |
| 1910 | Hunky Shaw | 155 | 146 | .281 | Ping Bodie | 110 |
| 1911 | Watt Powell | 175 | 195 | .290 | Watt Powell | 94 |
| 1912 | Chick Hartley | 119 | 129 | .305 | Roy Corhan | 76 |
| 1913 | Jimmy Johnston | 201 | 228 | .304 | Jimmy Johnston | 111 |
| 1914 | J. Fitzgerald | 170 | 185 | .308 | Biff Schaller | 107 |
| 1915 | Ping Bodie | 192 | 234 | .325 | Biff Schaller | 143 |
| 1916 | J. Fitzgerald | 132 | 133 | .315 | Biff Schaller | 131 |
| 1917 | J. Fitzgerald | 176 | 226 | .324 | Charlie Pick | 123 |
| 1918 | Charlie Pick | 102 | 127 | .333 | Charlie Pick | 65 |
| 1919 | J. Fitzgerald | 161 | 210 | .334 | J. Fitzgerald | 110 |
| 1920 | J. Fitzgerald | 171 | 208 | .336 | Maurie Schick | 100 |
| 1921 | Jim O'Connell | 170 | 202 | .342 | Bert Ellison | 124 |
| 1922 | Willie Kamm | 170 | 222 | .342 | Willie Kamm | 137 |
| 1923 | Paul Waner | 112 | 120 | .369 | Bert Ellison | 145 |
| 1924 | Bert Ellison | 201 | 307 | .381 | Eddie Mulligan | 150 |
| 1925 | Paul Waner | 174 | 280 | .401 | Paul Waner | 167 |
| 1926 | Earl Averill | 188 | 236 | .348 | Earl Averill | 131 |
| 1927 | Smead Jolley | 168 | 248 | .397 | Lefty O'Doul | 164 |

| 1928 | Smead Jolley | 191 | 309 | .404 | Earl Averill | 178 |
|---|---|---|---|---|---|---|
| 1929 | Smead Jolley | 200 | 314 | .387 | Gus Suhr | 196 |
| 1930 | Earl Sheely | 183 | 289 | .403 | Frank Crosetti | 171 |
| 1931 | Jimmy Keesey | 163 | 238 | .356 | Frank Crosetti | 141 |
| 1932 | Mike Hunt | 151 | 167 | .316 | Jerry Donovan | 134 |
| 1933 | Augie Galan | 189 | 265 | .356 | Augie Galan | 164 |
| 1934 | Jack Fenton | 146 | 146 | .293 | Elias Funk | 103 |
| 1935 | Joe DiMaggio | 172 | 270 | .398 | Joe DiMaggio | 173 |
| 1936 | Joe Marty | 164 | 215 | .359 | Joe Marty | 110 |
| | Brooks Holder | 110 | | | | |
| 1937 | Frankie Hawkins | 132 | 155 | .324 | Dominic DiMaggio | 109 |
| 1938 | Brooks Holder | 172 | 193 | .330 | Brooks Holder | 122 |
| 1939 | Dominic DiMaggio | 170 | 239 | .360 | Dominic DiMaggio | 165 |
| 1940 | Ted Norbert | 173 | 190 | .320 | Johnny Barrett | 111 |
| 1941 | Nanny Fernandez | 177 | 231 | .327 | Ferris Fain | 122 |
| 1942 | Ralph Hodgin | 172 | 216 | .320 | Brooks Holder | 113 |
| 1943 | Hank Steinbacker | 156 | 181 | .318 | Bernie Uhalt | 78 |
| 1944 | Joe Futernick | 120 | 116 | .391 | Bernie Uhalt | 86 |
| 1945 | Gus Suhr | 138 | 124 | .311 | Bernie Uhalt | 93 |
| 1946 | Ted Jennings | 136 | 150 | .303 | Ferris Fain | 117 |
| 1947 | Ray Orteig | 142 | 138 | .299 | Hugh Luby | 122 |
| 1948 | Gene Woodling | 146 | 202 | .385 | Gene Woodling | 121 |
| 1949 | Mickey Rocco | 163 | 174 | .276 | Jackie Tobin | 93 |
| 1950 | Joe Grace | 165 | 174 | .335 | Brooks Holder | 113 |
| 1951 | Joe Grace | 133 | 117 | .302 | Eddie Lake | 106 |
| 1952 | Joe Grace | 164 | 170 | .299 | Joe Grace | 88 |
| 1953 | Sal Taormina | 156 | 133 | .297 | Reno Cheso | 80 |
| | Reno Cheso | 155 | 157 | .297 | | |
| 1954 | Ted Beard | 160 | 169 | .300 | Ted Beard | 104 |
| 1955 | Mike Baxes | 143 | 163 | .323 | Ted Beard | 90 |
| 1956 | Gordy Windhorn | 127 | 137 | .306 | Ken Aspromonte | 80 |
| 1957 | Ken Aspromonte | 143 | 171 | .334 | Frank Kellert | 102 |

## OAKLAND A's—AMERICAN LEAGUE

| YEAR | PLAYER | GAMES | HITS | PCT. | PLAYER | RUNS |
|---|---|---|---|---|---|---|
| 1968 | Danny Cater | 147 | 146 | .290 | Bert Campaneris | 86 |
| 1969 | Sal Bando | 162 | 171 | .281 | Reggie Jackson | 123 |
| 1970 | Bert Campaneris | 147 | 168 | .279 | Bert Campaneris | 97 |
| 1971 | Reggie Jackson | 150 | 157 | .271 | Reggie Jackson | 87 |
| 1972 | Joe Rudi | 147 | 181 | .305 | Joe Rudi | 94 |
| 1973 | Reggie Jackson | 151 | 158 | .293 | Reggie Jackson | 99 |
| 1974 | Joe Rudi | 158 | 174 | .293 | Reggie Jackson | 90 |
| 1975 | Cl. Washington | 148 | 182 | .308 | Reggie Jackson | 91 |
| 1976 | Bill North | 154 | 163 | .307 | Bill North | 91 |
| 1977 | Mitchell Page | 145 | 154 | .307 | Mitchell Page | 85 |
| 1978 | Mitchell Page | 147 | 147 | .285 | Mitchell Page | 62 |
| 1979 | Dave Revering | 125 | 136 | .288 | Dave Revering | 63 |
| 1980 | Rickey Henderson | 158 | 179 | .303 | Rickey Henderson | 111 |
| 1981 | Rickey Henderson | 108 | 135 | .319 | Rickey Henderson | 89 |
| 1982 | Jeff Burroughs | 113 | 79 | .277 | Rickey Henderson | 119 |
| 1983 | Carney Lansford | 80 | 92 | .308 | Rickey Henderson | 105 |
| 1984 | Carney Lansford | 151 | 179 | 300 | Rickey Henderson | 113 |
| 1985 | Bruce Bochte | 137 | 125 | .295 | Michael Davis | 92 |
| 1986 | Alfredo Griffin | 162 | 169 | .285 | Jose Canseco | 85 |
| 1987 | Carney Lansford | 151 | 160 | .289 | Mark McGwire | 97 |
| | Mark McGwire | 151 | 161 | .289 | — | |
| 1988 | Jose Canseco | 158 | 187 | .307 | Jose Canseco | 120 |
| 1989 | Carney Lansford | 148 | 185 | .336 | Carney Lansford | 81 |
| 1990 | Rickey Henderson | 136 | 159 | .325 | Rickey Henderson | 119 |
| 1991 | Harold Baines | 141 | 144 | .295 | Jose Canseco | 115 |
| 1992 | Mike Bordick | 154 | 151 | .300 | Mark McGwire | 87 |
| 1993 | Troy Neel | 123 | 124 | .290 | Rickey Henderson | 77 |
| | Brent Gates | 139 | 155 | .290 | Ruben Sierra | 77 |

## SAN FRANCISCO GIANTS—NATIONAL LEAGUE

| YEAR | PLAYER | GAMES | HITS | PCT. | PLAYER | RUNS |
|---|---|---|---|---|---|---|
| 1958 | Willie Mays | 151 | 208 | .347 | Willie Mays | 121 |
| 1959 | Orlando Cepeda | 151 | 192 | .317 | Willie Mays | 125 |
| 1960 | Willie Mays | 152 | 190 | .319 | Willie Mays | 107 |
| 1961 | Orlando Cepeda | 152 | 182 | .311 | Willie Mays | 129 |
| 1962 | Felipe Alou | 150 | 177 | .316 | Willie Mays | 130 |
| 1963 | Orlando Cepeda | 156 | 183 | .316 | Willie Mays | 115 |
| 1964 | Orlando Cepeda | 142 | 161 | .304 | Willie Mays | 121 |

| 1965 | Willie Mays | 151 | 177 | .317 | Willie Mays | 118 |
|---|---|---|---|---|---|---|
| 1966 | Willie McCovey | 150 | 148 | .295 | Willie Mays | 99 |
| 1967 | Jesus Alou | 129 | 149 | .292 | Jim Ray Hart | 98 |
| 1968 | Willie McCovey | 148 | 153 | .293 | Willie Mays | 84 |
| 1969 | Willie McCovey | 149 | 157 | .320 | Bobby Bonds | 102 |
| 1970 | Bobby Bonds | 157 | 200 | .302 | Bobby Bonds | 134 |
| 1971 | Bobby Bonds | 155 | 178 | .288 | Bobby Bonds | 110 |
| 1972 | Chris Speier | 150 | 151 | .269 | Bobby Bonds | 118 |
| 1973 | Garry Maddox | 144 | 187 | .319 | Bobby Bonds | 131 |
| 1974 | Gary Matthews | 154 | 161 | .287 | Gary Matthews | 87 |
| 1975 | Von Joshua | 129 | 161 | .318 | Derrel Thomas | 99 |
| 1976 | Gary Matthews | 156 | 164 | .279 | Gary Matthews | 79 |
| 1977 | Bill Madlock | 140 | 161 | .302 | Derrel Thomas | 75 |
| 1978 | Bill Madlock | 122 | 138 | .309 | Jack Clark | 90 |
| 1979 | Jack Clark | 143 | 144 | .273 | Billy North | 87 |
| 1980 | Jack Clark | 127 | 124 | .284 | Jack Clark | 77 |
| 1981 | Milt May | 97 | 98 * | .310 | Jack Clark | *60 |
| 1982 | Joe Morgan | 134 | 134 | .289 | Jack Clark | 90 |
| 1983 | Jeff Leonard | 139 | 144 | .279 | Darrell Evans | 94 |
| 1984 | Chili Davis | 137 | 157 | .315 | Chili Davis | 87 |
| 1985 | Chili Davis | 136 | 130 | .270 | Dan Gladden | 64 |
| 1986 | Chili Davis | 153 | 146 | .278 | Robbie Thompson | 73 |
| 1987 | Will Clark | 150 | 163 | .308 | Will Clark | 89 |
| 1988 | Brett Butler | 157 | 163 | .287 | Brett Butler | 109 |
| 1989 | Will Clark | 159 | 196 | .333 | Will Clark | 104 |
| 1990 | Brett Butler | 160 | 192 | .309 | Brett Butler | 108 |
| 1991 | Willie McGee | 131 | 155 | .312 | Will Clark | 84 |
| 1992 | Will Clark | 144 | 154 | .300 | Will Clark | 69 |
| 1993 | Barry Bonds | 159 | 181 | .336 | Barry Bonds | 129 |

* 1981 season reduced to 111 games due to mid-season player strike.

# LEADING PITCHERS

## OAKLAND—PACIFIC COAST LEAGUE

| YEAR | PITCHER | RECORD | PCT. | PITCHER | ERA |
|---|---|---|---|---|---|
| 1903 | Jack Lee | 17-17 | .50 | Earned Run Average | |
| 1904 | Jim Buchanan | 33-21 | .611 | not calculated until | |
| 1905 | Oscar Graham | 28-25 | .528 | 1914. | |
| 1906 | No records kept. | | | | |
| 1907 | Willie Hogan | 20-14 | .588 | | |
| 1908 | Wright | 16-15 | .516 | | |
| 1909 | Tyler Christian | 18-17 | .514 | | |
| 1910 | Jack Lively | 31-15 | .674 | | |
| 1911 | Harry Ables | 22-11 | .667 | | |
| 1912 | Bill Malarkey | 20-11 | .645 | | |
| 1913 | Bill Malarkey | 25-16 | .610 | | |
| 1914 | Al Klawitter | 20-26 | .435 | Harry Ables | 2.02 |
| 1915 | Al Klawitter | 26-18 | .591 | Boyd | 2.64 |
| 1916 | Elwood Martin | 16-18 | .471 | Bill Burns | 2.42 |
| 1917 | Harry Krause | 28-26 | .518 | Elwood Martin | 2.06 |
| 1918 | Bill Prough | 13-12 | .520 | Bill Prough | 2.03 |
| 1919 | Buzz Arlett | 22-17 | .564 | Harry Krause | 1.75 |
| 1920 | Buzz Arlett | 29-17 | .630 | Ernie Alten | 2.41 |
| 1921 | George Winn | 14-7 | .667 | Harry Krause | 2.91 |
| 1922 | Buzz Arlett | 25-19 | .568 | Buzz Arlett | 2.77 |
| 1923 | Ray Kremer | 25-16 | .610 | Walter Mails | 2.96 |
| 1924 | Earl Kunz | 23-18 | .561 | George Foster | 3.59 |
| 1925 | Art Delaney | 17-16 | .515 | Hub Pruitt | 2.92 |
| 1926 | Hub Pruitt | 22-13 | .629 | Hub Pruitt | 2.47 |
| 1927 | Pudgy Gould | 17-5 | .773 | Art Delaney | 3.05 |
| 1928 | Pete Daglia | 18-11 | .621 | Martin Dumovich | 3.05 |
| 1929 | Lou McEvoy | 22-12 | 647 | Bub Hurst | 2.88 |
| 1930 | Pete Daglia | 18-16 | .529 | Howard Craghead | 3.64 |
| 1931 | Fay Thomas | 12-10 | .545 | Fay Thomas | 3.86 |
| 1932 | Ed Walsh, Jr. | 19-15 | .559 | Willie Ludolph | 2.76 |
| 1933 | Willie Ludolph | 19-9 | .679 | Willie Ludolph | 3.09 |
| 1934 | Willie Ludolph | 16-14 | .571 | Tom Conlan | 3.57 |
| 1935 | Willie Ludolph | 20-13 | .606 | Willie Ludolph | 3.09 |

| 1936 | Willie Ludolph | 21-6 | .778 | Willie Ludolph | 2.69 |
|---|---|---|---|---|---|
| 1937 | Jack LaRocca | 13-6 | .684 | Jack LaRocca | 3.20 |
| 1938 | Bob Joyce | 18-18 | .500 | Bob Joyce | 3.01 |
| 1939 | Ralph Buxton | 13-10 | .565 | Ralph Buxton | 2.88 |
| 1940 | Ben Cantwell | 13-5 | .722 | Jack Salveson | 2.30 |
| 1941 | Cotton Pippen | 17-16 | .515 | George Darrow | 3.32 |
| 1942 | Jack Salveson | 24-12 | .667 | Jack Salveson | 2.58 |
| | | | | Italo Chelini | 2.58 |
| 1943 | Cotton Pippen | 20-15 | .571 | Ralph Buxton | 2.75 |
| 1944 | Manny Salvo | 18-7 | .720 | Manny Salvo | 2.14 |
| 1945 | Garth Mann | 15-9 | .625 | Garth Mann | 2.88 |
| 1946 | Spec Shea | 15-5 | .750 | Spec Shea | 1.66 |
| 1947 | Gene Bearden | 16-7 | .696 | Gene Bearden | 2.86 |
| 1948 | Chas. Gassaway | 15-8 | .652 | Chas. Gassaway | 3.09 |
| 1949 | Lou Tost | 14-7 | .667 | Forrest Thompson | 3.16 |
| 1950 | Allen Gettel | 23-7 | .767 | Allen Gettel | 3.62 |
| 1951 | Bill Ayers | 20-13 | .606 | Lloyd Hittle | 3.74 |
| 1952 | Hal Gregg | 11-3 | .786 | Milo Candini | 2.57 |
| 1953 | Allen Gettel | 24-14 | .632 | Allen Gettel | 3.20 |
| 1954 | Don Ferrarese | 18-15 | .545 | Allen Gettel | 3.07 |
| 1955 | Hector Brown | 9-2 | .818 | Hector Brown | 2.95 |

## MISSION—PACIFIC COAST LEAGUE

| YEAR | PLAYER | RECORD | PCT. | PLAYER | ERA |
|---|---|---|---|---|---|
| 1926 | Bert Cole | 29-12 | .707 | Bert Cole | 2.63 |
| 1927 | Phil Weinert | 17-12 | .586 | Phil Weinert | 2.14 |
| 1928 | Ernie Nevers | 14-11 | .560 | Herm Pillette | 3.11 |
| 1929 | Herm Pillette | 23-13 | .639 | Bert Cole | 3.45 |
| 1930 | Ted Pillette | 14-9 | .609 | Herm Pillette | 4.34 |
| 1931 | Herm Pillette | 16-11 | .593 | Herm Pillette | 3.52 |
| 1932 | Ted Pillette | 13-14 | .481 | Bert Cole | 3.52 |
| 1933 | Johnny Babich | 20-15 | .571 | Johnny Babich | 3.62 |
| 1934 | Clarence Mitchell | 19-12 | .613 | Johnny Babich | 2.03 |
| 1935 | Wayne Osborne | 18-11 | .621 | Wayne Osborne | 3.53 |
| 1936 | Wayne Osborne | 12-9 | .571 | Otho Nitcholas | 3.63 |
| 1937 | Johnny Babich | 12-8 | .600 | Walter Beck | 4.22 |

## SAN FRANCISCO—PACIFIC COAST LEAGUE

| YEAR | PLAYER | RECORD | PCT. | PLAYER | ERA |
|---|---|---|---|---|---|
| 1903 | Jimmy Whalen | 29-21 | .580 | Earned Run Average | |
| 1904 | George Wheeler | 18-13 | .600 | not calculated until | |
| 1905 | Roy Hitt | 24-14 | .632 | 1914. | |
| 1906 | Roy Hitt | 36-14 | .720 | | |
| 1907 | Cack Henley | 24-15 | .616 | | |
| 1908 | Harry Sutor | 26-20 | .545 | | |
| 1909 | Cack Henley | 31-10 | .756 | | |
| 1910 | Cack Henley | 34-19 | .642 | | |
| 1911 | Cack Henley | 17-14 | .549 | | |
| 1912 | Frank Miller | 20-22 | .476 | | |
| 1913 | Skeeter Fanning | 28-15 | .651 | | |
| 1914 | Spider Baum | 21-12 | .636 | Spider Baum | 2.02 |
| 1915 | Chief Smith | 17-7 | .680 | Bill Steen | 1.55 |
| 1916 | Johnny Couch | 18-15 | .545 | Red Erickson | 2.37 |
| 1917 | Red Erickson | 21-15 | .674 | Red Erickson | 1.93 |
| 1918 | Lefty O'Doul | 12-8 | .600 | Spider Baum | 2.13 |
| 1919 | Tom Seaton | 25-16 | .622 | Jim Scott | 2.43 |
| 1920 | Jim Scott | 23-14 | .622 | Bert Cole | 1.87 |
| 1921 | Lefty O'Doul | 25-9 | .735 | Lefty O'Doul | 2.39 |
| 1922 | Jim Scott | 25-9 | .735 | Jim Scott | 2.22 |
| 1923 | Harry Courtney | 19-6 | .760 | Harry Courtney | 2.80 |
| 1924 | Oliver Mitchell | 28-15 | .651 | Marty Griffin | 3.20 |
| 1925 | Doug McWeene | 20-5 | .800 | Doug McWeeney | 2.70 |
| 1926 | Oliver Mitchell | 18-12 | .600 | Dick Moudy | 3.21 |
| 1927 | Dick Moudy | 18-11 | .633 | Dick Moudy | 3.46 |
| 1928 | Dutch Reuther | 29-7 | .806 | Elmer Jacobs | 2.56 |
| 1929 | Hollis Thurston` | 22-11 | .667 | Lefty Gomez | 3.42 |
| 1930 | Jimmie Zinn | 26-12 | .614 | Hal Turpin | 3.86 |
| 1931 | Sam Gibson | 28-12 | .700 | Sam Gibson | 2.48 |

| 1932 | Bill Henderson | 17-12 | .586 | Curtis Davis | 2.24 |
|------|----------------|-------|------|--------------|------|
| 1933 | Curtis Davis | 20-16 | .556 | Curtis Davis | 3.97 |
| 1934 | LeRoy Herrmann | 27-13 | .675 | Sam Gibson | 2.96 |
| 1935 | Sam Gibson | 22-4 | .846 | Pard Ballou | 3.28 |
| 1936 | Sam Gibson | 18-15 | .545 | Sam Gibson | 2.81 |
| 1937 | Sam Gibson | 19-8 | .708 | Bill Shores | 2.87 |
| 1938 | Sam Gibson | 23-12 | .657 | Sam Gibson | 2.66 |
| 1939 | Sam Gibson | 22-9 | .710 | Sam Gibson | 2.34 |
| 1940 | Eddie Stutz | 19-14 | .576 | Sam Gibson | 2.83 |
| 1941 | Sam Gibson | 13-7 | .650 | Larry Jansen | 2.80 |
| 1942 | Bob Joyce | 22-10 | .688 | Sam Gibson | 2.78 |
| 1943 | Al Epperly | 16-5 | .762 | BobJoyce | 2.43 |
| 1944 | Tom Seats | 25-13 | .658 | Tom Seats | 2.36 |
| 1945 | Bob Joyce | 31-11 | .738 | Bob Joyce | 2.17 |
| 1946 | Larry Jansen | 30-6 | .833 | Larry Jansen | 1.57 |
| 1947 | Bob Chesnes | 22-8 | .733 | Bob Chesnes | 2.32 |
| 1948 | Bill Werle | 17-7 | .708 | Con Dempsey | 2.10 |
| 1949 | Con Dempsey | 23-17 | .548 | Steve Nagy | 2.65 |
| 1950 | Chet Johnson | 22-13 | .629 | Chet Johnson | 3.51 |
| 1951 | Al Lien | 13-10 | .565 | Elmer Singleton | 3.04 |
| 1952 | Bill Bradford | 15-11 | .577 | Bob Muncrief | 2.69 |
| 1953 | John McCall | 12-7 | .632 | Bob Muncrief | 2.66 |
| 1954 | Frank Hiller | 11-8 | .579 | Frank Hiller | 2.92 |
| 1954 | Adrian Zabala | 11-8 | .579 | | |
| 1955 | Bill Bradford | 12-5 | .706 | Bill Bradford | 3.13 |
| 1956 | Jerry Casale | 19-11 | .633 | Max Surkont | 2.38 |
| 1957 | Leo Kiely | 21-6 | 778 | Leo Kiely | 2.20 |

## OAKLAND A's—AMERICAN LEAGUE

| YEAR | PLAYER | RECORD | PCT. | PLAYER | ERA* |
|------|--------|--------|------|--------|------|
| 1968 | Blue Moon Odom | 16-10 | .615 | Jim Nash | 2.28 |
| 1969 | Blue Moon Odom | 15-6 | .714 | Jim Roland | 2.20 |
| 1970 | Catfish Hunter | 18-14 | .563 | Diego Segui | 2.56 |
| 1971 | Vida Blue | 24-8 | .750 | Vida Blue | 1.82 |
| 1972 | Catfish Hunter | 21-7 | .750 | Catfish Hunter | 2.04 |
| 1973 | Catfish Hunter | 21-5 | .808 | Rollie Fingers | 1.92 |
| 1974 | Catfish Hunter | 25-12 | .676 | Paul Lindblad | 2.05 |
| 1975 | Vida Blue | 22-11 | .667 | Jim Todd | 2.29 |
| 1976 | Vida Blue | 18-13 | .581 | Vida Blue | 2.35 |
| 1977 | Doc Medich | 10-6 | .625 | Pablo Torrealba | 2.62 |
| 1978 | John H. Johnson | 11-10 | .524 | Elias Sosa | 2.64 |
| 1979 | Rick Langford | 12-16 | .429 | Steve McCatty | 4.11 |
| 1980 | Mike Norris | 22-9 | .710 | Mike Norris | 2.53 |
| 1981 | Steve McCatty | 14-7 | .667 | Steve McCatty | 2.32 |
| 1982 | Tom Underwood | 10-6 | .625 | Tom Underwood | 3.29 |
| 1983 | Chris Codiroli | 12-12 | .500 | Bill Krueger | 3.61 |
| 1984 | Ray Burris | 13-10 | .565 | Ray Burris | 3.15 |
| 1985 | Don Sutton | 13-8 | .619 | Don Sutton | 3.89 |
| 1986 | Curt Young | 13-9 | .591 | Moose Haas | 2.74 |
| 1987 | Dave Stewart | 20-13 | .606 | Dennis Eckersley | 3.03 |
| 1988 | Dave Stewart | 21-12 | .636 | Gene Nelson | 3.06 |
| 1989 | Dave Stewart | 21-9 | .700 | Mike Moore | 2.61 |
| 1990 | Bob Welch | 27-6 | .818 | Dave Stewart | 2.56 |
| 1991 | Mike Moore | 17-8 | .680 | Mike Moore | 2.96 |
| 1992 | Mike Moore | 17-12 | .586 | Bob Welch | 3.27 |
| 1993 | Bobby Witt | 14-13 | .519 | Bobby Witt | 4.21 |

* Based on 100-plus innings

## SAN FRANCISCO GIANTS—NATIONAL LEAGUE

| YEAR | PLAYER | RECORD | PCT. | PLAYER | ERA* |
|------|--------|--------|------|--------|------|
| 1958 | John Antonelli | 16-13 | .552 | Stu Miller | 2.47 |
| 1959 | Sam Jones | 21-15 | .583 | Sam Jones | 2.82 |
| 1960 | Sam Jones | 18-14 | .563 | Mike McCormick | 2.70 |
| 1961 | Stu Miller | 14-5 | .737 | Stu Miller | 2.66 |
| 1962 | Jack Sanford | 24-7 | .774 | Juan Marichal | 3.32 |
| 1963 | Juan Marichal | 25-8 | .758 | Juan Marichal | 2.41 |
| 1964 | Juan Marichal | 21-8 | .724 | Juan Marichal | 2.48 |
| 1965 | Juan Marichal | 27-13 | .629 | Juan Marichal | 2.14 |
| 1966 | Juan Marichal | 25-6 | 806 | Juan Marichal | 2.23 |
| 1967 | Mike McCormick | 22-10 | .688 | Gaylord Perry | 2.61 |
| 1968 | Juan Marichal | 26-9 | .743 | Bob Bolin | 1.98 |
| 1969 | Juan Marichal | 21-11 | .656 | Juan Marichal | 2.10 |
| 1970 | Gaylord Perry | 23-13 | .629 | Gaylord Perry | 3.20 |
| 1971 | Juan Marichal | 18-11 | .621 | Gaylord Perry | 2.76 |
| 1972 | Ron Bryant | 14-7 | .667 | Jim Barr | 2.87 |
| 1973 | Ron Bryant | 24-12 | .667 | Ron Bryant | 3.53 |
| 1974 | Mike Caldwell | 14-5 | .737 | Jim Barr | 2.74 |
| 1975 | John Montefusco | 15-9 | .625 | John Montefusco | 2.88 |
| 1976 | John Montefusco | 16-14 | .533 | John Montefusco | 2.85 |
| 1977 | Ed Halicki | 16-12 | .571 | Ed Halicki | 3.31 |
| 1978 | Vida Blue | 18-10 | .643 | Bob Knepper | 2.63 |
| 1979 | Vida Blue | 14-14 | .500 | Gary Lavelle | 2.51 |
| 1980 | Vida Blue | 14-10 | .583 | Vida Blue | 2.97 |
| 1981 | Doyle Alexander | 11-7 | .611 | Vida Blue | 2.45 |
| 1982 | Bill Laskey | 13-12 | .520 | Bill Laskey | 3.14 |
| 1983 | Bill Laskey | 13-10 | .565 | Atlee Hammaker | 2.25 |
| 1984 | Mike Krukow | 11-12 | .478 | Gary Lavelle | 2.76 |
| 1985 | Scott Garrelts | 9-6 | .600 | Mike Krukow | 3.38 |
| 1986 | Mike Krukow | 20-9 | .690 | Mike Krukow | 3.05 |
| 1987 | Mike LaCoss | 13-10 | .565 | Atlee Hammaker | 3.58 |
| 1988 | Rick Reuschel | 19-11 | .633 | Don Robinson | 2.45 |
| 1989 | Rick Reuschel | 17-8 | .680 | Scott Garrelts | 2.28 |
| 1990 | John Burkett | 14-7 | .667 | John Burkett | 3.79 |
| 1991 | Trevor Wilson | 13-11 | .542 | Trevor Wilson | 3.56 |
| 1992 | John Burkett | 13-9 | .591 | Bill Swift | 2.08 |
| 1993 | John Burkett | 22-7 | .759 | Bill Swift | 2.82 |

## BAY AREA PLAYERS IN THE HALL OF FAME

Through 1994, 23 men who either were born in the San Francisco/ Oakland Bay Area or who played a significant role in Bay Area baseball have been inducted into the Hall of Fame. With players such as the Oakland A's Rickey Henderson and the San Francisco Giants' Barry Bonds still active, this total is certain to grow in the 21st century.

(PHOTOGRAPHS COURTESY OF THE NATIONAL BASEBALL LIBRARY, COOP-ERSTOWN, NEW YORK).

EARL AVERILL
Inducted 1975

JOE CRONIN
Inducted 1956

JOE DiMAGGIO
Inducted 1955

ROLLIE FINGERS
Inducted 1992

LEFTY GOMEZ
Inducted 1972

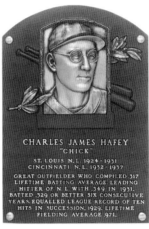

CHICK HAFEY
Inducted 1971

HARRY HEILMANN
Inducted 1952

HARRY HOOPER
Inducted 1971

CATFISH HUNTER
Inducted 1987

HIGHPOCKETS KELLY
Inducted 1973

REGGIE JACKSON
Inducted 1993

**ANTHONY MICHAEL LAZZERI**
"POOSH 'EM UP TONY"
NEW YORK, A.L. 1926-1937
CHICAGO, A.L. 1938
BROOKLYN, N.L. 1939
NEW YORK, N.L. 1939
FEARED CLUTCH HITTER WITH LONG BALL POWER.
PLAYED SECOND BASE WITH QUIET PROFICIENCY
ON FAMED "MURDERER'S ROW" YANKEE TEAMS WITH
RUTH AND GEHRIG. A .300 HITTER FIVE TIMES WITH
CAREER .292 MARK. DROVE IN OVER 100 RUNS
SEVEN TIMES. SET A.L. SINGLE GAME RECORD WITH
2 GRAND SLAMS AND 11 RBI'S, 5/24/36. BELTED 60
HOMERS FOR SALT LAKE CITY (PCL) IN 1925.

**TONY LAZZERI**
Inducted 1991

**ERNEST NATALI LOMBARDI**
BROOKLYN, N.L. 1931
CINCINNATI, N.L. 1932-1941
BOSTON, N.L. 1942
NEW YORK, N.L. 1943-1947
HIT .306 OVER 17 SEASONS DESPITE SLOWNESS AFOOT-
TEN TIMES BATTING OVER .300. WON N.L. BATTING
TITLE WITH .342 IN 1938 AND AGAIN IN 1942 WITH
.330. HELD HANDS LOW, WITH INTERLOCKING GOLF
GRIP AND QUICK STROKE. N.L. MVP IN 1938. SKILLED
RECEIVER AND HANDLER OF PITCHERS. OUTSTANDING
ARM FROM CROUCH POSITION, RIFLING THROWS
WITH SIDE-ARM RELEASE.

**ERNIE LOMBARDI**
Inducted 1986

**JUAN ANTONIO
(SANCHEZ) MARICHAL**
SAN FRANCISCO N.L. 1960-1973 BOSTON A.L. 1974
LOS ANGELES N.L. 1975
HIGH-KICKING RIGHT-HANDER FROM DOMINICAN
REPUBLIC WON 243 GAMES AND LOST ONLY 142
OVER 16 SEASONS. WON 20 GAMES SIX TIMES AND
NO-HIT HOUSTON IN 1963. LED N.L. IN COMPLETE
GAMES AND SHUTOUTS TWICE AND IN ERA WITH
2.10 IN 1969. COMPLETED 244 GAMES DURING
CAREER, STRIKING OUT 2,303 , AND FINISHING
WITH 2.89 ERA.

**JUAN MARICHAL**
Inducted 1983

**WILLIE HOWARD MAYS, JR.**
"THE SAY HEY KID"
NEW YORK N.L., SAN FRANCISCO N.L.
NEW YORK N.L., 1951-1973
ONE OF BASEBALL'S MOST COLORFUL AND
EXCITING STARS. EXCELLED IN ALL PHASES OF
THE GAME. THIRD IN HOMERS (660), RUNS (2,062)
AND TOTAL BASES (6,066) ; SEVENTH IN HITS
(3,283) AND RBI'S (1,903). FIRST IN PUTOUTS
BY OUTFIELDER (7,095). FIRST TO TOP BOTH
300 HOMERS AND 300 STEALS. LED LEAGUE IN
BATTING ONCE, SLUGGING FIVE TIMES, HOME
RUNS AND STEALS FOUR SEASONS. VOTED N.L.
MVP IN 1954 AND 1965. PLAYED IN 24
ALL-STAR GAMES - A RECORD.

**WILLIE MAYS**
Inducted 1979

**WILLIE LEE McCOVEY**
"STRETCH"
SAN FRANCISCO, N.L. 1959-1973, 1977-1980
SAN DIEGO, N.L. 1974-1976
OAKLAND, A.L. 1976
TOP LEFT-HANDED HOME RUN HITTER IN N.L.
HISTORY WITH 521. SECOND ONLY TO LOU GEHRIG
WITH 18 CAREER GRAND SLAMS. LED N.L. IN HOMERS
THREE TIMES AND RBI'S TWICE. N.L. ROOKIE OF
YEAR IN 1959, MVP IN 1969 AND COMEBACK PLAYER
OF THE YEAR IN '77. TEAMED WITH WILLIE MAYS
FOR AWESOME 1-2 PUNCH IN GIANTS' LINEUP.

**WILLIE McCOVEY**
Inducted 1986

**JOE LEONARD MORGAN**
HOUSTON, N.L. 1963-1971, 1980
CINCINNATI, N.L. 1972-1979
SAN FRANCISCO, N.L. 1981-1982
PHILADELPHIA, N.L. 1983
OAKLAND, A.L. 1984
IMPACT PLAYER WHO LIFTED CINCINNATI'S "BIG RED
MACHINE" TO HIGHER LEVEL WITH HIS MULTI-FACETED
SKILLS. TRADEMARK WAS FLAPPING LEFT ARM AS HE
AWAITED PITCH. PACKED UNUSUAL POWER INTO
EXTRAORDINARILY QUICK 150-LB. FIREPLUG FRAME. PLAYED
22 SEASONS AND ALSO HOLDS HOME RUN AND GAMES
PLAYED RECORDS FOR 2B. MVP, 1975-76.

**JOE MORGAN**
Inducted 1990

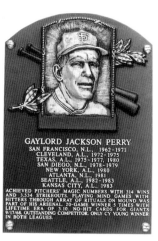

**GAYLORD JACKSON PERRY**
SAN FRANCISCO, N.L. 1962-1971
CLEVELAND, A.L. 1972-1975
TEXAS, A.L. 1975-1977, 1980
SAN DIEGO, N.L. 1978-1979
NEW YORK, A.L. 1980
ATLANTA, N.L. 1981
SEATTLE, A.L. 1982-1983
KANSAS CITY, A.L. 1983
ACHIEVED PITCHERS' MAGIC NUMBERS WITH 314 WINS
AND 3,534 STRIKEOUTS. PLAYING MIND GAMES WITH
HITTERS THROUGH ARRAY OF RITUALS ON MOUND WAS
PART OF HIS ARSENAL. 20-GAME WINNER 5 TIMES WITH
LIFETIME ERA OF 3.10. NO-HIT CARDS FOR GIANTS
9/17/68. OUTSTANDING COMPETITOR. ONLY CY YOUNG WINNER
IN BOTH LEAGUES.

**GAYLORD PERRY**
Inducted 1991

**FRANK ROBINSON**
CINCINNATI N.L., BALTIMORE A.L.,
LOS ANGELES N.L., CALIFORNIA A.L.,
CLEVELAND A.L.,1956-1976
FIRST TO BE CHOSEN MOST VALUABLE PLAYER
IN BOTH LEAGUES - N.L. IN 1961 AND A.L.
IN 1966. SET RECORDS BY HITTING HOMERS
IN 32 DIFFERENT PARKS AND WITH PAIR OF
GRAND-SLAMMERS IN SUCCESSIVE INNINGS IN
1970. FOURTH IN HOMERS (586), FIFTH IN
EXTRA BASES ON LONG HITS (2,450), SIXTH
IN TOTAL BASES (5,373). ON RETIRING, LED
N.L. IN SLUGGING PCT. IN 1960-61-62 AND
A.L. IN BATTING, HOMERS, RUNS BATTED IN,
TOTAL BASES AND SLUGGING PCT. IN 1966.

**FRANK ROBINSON**
Inducted 1982

**WILVER DORNEL STARGELL**
"WILLIE"
PITTSBURGH, N.L. 1962-1982
INTIMIDATING PRESENCE BETWEEN THE LINES
AND CHARISMATIC PATRIARCH IN CLUBHOUSE
AND DUGOUT. HIT 475 HOMERS. MANY
OF TAPE-MEASURE VARIETY AND HIT MOST
BY ANY PIRATE DURING 1970'S. LIKE HIS
ROUND-TRIPPERS, HIS 1,540 RBI'S ALSO MOST
EVER BY A PIRATE. BATTED .282 OVER 21
SEASONS, ALL WITH PITTSBURGH. SHARED N.L.
MVP HONORS IN 1979, AND NAMED MVP IN '79
N.L. CHAMPIONSHIP SERIES AND WORLD SERIES.

**WILLIE STARGELL**
Inducted 1987

**CHARLES DILLON STENGEL**
"CASEY"
MANAGED NEW YORK YANKEES 1949-1960,
WON 10 PENNANTS AND 7 WORLD SERIES WITH
NEW YORK YANKEES. ONLY MANAGER TO WIN
5 CONSECUTIVE WORLD SERIES 1949-1953.
PLAYED OUTFIELD 1912-1925 WITH BROOKLYN,
PITTSBURGH, PHILADELPHIA, NEW YORK AND
BOSTON N.L. TEAMS. MANAGED BROOKLYN
1934-1936, BOSTON BRAVES 1938-1943,
NEW YORK METS 1962-1965.

**CASEY STENGEL**
Inducted 1966

**LLOYD JAMES WANER**
"LITTLE POISON"
PITTSBURGH N.L., BOSTON N.L.,
CINCINNATI N.L., PHILADELPHIA N.L.,
BROOKLYN N.L. 1927-1945
MADE 223 HITS IN 1927 FIRST YEAR
WITH PITTSBURGH INCLUDING 198 SINGLES,
A MODERN MAJOR LEAGUE RECORD.
LED N.L. IN MOST SINGLES 1927-1928-1929-1931.
LIFE TOTAL 2459 HITS. BATTING AVERAGE .316.
WITH BROTHER PAUL, "BIG POISON"
STARRED IN PITTSBURGH OUTFIELD
1927-1940

**LLOYD WANER**
Inducted 1967

**PAUL GLEE WANER**
(BIG POISON)
PITTSBURGH-BROOKLYN-BOSTON-N.L.
NEW YORK, A.L.
1926-1945
LEFT HANDED HITTING OUTFIELDER BATTED
.300 OR BETTER 14 TIMES IN NATIONAL
LEAGUE. ONE OF SEVEN PLAYERS EVER TO
COMPILE 3,000 OR MORE HITS. SET MODERN
N.L. RECORD BY COLLECTING 200 OR MORE
HITS EIGHT SEASONS. MOST VALUABLE PLAYER
IN 1927 AND FOUR TIMES SELECTED FOR
ALL STAR GAME.

**PAUL WANER**
Inducted 1952

# INDEX

*photographs in italics*